Also by Roger Ebert

An Illini Century
A Kiss Is Still a Kiss
The Perfect London Walk (with Daniel Curley)
Roger Ebert's Movie Home Companion
Two Weeks in the Midday Sun: A Cannes Notebook
Future of the Movies (with Gene Siskel)
Behind the Phantom's Mask
Ebert's Little Movie Glossary
Ebert's Bigger Little Movie Glossary
Roger Ebert's Book of Film
Questions for the Movie Answer Man
I Hated, Hated, Hated This Movie
The Great Movies
The Great Movies II
Awake in the Dark: The Best of Roger Ebert
Your Movie Sucks
Roger Ebert's Movie Yearbook
Roger Ebert's Four-Star Reviews 1967–2007
Scorsese by Ebert
The Great Movies III
*The Pot and How to Use It: The Mystery
and Romance of the Rice Cooker*

LIFE
ITSELF

A Memoir

ROGER EBERT

GRAND CENTRAL
PUBLISHING

LARGE PRINT

Grand Central Publishing
Hachette Book Group
237 Park Avenue
New York, NY 10017

www.HachetteBookGroup.com

Printed in the United States of America

First Edition: September 2011
10 9 8 7 6 5 4 3 2 1

Grand Central Publishing is a division of Hachette Book Group, Inc.
The Grand Central Publishing name and logo is a trademark of
Hachette Book Group, Inc.

The publisher is not responsible for websites (or their content) that are
not owned by the publisher.

Library of Congress Cataloging-in-Publication Data
Ebert, Roger.
  Life itself : a memoir / Roger Ebert. — 1st ed.
    p. cm.
  ISBN 978-0-446-58497-5 (regular edition) —
ISBN 978-1-4555-0412-1 (large print edition)   1. Ebert,
Roger.   2. Film critics—United States—Biography.   I. Title.
  PN1998.3.E327A3 2011
  791.43092—dc23
  [B]
                        2011022442

For Chaz
and
For my parents

CONTENTS

CONTENTS

CONTENTS

CONTENTS

LIFE
ITSELF

MEMORY

I WAS BORN inside the movie of my life. The visuals were before me, the audio surrounded me, the plot unfolded inevitably but not necessarily. I don't remember how I 'got into the movie, but it continues to entertain me. At first the frames flicker without connection, as they do in Bergman's *Persona* after the film breaks and begins again. I am flat on my stomach on the front sidewalk, my eyes an inch from a procession of ants. What these are I do not know. It is the only sidewalk in my life, in front of the only house. I have seen grasshoppers and ladybugs. My uncle Bob extends the business end of a fly swatter toward me, and I grasp it and try to walk toward him. Voices encourage me. Hal Holmes has a red tricycle and I cry because I want it for my own. My parents curiously set tubes afire and blow smoke from their mouths. I don't want to eat, and my aunt Martha puts me on her lap and says she'll pinch me if I don't open my mouth. Gary Wikoff is sitting next to me in the kitchen. He asks me how old I am today, and I hold up three fingers. At Tot's Play School, I try to ride on the back of Mrs. Meadrow's dog, and it bites me on the cheek. I am taken to Mercy Hospital to be stitched up. Everyone there is shouting because the Panama Limited went off the rails north of town. People crowd around. Aunt Martha brings in Doctor Collins, her boss, who is a dentist. He tells my mother, Annabel, it's the same thing to put a few stitches on the outside of a cheek as on the inside. I start crying. Why is the thought of stitches *outside my cheek* more terrifying than stitches anywhere else?

The movie settles down. I live at 410 East Washington Street in Urbana, Illinois. My telephone number is 72611. I am never to forget those things. I run the length of the hallway from the living room to my bedroom, leaping into the air and landing on my bed. Daddy tells me to stop that or I'll break the bed boards. The basement smells like green onions. The light beside my bed is like a water pump, and the handle turns it on and off. I wear flannel shirts. My gloves are attached to a string through the sleeves because I am always losing them. My mother says today my father is going to teach me to tie my shoes for myself. "It can't be explained in words," he tells me. "Just follow my fingers." I still do. It cannot be explained in words.

When I returned to 410 East Washington with my wife, Chaz, in 1990, I saw that the hallway was only a few yards long. I got the feeling I sometimes have when reality realigns itself. It's a tingling sensation moving like a wave through my body. I know the feeling precisely. I doubt I've experienced it ten times in my life. I felt it at Smith Drugs when I was seven or eight and opened a nudist magazine and discovered that all women had breasts. I felt it when my father told me he had cancer. I felt it when I proposed marriage. Yes, and I felt it in the old Palais des Festivals at Cannes, when the *Ride of the Valkyries* played during the helicopter attack in *Apocalypse Now.*

I was an only child. I heard that over and over again. "Roger is an only boy." My best friends, Hal and Gary, were only children, too. We were born at the beginning of World War II, four or five years earlier than the baby boomers, which would be an advantage all of our lives. The war was the great mystery of those years. I knew we were at war against Germany and Japan. I knew Uncle Bill had gone away to fight. I was told, your father is too old so they won't take him. He put bicycle clips on his work pants and cycled to work every morning. There was rationing. If Harry Rusk the grocer had a chicken, we had chicken on Sunday. Many nights we had oatmeal. There was no butter. Oleo came in a plastic bag, and you squeezed the orange dye and kneaded it to make it look like butter. "It's against the law to sell it already looking like butter," my parents explained. Daddy and Uncle Johnny ordered cartons of cigarettes through the mail from Kentucky. Everybody smoked. My mother, my father, my uncles and aunts, the neighbors, everybody. When we gathered at my grandmother's for a big dinner, that meant nine or ten people sitting around the table smoking. They did it over and over, hour after hour, as if it were an assignment.

After the war, you could buy cars again. The cars were long, wide, and deep, and I was barely tall enough to see out the window. Three could sit across in the front seat, and three and a child in the back. You filled up at Norman Early's Shell station. He pumped the gas by hand into a transparent glass cylinder. He gave you Green Stamps. The great danger was having a blowout. We drove on the Danville Hard Road. It was a one-lane slab. When another car approached, you slowed down and put two wheels over on the side. That was when you had to be afraid of a blowout.

One of the rewards of growing old is that you can truthfully say you lived in the past. I remember the day my father sat down next to me and said he had something he wanted to tell me. We had dropped an atomic bomb on the Japanese and that might mean the war was over. I asked him what an atomic bomb was. He said it was a bomb as big as a hundred other bombs. I said I hoped we dropped a hundred of them. My father said, "Don't even say that, Roger. It's a terrible thing." My mother came in from the kitchen. "What's terrible?" My father told her. "Oh, yes, honey," she told me. "All those poor people burned up alive."

How can I tell you what they said? I remember them saying it. In these years after my illness, when I can no longer speak and am set aside from the daily flow, I live more in my memory and discover that a great many things are safely stored away. It all seems still to be in there somewhere. At our fiftieth high school reunion, Pegeen Linn remembered how self-conscious she was when she acted in a high school play and had to kiss a boy on the stage in front of the whole school. She smiled at me. "And that boy was you. You had this monologue and then I had to walk on and kiss you, with everybody watching." I discovered that the monologue was still there in my memory, untouched. Do you ever have that happen? You find a moment from your past, undisturbed ever since, still vivid, surprising you. In high school I fell under the spell of Thomas Wolfe: "A stone, a leaf, an unfound door; of a stone, a leaf, a door. And of all the forgotten faces." Now I feel all the faces returning to memory.

The British satirist Auberon Waugh once wrote a letter to the editor of the *Daily Telegraph* asking readers to supply information about his life between birth and the present, explaining that he was writing his memoirs and had no memories from those years. I find myself in the opposite position. I remember everything. All my life I've been visited by unexpected flashes of memory unrelated to anything taking place at the moment. These retrieved moments I consider and replace on the shelf. When I began writing this book, memories came flooding to the surface, not because of any conscious effort but simply in the stream of writing. I started in a direction and the memories were waiting there, sometimes of things I hadn't consciously thought about since. Hypnosis is said to enable us to retrieve past memories. When I write, I fall into the zone many writers, painters, musicians, athletes, and craftsmen of all sorts seem to share: In doing something I enjoy and am expert at, deliberate thought falls aside and it is all just *there*. I think of the next word no more than the composer thinks of the next note.

I lived in a world of words long before I was aware of it. As an only child I turned to books as soon as I could read. There was a persistent need not only to write, but to publish. In grade school I had an essay published in the mimeographed paper, and that led me directly to a hectograph, a primitive publishing toy with a tray of jelly. You wrote in a special purple ink, the jelly absorbed it, and you could impress it on perhaps a dozen sheets of paper before it grew too faint. With this I wrote and published the *Washington Street News*, which I solemnly delivered to some neighbors as if it existed independently of me. I must have been a curious child. In high school and college I flowed naturally toward newspapers. In the early days I also did some radio. I'll return to these adventures later in the book.

I realize that most of the turning points in my career were brought about by others. My life has largely happened to me without any conscious plan. I was an indifferent student except at subjects that interested me, and those I followed beyond the classroom, stealing time from others I should have been studying. I was no good at math beyond algebra. I flunked French four times in college. I had no patience for memorization, but I could easily remember words I responded to. In college a chart of my grades resembled a mountain range.

My first real newspaper job came when my best friend's father hired me to cover high school sports for the local daily. In college a friend told me I must join him in publishing an alternative weekly and then left it in my hands. That led to the *Daily Illini*, and that in turn led to the *Chicago Sun-Times*, where I have worked ever since 1966. I became the movie critic six months later through no premeditation, when the job was offered to me out of a clear blue sky.

I first did a regular TV show when Dave Wilson, a producer for the Chicago PBS station, read my reviews of some Ingmar Bergman films and asked me to host screenings of a package of twenty of his films. I was very bad on television. In person I could talk endlessly, but before the cameras I froze and my mind became a blank. One day Dave asked me to speak while walking toward the camera. To walk and talk at the same time? I broke out in a cold sweat. Later talking on TV became second nature, but that was after some anguish on my part and astonishing patience on the part of others. I found that if I did it long enough, it stopped being hard. In the early days of doing shows with Gene Siskel, part of our so-called chemistry resulted because, having successfully made my argument and feeling some relief, I felt personally under assault if Siskel disagreed. This led to tension that, oddly, helped the show.

Gene and I did the show because a woman named

Thea Flaum cast us for it. She will also appear again later. The point for now is: I had no conception of such a show and no desire to work with Siskel. The three stages of my early career (writing and editing a newspaper, becoming a film critic, beginning a television show) were initiated by others.

Between college and 2006, my life continued more or less on that track. I was a movie critic and I had a TV show. It could all have been lost through alcoholism (I believe I came closer than many people realized), but in 1979 I stopped drinking and the later chapters became possible. Had it not been for cancer, I believe that today I would be living much as I did before: reviewing movies, doing a weekly television program, going to many film festivals, speaking cheerfully, traveling a great deal, happily married to my wife, Chaz.

Marriage redefined everything. Although proposing to Chaz was indeed something I did freely, there is a point in a romance when you find your decision has been made for you. I wasn't looking for a wife. I didn't feel I "had" to be married. I didn't think of myself as a bachelor but as a soloist. Yet when I proposed marriage it seemed as inevitable as going into newspaper work. I hope you understand the spirit in which I say that. I am speaking about what seems ordained.

I deceived myself that I had good luck with my

health. I had my appendix taken out when I was in the fourth grade and was never in a hospital again except for two days in 1988 when I had a tumor removed from my salivary gland, the same tumor that would return almost twenty years later with such effect. Yes, I was fat for many years, but (as fat people so often say) "my numbers were good." Then I moved to a more vegetarian diet and for several years faithfully followed the ten thousand steps a day regime, lost one hundred pounds, and was in good shape for my age when everything fell apart.

The next stage of my life also came about for reasons outside my control. I was diagnosed with cancers of the thyroid and jaw, I had difficult surgeries, I lost the ability to speak, eat, or drink, and two failed attempts to rebuild my jaw led to shoulder damage that makes it difficult to walk easily and painful to stand. It is that person who is writing this book.

One day in the Rehabilitation Institute of Chicago, still in a wheelchair, I got a visit from Cyrus Freidheim, who had come to Chicago from Philadelphia to publish (rescue) my paper after it was bankrupted by crooks. My reviews had appeared online for several years, but now he advised me to start blogging, tweeting, and facebooking. At the time I wanted nothing to do with the social media. I feared, correctly, that they would consume alarming amounts of time.

In late 2007 I had my third unsuccessful surgery, at MD Anderson in Houston, and had returned to Chicago to learn to walk again. After all three surgeries, I was not to move so the transplants would not be disturbed. Being bedridden caused my muscles to atrophy, and three times I had gone through rehabilitation. From summer 2006 to spring 2007 I'd essentially been in the hospital, but now I was walking again.

Chaz took me down to the Pritikin Longevity Center in Aventura, Florida, for exercise and nutrition; they'd liquefy their healthy diet for my G-tube. She marched me in the sunlight and lectured me on how my skin was manufacturing vitamin D. On the second or third day there, I stood up to get a channel-changer, my foot caught on a rug, and I fell and fractured my hip. We came back to Northwestern Memorial Hospital in Chicago, and after enduring the exquisite pain of putting weight on that hip two days after a rod was inserted, I returned to the Rehabilitation Institute to start learning to walk all over again for the fourth time.

That was in April 2008, when I'd been planning to attend the tenth annual Ebertfest, my annual film festival at the University of Illinois. I was plenty pissed off at myself for having broken my hip instead. Then and there, I wrote my first blog entry and began this current, probably final, stage of my life.

My blog became my voice, my outlet, my "social media" in a way I couldn't have dreamed of. Into it I poured my regrets, desires, and memories. Some days I became possessed. The comments were a form of feedback I'd never had before, and I gained a better and deeper understanding of my readers. I made "online friends," a concept I'd scoffed at. Most people choose to write a blog. I needed to. I didn't intend for it to drift into autobiography, but in blogging there is a tidal drift that pushes you that way. Getting such quick feedback may be one reason; the Internet encourages first-person writing, and I've always written that way. How can a movie review be written in the third person, as if it were an account of facts? If it isn't subjective, there's something false about it.

The blog let loose the flood of memories. Told sometimes that I should write my memoirs, I failed to see how I possibly could. I had memories, I had lived a good life in an interesting time, but I was at a loss to see how I could organize the accumulation of a lifetime. It was the blog that taught me how. It pushed me into first-person confession, it insisted on the personal, it seemed to organize itself in manageable fragments. Some of these words, since rewritten and expanded, first appeared in blog forms. Most are here for the first time. They come pouring forth in a flood of relief.

1   410 EAST WASHINGTON

I LIVED AT the center of the universe. The center was located at the corner of Washington and Maple streets in Urbana, Illinois, a two-bedroom white stucco house with green canvas awnings, evergreens and geraniums in front, and a white picket fence enclosing the backyard. Hollyhocks towered above me by the fence. There was a barbeque grill back there made by my father with stone and mortar, a dime embedded in its smokestack to mark the year of its completion.

There was a mountain ash tree in the front yard, and three more next to the sidewalk on the side of the house. These remarkable trees had white bark that could be peeled loose, and their branches were weighed with clusters of little orange berries. "People are always driving up and asking me about those trees," my father said. He had planted them himself, and they were the only ones in town—perhaps in the world, I gathered. They needed watering in the summertime, which he did by placing five-gallon cans next to them with small holes drilled in their bottoms. These I carefully filled with the garden hose from the backyard, while making rainbow sprays over the grass around.

After they married, my parents lived in a small apartment in downtown Urbana, and then bought this house not long before I was born. My father took great pride in it. Not only the trees were unique. It was one of the few stucco houses in Urbana. The green awnings were handmade and were taken in and repainted every winter. We had a peaked roof over the living room, which also had stucco walls. There was a Spanish feeling, which reminded my father of the years he had lived in Florida.

My bedroom was the one with the window overlooking Maple Street. The walls were pale yellow, the ceiling red. It had a two-way fan, posing the fundamental scientific question, is it more helpful on a hot night to blow cooler air in, or warmer air out? I had better get to sleep quickly, because Harry with His Ladder would come around to look in to be sure my eyes were closed. I lived in fear of Harry and kept my eyes screwed tight until I drifted off to sleep. I can tell you even now what Harry looked like, because I saw him many times, perched on top of his ladder, when I allowed my eyes to flicker open.

Of this room as a very young child I remember only a few things. My mother putting me to sleep in a bed with sides that lifted up to prevent me falling out. A nightly ritual of love pats. My small workbench on which I hammered round pegs into round holes. A glass of water that was filled to the rim, but that I could see straight through, so obviously there was room down there for more water. My tears when I was accused of playing with water and spilling it, when I had been following strict logic.

My own little radio. I would lie on the floor under my bed, for safety, while listening to *The Lone Ranger*. I thought *Arthur Godfrey and His Friends* were friends about my age. I listened carefully to the lists of the FBI's most wanted men, whose descriptions were read by J. Edgar Hoover at the end of *The FBI in Peace and War. Caution—do not attempt to apprehend them yourselves!* From my hideout under the bed I used binoculars to search for them in the clothes closet. I had a bookcase in which I carefully arranged first childhood books, and then books about Tarzan, Penrod, the Hardy Boys, and Tom Corbett, Space Cadet.

Also *Huckleberry Finn*, the first real book I ever read and still the best.

When I was sick it was the best time. I could stay in bed and listen to *Our Gal Sunday*, which asked the question, "Can this girl from a little mining town in the West find happiness as the wife of a wealthy and titled Englishman?" Before that there was a local program *Penny for Your Thoughts*, where people got a penny just for calling up Larry Stewart and talking to him. Larry Stewart was also "the voice of the Fighting Illini," my father informed me. The Illini were the University of Illinois, the world's greatest university, whose football stadium my father had constructed— by himself, I believed. It was there that he had seen Red Grange, the greatest player of all time. Also in that stadium were seen the world's first huddle, the world's first homecoming, and Chief Illiniwek, the world's greatest sports symbol ("Don't ever call him a mascot," my father said. "Chief Illiniwek stands for something.")

The university also had the world's largest arched roof, over the Armory. The cyclotron, where they worked with atoms. The ILLIAC computer, in a building filled with vacuum tubes that could count faster than a man. My dad worked in there sometimes. "Your father is an electrician for the university," my mother told me. "It can't run without him.

But I'm afraid every day that he'll get shocked." I didn't know what that meant, but it sounded almost as bad as being "fired," a word I also didn't understand, although thank God that had never happened to my father. There was the Natural History Museum, with its stuffed owls and prehistoric bones. Altgeld Hall and its bells, which could be heard all over town in the summer, and which my father had personally installed, I believed.

The town also contained a cemetery where we would go to see swans float on the pond. And a Cemetery Graveyard, next to the Atkinson Monument Company in a lot overgrown with trees and shrubbery, where the corpses of broken gravestones could be picked through for the rock garden my father was building in the backyard. If you got lost in the Cemetery Graveyard, the ghosts might come for you. There was the Boneyard, a creek running through town, where the Indians had buried their dead and at midnight you could see their bones. An airport where we could see Piper Cubs taking off. A train station north of town, in Rantoul, where we could watch the Panama Limited and the City of New Orleans hurtling through, the world's fastest trains.

I attended Mrs. Meadrow's Tot's Play School during the day. This was because my mother was a Business Woman—in fact, the president of the Urbana

Business Women's Association. She was a bookkeeper for the Allied Finance Company, up a flight of stairs over the Champaign County Bank and Trust Company. It was run by Mr. R. V. Willis. On the first of every year they worked all day to get the books to balance. When they succeeded, Mr. Willis would take us all, including my father and me, to dinner at Mel Root's two doors down Main Street. In between the bank and Mel Root's was the Smith Drug Company, where Mr. Willis bought me by first chocolate soda. My parents smoked Lucky Strikes, but Mr. Willis smoked Chesterfields.

Our house had a concrete front porch on which rested four steel chairs that bounced on springy legs. My father painted them in pastel colors. On summer nights my mother would make lemonade and we would all sit out there. They would smoke and read the papers, and talk to neighbors walking past. Later you could see fireflies. The sounds of radios, voices, distant laughter would float on the air. On spare days, there were jobs to do. Pulling up dandelions. Picking tomato worms off the tomato plants in our vacant lot. A riskier job, climbing a stepladder to pick bagworms off the tallest evergreens. The paper bags containing the worms would be gathered in a pile, sprinkled with kerosene, and set alight. "Don't worry, boy. They're only worms and can't feel anything."

The most exciting job, in the autumn, was putting on old clothes and swimming goggles and crawling up the big air pipes of the furnace while dragging the vacuum cleaner hose, to pull the dust out.

In winter I was awakened by the sound of my dad shoveling coal into the stoker. In summer, by the clip-clops of the horse wagons of the Urbana Pure Milk Company. The horses knew their routes by heart and stopped at the doors of customers. Sally Hopson's family owned the milk company. In summer, the whistles of passing trains could be heard through open windows all through the night.

When you entered the house from the front porch, you were in the living room, with our fireplace. My father would place tablets on the burning logs that would make the flames burst into colors. Here we sat on Christmas Eve listening to Bing Crosby and his family. He had a son named Gary Crosby who I thought was just about my age. Off the living room was the dining room, nearly filled by the table. Most of the time the table's center boards were out, so my mother could let down the ironing board from the wall. Then came the kitchen, where my father made his chili and let it sit in the icebox overnight.

A hallway had doors opening to the living room, the kitchen, the bathroom, and both bedrooms. When Chaz and I revisited the house in 1990, a woman named Violet Mary Gaschler, who bought the house from my mom, asked us to come in and look around. I saw the alcove in the hallway where our telephone rested. We were on a party line. When the phone would ring at night, my mother would hurry to it, grab the receiver, and say, "Is it Mom?" My grandmother had heart trouble. Having a Heart Attack was worse than being shocked or fired. On that same visit with Chaz, I went to the basement and felt chills down my spine. Hardly anything had even been touched. On my father's workbench, a can of 3-in-One oil still waited. The chains on the overhead electric light pulls still ended in toy letters spelling out E-B-E-R-T. Violet Gaschler let me take an "E." The basement's smell was the same, faintly like green onions, and evoked summer afternoons in a lawn chair downstairs, reading *Astounding Science Fiction*.

It was from the basement that I operated the Roger Ebert Stamp Company, buying ten-cent ads in little stamp magazines and mailing out "approvals" to a handful of customers, who must have been about my age. These I addressed on an old typewriter. One day two men came to the door and said they might want to buy some stamps. I proudly took them downstairs and showed them my wares. My mother hovered nervously at the head of the stairs. The men left quickly, saying they didn't see anything they needed for their collections. Nevertheless, they seemed to be in a good mood. As they were driving away, my dad walked in from work. "What did those men want?" he asked. We told him. "Their car said Department of Internal Revenue," he said.

On April 22, 2009, the city of Urbana honored me by placing a plaque at my childhood home. At first I resisted. Far greater figures had lived in Urbana, such as the sculptor Lorado Taft; the poet Mark Van Doren; the novelists William Gibson, David Foster Wallace, Larry Woiwode, and Dave Eggers; the newspapermen William Nack, James Reston, Robert Novak, and George F. Will; the Nobel winner John Bardeen, who invented the transistor; and the Galloping Ghost himself, Red Grange. You see that Urbana truly was the Center of the Universe.

The city fathers assured me they planned to dedicate plaques to many other worthy sons and daughters of Urbana, and so I agreed to the ceremony. As I stood in front of 410 East Washington, I reflected that this was the first and only home my parents owned. Here they brought the infant Roger home from Mercy Hospital. Here they raised me, and encouraged me in my dream to be a newspaperman, even if it meant working after midnight on Fridays and Saturdays. Here my father refused to let me watch him doing any electrical wiring. Here he told me, "Boy, I don't want you to become an electrician. I was working in the English Building today, and I saw those fellows with their feet up on their desks, smoking their pipes and reading their books. That's the job for you." Among the old neighbors who turned out for the occasion was Sally Ormiston, who lived across the street and used a big toy clock face to teach me to tell time.

In the 1970s, an article appeared in the *News-Gazette* about the restoration of the bells in Altgeld Hall. It said the crew had found a note tacked to a beam up in the tower. It read "We repaired these bells on..." I forget the date. It was signed with three names, one of them Walter H. Ebert. On that early visit to Urbana, I took Chaz to visit my parents' graves. Close by, my father's parents are buried. My grandfather's name was Joseph Ebert. Joseph is my middle name. I must have noticed that many times when I visited those graves with my father, but that day, for the first time, I felt a bond with the man in that grave.

2   MY PEOPLE

MANY YEARS AGO during a drinking dinner at the house of the sociologist Howard Higman in Boulder, he refused to serve me dessert until I had heard him explain the difference between the European and American ideas of family. In Europe, he said, one's family roots went down, down, into the past. In America, they went out, out into the society. "An Englishman knows who his great-great-great-grandfather was," Howard said. "An American knows who's on his bowling team."

By his definition I am an American. I didn't realize until I began to write this book how little I know about my ancestors on either side of the family. It is a custom that all memoirs contain a chapter about the author's descent from long lines of Italian aristocrats and Mongolian yurt-dwelling camel hair jobbers, with an American bootlegger or Nazi sympathizer thrown in. I will disappoint.

I was a late child. My father was forty when I was born, my mother thirty-one. On my father's side, my grandparents died before I was born. On my mother's side, there was one grandmother. My father had three sisters. Two of them died spinsters, and from the third descended all my cousins. My mother had two sisters and three brothers, who together produced two children. I have three first cousins, which a European would find inadequate.

My father's parents appear in America from Germany in the late nineteenth century, leaving no memories. I never heard a word about my German relatives, nor do I know the names of my great-grandparents. My mother's Irish grandmother, known to me only as Grandma Gleeson, sailed to America during the potato famine, and my cousin Ethel Doyle produced a mimeographed record of Grandma's memories, with photographs mounted in it, which I cannot find. The only oral history I remember is that her sailing ship was blown back to shore by fierce storms six times, or eight. No Irish immigrant ever had a pleasant crossing.

My grandmother Anna Gleeson married a Dutch-American farmer named William Stumm, who was adopted and possessed no blood ancestors he knew about. He knew about his adoptive parents, but I don't. He must have had the spark of wit, because in my aunt Mary's family album I find a small display ad from September 12, 1901, reading: "W. H. STUMM. The game of billiards is brain-food for the over-worked businessman; an invigorator of the system that is exhausted thru studious attention to the routine of worldly affairs. East Side Billiard Parlors." This shred suggests he had a gift for drollery.

Anna had a sister I knew and visited, my aunt Ida in Chicago. Her daughters Ethel and Blanche lived with her, and died spinsters. Anna had other brothers and sisters, but none I remember meeting, except Uncle Charlie. I remember visiting his house in Taylorville as a little boy. He stood on the front steps and played "Turkey in the Straw" on his fiddle. After his death he wasn't much mentioned. When he was, his name was used as if everyone knew who he was, but I didn't. There was also an Aunt Mary Magner, but I believe she was an honorary aunt. She lost her only son when a two-by-four fell off a truck and flew through the window of the car he was driving, beheading him. He was an exemplary son who remained faithful to his pledge to his mother never to smoke or miss Sunday Mass, "although he was such a good man that he always carried a pack of cigarettes in his pocket so he could give them to friends."

On that side of the family I have two first cousins, Colonel Tom Stumm in Virginia and Marianne Dull in Colorado, who I see from time to time. Tom and I met in South Bend to bury his mother, Margaret, and I've visited Tom and Gloria in Virginia. Marianne and I have met when I've been in Colorado, and Tom's daughter Kathryn, an assistant district attorney and now a teacher, lives in Denver with her children. Many second cousins in the Stonington and Taylorville area were well known and frequently visited by us, and I am in touch with Tom Stumm and his children to this day, but distantly: weddings, a funeral, a Thanksgiving, a Fourth of July, Christmas cards. Tom's children and some grandchildren came to visit in Michigan. We like each other and are happy when we meet, but we have gone our own ways.

On my father's side, there are also two close cousins. I was raised with Jim and Karol Ann Pickens in Champaign-Urbana, and Jimmy inflamed my envy at family gatherings by playing "Lady of Spain" at breakneck speed on his accordion. Their mother, Reba, was the daughter of my father's sister Mame. This would have been on Christmas Eves at the Ebert family home on Clark Street, where my aunts Hulda and Wanda still lived. Karol Ann married Dwayne Gaines, and they had Tim and Shelly. Karol Ann helped run the University of Illinois Employees Credit Union, which her parents Glen and Reba had founded. Dwayne, Karol Ann, and Tim were heroic in the care of my mother, Annabel, in her later years. This often involved expeditions into dangerously drifting snow to carry her to hospitals or department stores. Dwayne has spent years restoring a Ford Coupe to such perfection it can hardly be risked to exposure at auto shows. I have good contact with Tim, who is the only person on either side of the family who can be called a movie fanatic, and thus can make good use of his old cousin. Jimmy Pickens spent his life as the town pharmacist in Watseka, Illinois. He and his wife, Bev, have four children, Todd, Susan, Steve, Kristin, and with them at last we strike gold in the reproduction department. They produced so many children and grandchildren that a photo taken at their fiftieth wedding anniversary looks like a church social.

In general, however, my grandparents on both sides began a population implosion. This fact, and age and geography, have resulted in my sense that I grew up pretty much alone in the world. I had warm relations with my mother's sisters Martha and Mary, and her brothers Everett, Bill, and Bob, but they were more than usually older than me, and after Bill died twenty years ago there was no one left.

Fortunately, it was at about that time I married Chaz Hammel Smith, or as she later became, Chaz Hammelsmith Ebert, because an American can have a double-barreled last name but there is little practice for a triple-barreled one. By marrying an African American, I was suddenly propelled from a void with few relatives into a world with relatives without number. Some months before my marriage, a reader wrote me about African-American families, "What you won't be prepared for is the relatives. The entire extended family is in continual communication, and it is a slow year without at least three weddings and three funerals." This is true. My white family valued and kept in touch with what few relatives they had, but in moderation. Chaz and her family are living genealogists. I once heard her on the phone asking about how Sharon was. I know two of her cousins named Sharon, and asked her which she was asking about. "Neither one," she said. "This Sharon is the daughter of a former neighbor of one of my brother Andre's girlfriends."

Many of her family have become my own family. I love and am loved. There are no strangers in her family, and as a member of another race I have without exception been accepted and embraced. Her children and grandchildren are mine. The grandchildren have six living grandparents. These people are good and kind to such an extent that I am on warm terms with Chaz's first husband, Merle Smith, and his wife Donna. Chaz's niece, Ina New-Jones, is greatly valued by me because she's one of those rare people who always think I am funny. A bad comedian would never learn the truth from Miss Ina. She and I can instigate laughter in each other almost to the point of unconsciousness. I have spent most of my life perfecting the skills and compulsions of a very funny guy, and Ina is the only person who always agrees with me.

Chaz's family transcends time and distance to stay in touch. Road journeys between Minneapolis, Chicago, and Atlanta are undertaken not only for weddings and funerals, but for birthdays, anniversaries, and graduations from college, high school, grade school, and kindergarten. At the other end of the age scale, there are retirement dinners and testimonials not to be missed.

My two families overlapped just barely. After my grandmother's death in 1960, Martha and her lifelong friend Jean Sabo continued to live in a house at 807 West Clark with Martha's brother Bob. After he moved to the Champaign County Nursing Home, crippled by emphysema, my uncle Bill retired from teaching and with Martha and Jean bought houses in Cape Girardeau, Missouri, and later in Wapella, Illinois.

Bill, Martha, and Jean came to live in my guest cottage in Michigan during the summer of 1988. "I love you and I don't have much time left," Martha explained. She had a heart attack on the evening of Bill's Thanksgiving dinner in 1988 and died in a nearby hospital three days later. On her deathbed she desperately tried to tell me something but failed, and shook her head "no" when I tried to guess. It wasn't "I love you." It was something very important. The two of us looked more alike than anyone else in the family, and I wondered if she was trying to tell me she was my real mother. That would have been unlikely. I have my birth certificate and a photo record of myself in my mother's arms beginning on the day of my birth. All the same, haunted by her urgency, I asked Jean if she knew of *any* family secrets she could share with me. "Not that I can think of," she said.

At Martha's funeral Mass in Wapella, Father Richard Brunskill, their next-door neighbor, noticed that as a lapsed Catholic I remained in my pew, and walked over to me. He held up the Host and said, "Take this for Martha." The village held a crowded potluck dinner in the church basement, and Martha was buried in the plot she and Jean had purchased in Wapella. Then Bill and Jean moved into separate retirement homes.

My uncle Bill and aunt Mary attended my

wedding. Mary, learning I would marry a black woman, asked me, "Honey, that's never been done in our family, so why do you want to start now?" I said I loved Chaz and wanted to make her my wife. "Well the good lord knows you've waited long enough," she said, "and it's better to marry than to burn." At the wedding, Mary and Bill sat with Chaz's mother, known universally as Big Mama, and enjoyed their celebrity.

Aunt Mary had a childless marriage with John J. O'Neill, a former state trooper who became the Champaign postmaster. Tall, jocular, a glad-handing Democrat with a patronage job in a Republican city, he ganged up with my father against Uncle Everett the Republican at family gatherings. He and Mary moved house at least every two years. "Johnny has Mary work like a slave to fix up those places, and then he sells them," my father said. "She loves it," said my mother, who may have been right. Some people enjoy being in eternal interior decorating mode.

Uncle Bill, a lifelong bachelor, was a retired high school agriculture teacher who taught in Elkhart, Indiana, and Elkhart, Illinois. Bill and Mary visited us in Chicago frequently, and we often drove down to Urbana. Bill and Mary by then lived in the Clark-Lindsey retirement home, where both remained alert until the end, although Bill in his eighties began counting on a visit from Ed McMahon with a $1 million check from Publishers Clearing House, and after his death we had to cancel his subscriptions to *Rolling Stone* and *Crawdaddy.*

Bill came to visit in Michigan many times, Mary only once. As I proudly turned into our wooded dirt lane, she shrank in her seat and said, "Oh, honey! Cut down these trees! They'll never be able to get in here to get you out!" Mary slowed in her later years because of emphysema. All those cigarettes. Bill was still planting tomatoes and cooking family dinners into his nineties. Every summer in the 1980s, he and Martha and Jean Sabo would take long road trips with their close friends Dave and Dot Sparrow of Kenney, Illinois, near Wapella. It was Bill's bitter disappointment that they wouldn't allow him, at eighty-six, to ride a mule to the bottom of the Grand Canyon. He dismissed their fears. "The mule isn't about to fall. Just strap me to the saddle and I'll get there one way or another." He was very serious, and there was lingering resentment over the issue. At the very end, on his last birthday visit to Michigan, he said he thought his brother Everett had died and yet there he was sitting at the table big as life. He was looking directly at me. Dot Sparrow said, "Well then you'd all better have some cake and ice cream!"

3   MY OLD MAN

UNTIL THE DAY he died, I always called him "Daddy." He was Walter Harry Ebert, born in Urbana in 1902 of parents who had emigrated from Germany. His father, Joseph, was a machinist working for the Peoria and Eastern Railway, known as the Big Four. Daddy would take me out to the roundhouse on the north side of town to watch the big turntables turning steam engines around. In our kitchen, he always used a knife my grandfather made from a single piece of steel. "That is the only thing you have from your grandfather." There was a railroad man's diner next to the roundhouse where we would go for meat loaf and mashed potatoes, but my first restaurant meal was at the Steak 'n Shake on Green Street. "A hamburger for the boy," my father said.

What have I inherited from those Germans who came to the new land? A group of sayings, often repeated by my father: *If the job is worth doing, it's worth doing right. A good workman respects his tools. Don't go to sleep at the switch.* They spoke German at home until the United States entered World War I. Then they never spoke it again. He was taken out of the Lutheran school and sent to public school, "to learn to speak American." He spoke no German, apart from a few words.

There is a story he told many times, always with great laughter. It was from Joseph. Before a man left Germany for America, the schoolmaster taught him to say "apple pie" and "coffee." When he got off the boat, this man was hungry and went into a restaurant. "Apple pie," he said. The waiter asked, "Do you want anything on top?" The man replied, "Coffee!"

My father was raised in a two-story frame house with a big porch, on West Clark Street. His parents believed they couldn't conceive, and adopted a daughter, Mame. Then they had three children: Hulda, Wanda, and Walter. Aunt Mame and Uncle Ben lived north of Champaign in a small house made of tar paper, heated by a stove. This was not considered to be living in poverty, but simply was their home.

It was always comfortable and warm, and I loved to visit. Uncle Ben drove a heating oil truck and would sometimes drive past our house and wave. Always with a cigar stuck in his mug.

Hulda and Wanda remained at home. I spent hours with coloring books on their floor or at their kitchen table, and tiptoeing up and running down the scary staircase. They had an actual icebox, and they had me hang the sign on the porch so the iceman could see from his horse-drawn wagon how much ice they needed. We sat around a kitchen table covered with oilcloth and ate beef and cabbage soup. Hulda contracted tuberculosis, and I heard, "She has to go live in the sanitarium up on Cunningham." This was spoken like a death sentence. She died, and the body was laid out in the living room. I was allowed to approach her and regarded her body solemnly. The occasion itself made more of an impression than the dead body: A coffin was in the living room. How strange.

I never knew Wanda as well as I knew my uncles and aunts on my mother's side. There was tension between my parents about their families, and I was always at the Stumm house, rarely at the Ebert house, although they were only six blocks apart on the same street. This was never really discussed, and my mother and Wanda always seemed friendly. I vaguely gather it involved how their financial assistance was divided. Perhaps their difference in religion. Because my father wasn't a Catholic, their marriage couldn't take place in St. Patrick Church, and my mother often observed, "We had to be married in the rectory." This wasn't my father's fault. Religion was never mentioned by Hulda and Wanda. I never went to their Lutheran church with them, because that would have been a mortal sin.

Wanda worked most of her life as a saleswoman for the big G. C. Willis store in downtown Champaign, and we'd visit her there, my father buying something. Everybody seemed to know her. The last time I saw her was in the 1970s, after she moved to a nursing home. My mother and I took her out to dinner. I was a little surprised by her warmth and humor. I felt her love. When I was a child she seemed tall, spare, and distant. "Your father's initials are still carved in the concrete on the curb in front of the old house," she told me. I went to look, and they were.

My father as a young man moved to West Palm Beach, Florida, and opened a florist shop with a man named Fairweather. "We delivered a lot of flowers to the Kennedys in their mansion," he said when Jack was elected president. There was a photo of him, trim and natty, standing beneath palm trees with a cigarette in his fingers. He and Fairweather lost the shop during the Depression and he had to move back home. He apprenticed as an electrician at McClellan Electric on Main Street in Urbana and then "got on" at the University of Illinois, where he worked for the rest of his life.

After the war, Bill and Betty Fairweather moved to Urbana, where Bill, the son of my father's partner, would study for his Ph.D. in psychology. He'd been a bomber pilot. Night after night, the voices of Bill and Walter drifted in from the front porch, as they talked late and smoked cigarettes. In the 1980s, the Fairweathers came to visit us in our Michigan house. "Rog," he asked me, "did you ever wonder why a Ph.D. candidate and an electrician would spend so much time talking? It was because your dad was the smartest man I ever met."

One day years later I was out to dinner with Glen and Reba Pickens. Reba was the daughter of Ben and Mame. In the years after the war they founded the University of Illinois Employees Credit Union, which began in idealism in dingy basement quarters and later grew into a big new building and millions in deposits. Glen and Reba were two of the sunniest people in my family, popular all over town. Their children were Jim and Karol Ann, who are the only cousins near my age I have from my father's side. At dinner I asked Glen and Reba what they knew about my dad's life in Florida. Not much, it turned out, although they thought the florist business had been doing well until the Depression.

"Your dad wrote a lot of letters home," Glen said. "He wrote about good times and then times turned bad and he started to think he would have to come back home. There were some sad things in there. We found all those old letters after Wanda died." I asked what had happened to them. "We threw them out," he said. "That house was filled with things. She never left home, you know." It hadn't occurred to him I would have given anything to read letters written by my father in the 1920s. My father was thirty-seven when he married, fifty-eight when he died. He lived twice as much of his life before I was born as after. How did he write? What did he dream? What were the sad things? I loved Glen and Reba, but what were they thinking? One Sunday in the 1950s, during the Rose Bowl game, the phone rang, and it was an old girlfriend of "Wally" from Florida, who told my mother she'd found his number from information. My mother handed him the phone. There was ice in her eyes. After the call was finished, I was told to go back downstairs and watch the game.

Growing up, there were always books in the house. Daddy's living room chair had a couple of bookcases behind it, which held best sellers like *USA*

Confidential, and matching volumes of Hugo, Maupassant, Chekhov, Twain, and Poe. We took both local papers, and the *Chicago Daily News*. He told me that if I read *Life* magazine every week and the *Reader's Digest* every month, I'd grow up to be a well-informed man. Every night at dinner we listened to *Edward P. Morgan and the News*, "brought to you by the thirteen and a half million men and women of the AFL-CIO." He told me I should never cross a picket line, and I never have. He was a member of the International Brotherhood of Electrical Workers, and my mother told me, "Your father may have to go on strike." I pictured him consumed in flames and wept until it was all explained.

He told me, "The Democratic Party is the friend of the working man." On election night in 1952 I was allowed to stay up as late as I could, listening with my parents to the radio. I must have been carried to bed. They came in together to wake me the next morning with the news that Eisenhower had defeated Stevenson. I had no idea what this meant, but I saw they were depressed. I knew Stevenson was the Democrat and had been governor of Illinois. "He gave a speech," my father said, "saying that he felt like the little boy who stubbed his toe. He said it hurt, but he was too big to cry." I burst into tears. He bought me *The Major Campaign Speeches of Adlai Stevenson*, and in

1956 when Stevenson came to the University of Illinois for a speech, I took it to him for a signature. He was surrounded by Secret Service agents, but when he saw the book he reached out to sign it. "Haven't signed one of these in a while," he said.

The TV set in the early days was banished to the basement, because my mother didn't want it "cluttering up the living room." Half of the basement held my father's workbench, the washer-wringer, and clotheslines. The other half had been supplied with reclining aluminum deck chairs. Later there was room for my science fiction collection and the desk that represented the offices of the Ebert Stamp Company. Daddy and I faithfully watched Jack Benny, Herb Shriner on *Two for the Money*, *Omnibus*, and particularly *The Lawrence Welk Show*. Welk reminded him of his father. When something good came on, my father would shout, "Bub, you'd better see this." She was often right upstairs at the kitchen table, reading the papers, listening to music on the radio. When she came down, she usually remained standing, as if she didn't want the TV set to get any ideas. Otherwise she could have my chair, and I'd sit cross-legged on the floor.

My father woke up about five thirty every morning, and listened to Paul Gibson on WBBM from Chicago. Gibson had no particular politics; he just talked for two or three hours. Daddy would make coffee and liked his toast almost burnt, and the aromas would fill the small house. I'd stumble in and he'd hand me a slice, slathered with clover honey from the university farms. Gibson didn't play much music, but one day he played "The Wayward Wind" by Gogi Grant. I walked into the kitchen. "You like that?" my father asked, nodding. The song has haunted me ever after.

My parents took me to see my first movie, the Marx Brothers in *A Day at the Races*. I had to stand to see the screen. I'd never heard Daddy laugh more loudly. He had seen the real Marx Brothers in vaudeville at the Virginia Theatre in Champaign. We went to see *Gentlemen Prefer Blondes*, and I was prepared to clap my hands over my eyes because *Our Sunday Visitor*, the newspaper distributed in church on Sundays, said the movie was racy. Together we saw *Bwana Devil*, the first movie made in 3-D. Those were the three movies I remember us seeing together. My aunt Martha took me to most of my movies.

At Walter's lunch hour, he'd come home and fix himself something. His favorite meal was a peanut-butter-and-jam sandwich and pickled herring in wine sauce. "The sweet and sour go against each other and make every bite fresh." When he cooked at dinner—rarely—it was usually hamburgers, pressed on a device of his own manufacture, or round steak, pounded with the side of a saucer, sprinkled with Accent and flour, and fried. He made chili with some bacon in it and let it improve in the refrigerator overnight. He always drew onion-chopping duty, with his father's knife.

He'd take me to Illinois home games at Memorial Stadium. "See those electrical pipes? I installed them." When the All-American J. C. Caroline broke away for a touchdown, he and everyone around us yelled so loudly it could be frightening. When it was very cold, he'd send me under the stands for cans of hot chocolate, to hold in our pockets. In the cold air the smoke of his Luckies was sharp. Everybody smoked. Ray Eliot, the legendary Illini coach, smoked on the sidelines. After my father was told he had lung cancer, he switched to filter-tip Winstons.

Walter was a tall man for his generation, six feet two inches. I never saw him angry with anyone except my mother, and that was mostly shouting at her to calm down: "Cut out that noise!" Their fights were mostly about money: how much they were helping her family, and how much they were helping his. Sometimes my mother would lie on my bed at night, sobbing after a fight, but I pretended I was asleep. My stomach would hurt. I have never been able to process anger.

They pushed me. I would go to the university and get an education. I wouldn't be an electrician like

my father. Daddy refused to teach me a single thing
about his work. When I was in grade school and used
a new word, they would laugh with delight and he'd
say, "Boy, howdy!" When I won the radio speaking
division of the Illinois High School Speech Contest
in 1957, the state finals were in a room in Gregory
Hall. My aunt Martha told me years later that he had
hidden in a closet to listen to me.

When I was around twelve he spotted an ad for
a fishing resort in Wisconsin and mailed off for the
brochure. We studied it. He was especially impressed
by their seven-course meals. "Boy, howdy!" We drove
north for a fishing trip, the two men in the family,
who had never been fishing together in our lives. I
guessed I was about to be told the facts of life, which
I already knew from a leaflet hidden in the night
table of my friend Jerry Seilor's father, who was never
able to bring himself to give it to him. No facts were
mentioned in Wisconsin. The resort was small and
inexpensive, knotty pine with stuffed deer heads and
painted sunsets on the walls. I remember little about
the food except that my father carefully counted the
courses. Combination salad. Split pea soup. Cottage cheese with chives. We rented a boat and fishing
tackle and sat upon the glassy lake in the sun. The
weather was one degree above cool. I don't remember if we caught anything. I remember our contented

silence together, the smoke from his Luckies, the hiss when a spent cigarette would hit the water, the songs from our portable radio: "The Wayward Wind." "Oh, Mein Papa," by Eddie Fisher. "That makes me think about my father," he said.

In 1956, I entered Urbana High School and joined the staff of the student paper. That autumn, Senator Estes Kefauver was Stevenson's running mate, and my father learned that after his speech Kefauver would be spending the night in a guest room of the Illini Union building on campus. He hatched a plan for me to interview the senator. He found someone on campus to letter an official-looking badge reading:

ROGER EBERT

URBANA HIGH SCHOOL ECHO

At six in the morning, we took up our post with other reporters and photographers outside the senator's room, and when his aide looked out and saw me, he saw a photo op. I was brought in to "interview" Kefauver and had my photo taken. "Are you deeply concerned that we are all in danger from strontium ninety?" I asked him, because we had been at his speech the night before as he lectured about the dangers of nuclear testing. "That's an excellent question," he said, smiling for the photographer.

I always worked on newspapers. Harold Holmes, the father of my friend Hal, was the managing editor at the *News-Gazette* and took us down to the paper. A Linotype operator set my byline in lead, and I used a stamp pad to imprint everything with "By Roger Ebert." I was electrified. I wrote for the St. Mary's grade school paper. I used a primitive hectograph kit to duplicate copies of the *Washington Street News*, which I distributed to neighbors, and *Ebert's Stamp News*, which I mailed to the six or so customers of my mail-order stamp company. Both were hand lettered in the purple ink that was absorbed by the hectograph gel and produced copies until the ink faded.

Harold Holmes asked me before my junior year in high school if I wanted to cover the Urbana Tigers for the *News-Gazette*. This caused a debate at the kitchen table. I was not yet sixteen. I would have to work until one or two a.m. two nights a week and drive myself home on a learner's permit. My mother said, "Those newspapermen all drink, and they don't get paid anything." There was some truth in this. My father said: "If Harold thinks the boy can do the job, we'll always regret not giving him the chance."

As a younger man, he drank. My mother determined to put an end to this. "She put your father through hell on earth," Aunt Martha told me. Advised by a family doctor, my mother added some substance like Antabuse to his coffee. When he had his next beer, it made him deathly ill: "He didn't get up off that davenport for two days." This was before I was born, and I never saw him take a drink. When the old Flat Iron Building in downtown Urbana burned, he took me down to witness the flames, and I saw tears in his eyes. It had been the home of the Urbana Elks Lodge. "Why are you crying, Daddy?" "I had some good times in that building."

We went for drives. We went to Westville, south of Danville, to eat Coney Island hot dogs made the same way they made them in West Palm Beach. We went up to Wings, north of Rantoul, to have Sunday dinner, and they brought a tray with kidney bean salad, celery sticks (stuffed with canned cheese), carrots, green onions, radishes, pickled peppers, candied watermelon rinds, quartered tomatoes, and coleslaw (pronounced "cold slaw"). Every single time my father beheld this sight, he said exactly the same thing: "They fill you up before you even get your meal." Then he would glance at me, to signal that he knew he said it every time. That's how I gained a lifelong fondness for repeating certain phrases beyond the point of all reason. These included: "Too long a sacrifice can make a stone of the heart," from my best friend John McHugh, via Yeats; "A wee drop of the dew," from my great editor Bob Zonka; "Irving! Brang 'em on!" from my Cannes buddy Billy Baxter; "Not by foot, I hope!" from Tintin's dog, Milou. These phrases are not tics, they are rituals in the continuity of life.

We drove to Starved Rock State Park. Turkey Run State Park. The Great Smoky Mountains. Rockome Gardens, the big rock garden in Amish country down around Arthur, Illinois. These destinations I found interesting, the drives boring. I read books in the backseat. Sometimes we'd drive with our neighbors the Wikoffs up to Mickelberry's Log Cabin on Ninety-Fifth Street in Chicago. This was a long drive in the years before the interstates. Sometimes we'd just drive up to Rantoul to see the Panama Limited go barreling through. "It must have been going ninety miles an hour," my father would say, glancing at me because he said exactly the same thing every single time, no matter how fast it was going. Then my mother would run into the Home Theater to get popcorn and Necco wafers, which we would share when, on our drive home, we parked at Illini Field, north of Urbana, to watch the planes land.

Daddy loved music, and as a member of the university staff he let us into the balcony at Huff Gymnasium to "keep an eye on the lights" while we watched the orchestras of Harry James, Count Basie, Les Baxter, Stan Kenton, Les and Larry Elgart. I absorbed popular music through my pores. In the basement

I would use a tape recorder he bought me to record radio shows on which I played my 45 rpm records and pretended to be a deejay.

On his belt he carried a leather pouch with his smaller tools and a key ring large enough for a prison warden. He needed to be able to walk in anywhere. On nights when a fierce thunderstorm would descend, the phone might ring. I would lie awake waiting for my father to say, "Come on, boy, the lights are out." We would drive in the maroon Plymouth through the darkened streets to the power plant, a looming coal-smelling building that my father would enter with a flashlight and do something. "All right, boy," he would say. "Stand by the door." All of the lights on the campus would come back on, and we would drive home, me dozing in the car, although I could tell when we came closer, on Race Street, because the bricks rumbled beneath the wheels.

The university was smaller then, and so was Champaign-Urbana. We went as a family to every dairy that had an ice cream counter. Daddy scouted out little restaurants. There was the Huddle House on University Avenue, which had a counter with perhaps fifteen stools in the front of an enormous building with no apparent purpose. Every time we went there, he speculated that the Huddle House was a front for Russian spies. He liked the Race Inn on Race Street, where you get all the fried smelts you could eat on Fridays. And Mel Root's on Main Street. I joke about movies with a café where everybody in town comes and they all know one another. Mel Root's was that place in Urbana.

I wonder what my father really thought about his life. He married a beautiful woman, and I believe they loved each other. Whatever had happened in West Palm Beach stayed in West Palm Beach. He married in his late thirties, held a good-paying job, owned his own home on a corner lot. He debated politics with my Republican uncle Everett Stumm, was militantly pro-union, had me worried when Eisenhower defeated Stevenson the second time. He never said so, but I got the notion that the Republicans were not good people. He read all the time. In another generation, he would surely have gone to university and read books with his feet up on the desk, and he wanted me to do that for him. Sometimes I resented him, as when blinded by summer sweat while pulling bagworms from evergreens while he repeated, "If the job's worth doing, it's worth doing well." He wouldn't let me have my dog Blackie in the house. He thought rugs were more important than dogs. Did I know how much I loved him? I do now.

In the spring of 1960 I announced that I didn't want to go to Illinois, I wanted to go to Harvard, like Jack Kennedy and Thomas Wolfe. This was on a warm day, the screen door open in the living room. "Boy, there's no money to send you to Harvard," he said. "But I have my own job," I said. To my astonishment he began to cry. Then I learned what my mother already knew, that a month earlier he had taken the train to Chicago and consulted a specialist who told him he was dying of lung cancer.

Surgery was at Cole Hospital. I waited in a small rose garden; my mother was inside. The surgeon closed up his chest and told us he might live two years at the most. He came home, worked for a few weeks, then went on sick leave. He read. Harry Golden, the liberal North Carolina Jew, had a new book out, and he loved Harry Golden. He never missed Lawrence Welk. I was busy, pledging a fraternity, dating, working for the *News-Gazette*, publishing my science fiction fanzine. I would sit in the living room or the basement and read with him or watch TV. He told me he was doing fine. Lighting up a Winston. I saw my mother's eyes, but we didn't speak of the unthinkable. He went back to the hospital, and I brought the new Harry Golden book over for him.

That day I saw something I am so grateful to have seen. He sat up on the edge of his bed. "Hold me, Bub," he said. "It hurts so much." She took him in her arms. "Oh, Wally," she said, "I love you so much."

4   MY MOTHER

ANNABEL STUMM WAS born outside Taylorville, Illinois, on the family farm. Her father, William, was of Dutch stock, had been adopted as a boy, and that is all I ever learned about his family. Her mother, Anna Gleeson, was a second-generation Irish American whose own mother immigrated to America on a sailing vessel. How the two families came to farm in Illinois I was never told. It wasn't a closed subject, but simply never an open one. Because I was a late child and my relatives were a good deal older, it belonged to the past. William must have operated a billiard parlor in Taylorville, or perhaps the smaller town of Stonington, because someone pasted his tiny newspaper advertisement from 1901 in a family album.

After William died Anna moved her family to Urbana so two of her sons could attend the university. She opened a boardinghouse for students, and in that establishment Annabel was raised with her brothers Everett, Robert, and William, and her sisters Mary and Martha. There was another brother, Gleeson, a tow-headed playmate in old photographs, who died on the farm: "He fell down the steps carrying a bottle."

One day in the 1970s I drove with my mother, Martha and Bill, and our cousin Bernardine Gleeson to visit the old farmhouse, which stood, abandoned by later tenants, open to the weather. They walked cautiously inside and thought maybe they remembered one patch of wallpaper. They were shocked by how small it was: "How did our whole family ever fit in here?" There was a creek at the bottom of the yard and my mother remembered they ran barefoot to it all summer long. This was almost the only time I ever heard them discuss their brother who had died there.

I read the memoirs of Europeans who trace their ancestry back for centuries. My ancestors appeared as if from nowhere in the New World, and I know so little about any relatives of the great-grandparent generation. They were Irish, Dutch, and Germans, immigrating on my mother's side from need and on my father's side from the demand for skilled labor in the railroad shops. I only knew one of my four grandparents, Anna, who lived on Clark Street in Urbana with her children Bob and Martha, and Martha's lifelong friend Jean Sabo. This house was always referred to by Annabel as Home.

My parents were scarred by the Depression. My father lost his business. My mother, a decade younger and more vulnerable, remembered the hard times on the farm and the crowded boardinghouse where the boarders took precedence. I would take her on drives around town and sometimes our route would take us past the Champaign County Nursing Home. She always called it the "poor farm," and predicted, "That's where I'll end up." I told her I would not allow that, but the dread was too deeply embedded. I thought I could count on things to turn out right. She never learned to do that. For some time after I moved to Chicago, she didn't know how to explain to her friends how I earned a living. "And does Roger still just...go to the movies?" she was asked.

Annabel and Mary were beauties. Martha, with whom I felt an instinctive sympathy, was plain. Everett, the oldest, was the vice president of a gravel quarry somewhere near Crystal Lake, Illinois. He was the only Republican in the family. His children Tom Stumm, a West Point graduate and retired colonel, and Marianne

Dull, wife of a Colorado veterinarian, are my only first cousins on my mother's side. Bill, Bob, and Martha never married. Bob, who wasn't as smart, worked as a janitor at the University of Illinois library. He was always more of a bystander at family gatherings.

After high school, my mother attended secretarial school and then went to work for the Allied Finance Company, which had four rooms above the bank in downtown Urbana. Working outside the house was an unconventional, even dashing, decision. She was at one time president of the Urbana Business Women's Association, and involved in some kind of infighting that inspired conspiratorial phone calls late into the night. When the owner of Allied Finance, Russell Willis, was drafted into the war, she managed the business by herself, hiring an assistant to help her repossess cars whose owners had fallen behind on their payments. Such deadbeats were known as "No Pays." It was a term of disparagement, given meaning because she lived in lifelong fear of someday becoming a No Pay herself. The company supplied her with a car, so we had two cars in the driveway when that was rare. And there were two paychecks, so I grew up in security and comfort although I realize now my parents never really had much money.

When Walter returned to Urbana from Florida, I was told, he set eyes on Annabel and began courting her. They were a fashionable couple, both stylish dressers, he at the time with a movie star mustache, she with a knockout figure. After their marriage they lived in Tuscan Court, an Italianate apartment compound behind the Flat Iron Building in downtown Urbana. It was two blocks from Walter's job at McClellan Electric before he got his university job, three blocks from Allied Finance. In about 1940 they bought 410 East Washington on a twenty-year mortgage.

During the war, my mother was a Gray Lady and left home two nights a week in her uniform to do wartime volunteer work. After the war, Russ Willis returned and hired his son, a nice enough man, but my mother felt hurt that he was promoted over her after she had kept the company running in the war years. Feminism was not heard of in those days, but she would have been in favor.

A great deal of Annabel's life revolved around St. Patrick Catholic Church. It stood on Main Street, only half a block from Home. At three or four I began to think of the church as a realm apart from life, perhaps in another dimension, where the priest spoke an unknown language and moved through incense and music, vestments and processions, awesome and boring. Annabel wasn't concerned with theology but with ritual, centering on the public display of devotion. She and some of her friends were much taken with a woman named Jean Shroyer, who lived in an apartment two doors down from the church and never missed a service, even attending every Mass on Sunday. In 1952 Jean made the Marian Year pilgrimage to Rome and returned with the papal blessing, holy water, Kodak slides, and prayer books. She began a study group devoted to the Virgin, which they all attended, and was greeted in our home as a temporal saint. My father remained detached during these occasions.

Walter and Annabel were stage parents, encouraging situations in which I might draw attention. When the Urbana Police started the Junior Police, it was my photograph that appeared in the paper, being fitted with my official hat. I remember not one thing more about the Junior Police. I heard over and over that I was "gifted," although I never had any special gifts in school other than those, like reading and writing, that seemed to come naturally. Much was made when, in the eighth grade, I won an essay contest held by Chanute Air Force Base in Rantoul, north of Urbana. Again my picture was in the paper. My award, a desk pen, was presented by David Dodds Henry, president of the University of Illinois. That such a great man would officiate at an essay contest for eighth graders strikes me as peculiar.

My mother's life revolved around our family, her family, and her job. I often visited the Allied Finance offices, where Mr. Willis supplied me with a copy of *Swiss Family Robinson* and allowed me the use of a typewriter on which I taught myself to hunt and peck more or less the way I do today. When we went outside for lunch at Mel Root's or the counter at Smith Drugs, everybody knew Annabel. To be a "businesswoman" was a form of celebrity, and her friends included Frances Renner, president of Urbana Home Loan, whose husband was later to be framed in the death of my dog Blackie.

There was some kind of upheaval at Allied Finance, unclear to me, and Annabel left the company. It may have involved the promotion of a man into a job she thought should have been hers, and there were endless evening phone conversations that could be overheard but not understood. In about 1956 she went to work as the bookkeeper for Johnston's Sport Shop in Champaign, and I got a Saturday job there at fourteen, as a salesclerk. After my father died in 1960, she supported us as a bookkeeper for a plumbing supply and two florists. She paid off the family home and sold it, and we rented a two-bedroom house a few blocks north, which is where I lived while going to the university.

In all those years there were half-understood

conversations about the fact that Jean Sabo continued to live at Home with my grandmother, Martha, and Bob. She and Martha had met in nursing
school; Jean became an army nurse, took an apartment after the war, and later moved in. Martha was
the youngest, and always the most self-confident, and
she announced that Jean would be moving in as a
fact. Anna Gleeson died in 1960, attended by all of
her children, and Jean and Martha continued to live
together, eventually buying homes where Bill joined
them after retirement. Not once was the relationship between Martha and Jean ever discussed in my
hearing.

Annabel began to date a man named George
Michael, who had lived with his late wife, Berenice,
a few blocks down Maple Street. He was an accountant for the university's computer division. Stable,
reticent, a pipe smoker, he introduced her to the
social life of the American Legion post in Urbana,
and for the first time in her life she began to drink.
I started drinking in college at about the same time,
and gradually we both began drinking more. One
night I returned early to our house and found Annabel and George in bed together. I went to my room
and after half an hour George came in and told me
he loved my mother and he "planned to do the right
thing." They were married in a simple ceremony in

the St. Patrick rectory and there was a little reception at Home. "Now you listen to me," Martha said, as she often did. "George Michael is a good man and he likes you. He has his work cut out for him with your mother."

He bought a new three-bedroom house on Vawter Drive in a new subdivision and told me, "All of my life I've dreamed of a house like this." There were happy times there, as I essentially lived my life on campus and moved into my fraternity for one semester. But the social life at the Legion post expanded into more drinking, more for Annabel than George, and there began to be arguments centering on Annabel's jealousy of Berenice; let her find one thing in the house that had belonged to her, and George was "holding on to it." This reached such a pitch that in 1964 I moved out for good and rented an attic apartment on Green Street, near campus.

George and Annabel sold the house and became managers of a nearby apartment complex, living rent free. I by now had spent a year in Cape Town and was living in Chicago, where they would visit for Cubs games. One day my mother called and said George had moved out. He disappeared without a word, reportedly went to live in California, and I never heard another word from him. "I'm not surprised," Martha told me. Annabel went to the church to have the marriage annulled, for reasons never clarified: "It's between me and the church."

Although alcoholism was in my family, my parents never drank during my formative years, and my memories of life at 410 East Washington are of happiness and encouragement. I had an idyllic childhood, and no more than the usual tumultuous adolescence. I can see now that the Daddy I knew was preceded by a different young man who left to try his luck in Florida. After he stopped drinking, he retired completely into our family and his work. He had no separate social life with friends and never went to places where drinking was expected. That must have been the nature of his bargain with alcohol. He was a rock of my childhood. I wonder what he was really thinking. I know my parents were mostly happy together and in love.

My mother passed all those years in innocence of alcohol. George wasn't responsible for her change, but only the occasion for it, and I don't believe he was an alcoholic. He was kind to me and patient with my mother. I often saw them happy together and enjoyed being with them. But as I understand alcoholism, Annabel's first drink filled a place in her she never knew existed, and she was not a person who could drink. I took her to an AA meeting in Chicago once, at which she told the group she was so proud of me for all I was doing to help them. She didn't believe I was really an alcoholic, and she knew she wasn't.

People liked Annabel. She was funny, chatty, a character. She made an impression. Whenever I return to Champaign-Urbana, I meet people who smile when they remember her. Her employers liked her. Neighbors, friends, companions, nurses. Students she met when she was working in the office at Hendrick House, the student residence owned by her friend and mine, Betsy Hendrick.

My mother continued to smoke and drink. She moved into a new two-bedroom apartment and began to employ women to look after her. The first of these was Ruby Harmon, whom we'd known since she started doing my family's laundry in the 1950s. Ruby was her best and most loyal friend, and one day in the 1980s she called me and told me there was something I should know: My mother was drinking too much and had to be put to bed drunk every night, "although she pulls herself together when you visit." She was being treated for emphysema and osteoporosis. I was then three or four years sober and called her doctor to tell him this news. My mother must have guessed my source of information and banished Ruby from her life. I don't believe the doctor took me very seriously; Annabel would have never let him suspect the nature of her drinking.

What then followed were a series of enablers, some who drank with her, some who did not. Her emphysema worsened, she grew thin and frail and moved into a nursing home. Here she couldn't drink, and our conversations grew happier. Betsy Hendrick and her daughter Becky were regular visitors, like members of the family. Karol Ann and Dwayne were always helpful. Other friends filled her room. The nurses told me with some pride that she insisted on always looking her best for her visitors.

She continued to smoke, and when she was on oxygen would remove the tube to have a cigarette: "Honey, it's all I have left." Her circulation began to fail, her blood pressure dropped too low, and she was moved to Mercy Hospital, where I had been born. In her last days she fell into a coma, although when asked how she was, she would faintly reply "fine." On her last day and night, she recited the Hail Mary unceasingly, hour after hour. At four that morning she seemed to fall into a deep sleep, and I told a nurse I'd go home for a nap. She looked at me curiously but hesitated to tell me what she must have been thinking. At six that morning, I received the call that my mother had died. I fell to my knees and sobbed.

I remember her with a sense of great loss. She was a good mother during all the years that counted. After my father's death she worked full-time to help me in school. I never felt a moment's poverty, and after her death I found an old checkbook and was astonished to find that during some years her income was little more than $2,500. We must also have been living on the proceeds of the house my parents bought. She never asked me for money from my *News-Gazette* job but was happy for me to take her out for dinner.

She was smart and canny. In the 1970s I sent her on a trip to Europe and she found her way around easily and came back loaded with stories. She made friends everywhere. In Ireland, she bonded with my friend John McHugh's family. In line at the Rome airport, the people behind her heard her name and introduced themselves as the Rotarians who'd met me when I got off the plane in Cape Town. The tension between us grew during the 1970s as we both drank more, and possibly became worse for her when I stopped drinking in 1979. But she never let down her guard or expressed a single worry about herself. She was always "fine."

Don and Ruth Wikoff, our old neighbors, ran her funeral from the Renner-Wikoff Chapel. Martha, Bill, Jean, cousin Bernardine from Stonington, and Karol Ann and Dwayne Gaines and Jimmy and Bev Pickens, cousins from my father's side, stood with me. Ruby Harmon came and hugged me and said, "She always loved you, Roger, and I always loved her." I told her she had done the right thing by calling me.

5

ST. MARY'S

My GRADE SCHOOL probably couldn't get state approval today. The teachers were unpaid and lived communally. Two grades were taught in one classroom. There were no resources for science, music, physical education, or foreign languages except the Latin of the Mass and hymns. No playground facilities. The younger students were picked up by the single school bus; as soon as we were old enough, we rode our bikes to school, even in winter. A typical meal in the lunchroom might consist of a peanut butter and jelly sandwich on white bread, a dish of corn, a dish of fruit cocktail, and a carton of milk. If you had a penny, you might buy a jawbreaker afterward.

I received a first-rate education. At St. Mary's

Grade School in Champaign, one block across Wright Street from Urbana, we were taught by Dominican nuns who knew their subjects cold, gave us their full-time attention, were gifted teachers, and commanded order and respect in the classroom. For eight years we were drilled in reading, writing, arithmetic, and religion. Periods were devoted to history, geography, and science, taught from textbooks without visual aids or any other facilities. We learned how to write well, spell, and God knows we learned how to diagram a sentence.

I can't prove that a St. Mary's graduate had a better education than a majority of today's high school graduates, but that's my impression. Some of the high school kids who write thoughtful comments on my blog say they've taken charge of their own education, at least in reading and writing. At some point they needed to because their classes had become boring. I taught rhetoric in a Chicago city college for a year. The impression I got was that some students always could write, and some of the others would never be able to. For years during grade and high school I read secretly at my desk while following the class elsewhere in my mind.

I attended St. Mary's for an excellent reason: I would go to heaven. I liked my public school friends, but they were non-Catholics and couldn't look forward to that. It was their misfortune they weren't pagans; pagans at least could spend eternity in limbo because they were not lucky enough to have learned about the Roman Catholic Church. Protestants and Jews had their chance and blew it. "Hindus" and "Muhammadans," the titles under which I mentally filed all the peoples and religions of Asia, India, Arabia, and the Holy Land, were, I suppose, given a pass as honorary pagans.

We put dimes into envelopes that were mailed by Sister to the Society for the Propagation of the Faith. We were each "sponsoring" a little African child, who would now be able to learn about the Church from missionaries and look forward to spending eternity gazing upon the face of God. The first hour of every day was devoted to the study of religion, which began with memorizing the Baltimore Catechism and in upper grades developed into fascinating discussions of theological loopholes. I asked in class one day if the little African children wouldn't be better off without missionaries, because if they never learned about salvation through the Church, they wouldn't run the risk of hell. Sister Rosanne looked at me sadly. "Those poor little children have just as much a right as you do to enjoy the love of God."

This was, if you think about it, a liberal argument. We never discussed politics in class, but I came away with the firm impression that Franklin Roosevelt was our greatest president after Lincoln. In general the Dominicans applied Catholicism toward liberal ends, such as support for equal rights, freedom of speech, separation of church and state, and the rights of workingmen. We especially valued separation of church and state because it was all that protected us from a Protestant takeover. Abortion was off the table as a subject fit for the classroom. Birth control was also not discussed; it was assumed you saved yourself for marriage and then had as many little Catholics as the Lord desired. Religion class did however cover such topics as tattoos (a sin against the body, which is the temple of the Holy Ghost) and naming pets after saints (a sacrilege; Rover was allowed but not Max). One day in eighth grade the boys and girls were separated and the assistant priest took us into the auditorium and warned us never to touch ourselves. He didn't specify where we were not to touch.

The school building had a basement for Sister Ambrosetta's first-grade room, the cafeteria, and the gymnasium. The gym was just slightly larger than a basketball court and had two or three rows of seats across one of the short ends. Pads under the baskets protected us from crashing into the walls. Our coach was the tomboy Sister Marie Donald, who tucked the hems of her habit into the rosary she wore around her waist and dribbled and shot better than any of us. She taught second and third grades on the second floor, and it was there we had what passed for school band practice. She passed around triangles, tambourines, ratcheted sticks, maracas, and wooden blocks, and we formed a rhythm section to pound, scrape, ding, and rattle along with music on 78 rpm records. Fifth and sixth grades were taught by Sister Nathan, a fresh-faced favorite who usually seemed amused by us. We took this as a sign of favor.

Now my memory fails. I know Sister Rosanne, an immensely kind woman, very smart about current events, taught seventh and eighth grades, and Sister Emma taught third and fourth. Did Sister Gilberta, the principal, come in there somewhere? To be sent to the principal's office was a special damnation. We feared her, because we feared the feeling of guilt. The nuns weren't "strict" in the sense usually meant. No sister ever laid a hand on any student as far as I know. Nor did they raise their voices. It was an orderly school. We regarded the nuns with a species of awe, because they were the brides of Christ and had the entire One, Holy, Catholic, and Apostolic Church backing them up.

The school year mirrored the church year. We turned the pages on a big Advent calendar, observed saints days, wore ashes on Ash Wednesday, announced what we were giving up for Lent. After a long winter, relief came on May 1, and the crowning of Mary. We held a May Day parade, the boys in ties, the girls in frocks. In eighth grade our queen of the May was Jeanne Rasmussen, whom I was smitten with, but too shy to tell her. We marched in procession from the school to the statue of Mary next to the church, and placed little bouquets at her feet, singing:

Bring flowers of the rarest
bring blossoms the fairest,
from garden and woodland and hillside and dale;
our full hearts are swelling,
our glad voices telling
the praise of the loveliest flower of the vale!

O Mary we crown thee with blossoms today!
Queen of the Angels and Queen of the May.

For recess, we raced from the school to the playgrounds, which were dirt lots ringed with shrubbery on either side of the convent. The nun who was cook and housekeeper kept an eye on us from her kitchen steps. There was no playground equipment, not even a swing or a slide. Bringing our own gear, we played softball, dodgeball, football, marbles, jacks, hopscotch, and mumblety-peg. There was a fallen tree trunk on which we played king of the hill, which involved two boys mounting the log and trying to push each other off. Girls fanatically jumped rope, which boys would not and as a result could not do.

I was not gifted at sports but was sought after as an entertainer. I had the knack of reading a book and repeating its dramatic highlights, and I'd walk around the block regaling my followers with the career of Harry Houdini. I went through a particularly devout period after I took the confirmation name of Blessed Dominic Savio, the saintly young pupil of St. John Bosco. I was allowed this choice by the special dispensation of Father J. W. McGinn, since technically my choice should have been a saint. Dominic made the grade a few years later, one of the youngest saints in church history. A large image of him can be seen on the wall of the grade school in Fellini's *8 1/2*.

I became inflamed by a biography of Savio in which, as a lad in school, he attempted to teach his schoolmates the folly of violence as a means of ending disputes. Two of them had a grudge and announced they would settle it with a fight. Vainly did the Blessed Dominic attempt to talk them out of this. When they squared off, he removed a crucifix from his pocket and stepped between them, holding it aloft and telling them, "Throw the first stones at me." Shamed, they lowered their heads, and he urged them to make a good confession. This struck me as exemplary behavior, and I went to school with a small crucifix in my pocket and asked two of my friends, Dougie Pierre and Jimmy Sanders, to start a fight so I could step between them. They said they weren't mad at each other. "Then start one anyway," I pleaded, not quite capturing the spirit of Blessed Dominic's message.

I was a case study. I threw myself into winning the school's annual magazine subscription contest, sponsored by the Curtis Circulation Company. A portion of each subscription went to the school, and the best salesman won a trophy. I won two years in a row, flogging the *Saturday Evening Post, Ladies' Home Journal, Popular Mechanics,* and dozens of other titles (the nuns neatly crossed out *Esquire* on every form). A pitchman arrived to kick off the next year. "Everyone you know is a sales opportunity!" he lectured us in the auditorium. "Your parents, your neighbors, even people you meet! Don't be shy! Sell those subscriptions!" I raised my hand. "Sir," I asked, "would you like to buy a subscription?" I expected laughter, applause, and his congratulations. What I got was total silence and Sister Gilberta ordering me to meet with her in the hall to explain why I had embarrassed my whole school. Then followed talks with my parents. I felt humiliated and outraged. It seemed to me

I had been mistreated by people with no imagination or sympathy. I suppose in another sense I was being a little jerk. That pattern has persisted.

Something happened the summer after eighth grade that puts St. Mary's in a new light. It was my last year at St. Joseph's Camp for Boys, on Bankson Lake in Michigan. One of my buddies was Mole Hasek from Ohio. One day the kids were grabbing off his glasses, putting them on, and staggering around: "I'm blind! I'm blind!" I took my turn and suddenly the entire world shifted into focus. I didn't want to ever take them off again. I wrote to my parents: "I need glasses!"

The optometrist had me read the charts and slowly straightened up. "Has Roger ever worn glasses?" he asked my mother. "No. He hasn't needed them." The doctor said: "He's probably always needed them. He's very shortsighted." He wrote me out a prescription. "Wasn't he ever tested?" It had never occurred to anyone. My parents and my aunt Martha the nurse monitored my health, which was good; I was in the hospital only twice, to have my tonsils and appendix removed, and had monthly radiation treatments for ear infections (they were probably responsible for the salivary cancer I developed in my sixties). I'd never complained about eyesight, and no one noticed any problems. My father said, "Now we know why you always had your nose in a book." I also knew why I was no good at sports: I couldn't see well enough. I remember in seventh and eighth grades having a desk in the back row of the room. Apparently I couldn't read the blackboard very well—then, or ever before. How did I get through grade school? I have no idea. Maybe Blessed Dominic coached me.

6   DAN-DAN THE YO-YO MAN

WHEN APRIL WITH its sweet showers brought flowers to the lawns of May and birds filled the air with melodies, Dan-Dan the Yo-Yo Man made his annual pilgrimage to our playground at St. Mary's School. He drove up in a dark maroon 1950 Hudson we all recognized on sight: It had the Step-Down Ride that allowed it to outcorner Fords and Chevys at the stock car races out at the fairgrounds. To own a car like that was to be a Duncan Yo-Yo professional.

Dan-Dan dismounted on the far side of the big Hudson, and when he walked into view there were already two Yo-Yos spinning in the air before him, a whirl of red and yellow. He walked smiling toward home plate, let the Yo-Yos bounce off it, and snapped them on the fly into his pockets. He took out one and rocked the baby, walked the dog, skinned the cat, made the monkey climb the string, and went around the world. Then he pulled out a Camel, lit up, and passed out flyers for the citywide Duncan Yo-Yo contest that would be held on the stage of the Princess Theater on Main Street in Urbana for the following three Saturdays.

The marathon began with an elimination contest. Whoever couldn't do a sleeper, the easiest trick of all, had to leave the stage in shame. This first Saturday was run like a cattle call: Contestants onstage at the right, sleep or wake, offstage to the left, keep it moving. Ushers made sure no one sneaked through for a second chance. Survivors were given a Yo-Yo Club card to show the next weekend.

The Saturday matinee at the Princess at one time cost nine cents. Popcorn was a nickel. Candy bars were a nickel. So were bags of drops: licorice, lemon, root beer, or horehound. An all-day sucker with Mickey Mouse on it was two cents. Jawbreakers a penny. Girls would buy a roll of Necco wafers, ten cents, and share them out. Urban legends were passed along about the kid who was running with a Holloway bar in his mouth, and he fell and the stick got driven through his brain. You gave your ticket to the usher and got your serial card punched. The serials had twelve episodes. Eleven punches, and you got into the twelfth show for free. What if you gave your card to a buddy? The Princess didn't care. Then the buddy had to buy a ticket.

We raced inside and grabbed our favorite seats. Then big kids took them and told us to get lost. The interior would be flooded with light as someone let a buddy in free by the alley door. Much whistling and stamping of feet. An usher would race to collar the sneak before the door slammed and he took cover in protective darkness. Boys sat with boys and girls with girls. Sometimes older kids might be going steady. She would have his class ring around her neck, its weight ever so slightly depressing the uncanny valley between the sweet little bumps of her cashmere. If you sat behind them and said anything, you might get a knuckle sandwich.

Saturdays at the Princess involved a time commitment, a fact not lost on our parents. The show started about noon, with a slide offering a five-dollar reward for the apprehension of vandals. Then a slide reading *Ladies! Hold onto your bags! Do not place them on the seat next to you! Your cooperation will help them in not getting lost!* Then the ads. Busey Bank. Hudson Dairy. Urbana Pure Milk Company. Lorry's Sport Shop. Mel Root's, *Serving fine food at affordable prices 24 hours a day—we never close!* Then the coming attractions. Next week! Roy Rogers, King of the Cowboys! Cheering! Dale Evans, Queen of the Cowgirls! Booing! Coming soon! Hoppy! Rex Allen! The Bowery Boys! Then five color cartoons. Mickey Mouse. Daffy Duck. Tom and Jerry. Mr. Magoo. Goofy. Then the serial. Batman, Superman. Rocket Man. Flash Gordon. Cheering as the hero escaped from last week's fatal trap, only to fall into another one ten minutes later. Then the newsreel. Commie defeat in Korea! A-bomb tests! Premiering the new Studebakers! *It looks speedy—but which way is it going?* Yankees off to a good start! *At Florida's beautiful Cypress Gardens, syncopated mermaids parade on water skis! Their smiles say, come on in—the water's fine!*

By this time only the girls doling out Neccos to themselves were still in business. Even the all-day suckers were gone; they hadn't been licked, but crunched in greed. There was a sudden fanfare, as on the screen searchlights crossed over the words *Our feature presentation.* There was a preshow rush downstairs to the boys' room. It had a semipermanent population of underage smokers, looking like they were ready to paste you.

It was always a double feature: A Western and a comedy. Of the comedies, usually the Bowery Boys or Abbott and Costello. When Bud and Lou met

Frankenstein, it scared the shit out of us. Then the Western. For some reason, I have vivid memories of two enigmatic cowboys, Whip Wilson and Lash LaRue. They packed wicked bullwhips. It was incorrectly believed by some that they didn't carry guns. Untrue. They carried them, but they didn't need them, because their whip snatched your gun out of your holster faster than you could draw. I wished they'd been married, like Roy and Dale. I fantasized about their wives Whippet Wilson and Lashes LaRue.

As the afternoon came to an end, the theater, now hot and humid and smelling of sweaty T-shirts, grew quiet in suspense. Dan-Dan the Yo-Yo Man strode onstage—from the steps, because there was no backstage—with twin Yo-Yos spinning, maybe Whistlers. The Yo-Yo showdown began. The second Saturday, the prizes were cartons of six Coke bottles, courtesy of the Champaign-Urbana Coca-Cola Bottling Company on South Neil Street. Third weekend, after a surviving handful met the challenges of advanced tricks, the winner got a brand new Schwinn. I assume the Duncan Company paid for this and Dan-Dan's salary out of the Yo-Yos they sold across the street at Woolworth's. What Dan-Dan did to pass the time Monday through Friday, I have no idea.

After some lucky kid had his new bike handed down to him from the stage and pushed it up the aisle, we staggered out into the sunshine with sugar headaches and went to the dime store to buy a professional Yo-Yo; those cheap red and black models would never win you a Schwinn. But one year I lingered over a display for the Miracle-Gro Garden in a Pan and brought it home to my bedroom windowsill. It was an aluminum pan like chicken pot pies came in, filled with vermiculite and embedded with eager seeds. I bathed them with water, and they brought forth young shoots, and it was spring, and everyone was in love, and flowers picked themselves.

7 SUMMER

ON THE LAST day of school, time stretched forward beyond all imagining. There was a heightened awareness in the room as the second hand crept toward our moment of freedom. We regarded the nuns as a discharged soldier does his superior officer. Here had existed a bond that would never be again. We didn't run screaming out the door. We sauntered. We had time. We were aware of a milestone having passed.

Some kids would go to second homes, or to visit relatives, or to summer camp. My friends and I would stay at home. We would have nothing planned. The lives of kids were not fast-tracked in those days. We would get together after breakfast and make desultory conversation, evaluate suggestions, and maybe play softball, shoot baskets, go down into somebody's basement, play cards, go to the Urbana Free Library for Miss Fiske's Summer Reading Club, rassle on the lawn, listen to the Cardinals, play with our dogs, or lay on our stomachs on the grass and read somebody's dad's copy of *Confidential* magazine. Somebody's mom was probably keeping an eye on us through a screened window.

Our bicycles were our freedom. We would head out for Crystal Lake Park, dogs barking behind us until they grew uninterested in this foolishness and fell back. Or maybe this would be a day when we would earn money. This we did by mowing lawns, or when we were younger taking a card table out to the sidewalk and opening a Kool-Aid stand. Some kid would announce he was "opening," and we would look at him in envy, because he was in retail, and we wished we had thought of it first. It was nothing for two adults, perfect strangers, to pull over and invest a dime to drink from two jelly glasses, washed out in a soup pot full of dishwater. When the sun fell lower in the sky, the newspaper trucks would come around pitching bundles, and I would ask a pal, "Want to walk me on my route?" Always "walk me." Never "walk with me."

In all of our movements away from home base, we peed when we had to and where we could. Behind trees, in shrubbery, against back walls, in the alley. This we called "going to see a man about a dog." When the City of Urbana dedicated a plaque on the sidewalk marking my childhood home, from my seat on the little platform I could see several of my boyhood pissoirs. Why didn't we just go home to pee? Your mom might grab you and make you do something.

As an only child I was sometimes content with my own company, especially after I discovered science fiction. In a corner of the basement I positioned my cast-metal bookshelves, for which I redeemed three books of Green Stamps each. On these I placed the old s-f magazines that two foreign brothers, graduate students on my *Courier* route, had given me. *Astounding, Galaxy, Fantasy & Science Fiction*. Then I discovered, more to my taste, *Amazing Stories, Imagination*, and the final issues of the full-size pulp *Thrilling Wonder Stories*. Science fiction itself somehow had an aura of eroticism about it. It wasn't sexually explicit, but it often seemed almost about to be.

Down there in the basement it was cooler. I reclined in an aluminum lawn chair and played albums on my record player—Pat Boone, Doris Day, the McGuire Sisters, Benny Goodman, Les Paul and Mary Ford, Polly Bergen, who sent me an eight-by-ten autographed photo. I wrote to Percy Faith and he mailed me a dozen of his 45s. I wrote asking Stan Freberg for an autographed photo, and he wrote back regretting that he was all out of photos, but as a consolation was enclosing a hairpin from Betty Furness. A lot of my records evoked thoughts of lost romance, about which I knew nothing. I grew sentimental at second hand.

Sometimes a central Illinois thunderstorm would come ripping out of the sky, loud and violent. All hell broke loose. Afterward the rainwater would be backed up at the corner drains, and we would ride our bikes through it, holding our Keds high to keep them dry. The rest of the time it was hot outside, sometimes for a few days even "above one hundred degrees Fahrenheit," we said in an official tone. Air-conditioning was rare except at the movies. Windows and screen doors stood open day and night. The idea was to get a "cross breeze," although actually you just left everything open and the breeze did what it wanted.

Eventually my parents bought a Philco window air conditioner for their bedroom. After they finished their iced tea and their last cigarettes on the front porch, my father would say, "Time to turn on the air conditioner." In my room I read late into the night in the heat and humidity, the book balanced on my chest. I was decked out in what my aunt Martha described approvingly as "shorty pajamas." I read far later than I should have. I'd joined the Book-of-the-Month Club with a twenty-five-dollar gift certificate from my aunt Martha, at a time when few books were as much as five dollars. I read *By Love Possessed* with fascination for the adult characters entirely outside my experience. Countless science fiction books. Erle Stanley Gardner. The angry screeds of Vance Packard, like *The Hidden Persuaders* with the attack on "ad men" and its photos discovering subliminal images of genitalia in the ice cubes of vodka ads. *Julius Caesar* by Shakespeare, feeling smug. *All the King's Men*, recommended to me by the lady at Robeson's Book Department. I read it four or five times, absorbed in its portrait of its hero Jack Burden, the cynical newspaper reporter and enabler for the corrupt governor.

In my teens I began to read Thomas Wolfe, and felt I'd met my soul mate. From a small town he went north to Harvard and then to the great city of New York. He was a Writer, filled with fierce energy, pouring out a stream of passionate prose. His hero stalked through the stacks of the Harvard library, feeling driven to read every book. On the train north, he had dreamed of the soft white thighs of the farm women of the night. He walked the campus, uttering wild goat cries to the moon. Through my window, a lonesome train whistle blew. My chin made a puddle of sweat on my neck. No writer since has been able to sweep me up like Thomas Wolfe when I was thirteen and fourteen. I read all his novels nonstop. We all grow less sweepable. I read *Look Homeward, Angel* again a few years ago and expected it to seem overwrought and dated, but it held up pretty well. Then I began again on *Of Time and the River* but got bogged down. I still have my Universal Library reprints of *The Web and the Rock* and *You Can't Go Home Again*, but they remain on the shelf.

In the summer mornings, I remember the freshness of the new air, and my father in the kitchen listening to the radio. Television came late to Champaign-Urbana, because the *News-Gazette* and the *Courier* were fighting for the license. But we had radio. The fifty-thousand-watt clear-channel stations boomed in from Chicago: WBBM (CBS), WGN (Wally Phillips with *Your Top Ten on WGN* and the Cubs), WMAQ (NBC), WLS (ABC and Dick Biondi). And from St. Louis: KMOX (Harry Caray doing the Cardinals, until, every kid repeated, "Augie Busch caught him in bed with his wife and threw him out of town"). The local stations were WDWS, WKID, and WILL, the university station. WDWS had CBS and news about flooded viaducts, farm reports, local election results. WKID had Joe Ryder, the "Country Gentleman," in the morning, and a mix of pop and country all day. It was only on sunup to sundown. In the evening sometimes I would ride my bike out to the Philo Hard Road and visit the Dog n Suds, where the Dog in a Basket, including coleslaw, fries, and a root beer, seemed to me a spectacular feast. WKID was next door in a hunched concrete-block building, and once on a long summer evening when the station was on late, I shyly knocked on the screen door. Don McMullen invited me in. He was the deejay, news reader, engineer, everything. Joe Ryder was the station manager, long gone home. Don let me sit in the studio and watch him cue records, holding them in place with a thumb while he finished reading a commercial, then announcing a song and lifting his thumb, perfectly timed.

While a song was playing he showed me into a closet where the UPI wire was pounding, ripped off yards of news and threw it away, ripped off the weather forecast, and went back to the broadcast booth. "Something Smith and the Redheads," he said, and then: "We have a young announcer here named Roger who is going to tell us about the weather." He pointed to the paper in front of me and swiveled the mike over. I was almost dizzy with a flush of excitement. "Sunny and warmer tomorrow, with a high around eighty," I read. "Good job, Roger," Don said. I had been on the radio. There was no turning back. When Don got married I gave him steak knives.

My best friends were Hal Holmes, Jerry Seilor, Larry Luhtala, George Reiss and Danny Yohe from across Washington Street, and on my side of the street the Shaw Boys (Steve, John, and Chuck Shaw), Johnny Dye, Karen Weaver, and Steve and Joe Sanderson. Gary Wikoff and Jackie Yates were around the corner on Maple Street. We boys would form circles with our bikes, one foot braced on the ground, as a girl would sit on her porch steps and hold court. I sensed these conversations were about more than they seemed. Hal and Gary were a little older and seemed to understand more.

The Four Stampers Stamp Club would meet in my basement to trade stamps, allegedly, and look up years and prices in our "Elmers," the thick orange booklets from Elmer R. Long in Harrisburg, Pennsylvania. I say "allegedly" because the talk quickly turned to girls—those at school, and then, with wonder, Jayne Mansfield. One night a Four Stamper explained to me what men and women "did" together, demonstrating with the fingers of one hand forming a circle and a finger from the other hand poking into it. "You know, like this," he said. All became clear to me, although I couldn't figure out what the circle stood for. The navel, probably?

A lot of time was spent trying to get cool. Riding our bikes worked, but when we stopped we'd be streaming with sweat. All of us would ride over to Harry Rusk's grocery, lean our bikes against his wooden porch, and reach into his cooler, a block of ice floating in the water, and haul out a Grapette, a Choc-Ola, or maybe an RC, because for the same money you got more. Never a Coke or 7Up, which you got at home, and you didn't see the point of 7Up anyway, although "You Like It—It Likes You!"

If we rode our bikes out to Crystal Lake, we would pass the A&W Root Beer stand at Race and University. A five-cent beer in a frosted mug. Then we would go to the swimming pool and wash off our bike sweat in the water. In high school I was hired by the pool manager Oscar Adams to be an assistant lifeguard. My duties included the Poop Patrol, my tools a face mask, a waste basket, and a spatula. General cheering each time I emerged triumphant from the deeps. Oscar Adams was also the high school basketball coach, driving instructor, physical education teacher, and chaperone at the Tigers' Den on Friday nights. Urbana couldn't do without him. He had one daughter in particular, Barb, who brought to life the wonderful qualities of a bathing suit.

Movie theaters advertised *It's Cool Inside!* To make this difference more dramatic, the Princess on Main Street made the temperature as cold as possible. Returning to the blinding sunlight, we got headaches between our eyes. Hal and I called each other Holmesy and Stymie. Sometimes Holmesy and I would head across the street to the fountain at McBride's Rexall Drugs where he introduced me to the Cherry 7Up, and my prejudice against 7Up disappeared. We sipped them so slowly they could have been liquid gold. We agreed it was the best-tasting drink in the world. There I also searched the paperback racks for Robert Sheckley, Arthur C. Clarke, and Theodore Sturgeon. Also the Ace Doubles, two s-f novels in the same binding, the cover of one novel on one side. Turn it over and there, upside down, was the other cover. I read my first Philip K. Dick in an Ace Double. To sell Philip K. Dick in those days, Ace had to bundle him with someone else. Today he has two volumes in the Library of America.

Sunday Mass at St. Patrick's was sweltering. The doors stood open, the lower panes of the stained glass windows were propped wide, and big oscillating fans swept the congregation, although these were turned off during the sermon by Father Martel, who followed Father McGinn. The longer he talked, the more we sweated. We worked the fans that were Compliments of Renner-Wikoff funeral home.

The midday meal was the big one on Sundays, and after a nap, for his dinner on Sunday my father liked oatmeal. Then we watched Ed Sullivan. Then my father would say, "My oatmeal has worn off. Does anyone feel like a chocolate malted?" In my high school years there was the Dairy Queen, but in grade school we went to Hudson Dairy on Race Street, a counter lined with stools, a strong aroma of milk, a malt that came with a metal can to hold the part that didn't fit in the glass. "They give you a smaller glass so it feels like you're getting more," my father explained several dozen times.

The nature of summer changed as I grew older. I got a part-time job at Johnston's Sport Shop in 1956, and my first newspaper job at the *News-Gazette* in 1958. Holmesy got an early 1950s Chevy. We'd go out to the new McDonald's at Five Points, across the street from Huey's Store ("What's not on the shelf is on the floor. If it ain't on the floor we ain't got it no more"). A couple of years later I got my first car, $395, a 1954 Ford, sky blue. I painted the wheel rims red, bought stick-on white sidewalls, and hung a pair of foam dice from the rearview mirror. Left sitting in the sun, it smelled inside like scorched plastic, and the steering wheel was too hot to touch. The last day of summer came sooner.

8

CAR, TABLE, COUNTER, OR TAKHOMASAK

IN MY THIRD or fourth year I ate my first restaurant meal, at the Steak 'n Shake on Green Street near the University of Illinois campus. The eyes of the world were on this capable little man, sitting on a stool at the counter, grasping a Steakburger in his hands and opening up to take the first bite. My dad passed me the ketchup bottle and authority flowed into my hands as I smacked it on the bottom. "Aim it on your plate next to the fries," he advised. I did. "Good job."

If I were on death row, my last meal would be from Steak 'n Shake. If I were to take President Obama and his family to dinner and the choice was up to me, it would be Steak 'n Shake. If the pope was to ask where he could get a good plate of spaghetti in

America, I would reply, "Your Holiness, have you tried the Chili Mac or the Chili 3-Ways?" A downstate Illinois boy loves the Steak 'n Shake as a Puerto Rican loves rice and beans, an Egyptian loves falafel, a Brit loves bangers and mash, a Finn loves reindeer jerky, and a Canadian loves doughnuts. This doesn't involve taste. It involves a deep-seated conviction that a food is right, has always been right, and always will be.

Steak 'n Shake is a fast food chain, the first except probably for White Castle. Certainly it's the best. How many fast food chains bring you a glass of water and silverware, and serve you on china? Friends in Los Angeles took me to In-N-Out Burger, and I consumed a mushy mess on a soft bun and shook my head sadly. The very names of the two chains describe the difference in styles of sexual intercourse between California and the Heartland.

The motto of Steak 'n Shake is "In Sight It Must Be Right." No comma. This achieves the perfection of a haiku. There is no skullduggery going on in the back room. Take a seat at the counter and everything happens before your eyes. You watch acolytes in ecclesiastical black and white and little paper soldier caps. The griddle man spears ground beef in the shape of a big marshmallow, positions it on the griddle, mashes it with his spatula. Two, four, six, eight patties, consulting the green and white guest checks lined up before him. He positions the buns facedown on the grill and places a thin wooden plank over them. He turns over each patty and mashes it again. He lifts the plank and places it on the stainless steel shelf before him. He lines up buns on the plank. He blesses a few chosen patties with a slice of cheese. He lifts up the patties and distributes them on the buns. He slides the plank along toward the sous chef in charge of condiments.

The Steakburger is a symphony of taste and texture. Steak 'n Shake has always boasted "We grind all the select cuts—sirloin, porterhouse, ribs, filet." This they do in "Our Own Government-Inspected Commissary," located in, of course, Normal, Illinois. The sandwich is Served on a Toasted Bun. If you order onion, it will be a perfect slice of sweet Bermuda. If you order pickles, you will get two thin slices, side by side. Mustard, relish, tomato, lettuce can also be added. When you bite into the Steakburger, it is al dente all the way through: toasted bun, crispy patty, onion, pickle, crunch, crunch, crunch. The Steakburger has remained unchanged since 1945. They don't add ketchup in advance, because it lends itself to soggy buns. You find a bottle at your table. Also a little bottle of Steak 'n Shake Hot Sauce, which is whole hot peppers floating in water. My father said it was not for the likes of me. He liked to dash it on his Chili 3-Way. I would watch in awe as he sprinkled it on and took his first bite. He would glance at me sideways and elevate his eyebrows a fraction. You see why as a film critic I am so alert to the nuances of actors.

These days at Steak 'n Shake you can order such items as soups, taco salads, chef salads, and Philly cheesesteak. There is a three-page fold-out glossy menu, including even breakfast. I have never ordered an item that was not on the original menu. It is a rule with me. From the start my order was unchanging, unless I added a Tru-Flavor Shake. In Sight It Must Be Right, and you can see the soda jerk combining ice cream and milk in a stainless container, blending them in a mixer, and pouring it all into a big tall glass. Many of today's children think milk shakes are extruded from a spigot.

My Steak 'n Shake fetish is not unique. On an early visit to the Letterman show, I said to David during a commercial break, "I hear you're from Indianapolis, home of the head office of Steak 'n Shake."

"In Sight It Must Be Right," he said. Our eyes locked in communion.

"Four Ways to Enjoy," I said.

"Car, Table, Counter, or TakHomaSak," he replied.

"Specializing in Selected Foods..."

"...with a Desire to Please the Most Discriminating."

"Thanks for Your Liberal Patronage."

"Signed, A. H. (Gus) Belt, founder," he said, and we shared a nod of great satisfaction. Augustus H. Belt founded Steak 'n Shake in 1934, and despite changes in ownership over the years, it preserves the original logos, mottoes, typography, design, approach, philosophy, and recipes. The founder built well.

My wife, Chaz, having been raised in Chicago, knew nothing of Steak 'n Shake. For reasons obscure to me, Steak 'n Shake surrounded the city but never entered it. In 1990, driving downstate to Urbana for my high school reunion, we were passing Kankakee when she said, "Look! There's a sign for your restaurant." I smoothly took the interstate exit. The Kankakee store looked much as all Steak 'n Shakes always have, although in the 1970s they added red to the original color scheme of black and white. We took a booth. "Permit me to order for you," I said. Chaz enjoyed her meal. "I see what you mean," said the darling girl. That night the Urbana High class of 1960 met at the Crystal Lake Park pavilion for wine, fruit, and cheese. "Let's blow this Popsicle stand," said Chris Hastings after a few hours. "Steak 'n Shake!" said John Kratz. "You weren't kidding,"

Chaz said, for I had told her I was not the only devotee in Urbana.

Our cars formed a parade to the Steak 'n Shake on University Avenue, and I was reminded of the universal drive-in ritual: Find a place in the back row, wait until the cars in front of you move ahead, race your engine, jerk ahead in a cloud of burnt rubber, and brake precariously inches from the car ahead. We ordered from carhops, and I remembered a mystery that haunted our high school days: Why didn't we ever recognize a single carhop? Were they pod people? In recent years curb service has been replaced by drive-thru windows. Customers shout their orders into a squawk box, and if they don't plan to TakHomaSak, they find a parking space and dine meditatively. In the curb service days, the car windows were all rolled down. You could look straight through other cars to the end of the line, while currents of rivalry, gossip, and lust flowed back and forth. If your friend had his parents' convertible, you could sit on the trunk with your feet on the seat and command the big picture.

That was on the Friday night. On Saturday the class toured Urbana High School, and at lunchtime it was decided we should inspect the new Steak 'n Shake up on Route 45. "Your classmates are crazy," Chaz said. That evening we held our banquet at the

Urbana Country Club. The club had its own chef, but the dinner committee had decided on catering by Steak 'n Shake. On Sunday morning, as we got into our car at the Lincoln Lodge motel, Chaz took my hand and said, "Let's not stop at Kankakee."

9

BLACKIE

EVERY TIME I see a dog in a movie, I think the same thing: I want that dog. I see Skip or Lucy or Shiloh and for a moment I can't even think about the movie's plot. I can only think about the dog. I want to hold it, pet it, take it for walks, and tell it what a good dog it is. I want to love it, and I want it to love me. I have an empty space inside myself that can only be filled by a dog.

Not a cat. I have had cats and I was fond of them, fonder than they ever were of me. But what I want is unconditional love, and therefore I want a dog. I want to make its life a joy. I want to scratch behind its ears, and scratch its belly when it rolls over. I want to gently extend its tail so the dog can tell it has a fine tail indeed. I want to give it a shampoo, and sneak it bites from the table, and let it exchange the news with other dogs we meet on the street. I want it to bark at the doorbell, be joyous to see my loved ones, shake hands, and look concerned if I seem depressed. If I throw a ball I want the dog to bring back the ball and ask me to throw it again.

If you've read John D. MacDonald's Travis McGee books, you'll remember Meyer, the hairy economist, who lived on a neighboring houseboat. He went to dinner with some new boat owners at the marina, and when he got back McGee asked him what they were like.

"They were bores," Meyer said. "Do you know what a bore is?"

"I'm sure you'll tell me, Meyer."

"A bore, Travis, is someone who deprives you of solitude without providing you with companionship."

For me, that's the problem with cats. If they follow me all over the house, it's not because they want to play, it's because they think something edible might turn up, or that I will entertain them. If these prospects seem remote, a cat will simply stay where it is, idly regard me as I leave the room, lick itself a little, and go back to sleep. I had cats named White Cat, Orange Cat, and Sports Fan. They were swell cats and all that, but they could take me or leave me. After we got married, Chaz confided that she didn't enjoy the cats jumping on the table during dinner and staring intently at her plate.

"They won't grab anything unless you leave the table," I said.

"That isn't the point," she said.

I realized that one of the peculiarities of women is that they don't want their dinner anywhere near inquisitive little paws that have been busy in the litter box. Men aren't like that so much.

I never met a dog that didn't beg at the table. If there is a dog that doesn't, it has had all the dog scared out of it. But a dog is not a sneak thief like a cat. It doesn't snatch and run, except if presented with an irresistible opportunity. It is a dinner companion. It is delighted that you are eating, thinks it's a jolly good idea, and wants to be sure your food is as delicious as you deserve. You are under a powerful psychological compulsion to give it a taste, particularly when it goes into convulsions of gratitude. Dogs remember every favor you ever do for them and store those events in a memory bank titled Why My Human Is a God.

I can hardly pass a dog on the street without wanting to pet it. If you first let them slowly smell your hand, they'll usually let you. Some guys will admire a babe's dog so they can chat her up. With me, it's strictly a matter of getting to know the dog. Quality time with a dog calms me and makes me feel content. I came across an article from *Salon* that explained this phenomenon. Friendliness between Man and Dog releases a chemical into both the human and canine bloodstreams, which is why they both like it so much. The chemical is named oxytocin. You're already ahead of me: Yes, reader, that is the chemical associated with the emotion called Elevation.

I had two dogs when I was a boy, Blackie and Ming. They had those names because the Dominican sisters told us dogs didn't have souls, and so it would be a sin against the Holy Ghost to give them a saint's name. This sent me racing to the encyclopedia, because I had never heard of a Saint Roger, although probably it would seem strange to name a dog after yourself. You wouldn't want your mom shouting through the screen door for the whole neighborhood to hear: "Roger, get your nose out of that garbage and get back in the house!" Luckily, there was a Saint Roger Niger of Beeleigh Abbey, so the question didn't arise. He was consecrated bishop of London in 1229, so that was good. Blackie was half beagle and half spaniel. Ming was a Pekingese. But not a toy Pekingese, I hasten to add. He was a good-sized dog, earnestly dedicated to chasing things, chewing things, and barking at everything that could not be chased or chewed. You know how you associate certain memories with books? I can never look at Oscar Lewis's *Children of Sanchez* without observing that Ming chewed a good half inch off the spine.

On Ming I lavished the attention that Blackie was denied. The tragedy of Blackie was that he was not allowed in the house. My father wouldn't allow it. This was not because he disliked Blackie. "Boy," he said, "you picked a bad time to bring a dog home. We've just Installed Wall-to-Wall Carpeting." Somehow you could hear that the phrase was capitalized, right down to the "I" in "Installed." Wall-to-Wall Carpets were a big deal in the late 1940s, along with picture windows, always referred to as Big Picture Windows. You can see we were up to date at our house. But it is the nature of a dog to take an interest in carpets, and the threat to Wall-to-Wall Carpeting was particularly alarming to my father, because If Anything Happened to It We'd Have to Tear the Whole Thing Up.

Blackie lived in our backyard, and for a blessed summer we were a dog and his boy, running all over the neighborhood—for dogs and boys ran free in those days. He went to baseball games with me, and chased after my bike to Harry Rusk's market, and we went to the park. He knew all my friends. Blackie had an active circle of his own friends, including his brother Pepper, who lived next door at Karen

Weaver's house, and his pal Snookers, a dachshund who lived one door down on Maple Street with Jackie Yates. Then autumn leaves began to fall. Soon it was winter, with early snow on the ground. I was back in school. Pepper and Snookers went to live inside. As a shelter, Blackie was given my old playhouse in the backyard, with a dog house inside and blankets on the floor. "He'll grow his winter coat," my dad said. But Blackie spent long days and nights cold and lonely, and I was acutely aware of this. Blackie would hear the sound of the school bus and start barking for me, and I would run out to the backyard to comfort him, for he would be sobbing. "I'm sorry, Blackie boy. I'm sorry." My heart was breaking, but I couldn't stay out there forever. When I went indoors and stood over the hot air register to thaw out, I felt torn up inside. I had betrayed him. But I could understand that my father had a point.

Maybe that's why *Shiloh* hit me so hard. The father in that film was essentially right. I showed *Shiloh* one year at Ebertfest, the film festival I started with the University of Illinois, and our guest was the great actor Scott Wilson, who plays the reclusive squirrel hunter who is so mean to Shiloh. After the movie, we invited kids from the audience up on the stage. A little girl timidly asked Scott, "Mister, why are you so mean?" Scott could have replied by explaining how he was only an actor and it was only a role. He showed what a perfect instinct he has. He said, "Honey, I just don't know. But I learned my lesson."

A few months into Blackie's exile, Jackie Yates's father, a nice man, mentioned to my father that Blackie howled half the night under their bedroom window. I knew this was the truth, because his lonely cries kept me awake. Sometimes I would open the storm window and call out, "It's okay, Blackie boy." But I knew it wasn't okay, and my voice only inspired more laments. I tried peeking out from behind my curtain. Sometimes in the moonlight Blackie would be standing outside his little house, gazing reproachfully at my window. Through the bedroom door at night, I heard snatches of conversation from the living room: *Never stops barking... the boy... the dog... Roger loves that dog... I know, I know... Bob Yates... keeps me awake, too...*

It was announced that my cousin Bernardine in Stonington had invited me for a visit. That meant my first airplane ride, in an Ozark Air Lines DC-3 to Decatur. When I returned, we sat in the car at the airport and my mother said, "Your father has something he wants to tell you," and I knew what it was and my heart cried: *Blackie!* Blackie had run away from home. Ten blocks from 410 East Washington Street, he ran out in front of a car driven by Enos

Renner, husband of my mom's good friend Frances. The Renners called her after reading his dog tag. I sat in the car and knew this was a lie. Something broke inside of me. What was Blackie doing ten blocks away from home? Why had he conveniently been struck by a car driven by a witness we already knew? At home I fell on my bed and wept and knew that Blackie had not been killed, not by running under Enos Renner's wheels anyway, and he might be crying for me at that moment at the dog pound. Or he might be dead.

That is the Blackie story. Ming died of battle injuries. He jumped from my bed to snap at a fly, fell wrong, and broke his back. His hind legs were paralyzed. My friend Hal Holmes suggested maybe we could make him a little cart to haul himself around, but we both knew that wouldn't work. I would have been about twenty then. I have been the rest of my life without a dog. It never seemed like it would be fair to the dog. I was always going out of town on trips, I got home late, its meals would be missed, there was no one to walk it, and on and on. These days it just plain doesn't make sense. Chaz has her hands full taking care of me. That's the way it is. It just doesn't work out that I can have a dog. But there's still an empty space inside of me, about the size of Blackie.

10   MY VOCATION

IT WAS MY mother who decided I would be a priest. I heard this starting early in my childhood. It was the greatest vocation one could hope for in life. There was no greater glory for a mother than to "give her son to the Church." There was a mother in our congregation at St. Patrick's, Mrs. Wuellner, who had given *two* sons to the Church, Fathers Frank and George, and these two good men came once to visit us at our home, possibly to inspire me.

My father, raised as a Lutheran, attended St. Patrick's only on such occasions as midnight Mass on Christmas Eve. I remember sitting in a front pew with my First Communion class and noticing Father McGinn glancing toward the back of the church. I became convinced that my father was sitting down when he should be standing up, or otherwise indulging in disgraceful non-Catholic behavior, and I wanted to turn around but didn't dare.

My father stayed out of it. On most Sundays he stayed at home. He explained this gave him a chance to read the Sunday funnies before I wanted them. That seemed to me an excellent reason for staying home. There was also the problem that he would lose his immortal soul, having been offered the opportunity for salvation through the Church and renouncing it. I remember an occasion when my mother, briefing me in the kitchen, deployed me into the living room to pray on my knees beside his chair, beseeching heaven for his conversion. My father was a good sport about this and thanked me. He said he needed some time to think it over.

In my childhood the Church arched high over everything. I was awed by its ceremonies. Years later I agreed with Pauline Kael when she said that the three greatest American directors of the 1970s—Scorsese, Altman, and Coppola—had derived much of their artistic richness from having grown up in the pre–Vatican II era of Latin, incense, mortal sins, indulgences, dire sufferings in hell, Gregorian chant, and so on. Jews likewise had inspiring ceremonies. Protestants were victims of sensory deprivation.

The parish priest was the greatest man in the town. Our priest was Father J. W. McGinn, who was a good and kind man and not given to issuing fiery declarations from the pulpit. Of course in Catholic grade school I took the classes for altar boys. We learned by heart all the Latin of the Mass, and I believe I could serve Mass to this day. There was something satisfying about the sound of Latin.

Introibo ad altare Dei.
Ad Deum qui laitificat juventutem meum.

"I will go to the altar of God. The God who gives joy to my youth." There was a "thunk" to the syllables, measured and confident, said aloud the way they looked. We learned in our altar boy classes when you stood during the Mass. When you knelt. When you sat during the reading of scripture and the sermon. When you rang the bell, when you brought the water and wine. How to carefully hold the paten under the chins of communicants so a fragment of Holy Eucharist would not go astray. Later, there were dress rehearsals at the St. Pat's altar.

For years I served early Mass one morning a week, riding my bike to church and then onward to St. Mary's for the start of the school day. On First Fridays, the Altar and Rosary Society supplied coffee, hot chocolate, and sweet rolls in the basement of the rectory. When you served at a wedding, the best man was expected to tip you fifty cents. When you served at a funeral you kept a very straight face. During Lent there were the stations of the cross, the priest and servers moving around the church to pause in front of artworks depicting Christ's progress toward Calvary. Walking from one station to the next, we intoned the verses of a dirge.

> At the cross, her station keeping,
> Stood the mournful mother weeping,
> Close to Jesus to the last.

I enjoyed the procession around the walls of the church, the sweet smell of the incense smoking in the censer as I swung it. Out of the corners of my eyes I could survey everyone in the church and exchange furtive grins with my pals, although I was supposed to be attending our symbolic progress through Christ's sufferings.

I was never abused in any way by any priest or nun. One incident remains vivid to this day. When I was perhaps eight years old and new to serving Mass, my mind emptied one morning and I made a mess of it. When we returned to the sacristy, I burst into tears. "I'm sorry, Father!" I sobbed, and Father McGinn sat down and took me on his lap and comforted me, telling me that God understood and so did he. Today, tragically, the idea of an altar boy on a priest's lap has only alarming connotations. On that day Father McGinn was only being kind, and I felt forgiven.

My mother continued with her assumption that I would become a priest. There were times when I wondered if she had only given me birth for the high purpose of "giving me to the Church." When I was thirteen, I was sent for a three- or four-day retreat at a seminary run by the Diocese of Peoria. We boys were to be given a glimpse of the training ahead of us. I remember two things in particular: A fiery version of a sermon I believe was then known to all Catholic boys, with a lurid description of the unimaginable torments of infinite duration awaiting any boy who committed the sin of impurity. And then an interlude after lunch where we sat on the grass and chatted with actual seminarians, who were older and casually smoked as they discussed vocations, ours and theirs.

I was already a little smartass, and asked my seminarian: "If hell is the way they describe it, how can the punishment for impurity be worse than the punishment for anything else?" The seminarian smiled condescendingly. "The notion of levels of hell comes from Dante," he said. "He was a great poet but an amateur theologian. See, that's the sort of thing we study." I remember the sermon, the conversation with the seminarian, and only one more detail from my life as a seminarian: I came down with some insignificant complaint, maybe a fever, and spent a night in the infirmary listening to my portable radio and hearing Patti Page sing "Tennessee Waltz." It must have been June. The light lasted long, the windows stood open, a lazy breeze drifted in, I was in the only occupied bed, I was in early adolescence, and the song summoned confused feelings of regret for experiences I stood on the brink of having. Patti Page sang of a song that took her sweetheart from her. I was that sweetheart.

I was a voracious reader in grade school and early on began to question the logic of the faith. To be informed it was necessary for me to just simply *believe* was not satisfactory. Some things just didn't make any sense. If God was perfect, I reasoned, how could he create anything that contradicted his creation? This conclusion, reached in grade school, was later to lead me like an arrow to the wonderful theory of evolution. We were not taught creationism in grade school, and I learned that the Church was quite content to get along with Darwin. The questions that plagued me didn't have to do with science but with fairness. If you committed a mortal sin, it might depend on sheer chance whether you would get the opportunity to confess it before you died. Why had God, who was all-powerful, devised this merciless moral mechanism for his creatures? He created paradise and in no time at all his very first humans, Adam and Eve, did something that made perfect sense to me. I would have eaten the apple myself. Now humankind was condemned forever to the prospect of hell. Did hell even exist before there were people to occupy it? If only the fallen angels lived there, why didn't God in his infinite mercy choose to keep us someplace handy where he could encourage our rehabilitation? And who dreamed up the system of indulgences, even plenary indulgences, which reminded me uneasily of Get Out of Jail Free cards? The Church began to resemble a house of cards; remove only one and the walls fell.

At some point soon after my discovery of *Playboy* magazine I began to live in a state of sin, because I simply *could not* bring myself to confess certain transgressions to a priest who knew me and could see me perfectly well through the grid of the confessional. Logically I was choosing eternal torment over a minute's embarrassment. This choice was easy for me. When I saw Harvey Keitel placing his hand in the flame in *Mean Streets*, I identified with him. The difference between us was that long before I reached the age of Charlie in the film, I had lost my faith. It didn't make sense to me any longer. There was no crisis of conscience. It simply all fell away. I remained a cultural Catholic, which I interpret as believing in the Social Contract and the Corporal Works of Mercy. I didn't believe then, and don't believe now, that it is easy to subscribe to the teachings of the Church and not consider yourself a liberal.

I got my driving license and my first car at sixteen. By then I was working for the *News-Gazette* and came home at two a.m. after helping put the Sunday paper to bed and stopping off with Hal Holmes and Bill Lyon at Mel Root's restaurant across from the courthouse in Urbana. This was my excuse to sleep late and go to a later Mass than my mother. What I did instead was buy the Chicago papers and read them while parked in my car in Crystal Lake Park.

In high school, I was taking Latin at my mother's insistence. She said I would need it when I eventually got my vocation. Mrs. Link, our Latin teacher, was a cutie who wore smart tailored suits and high heels, and her classes were elegant performances. In diction and wit, she was like a crisp movie star, and we regarded her with wonder. I never told my mother I wouldn't become a priest, but she got the idea. Even after starting work in Chicago, I never found the nerve, when we were visiting, to not attend Sunday Mass with her. She knew well enough those were the only times I went to church. What I was doing, I suppose, was going through the motions to respect a tradition that was more important to her than to me. She believed in the faith until the hour of her death. She was buried from St. Patrick Church, and I tipped the altar boys.

11 NEWSPAPER DAYS

DICK STEPHENS, WHO must have been all of twenty at the time, chain-smoked Camels, drove a fast Mercury, and covered Urbana High School sports for the *News-Gazette*. The sports editor in those days was Bill Schrader, who called everybody "coach." He promoted Stephens and grandly ordered him to "hire your own successor." After talking to Hal's dad, Harold Holmes, the managing editor, Stephens hired me.

In that September of 1958, just turned sixteen, I was working part-time for Seely Johnston at his sports shop, where I functioned by listening to everything said by Mate Cuppernell, a weathered salesman, and repeating it. If a customer was shopping for fishing lures, I'd say, "The cats are taking that

Heddon spinner out at Kaufman's Clear Lake." I had never been fishing. Mate taught me how to spin-cast using a thumb-action reel and a plug at the end of the line. One day when I was demonstrating to a customer in front of the store, the plug flew through the air and snagged the back of a garbage truck. The line snapped. I was humiliated and quietly put the rod back on the rack. Later that day Herb Neff, the store manager, was out front doing a demonstration. He used the snap of the fiberglass pole that should have been good for fifty feet, and the plug flew five feet and stopped. He lost the sale and blamed me. He complained to Seely, who drove him crazy because every time he had a sale all written up, Seely would hurry out, grab the slip, and take off 10 percent.

Seely lived until nearly one hundred, running his store to the end. Every time I visited Champaign-Urbana, he would turn up to greet me, telling everyone in listening distance, "I gave him his start." Then he'd hold his hand under my chin. The first time I saw this gesture I was autographing my first book in Robeson's Book Department. I looked at him blankly. "Come on, young man!" he said sternly. "You know what I want!" I didn't. He shook his hand. "Right here in my hand!" The readers waiting in line regarded this. "What in your hand, Mr. Johnston?" I said. "Your chewing gum! You're at work now!"

Seely was paying me seventy-five cents an hour. The *News-Gazette* job represented a fifteen-cent hourly raise. To be hired as a real writer at a real newspaper was such good fortune that I could scarcely sleep. To be sure, the job paid poorly, but everything was cheaper in those days and I was already driving my own car, a 1954 Ford. I stayed past midnights on game nights, driving home after curfew on a pass from the police department.

My colleague late at night, a year or two older, was Bill Lyon, who covered Champaign High School sports and became a columnist for the *Philadelphia Inquirer.* Tall, with a crew cut, he smoked cigars while pounding out his copy. We'd be the only two in the newsroom at midnight on Fridays, writing our coverage of the football games.

Bill and I would labor deep into the night on Fridays, composing our portraits of the games. I was a subscriber to the Great Lead Theory, which teaches that a story must have an opening paragraph so powerful as to leave few readers still standing. Grantland Rice's "Four Horsemen" lead was my ideal. Lyon watched as I ripped one sheet of copy paper after another out of my typewriter and finally gave me the most useful advice I have ever received as a writer: "One, don't wait for inspiration, just start the damned thing. Two, once you begin, keep on until the end.

How do you know how the story should begin until you find out where it's going?" These rules saved me half a career's worth of time and gained me a reputation as the fastest writer in town. I'm not faster. I spend less time not writing.

Before each game I wrote a pregame story and walked across the street late at night to slip it through Harold Holmes's mail slot. I hardly seemed to sleep in those days, and it might be two or three a.m., sometimes with a new snow falling. One night there'd been an ice storm, and every tree branch sparkled in the light of the full moon. No lights in the windows, no traffic on Washington Street, and me with my next byline in my pocket.

Urbana that season had a great football team under the "tutelage" (a dependable sportswriting word) of Coach Warren Smith, a proponent of the single-wing offense. He even wrote a book on it. The Tigers were an underdog in the Big 12 (Champaign, Bloomington, Decatur, Springfield, Mattoon, and so on) but were undefeated with two games to go. The season closer, of course, would be with Champaign, a night fraught with Shakespearean drama, during which crosstown romances were destroyed, fenders bent, friendships ended, families divided. Perhaps the team was distracted by the Champaign game coming up in a week's time, but they were unexpectedly defeated and their hopes of a perfect season destroyed.

This was clearly the occasion for a Great Lead. I wrote: "The glass slipper was shattered and broken, the royal coach turned into a pumpkin, and the Cinderella Urbana Tigers stumbled and fumbled and fell." Saturday morning, I turned up at work, assembling area high school scores, and the news editor, Ed Borman, loomed over my desk and rumbled, "Young man, that's as good a piece of writing as we've had on high school sports in quite a while." I turned back to the sports section and read my Great Lead again, and as you can see I memorized it.

My euphoria was shattered at school on Monday, when Coach Smith slammed his door on me after thundering, "From this day forward, you are banned from all Urbana sports under my jurisdiction. You can buy a ticket to the games." He left me devastated. It was up to Stanley Hynes, our grizzled World War II veteran English teacher and advisor of the high school paper, to negotiate a truce. I admired him enormously because he addressed his students as "Mister" and "Miss" just as if we were in college, and he smoked in the classroom. "There has been a literary misunderstanding," he told me. "Coach Smith thinks you called him a pumpkin."

Borman entered my story in the Illinois Associated Press writing competition, and it won first place in the sportswriting category. That happened in summer of the next year. Daddy had been diagnosed with lung cancer the previous spring and was now in the last weeks of his life. I took the framed certificate to him in the hospital, and he was proud of me. I would never again win anything that meant more.

Coach Smith was the speaker at one of our class reunions. He recalled that long-ago season, and said, "You boys were the best team I ever coached. And remember that you were covered in the *Gazette* by Roger here, who would go on to work in Chicago." And who called him a pumpkin.

I worked full-time at the *News-Gazette* on Saturdays, when in season there was no story in town more important than the Illinois football game. Bill Schrader, the sports editor, commanded our field army. He would write the game story and the Illinois locker room story. Dick Stephens would handle the opposing coach, unless it was Woody Hayes, and then he and Schrader would switch. Curt Beamer, who at one time or another had possibly photographed a third of the local population, had a sidelines pass and his photos would be blown up big on the front page and in the sports section. It went without saying that the story would get the front page headline, eight columns in Railroad Gothic, a typeface we referred to as "World Ends."

In September 1958 I was assigned to Beamer as his caption writer. This was a lowly but crucial job. I knelt next to him on the sidelines, the perfect view, and wrote down the players in every frame of film. He briefed me: "You're not here to enjoy the game. Your number one duty is to grab my belt and yank me out of the way if I'm about to get creamed by a player I can't see through the viewfinder. Number two, make a list starting with "Roll one, Shot one" and write down the players in every shot I take, because when they get muddy they all look the same." When the ball was snapped, I hooked my fingers through Beamer's belt, ready to yank him hard if a play ran into our sidelines. Looking through his telephoto lens, he sometimes couldn't see them coming. "Pull me too soon and you spoil a great picture," he instructed me. "Wait too late, and we get creamed."

Beamer's photos from the first three quarters were rushed back to the office by a speed demon on a motorcycle. After the game we rushed back ourselves. His photos would supply the wire services. In the photo lab, Hal Holmes would be developing them as fast as he could, hanging them by clothespins to dry. I stood by with my caption notes. Bill Schmelzle, the city editor, would come back to the lab to get a look at what we had. Beamer would pick the best ones and Holmesy would lay them on rotating cylinders to go over the telephone to the AP.

By now it was maybe seven o'clock. In the newsroom, all attention focused on Schrader, pounding on his Smith-Corona in a cloud of cigar smoke. The rest of us went across to Vriner's Confectionery for dinner. Tyke Vriner was a local celebrity: He'd led the Champaign Maroons to an undefeated season around 1940, but when it turned out he was overage the team had to forfeit every game. Vriner's was a period piece even then: A marble counter with stools and a soda fountain, glass cases for the fudge and taffy he made in the rear room, and high-backed wooden booths. It was said that the mayor of Champaign and other notables joined in after-hours poker games back there. Hal and I would order cheeseburgers or maybe even a T-bone steak, which Tyke would fry right on the hamburger grill. All he had was a grill for meat and deep fat for fries, chicken, and shrimp.

After dinner, we went back up to the newsroom, where Ed Borman would have taken over the city slot from Schmelzle. He supervised T. O. White, the retired sports editor who was entrusted with writing headlines and reading copy. A few other local stories might come in: Crashes, fires. I would go over to Champaign Police to look at the blotter for newsworthy cases. Borman would be back with the Linotypes, leaning over the turtles that held the type and photo engravings, reading it upside down. The paper would be locked up, the press would roll, the building would shake, we'd all gather around the city desk, and Borman would produce six-packs of Old Style from a refrigerator in the publisher's office. That autumn he pushed a can over the desk to me, my first beer. The pressroom foreman came up with the paper, and we read it. As my mother prophesied, I was a newspaperman, underpaid and drinking.

In the summer of 1959 I was given a full-time job on the state desk, writing up obituaries, fires, traffic accidents, and county fair prizes in the paper's circulation area, always referred to as "East Central Illinois." My partner on the beat was Betsy Hendrick, also young and ambitious, who later went on to run the family business, Hendrick House. Our mentor in those days was Jari Jackson, a passionate young woman who took every story with dead seriousness and drilled me on the UPI style book. Her copy pencil would slash through my stories; she was not as forgiving as the sports desk, which granted itself infinite leeway in style. The high point of Jari's day would be a "fatal," a car accident with fatalities. She would growl down the line to the state police for more details, chain-smoking and growing impatient as the deadline approached. I learned from her that a news-paperman never misses a deadline, and I never have.

The city room in those days was filled with characters, and each desk was like an island of influence. All work flowed into and out from Schmelzle, a benign man who had round shoulders from years of bending over copy. He sat at the crossbar of the H-shaped city desk. Across from him sat a chief copy editor, often T. O. White, the former sports editor. To his left, Borman. To his right, Gracie Underwood, the former society editor. Gracie's best pal was Helen Stevick, mother of Marajen Stevick Chinigo, the paper's owner. Helen would appear in the news room around lunchtime with her poodles on a leash. She and Gracie would go out to lunch together, and after returning Gracie would put her head down on her arms and sleep soundly for an hour.

The state desk was next to the city desk. Across from us was the society desk, run by Bill Schmelzle's wife, Annabel. Sports was at the other end of the room. Across from them was a long desk for general assignment reporters, including Joe Black, who always smelled faintly of bourbon and wrote beatnik poetry. Right in the middle of the room, between the reporters and sports, was the desk of Fran Myers, the university editor, a formidable matron who embodied a Wodehousian aunt. Every single one of these people, with the exception of Fran Myers, was a smoker, and a grey cloud hung low over the room.

In a room off the newsroom were the desks of Willard Hansen, the editor, and Harold Holmes. They shared space with the morgue, in which countless clippings rested in file envelopes. Willard was a diffident, polite man whose editorials advised our readers to vote Republican in every possible circumstance. So Republican was the paper that in 2008, long after Marajen had died at an advanced age and even the *Chicago Tribune* broke with more than a century of tradition to endorse Obama, it faithfully endorsed Senator John McCain. Behind Harold and Willard was the conference room, lined with photographs of D. W. Stevick, founder of the paper, and his legendary daughter and countess, who had married Count Michael Chinigo, the International News Service bureau chief in Rome. Marajen, a great beauty in her youth, looked dashing as an early aviatrix and companion of senators, tycoons, and movie stars. She commuted between a mansion in Palm Springs, a villa in Ravello, Italy (where she lived on a hillside next to Gore Vidal), and her big childhood home in Champaign, which had the first private indoor pool in town. Regularly the *News-Gazette* railed against the "out of town ownership" of the *Champaign-Urbana Courier*, a member of the Lindsay-Schaub chain out of Decatur, forty miles away. Bob Sink, the crusty editor of the *Courier*, eventually wrote an editorial saying the paper was "weary of these complaints from the banks of the Tiber."

In those days the paper, then at 52 Main, was not air-conditioned. Huge windows opened to the summer heat, and every desk was covered with grime from the nearby Illinois Central tracks. Fran Myers's first task every morning was to scrub her domain with Windex. In August, millions of tiny black bugs from the cornfields would be attracted by the paper's big neon sign, and our desks would be covered in the morning by their corpses. We scraped them onto the floor with folded copy paper. The heat down the hall in the composing room, filled with Linotype machines, was unbearable when I raced with breaking stories on deadline to Bill Schmelzle, leaning over the type, reading it upside down, cutting stories while they were in lead, his sweat dripping on the headlines.

My first day of full time, Schmelzle pulled the oldest trick in the newsroom on me. "Ebert, take a day off," he called from his desk. Everyone looked up. "Look behind you," said Ruth Weinard, the sweet assistant society editor. I was standing in front of the wall calendar. The day began slowly. We received our "assignment sheets," individually prepared for every reporter by Schmelzle from his tickler file, which contained advance notes on everything of possible interest to East Central Illinois. "Check cause of Philo fatal," he might write to me. Or "new highway work at Hoopeston." I was not discriminated against because of age and sometimes drew plum assignments, like "Rantoul Rotary," "Holiday Inn opening," or "Paxton grain elevator fire."

As the morning progressed, the most important state desk stories defined themselves. There might be a farm machinery accident near Mahomet. Or Jari Jackson might have a fatal with three or even four deaths and would evacuate from her desk and commandeer a command post at city desk, racing back and forth puffing furiously. From her example I absorbed the frightening urgency of deadlines. By 11:30 a.m. every typewriter on the floor was being pounded with the velocity and rhythm of self-taught typists at incomprehensible speed. Deadline was 12:15. The city room would empty, with most reporters heading directly across the street to Vriner's for lunch. By then Schmelzle would be permanently in the composing room, putting the edition to bed. We had two editions, the state (two pages filled with news and photos from our small-town correspondents) and the city (those pages swapped out for more local news and last-minute updates).

The *News-Gazette* was a few blocks from city

hall, which housed the fire and police departments. Through the tall open windows we could hear the fire sirens as the trucks pulled out. One day, just after deadline, the sirens wailed and Schmelzle told me, "Wait five minutes, call the fire department, and see what it is." Champaign firemen told me it was "a still at Morris Brown's junkyard." I pounded out one paragraph on deadline: "A still caught on fire just after noon Tuesday at Morris Brown's junkyard. Champaign firemen said it was out on arrival." I rushed back to the composing room with my sheet of copy paper, which Schmelzle handed to the foreman without reading. It was "railroaded" into type, not copyread, slammed onto the bottom of page three, and the paper went to press.

At four that afternoon I was summoned to the desk of Harold Holmes.

"Roger," said Mr. Holmes, "I would like you to meet Morris Brown."

Morris Brown did not look like a happy man. He was a well-known bondsman who had once, I knew, stood bail for a circus elephant. I told him I was sorry to hear about his fire.

"There's more to be sorry about than that," Holmes said. "Do you know what a still is?"

"It's a machine used for...distilling? Something?" I said.

"True enough, but at the fire department, you see, it's also short for 'stillborn.' That's a fire that's already out when they get there."

Schmelzle, who had silently come up behind me, broke into laughter. Mr. Brown handed me his card, which read: "Can't make bail? You don't need the wings of an angel if you know Morris Brown."

12   HIGH SCHOOL

I went to Urbana High School between 1956 and 1960, walking the four blocks to school. We were the first generation after Elvis, and one of the last generations of innocence. We were inventing the myth of the American teenager. Our decade would imprint an iconography on American society. We knew nothing of violence and drugs. We looked forward to the future. We were taught well. We had no idea how lucky we were.

I realize now what good teachers I had. At the time I took them for granted. Because the university had a nepotism rule, some of them were spouses fully qualified to teach at the college level. I suspect high school teaching was bearable, even enjoyable, for them because the school was run smoothly under firm discipline and as far as I'm aware didn't have a single incompetent faculty member. Teachers controlled their classrooms. Hallways weren't fight zones. Boys wore slacks, girls wore dresses. It was like a cliché from the movies. We even had the Elbow Room, a malt shop on the corner, to hang out in, with a jukebox.

When I think of those days, they often come down to a Friday night in autumn, and a football game. I successfully auditioned for the job of game announcer, and watched the games from a third-floor window of the school building, where I first met Dick Stephens, who covered the Tigers for the *News-Gazette*. I grandly announced, "Ladies and gentlemen, please rise to join in the singing of our national anthem." I read announcements about homecoming dances and charity car washes and chanted "Touchdown, Urbana!" with enthusiasm, or "Touchdown, Champaign" with dejection.

After the game, I went to the Tigers' Den. This was a brick storefront a block from Main Street in Urbana. Customized cars cruised slowly past, thought to contain sexual predators from alien high schools on the hunt for our Urbana girls. Inside, there was only one chaperone, Oscar Adams, possibly the best-known and most popular man in town. Oscar's chaperoning duties consisted largely of sitting in the lounge watching *Gunsmoke* on TV.

There was a small dance hall with a stage at one end and a soft drinks bar at the other, chairs around the walls, and the sexes eyeing each other uneasily, for nothing is easier for a teenager to imagine than rejection. The boys dressed in chinos or corduroys, and plaid shirts from Penney's. Our hair was fixed in place by Brylcreem. The girls wore skirts that swirled when they danced.

If you knew what to look for, you'd catch guys cupping their hands in front of their mouths and sniffing to test themselves for halitosis. The cautious among us worked through packs of spearmint, or if we were really insecure, Dentyne. Halitosis was far worse than dandruff. The only thing more to be feared was an untimely erection on the dance floor, especially if you'd been slow dancing; at the end of the dance your buddies were watching you like hawks, ready to point and go, *Yuk! Yuk!*

One of the girls I had yearnings for might be there when I arrived at the Tigers' Den, studiously not noticing me. You could spend half an hour deliberately not making eye contact. It was a form of pre-dance foreplay. The evening began with rock and roll, the girls dancing with one another, and then a guy would sidle up to the deejay and ask for a "slow song." And now it was crunch time. With all of your courage you approached the girl of your dreams.

It might be that you were too slow, and another guy would get there first. Was that the faintest shadow of a hint of a sidelong teasing look of regret that Marty-Judi-Sally-Carol-Jeanne sent your way? Or had she forgotten you even existed? Halfway across the floor toward her, you saw her taken into the arms of a rival and made a studious course correction as if you'd only been walking across the room to get to the other side.

The legendary teacher of our time was Mrs. Marian Seward, whose senior rhetoric class we heard about as freshmen. She was exacting and unforgiving, and cultivated a studied eccentricity. Once she stood looking dreamily out the window, her arms crossed, and said, "Oh, students, this morning I walked into my farmyard and listened to the worms making love." She issued lists of Rhet Words—words we had to try to find in our reading. They counted heavily toward our grades. She had an eagle eye for cheating. Thomas Wolfe was a gold mine of Rhet Words. When I found a word, I'd copy it in pencil on the flyleaf. From my copy of *Look Homeward, Angel*: Scrofulous. Immanent. She was hard, but she was good. She intimidated us with her standards. When I walked into her class, I thought I knew it all. I was a professional newspaper reporter. She returned my first paper marked with a D, and I appealed to her. "Mr. Ebert," she said, "when, oh, when, will you learn that the paragraph is a matter of style, and not of punctuation?" Mrs. Carolyn Leseur, another English teacher, confided at our fiftieth reunion that when the faculty was voting on the members of a senior honor society, I was blackballed by one teacher for being a "smart-ass." And who was that teacher? "Mrs. Seward." True to her standards. This long-delayed information filled me with great happiness. We may have feared Mrs. Seward, but she demanded our best and I think we respected that.

Stanley Hynes was another English teacher, and for him I held great affection. He took us into Shakespeare so well that I never got out again. From other teachers, we heard bits of his story. While still too young to serve, he volunteered for the First World War, was gassed at the front, and his facial skin was darkened and pockmarked as a result. For World War II he might have been too old, but he volunteered again.

Hynes was a bachelor. It is conceivable he was gay. He treated his students as adults, and we responded. Our discussions of poetry in his classroom became serious and introspective, and students had a way of thinking deeper to impress him. He was the sponsor for the student paper, a volunteer for all school projects, yet existing above the daily flow with a gravity and intelligence that set him apart.

Some years after graduating, I came across him one night in the basement cafeteria of the Illini Union on campus, which functioned as a coffee shop and gathering place for those outside the mainstream—foreign students, nerds, geeks, writers, musicians, chess players, programmers with their shoe boxes of punch cards, students of the *New York Times* crossword puzzle. He was by himself, smoking a cigarette, drinking coffee, his finger keeping his place in his book. I had the impression he'd seen me before I'd seen him. "Good evening, Mr. Ebert." Just as always. I was happy to see him but caught a little off guard. I could have had a post–high school conversation with him, and I don't remember why I didn't. That might have been my opportunity to know him better. When I meet my classmates from those years, they remember him with warmth and we share our curiosity: What was his life like? What did he go through in two wars? Was he lonely? Was he always like...Mr. Hynes? If there were answers, we didn't have them, except perhaps in his passion for the literature he taught.

In those years I read endlessly, often in class, always late at night. There was no pattern; one book led randomly to another. The great influence was Thomas Wolfe, who burned with the need to be a great novelist, and I burned in sympathy. I felt that if I could write like him, I would have nothing more to learn. I began to ride my bike over to campus and steal quietly into the bookstores, drawn to the sections of books by New Directions and the Grove Press. I bought poems by Thomas Merton, *Tropic of Cancer* by Henry Miller, and in *The New American Poets* I found the Beats, whose values and references seemed alien and yet attractive to me.

Starting in grade school I consumed a great deal of science fiction, including four or five monthly magazines, but that tapered off in college as I began to choose "real" literature. Some of the sci-fi authors were better than I realized at the time. But even as I drifted from the genre itself, I found myself involved in Fandom, an underground culture of the fans of science fiction, fantasy, the weird in general, and the satire and irony of the time: Bob and Ray, Harvey Kurtzman, *MAD* magazine, Stan Freberg.

Fanzines were mimeographed magazines circulated by mail among science fiction fans in the days before the Internet. I first learned about them in a 1950s issue of *Amazing Stories* and eagerly sent away ten or twenty cents to Buck and Juanita Coulson in Indiana, whose *Yandro* was one of the best and longest running of them all. Overnight, I was a fan, although not yet a BNF (big name fan). It was a thrill for me to have a LOC (letter of comment) published on such issues as the demise of BEMs (bug-eyed monsters), and soon I was publishing my own fanzine, named *Stymie*.

I have always been convinced that the culture of fanzines contributed crucially to the formative culture of the early Web and generated models for websites and blogs. The very tone of the discourse is similar, and like fanzines, the Web took new word coinages, turned them into acronyms, and ran with them. Science fiction fans in the decades before the Internet were already interested in computers—first in the supercomputers of science fiction myth, and then in the earliest home-built models. Fans tended to be youngish, male, geeky, obsessed with popular culture, and compelled to circulate their ideas. In the reviews and criticism they ran, they slanted heavily toward expertise in narrow pop fields. The Star Trek phenomenon was predicted by their fascination years earlier with analysis of *Captain Video, Superman, X Minus One,* and *Sheena, Queen of the Jungle,* and there were detailed discussions about how Tarzan taught himself to read.

The Urbana High School Science Fiction Club went as a group to hear our hero, Arthur C. Clarke, speak on campus. Years later, tingles ran down my spine when I heard the voice of HAL 9000 in *2001: A Space Odyssey* announce that it had been born in the computer lab at the University of Illinois in Urbana. (Was there a connection? I interviewed Clarke on a cybercast from Sri Lanka, and he said he didn't recall having been to Urbana.)

I was demented in my zeal for school activities. I joined the swimming team, appeared in plays, founded the Science Fiction Club, coedited the newspaper, co-hosted the school's Saturday morning radio broadcast, won the state speech contest (radio speaking division), and was elected senior class president, all the time covering high school sports for the *News-Gazette*. It was not in my nature to attend classes and go home. Two nights most weeks I worked for the paper until well past midnight.

It was the duty of the class president to produce the senior talent show every spring, and I threw myself into this project. Larry McGehe and John Kratz, two of my friends, constructed a plywood time machine pierced by dozens of lightbulbs and stood behind it, furiously rotating a copper strip past contact points so the lights spun in a pinwheel effect. We synched a tape recorder to broadcast a satire of the school's morning loudspeaker announcements. We built the set, held rehearsals, worked with the UHS Jazz Band, stayed up all night.

I was the emcee. The show was a success. Afterward we had coffee and cake backstage and then I walked out and sat in my car and collapsed in sobs. I had spent four years in a frenzy of overachievement, and I was wrung out. I had come to the end of something. I had no good reason for sadness, but I've never forgotten that night. I drove for a while through the moonlit streets, torch songs playing on the radio, seeing myself, and the town, through eyes instructed by Thomas Wolfe.

13   UNIVERSITY

URBANA-CHAMPAIGN WAS GATHERED at the feet of the University of Illinois like a medieval town outside the walls of a great castle. It employed us, it fascinated us, it was our fame. Its professors were knights who deigned to live among us. I had a professor from Hungary on my *Courier* route, and my father told me to always walk the route clockwise "so the old professor will get his paper sooner."

Told that my father worked at the University of Illinois as an electrician in "the physical plant," I imagined it as a form of vegetation. On Saturdays he would sit close to the radio, following the Illinois game, reacting to the play-by-play by Marc Howard and later Larry Stewart. I watched him and laughed and frowned in sympathy. When the Illini scored, he always said, "Boy, howdy!" In the first postwar years our family would often go for dinner at a cafeteria on campus in a Quonset hut that had a wheelchair ramp. Here were budget-priced meals for faculty, staff, and war veterans in wheelchairs. "They like it here because they don't have to wheel those chairs up and down hills." One man was blind. My father whispered, "Watch him feel to make sure his apple pie is pointed at him." On pleasant days, we would stroll after dinner onto the Quadrangle, lined with trees and the biggest buildings I'd ever seen. "This is the greatest university in the world," my father told me. "Someday you'll go here."

My parents took me to my first home game in Memorial Stadium. We entered a vast hall with ramps leading overhead. We emerged into a dizzying expanse of space, 63,000 people all focused on the field below. The Marching Illini were playing "Hail to the Orange." Opposite us, intricate designs were being formed by the Block I. "This was the first card formation in the country," Daddy repeated before every game. "Illinois also had the first homecoming, the first forward pass, the first huddle. I was here on opening day and saw Red Grange running for seven touchdowns against Michigan." After the game we walked past the university Armory, beneath "the largest unsupported roof in the world." The university had the first, the biggest, or the best of everything.

When I was older, I rode my bike around the campus, a solemn kid, ignored and invisible, studying the students. There were Indian women in saris. There were Asians, Africans, Sikhs in turbans. One day Mr. R. V. Willis, my mother's boss at the Allied Finance Company, took me over to the University Library ("the world's largest," my father explained). We walked upstairs past a glass case containing a first edition of Audubon. "A page is turned every day," Mr. Willis explained. "It's one of the rarest books in the world." He showed me the Reading Room, a towering open space surrounded by books and lined by long tables with students bent over their three-by-five cards. We went to the main desk. "This is the boy's first visit to the library," Mr. Willis said. "I'd like him to see the stacks." A librarian asked me what I wanted to see. "The first issue of *Life* magazine," I said promptly. We entered into a labyrinth so awesome that now I picture it when reading Borges' "The Library of Babel." Floor after floor extended above and below, visible through steel catwalks. In cubicles students hunched over their work. We walked down a narrow corridor and found every issue of *Life*.

When I was a senior in high school, Principal R. H. Braun said he was recommending some students for the university's early entrance program. For the spring semester, I would take my first morning class at the university. This was Verbal Communications 101, taught by A. Tress Lundman, sweet as she sounds. I shyly entered the most magnificent of all university buildings, Altgeld Hall, built in 1897 as the first library. Its thick stone walls were intended to be fireproof. Its first architect was Daniel Burnham, fresh from masterminding the World's Columbian Exposition, later replaced by Governor John Peter Altgeld after a disagreement over design. In spirit and the medieval stones of its walls it resembles Louis Sullivan's Auditorium Building in Chicago, both lacking steel frames and held up by the stones in their walls. The tower with the University Chimes rises from it. I joined a class of students who were no more than six months older than I was. We learned to debate, recite, and declaim. It was a new world, and many of the students spoke with confident Chicago accents.

That summer I was back on full time again at the newspaper, going out to a field south of campus where the Assembly Hall was under construction. This involved building a massive circular base on which would rest a matching dome. The dome was supported from within by heavy scaffolding during construction, but then five hundred miles of steel cable would be wrapped around the rim, compressing it so it would stand in place entirely without interior columns. I was sent to the construction site to interview Max Abramovitz, the architect. "So this will be the world's largest rim-supported dome?" I asked him. He looked at the fearsome project. "It will be if it doesn't fall down."

Illinois was known as the Greek Capital, because it had more fraternities and sororities than anywhere else. We didn't have money for me to live in a fraternity, but I could pledge one as a townie and continue living at home. I made the rounds during Pledge Week, deciding on Phi Delta Theta and its handsome stone house on Chalmers. This was the top house on campus at the time, and in my senior year had the captain of the football team (Mike Taliaferro), one of the greatest scorers in Illini basketball history (Dave Downey), the president of the Student Senate (Larry Hansen), and the editor of the *Daily Illini* (me).

As a Phi Delt I could take meals, hang out to "study," and engage in the joys of Hell Week. We'd gather to serenade sororities. The song "Phi Delta Theta Girl" never struck me as particularly complimentary (*If you were the kind that sold, you'd be worth your weight in gold*). The house plunged me into undergraduate life. I memorized the names and years of all the upperclassmen, the names of their girlfriends, the names of the Founders, and much more arcana, and during Hell Week, desperately sleep deprived, I earned myself a night of sleep by winning the raw egg eating contest, with twenty-six. Some years later, when I saw it, the egg scene in *Cool Hand Luke* rang a bell.

Hell Week was an abomination, a bonding ritual in which pledges were worn down with a mental and physical sadism I believe has now been outlawed. All led up to the last night of the week, in which each candidate was led for the first time into the Chapter Room in the basement, now candlelit and with a medieval theme. I'm not certain the active members wore dark hoods, but that's how I remember them, like medieval torturers. The final test, which had been darkly hinted at for days, was called "Nails." We were placed barefoot on a tabletop and looked down in the dim light to see a plank with nails driven through it, facing up. There was about enough space for your two feet. Then we were blindfolded. The idea was to jump down to the plank and miss the nails. I believed this absolutely. The member chanted "Nails...nails." One of the members had reportedly been taken to an emergency room the year before after not missing a nail. I couldn't do it. I hesitated. I was terrified. I hadn't had two hours a night of sleep in days. How could I do it? If I didn't, I would never become a Phi Delt. I was eighteen years old. Becoming a Phi

Delt had become the most important goal in my life. I jumped. The nails were rubber.

This ritual struck me then as cruel, and strikes me now as bullshit. It was useful in helping me understand military basic training. The idea, at an early age, is to enforce bonding. Your loyalty to the group is more important than any ideas from the outside world, any ideas of reason and values you may have carried to the moment. In my case, Nails created an anger toward the house. I didn't express it. When I stopped going to the house it was for other reasons. But that's why I only attended one homecoming event at Phi Delt.

A turning point in my life came at 8:00 a.m. on the first day of classes at the university, when I walked into English 101, taught by Daniel Curley. He would become my mentor and the friend of a lifetime. I'd never met anyone like him before. He had a Massachusetts accent, wore clothes from the Sears catalog (walking boots, chinos, corduroy pants, work shirt), carried a book bag at a time when knapsacks weren't universal, had a haircut that looked as if it had been administered by trimming around a bowl on his head, was a noted author of fiction, had been one of the editors of the university's famous *Accent* literary magazine, and loved fiction and poetry with an unconcealed joy. Here in the flesh was one of those guys with his feet up on his desk, reading a book.

I was to take every class Curley offered, including Fiction Writing, where one of the other students was Larry Woiwode, then obviously already the real thing. Curley read our stories aloud anonymously, to encourage open discussion. There was never any doubt who wrote Woiwode's. Curley introduced me to many of the cornerstones of my life's reading: "The Love Song of J. Alfred Prufrock," *Crime and Punishment, Madame Bovary, The Ambassadors, Nostromo, The Professor's House, The Great Gatsby, The Sound and the Fury.* One day he handed out a mimeographed booklet of poems by E. E. Cummings, and told us to consider the typography as musical notations for reading the poems aloud. Cummings ever after was clear to me, and I know dozens of his poems by heart. He approached these works with undisguised admiration. We discussed felicities of language, patterns of symbolism, motivation, revelation of character. This was *appreciation*, not the savagery of deconstruction, which approaches literature as pliers do a rose.

Curley walked everywhere. I walked with him. I sat in his office in a dormer under the roof of the English Building. Remembering my father's ideas of English professors, I asked him one day if he'd ever smoked a pipe. "I tried to take one up, but it was no go." He always spoke to his students as equals. He observed instead of instructing, delivered information in asides, said such things as, "During the war the English fled to Trollope as a means of escape." He lived in a house on Professor's Row in Urbana with his wife, Helen, and four jolly daughters. One bedroom had become the office for *Ascent*, the literary quarterly he began when the English Department's J. Kerker Quinn called it a day after twenty years of *Accent*, during which Quinn had been early or first to publish such writers as Eudora Welty, William Maxwell, and Flannery O'Connor. Curley's home was lined with bookshelves. Sometimes I dropped off a class assignment and we sat in the living room, dark and comforting, drinking tea and discussing our reading.

My early role models were my father and Dan Curley. He appeared in my life almost precisely when my father died, and it occurs to me that he must have known that. Did he understand the need he began to fill? He spoke to us once of the "first-rate second-rate writer," someone who was good but not quite that good: John O'Hara or Sinclair Lewis, perhaps. In my junior or senior year, filled with myself, infatuated with my weekly column in the *Daily Illini*, I reviewed his latest novel *A Stone Man, Yes* and described him as a first-rate second-rate writer. How could I have done this? How could I have been so cruel to a man who had been so kind? I had been his student for twenty-six credit hours. He was my friend. I did not possess the right to publish such a thing. Sherman Paul, another professor I idolized, stood next to me at the coffeepot in the English Seminar Room and drily observed, "That must have taken some nerve."

Curley never discussed it with me. I should have apologized but lacked the courage. A year or so later at a crucial moment he made a course correction on my life. I had become a cocksure asshole. I was editor of the *Daily Illini*, president of the U.S. Student Press Association, still working for the *News-Gazette*, winner of a Rotary fellowship for a year of study at the University of Cape Town. In 1964, I applied for admission to the graduate program in English and would begin classes in the autumn semester before spending 1965 in South Africa. There was a technicality. My grades weren't good enough. The problem was French; I had failed it semester after semester. All my life I've been able to absorb stories and repeat them nearly verbatim, and all my life, I have been unable to actually memorize. This may have begun with the multiplication tables. I'd had my appendix removed while the class learned them at St. Mary's, and had to catch up. I capsized on the sevens and nines. Daddy wrote out the tables on a shirt cardboard and sat me down in the living room night after night until I learned them. This I could not do. My tears made the ink run. Eventually I got them, but either something broke, or I was born with it broken. I am a failure at rote memorization.

Thus it was with French. I can read it pretty well, speak badly, and understand it when pronounced by someone sensible, say a Vietnamese. I can get by at Cannes. But I could not get a passing grade in college, and although the English faculty was agreeable to admitting me into the graduate program, I didn't quite clear the grade-point bar. Curley did the math: If I took two credit courses in summer school of 1964 and got A's in both, I could be admitted. This was a done deal. One of my professors would be Richard Wasson, a brilliant hotshot who was the coming man. He liked me, but I tried his patience. I was insufferably full of myself. One day in class I disagreed with him, I have no idea what about. Our words grew heated. This passed the accepted limits of classroom discussion, and Wasson threw me out of the class. A day later I ran into Curley on the steps of the library: "If I were you, I'd make it right with Wasson. It seems as if you may have been in the wrong. He's willing to let you back in. If you don't get into graduate school, you may be in Vietnam before you go to South Africa." I made it right with Wasson, I was accepted into graduate school, I went to South Africa, I returned to graduate school, and I was accepted as a Ph.D. candidate at the University of Chicago, hired by the *Sun-Times*, and here I am today. The link in this chain of events was Daniel Curley, the first-rate second-rate man.

During my years at Illinois it seemed as if I followed a path laid out for me in childhood. "Someday you will go here," and one day I did. I loved the university. It took me from childhood to my life. My senior year coincided with the university's centennial, and I pitched an idea to the University of Illinois Press: I would leaf through one hundred years of the back issues of the *Daily Illini* and compile an informal anthology of items reflecting university life during the century. I returned again to the stacks where I'd discovered *Life* magazine and commenced this foolhardy project. I couldn't begin to read everything, but I made serendipitous discoveries, like a classified ad with Red Grange trying to sell his car ("goes like sixty"). This eventually became my first book, *An Illini Century*. As a wild shot, I wrote to the poet and professor Mark Van Doren, born and raised in Urbana, and he agreed to write the introduction.

There are a few classes I remember vividly. Although I was no good at science or math, I found myself fascinated with physical anthropology, and that set off my lifelong fascination with the perfection of the theory of evolution. I took a class on William

Faulkner and Willa Cather and was introduced to the power of Cather's stories and the clarity of her prose, as clear as running water. I had a typography course down in the basement of Gregory Hall with Glenn Hanson, in which I learned about typefaces, page design, and the history of printing. We composed full-page advertisements or broadsides, set them into type, conformed them, locked them up, and printed them out on an old flatbed press. One of my classmates was Jill Wine Volner, who not many years later was one of the Watergate prosecutors. I studied "The Organic Tradition in America" with Sherman Paul, one of the best-known academics in America, who wove together Thoreau, Emerson, Louis Sullivan, Veblen, Randolph Bourne, and others into an American voice distinct from Europe. He was a precise lecturer, giving the impression of an intelligence barely contained by speech, and a spellbinder. Once again, none of the stupidity of modern academic theory. He held the romantic notion that in order to study a text one must read it.

During these years my liberalism took clearer form. John Kennedy's run for president in 1960 was the occasion. I joined the Young Democrats. I was in the crowd that filled the Quad for his speech from the steps of the auditorium. I ran next to his convertible as it drove him away from the campus. A student from England, Si Sheridan, convinced me the *Daily Illini* was shamefully right-wing, and that it was necessary to start a liberal weekly in opposition to it. He suggested the name *Champaign-Urbana Spectator*, and I used my basement as our office. The paper appeared weekly for a year, and then I sold it for two hundred dollars at the beginning of my sophomore year and I went to work for the *Illini* as a columnist. Si Sheridan turned out to also be named Simon Hartog, a confusion involving his family matters, and in 1967 we met again in London when he gave me a dinner at one of the new psychedelic clubs named, I think, the Round House. Years later we met again at Cannes; he was now the buyer for the state television network of Mozambique. Years after that I heard from his brother, who said he had died. You meet someone glancingly in a lifetime who has an unforeseen influence; the *Spectator* gave voice to my liberalism, I learned from his opinions, and the weekly got me the column on the *Daily Illini*. So much of what happens by chance forms what becomes your life.

Liberal life for undergraduates centered on a smoky den named the "K Room," in the basement of the YMCA. It had a short-order grill and tables jammed together, and there a crowd of undergraduate leftists would meet for coffee, read the papers, read to one another from such books as *Growing Up Absurd* by Paul Goodman. On Thursdays we held the liberal Lunch Club, dominated by Rennie Davis, later to become one of the Chicago Seven. I was never that radical. One of the stars of the K Room was his girlfriend at that time, a chain-smoking young woman named Liz Krohne, who I recruited as a columnist for the *Daily Illini.* As a writer she had a gift and a clear voice, and we thought her destined for remarkable things. After we all moved to Chicago she disappeared from my life. There were reports she had moved to the South and was active in the civil rights movement, organizing and writing. I remember her vividly for her radicalism explained with a confiding smile.

I lacked the courage to commit myself by going south. Brendan Behan said critics reminded him of eunuchs in a harem: They see it done nightly, but are unable to do it themselves. I could argue with that, but in many ways I used journalism to stay at one remove from my convictions: I wouldn't risk arrest but would bravely report about those who did. My life has followed that pattern. I observe and describe at a prudent reserve. Now that life has deposited me for much of every day in a chair comfortable for my painful back and I communicate largely by computer, I suppose I must be grateful, for I seem to have been headed this way all along.

The autumn of 1966 was a conscious leave-taking from the university. Many of my friends were gone. My graduate courses in English had a new seriousness and could no longer be finessed without actual work. I had the good fortune to enroll in a class on Shakespeare's tragedies, taught by G. Blakemore Evans, who was a legendary Shakespearean. It was then that Shakespeare took hold of me, and it became clear he was the nearest we have come to a voice for what it means to be human. I confessed to Wasson that I hadn't read most of Shakespeare, and he observed that the plays were not terribly long. If you read a play every Sunday morning it would take thirty-eight weeks. I started, and after I went to Cape Town I plunged in deeply, in reading that was a form of prayer.

That fall was unusually long, and the autumn leaves unusually bright. As I drove around town, I thought, I am saying good-bye to all this. Whatever comes next, it will not happen in Urbana.

14 THE *DAILY ILLINI*

I SPENT MORE time working on the *Daily Illini* than I did studying. After selling the *Spectator*, I walked in cold and began writing a weekly column. I became the news editor, and then was appointed editor in my senior year. I can't say it was the best job I ever had, but...well, yes I can. It was the best job I ever had. The *Daily Illini* had been from the earliest days a commercial enterprise and not a "student activity." It was owned by the Illini Publishing Company, which also owned the yearbook and a campus low-power radio station. That was a great convenience in shielding the university from lawsuits and scandals involving the undergraduate editors.

The paper occupied the basement of Illini Hall at

Wright and John. It was in every sense a real newspaper, published five days a week on an ancient Goss rotary press that made the building tremble. Something was forever lost from newspapers when their buildings stopped trembling. We had three union employees, two printers and Phil Roach the pressman, and we knew they were union men because there was a shop grievance approximately weekly. These usually involved disagreements between editors and printers about what could and would be set into type, and how. There were some tense moments during the Cuban Missile Crisis when Dave Harvey, a member of the Young People's Socialist League, wrote a column questioning the facts we had been presented. Harvey later became a famous sociologist. I don't remember if the column was printed. What I remember is Orville Moore, the shop foreman, astonishing us with his vocabulary in denouncing it.

Our words were set into hot lead on Linotype machines. Pages were composed on heavy metal tables called turtles. Orville and the student night editor leaned over them facing each other, both reading backward, one reading upside down. Each page had to be justified to fit perfectly within the form, and this usually meant words had to be trimmed. This Orville did with a steel tool that cut them from the lead. All cuts had to come from the ends of paragraphs, which could lead to puzzling lapses. Resetting a shorter version of a story was forbidden under Orville's interpretation of the union rules.

I never saw Orville Moore without a cigar clamped into his teeth. He taught us as much about journalism as many of our professors, and it was all practical. He helped us understand that a newspaper, apart from being a stanchion of democracy, was a mass-produced product for sale at retail. It had to be produced on time and on budget, and the meaning of "deadline" took on terror when Orville would announce he would simply fill up remaining holes with something from the "overset," stories set in type that had never run. This never happened. We were convinced Orville would choose the most embarrassing overset at hand, for example heat wave coverage in the middle of January.

The paper ran twelve to twenty pages most days, tabloid. The press printed one color, black, on huge rolls of white newsprint, but for an ad, a Christmas shopping issue or homecoming, Phil Roach would add red, green, or the school colors, orange and blue. This he did with an intimate understanding of the linear path the paper traveled through the print rollers. He would map his strategy to assign a red roller or a green roller, say, and then suspend himself above the presses in an aluminum lawn chair and paint the colored inks on those rollers with a brush. Wade Freeman, the editor before me, told Phil that if he ever fell into the press we could also hope for shit brown, which was what his daring scheme was full of.

We had an old-fashioned semicircular copy editors' desk in the newsroom, a strange assortment of desks and typewriters, and an office up front ruled by Paul McMichael, the long-suffering publisher hired by the publishing company. He kept the books, handled the billing, settled disputes, and was the adult in the room. I have no idea how many speeches he had to listen to about freedom of the press, yet he tended to be permissive.

As editor I was a case study. I was tactless, egotistical, merciless, and a showboat. Against those character flaws I balanced the gift of writing well, a good sense for page layout, and ability as a talent scout. I took special satisfaction out of finding gifted writers and giving them a column. I found the young Liz Krohne, who was ahead of the curve on radicalism. I made a math student named Ron Szoke our film critic and learned as much from him as from anyone since. I recruited another mathematician, Paul Tyner, to write columns, and he was as funny as S. J. Perelman. He wrote a column based on his experiences as a waiter at the campus Spudnut Shop. Noticing a sign saying "No Reading," he asked the owner if that was appropriate for university students. "Somebody could start reading some book and never stop," the owner said. "My motto is, get 'em in, give 'em their Spuddies, and get 'em out again." This inspired a celebrated Tyner column titled "The University is a Spudnut Shop."

Tyner fascinated me. He wore his hair like the Beatles before they did. He was handsome in the Jean-Paul Belmondo manner. He largely supported himself, he said, by hustling pool in the Union's billiards room. On every men's room wall on campus he wrote: *Autofellatio is its own reward.* While getting a Ph.D. in math he sold a short story to the *New Yorker* and later expanded it into a novel, *Shoot It*, published by Atlantic Monthly Press/Little, Brown. He was a romantic, the lover of spectacular women. He often joined one of the communal tables at the Capitol Bar on Green.

Before dawn one morning in Chicago some years later, he hammered on my door and entered drunk, carrying a bottle of vodka. "I need a place to drink this," he said. I let him in and went back to bed. In the morning I left him unconscious on my sofa. At some later period—months? years?—he reappeared in my life on a Saturday afternoon when I was sitting at O'Rourke's, my favorite Chicago bar, dazed with drink.

"Roger," he said, "look at you. You're drunk in the afternoon. That's not good. It means you're an alcoholic." He told me he was an alcoholic and now was sober through Alcoholics Anonymous. He must have given me the kind of information any AA member would have shared, but I was in no condition to listen. I later learned that Tyner, still sober, had married and was working in San Francisco. The time frame for all this is hazy. At some later point I learned he was dead. On a flight from London to San Francisco, Paul had inexplicably started drinking again. He continued for a week and then shot himself in the head. I still have his novel on my shelf.

Another columnist I recruited was a philosophy student named Robert Jung. He was a good-looking, quietly funny guy whose column was somber and poetic about the big picture, which for him zoomed out to Existence itself. My sports editor was Bill Nack, the future *Sports Illustrated* star, who was no less poetic, and they spent hours huddled in the corner discussing deep matters. Jung's weekly column showed a mastery of the personal essay; he led you inexorably to a conclusion you didn't see coming. One of the professors who passed him on his Ph.D. oral exam was Frederick Will, a student of Wittgenstein and the father of George Will. Fred was as far to the right as Robert was to the left.

Nack followed me as editor. I stayed as a graduate student for the rest of 1964 and often saw Bill and Robert drinking coffee and explaining the universe to each other. Jung got his Ph.D., married, and found a job in the Philosophy Department at Southern Methodist. He stayed in contact; he was doing seminars around Dallas on existentialism. One day I got a call from Bill. Jung had checked into a hotel near Dallas to explore the border between life and death. As Bill understood it, he tried bleeding himself slowly. He was calling 911 when he passed out and died.

The *DI* was a real paper. We were a member of the Associated Press. We ran Walter Lippmann once a week and the comic strip *Pogo* every day. We had an ad department. We paid salaries; a night editor made three dollars, which would buy you a good dinner. Norman Thomas, the perennial presidential candidate of the Socialist Party of America, spoke on campus, and I interviewed him and asked if the *DI* could syndicate the column he wrote for the party newspaper, *New America*. This cost us two dollars a week. I got the impression he was not widely syndicated; once a week I received a letter from Thomas with a *carbon copy* of his new column. I ran conservative columns by Dave Young, later the transportation editor of the *Chicago Tribune*, and Bob Auler, who stayed in Urbana, opened a law office, and became famous for suing the university on behalf of athletes. For a time he owned the Champaign-Urbana minor league baseball team. We're still good friends. He calls me the Mad Bomber and I call him a Fascist Baby Eater.

As editor I loved to cover campus characters, and one was well known to us, because he had found a bedroom for himself in the small room where lead was remelted into bars for the Linotypes. This was an earnest young man named Richard McMullen, who helped circulate the paper and explained he could sustain life on almost no money by eating gelatin dissolved in water and an occasional apple. He walked the campus with a billboard proclaiming "Good News for Jews" and was arrested by the campus police for handing out the Bible in front of the University Library. The *Daily Illini* found this an outrage against freedom of speech, and I addressed a rally on the steps of the auditorium, using a battery-operated bullhorn. Effortlessly changing from activist to journalist, I pitched the story to the *Chicago Sun-Times* and had my first byline in the paper, on page one.

I bought the paper on November 22, 1963, and read my front-page story again and again while sitting in the Reading Room of the Illini Union. The sound of a radio broke the silence, where not even music had been heard, with the news from Dallas. I ran to our basement office. Everyone was there. On the radio, WILL, the university radio station, was playing Beethoven's Fifth.

In a dramatic gesture, I swept everything off the top of my desk into a large wastebasket and made it a command post. I deployed Dave Reed, the executive editor, to write a story of the mood of the campus, which he could have written by simply looking around. The news editor John Keefe went to interview Norman Graebner, the famous history professor, who had just been scheduled to address the campus that night from the auditorium stage. He was considered a Great Man. I telephoned Revilo P. Oliver, the classics professor notorious for writing an article in the John Birch Society magazine calling Kennedy a communist. There was no answer.

John Schacht, the journalism professor who was chairman of the Illini Publishing Company board, made his only visit in history to our offices and handed me a headline that would be a perfect fit in two lines of Railroad Gothic: NATION MOURNS SLAIN LEADER. Unable to improve on it, although I resented his trespass, I took it back to Orville Moore, who regarded it from under his green eyeshade and asked himself, "Where the hell is our Second Coming of Christ font?"

Kennedy had campaigned from the auditorium steps in autumn 1960, and I had run breathless beside his open convertible. An assassination was unthinkable then. In a second in 1963 America was turned upside down. Dave Reed sat in the copy desk slot. Our lead story would be from the AP. I went to the Capitol and ate dinner with Bob Jung, Bill Nack, Paul Tyner, Bob Auler, and others. It was as if someone had called a meeting. The bar was jammed, but hushed. At three a.m. I was back at the paper to watch Phil Roach push a button and start the press. The nation mourned its slain leader.

15   MY TRIP TO HOLLYWOOD

In 1963 the Illinois team won a trip to the Rose Bowl. I assigned myself and Dave Reed to cover the story. The U of I Foundation paid for our train tickets. My sports editor was Bill Nack, later to become one of the greatest of all American sportswriters, but I don't recall him on the train. He probably hitchhiked.

I'd watched the great 1963 team from the sidelines as Curt Beamer's caption writer, seeing Dick Butkus and Jim Grabowski close enough to get mud kicked in my face. I wanted to see Illinois in the Rose Bowl; that was an excuse. Much more urgently I wanted to see California. I'd been as far west as Peoria. Since reading *On the Road* I had subscribed to the whole

California mystique, and already I used "Hollywood" as a weary adjective for a world I knew nothing about.

We took the Illinois Central to Chicago and boarded the Santa Fe for Los Angeles. We slept sitting up. There were two cars chartered by the Student Senate, and the bar car became like Saturday night in Campustown. I became friendly with a voluptuous young woman and under a grey woolen railroad blanket in the middle of the night, rocking through the midlands, we made free with each other. I recall her warmth and enthusiasm; I wish I could recall her name. Many undergraduate women acted as if they were making a gift of something, but in her dexterity she seemed to be gifting herself, and I found it so exciting that it was a hungover dawn before we finally fell asleep.

Across the deserts and the plains we rocketed in a Thomas Wolfean journey, dismounting at lonely stations like Durango to toss footballs in the night air. Union Station was an art deco set. We moved into the Biltmore Hotel on Pershing Square, and in the ancient gilded bar with its two-story ceiling we ate peanuts and threw the shells on the floor. Six to a room, we slept on cots. I read the *Los Angeles Times* a page at a time, and Jim Murray's columns twice. I walked outside in shirtsleeves in winter. Nearby we bought Mexican street food and lingered uncertainly outside bars with women smiling at us through the windows.

This was all brand new. Dave and I stuck together like strangers in a new land. Hicks from the sticks. He played the mandolin, and we sat on a ledge in Pershing Square and together sang songs we knew from the Campus Folksong Club: "Amazing Grace," "May the Circle Be Unbroken," "Tennessee Waltz," "This Land Is Your Land." We put a cup on the sidewalk and made a few quarters, we two fresh-faced, tousled-haired, pink-cheeked lads from the cornfields, and never thought it odd that our fans were middle-aged men who avoided eye contact with one another.

I will spare you any mention of the Rose Bowl Parade and the game itself. What remains is one night. Dave and I found ourselves on Hollywood Boulevard, reading the stars on the Walk of Fame and examining the handprints at Grauman's Chinese. Half a block off the boulevard we found a club named Disco a Go-Go. We sat at a railing and watched the lights of a disco ball revolve upon the small and shabby dance floor, and the dancing couples seemed to be glamorous and cool. One girl in a black sweater and pleated skirt danced with a Troy Donahue type, his blond hair in a pompadour because the Beatles were only just happening. She had the largest breasts I had ever seen on a young and slim woman. She and her date pressed eagerly against each other. I was hypnotized. I remembered the girl with the white parasol that Mr. Bernstein would never forget in *Citizen Kane*. This was California. This was Hollywood. This was life. It was all ahead for me. Yes.

How we found ourselves later that night in front of the Mormon temple on Santa Monica Boulevard I cannot remember. We must have taken a taxi, although why we went to that address I can't say. Neither of us had any idea what it was. I remember standing with Dave, gazing up at the golden angel on the spire, and then noticing how late it was. I said we had better take a taxi to the Biltmore. Dave, who had matched me beer for beer, said he would walk. He wanted to see more of Los Angeles. Getting into a taxi, I asked him if he even knew the way. He asked me how many Biltmore Hotels I thought there were in Los Angeles.

The next morning all my roommates had already left when I awoke very late to a pounding on the door. It was Dave. He limped into the room and pulled off his penny loafers. The heels of his socks were soaked with blood. He limped for the rest of the trip. Now that I know Los Angeles I think it's impossible that he walked all the way back. I stay in touch with Dave, who became a journalism professor at Eastern

Illinois University, but he's never told me what happened. The bastard probably met up with the girl in the pleated skirt.

Illinois won the Rose Bowl, there was much celebration, and we boarded the train for the journey home. I found my makeout partner, but I had a painful earache and slipped the porter twenty dollars to put me in a Pullman sleeping compartment. So great was the pain I didn't even invite my friend to join me. I took three aspirins and a double scotch and far into the night read the Modern Library edition of *Fifty Stories* by John O'Hara.

16   CAPE TOWN

OUR NEIGHBOR HAROLD Holmes suggested me as a nominee for a Rotary fellowship, which paid for a year of postgraduate study overseas. It was the only scholarship I was likely to win, because it wasn't based entirely on grades but took student activities into account. My editorship of the *Daily Illini* may have helped. Asked to name the five schools I desired, I wrote down Cambridge, Trinity in Dublin, Calcutta, Melbourne, and the University of Cape Town. The only one of these I'd seen was Cape Town, on the slopes of Table Mountain, when I was with the wheelchair team from Illinois during their 1962 tour. Cape Town was the one I was offered.

I took the Panama Limited to Chicago. I was free.

I was out of Urbana and out of America for a year. My host Rotary district said I was welcome to speak to as many clubs as I wished, and I assured them I would speak to as many as possible. This provided me with the hospitality of locals throughout the Cape, as far north as Bloemfontein, and all over South-West Africa, now Namibia, where from Windhoek I was flown in a Rotarian's small plane down to the Diamond Coast and visited the towns of Oudtshoorn and Swakopmund, places out of time, the imposing civic buildings of German colonialism towering incongruously over the humble structures of what South Africans called a dorp town.

At the university I had a little room at University House, some way up the mountainside from Rondebosch. One afternoon I sat in my room and took inventory. This was in June, winter in the Southern Hemisphere, and it had been raining steadily for two weeks. I was alone in the residence; the others had packed off for vacation. Under an umbrella I ventured out to the Pig and Whistle on Main Road, where I favored the ploughman's lunch, but to sustain life I'd laid in a supply of tinned sardines, cheese, HobNobs, apples, Carr's Table Water Crackers, ginger cookies, Hershey bars, biltong, sausage, peanut butter, and a pot of jam. I had a little electric coil that would bring a cup of water to a boil, a jar of Nescafé, and a box of sugar cubes. I wrote in my journal: "I have not spoken to anyone since Monday. The radio is playing 'Downtown' by Petula Clark. I've been reading some Shaw, *Man and Superman*. I'm wearing jeans, my cable knit sweater and my Keds. I've made coffee and am waiting for it to cool. Let it be recorded that at this moment I am happy."

University House was a two-sided row of rooms opening onto covered porches. Built for troops during the war, it housed graduate students, mostly in the law or medicine. The water poured down the roof and collected in an exposed gutter, which carried it along somewhere downhill. All my life I've loved to sit very close to the rain and yet remain protected—in a café, on a porch, next to a window, or in that room, which had crank-open windows and a Dutch door. It was unheated, and after a warning from the housemother I'd gone to the OK Bazaar for an electric heater.

"What do I really need that isn't here in this room?" I wrote. "Its dimensions are a little more than twice as wide and deep as I am tall. I dunno, maybe 150 square feet? Here I have the padded wood chair in which I sit tilted against the wall, my feet braced against my straight desk chair. I am holding the three-inch-thick Paul Hamlyn edition of Shaw's complete plays. This room contains: A wood single bed, an African blanket covering it, a wood desk and its gooseneck lamp, a small dresser with a mirror over it, my portable typewriter, a wardrobe containing my clothes, a steamer trunk serving as a coffee table, and two bookcases, filled to overflowing. What more do I actually need?"

That year I walked all over downtown Cape Town, found used bookstores, read constantly while drinking tea in cafés or beer in pubs. I joined the Rondebosch Chess Club and huddled over its boards in a smoky little room near the train station, served coffee and ginger cookies by its servant. I read under trees on the slopes of Table Mountain. I became active in the National Union of South African Students, attended weekend retreats on a campsite near Cape Point, sang civil rights songs. I became a teacher one night a week at a night school in a Coloured township, where the students were desperately cramming to win university places. The University of Cape Town was not officially segregated but had the same entrance requirements for applicants from South Africa's separate and unequal schools. We studied *The Tempest*, that year's set book. The students needed no encouraging. This mysterious text written in their second or third language could unlock an education and open careers to them.

South Africa was then seventeen years into

apartheid, with twenty-nine to go before the election of Nelson Mandela. He would spend twenty-seven years as a prisoner. Every detail of racial segregation was ordered. The housemother had Joseph, the house servant, bring a mattress for my bed, and said in front of him, "It's been slept on by a kaffir but you Yanks don't care, do you?" There were Africans and Cape Coloureds everywhere, and whites walked among them as if separated by invisible walls. I noticed a similar separation in India, where street beggars didn't quite occupy the same dimension as others.

When I'd been in Cape Town for a few days, I looked over the movie ads and decided to see *From Russia with Love*. Using my map, I took the train and presented myself at the ticket window, not taking particular notice of the nonwhites everywhere until the cashier called the manager, who said it was illegal to admit me: "This is not a theater for whites." As I apologized he heard my accent and laughed with delight. "An American!" he said. "You don't know any better." He took me into the theater, where the lights were still on, and showed me a seat. The audience looked at me as if I must, by default, be in the Special Branch, until the manager made an announcement in Afrikaans and they all laughed and even applauded. I was an American and too ignorant to know what I'd gotten myself into. My University House friends assured me I could have gotten my throat slit by wandering off the map like that. I didn't feel a moment's unease, and after the movie a Coloured policeman materialized to walk with me back to the bus.

It was in Cape Town that I first slept the night with a black woman, Liz, whom I'd met at a NUSAS weekend. It didn't involve sex, but nevertheless we could have been jailed under the Immorality Act. She'd been stranded at one of the (not uncommon) mixed-race parties near campus, and I offered her a place to spend the night. "Do you know what that involves?" she asked. I did, but didn't take it as seriously as she did. We slept on my bunk and drank coffee in the morning behind the closed shades. "Now here is what we will do," she said. "You walk down to the bathrooms. Leave the door open. I will stand out of sight. Then I will call your name and stand in the doorway as if I've been looking for you."

On Rotary's free tickets I flew all over southern Africa. It was like returning to an alternative American South in the 1940s. Segregation was a matter of fact. As a guest I was awakened in the mornings with hot tea by a servant who called me "boss." Every meal at a club function without exception began with soup, salad, and a fish course and concluded with pie or pudding with hot cream poured over it. In those years Rotary with its international outlook was viewed as suspiciously liberal, and there were few Afrikaans members. Most Rotarians were affiliated with the "moderate" United Party, but I met a few members of the Liberal Party, which included the writers Alan Paton and Nadine Gordimer. There was no television, lest the nation be exposed to equitable treatment of Negroes. Movies and books were censored. *Playboy* was smuggled in from overseas.

Of all my hosts, I remember most clearly Felix and Naomi Harris of George, along the Garden Route from Cape Town to Durban. They had a house perched on a hillside and surrounded by a riot of vegetation. We went swimming in an Indian Ocean bay as warm as bathwater. They had a little old dog with a leg missing and said he had been near death when they moved to the hillside. One day he shuffled out the door, scented wild nature, and to their amazement trotted into the shrubbery to leave his mark. Now he tore around the yard chasing birds.

Up in South-West Africa, time was even more retrograde. In the evenings I played Monopoly or Scrabble with my hosts. Outside Swakopmund on the bed of a dry river they held a *braaivleis*, grilling chops and roasting potatoes over a driftwood fire. It was the edge of the Namib Desert, and no grass grew on their lawns, where servants raked the dirt into elaborate patterns. I returned to Windhoek by overnight train, sleeping with three other passengers on pull-down leather benches, buying roast chicken through the windows from the African cooks on station platforms.

At the university my advisor was R. G. Howarth, professor of English. He peered around books piled on his desk, spent much time filling his pipe, and asked me, "What do you plan to study?" The English literature of South Africa, I told him. "What have you read? *Cry, the Beloved Country?*" Also some Doris Lessing, I said. "Then you'd better start reading." I attended the graduate student seminars on Shakespeare in a room looking down Table Mountain, vines blowing through the window. In the English Seminar Room I held a reading of E. E. Cummings, and repeated it in a bohemian coffee shop on Main Road. Every weekend there was a boozy party. At an illegal mixed-race party in District Six I danced to the Beatles for the first time. That year I saw one, and only one, person smoking cannabis. The campus Catholic center was named Kolbe House. There every Saturday evening there was a celebration of the Mass, followed by a "social hour." The apartheid laws allowed people of different races to attend church services, and if those were followed by a get-together at which music was played and people danced, well, there you were.

On one drinking night my friend Tiki and I went to a shady club in Cape Town, which wouldn't admit her in jeans, so she went into a washroom, removed the camisole from under her blouse, and suspended it from her waist. I carried her jeans rolled up under my arm. It was a brandy and ginger ale night. We met a transsexual who complained that implants had made her breasts turn blue. Late the next morning I woke, vomited, and began reading *Homage to Catalonia* by Orwell.

My return trip was aboard the Lloyd Triestino *Europa*, sailing from Cape Town up the coast and through the Suez Canal to Venice. Friends came to wish me bon voyage, and Tiki, her long hair flowing behind her in the wind, stood on the dock and waved and waved until she grew too small to see. At the end of the journey in the Venetian lagoon, San Giacomo materialized out of the fog.

17   LONDON PERAMBULATING

I SAILED INTO Venice for the first time a little after dawn, standing at the bow, the fog so thick San Giorgio Maggiore seemed to float in the clouds. From Venice I went by train to Munich and then to London, where at American Express there was a letter from Dan Curley saying that he and his family were spending the year on sabbatical. Dan was a walker. He had waterproof shoes, a slicker, and a knapsack containing binoculars and a bird guide. Our first day he took me for the walk we later wrote about in our guidebook *The Perfect London Walk*. We started from the Belsize Park Tube stop and walked past Keats House and into Hampstead Heath and to the top of Parliament Hill, where all of London was at our feet. Then we set out across the Heath to the tumulus under which Boadicea, a queen of the Celts, is said to be buried, unless she's under the tracks at King's Cross, which is another legend.

On the Heath Curley pointed out the lane of trees where Keats first met Coleridge. We came up behind Kenwood House and had lunch at the Spaniard's Inn, where Mr. Pickwick so unwisely proposed marriage. It was there I first tasted a banger. It would not be my last. A sausage allegedly containing meat, the banger is so beloved by the British that they threatened to drop out of the Common Market when Europe disrespected its ingredients. In some pubs they're served with a fork, in most with a toothpick. They are much improved by Colman's English Mustard, which every pub supplies in a little pot with a tiny wooden spoon. No other mustard will do. If you insist on Dijon mustard you might as well drop your banger on the floor and grind it under your boot.

On that first day the Spaniard's was still broken up into cozy little spaces and cul-de-sacs, booths and hideaways. "Dick Turpin's Room," from which the highwayman picked out likely coaches to rob, was still there. Later corporate vandals "modernized" it, which meant ripping out the age-old walls and "opening it up." On another day we drank at the Blackfriar pub by the bridge of the same name when it, too, had a public bar, a private bar, a fireplace room, and so on. Also now ripped out and redecorated as an airport "pub." What gnaws at people until they're driven to destroy the past? It was at the Spaniard's that I acquired a meme that I now pass along to you. As Dan stood before a urinal he invariably intoned, "As the man says in the play, for this relief, much thanks." I rarely urinate without repeating that phrase. Now it's yours. Years from now, an atom of Dan Curley will persist as you quote your Shakespeare.

Down the way from the Spaniard's, we visited Kenwood House, the grandest country house near London, with Rembrandts, Romneys, and a trompe l'oeil library. There are gardens crowded with giant rhododendrons and azaleas, blinding with beauty in the springtime, concealing flower tunnels you can walk through. It was cold that first day, making a mockery of Dr. Johnson's Summer House. On later visits, if the weather was pleasant, I invariably rested on my back under the same tree on the lawn, my eyes shielded by my Tilley hat, and dozed half aware of the noises of children and dogs playing. I had been here before, I was here now, I would be back again.

Then we took the 210 bus into Highgate and walked down to the cemetery and to the graves of Karl Marx and George Eliot, and then across the way to Old Highgate Cemetery, because Marx and

Eliot were in New Highgate, you see. In those days the Friends of Highgate Cemetery hadn't yet started clearing the tangled growth that choked the cemetery during the war, when the groundsmen had been needed as air wardens. Tombstones leaned at crazy angles, graves gaped open, and the Columbarium looked like the set for Hammer horror films, which it often was. A daughter of Charles Dickens rests there, and Radclyffe Hall, with a plaque signed by her lover Una. The cemetery is overshadowed by the looming back wall of St. Michael's Church, where Coleridge is buried under the center aisle.

The Perfect Walk took place during one long day, ending in frigid twilight and assisted by buses. I go into such detail to spare you an account of countless nooks and crannies of the great city. Dan started me on a lifelong practice of wandering around London. From 1966 to 2006, I visited London never less than once a year and usually more than that. Walking the city became a part of my education, and in this way I learned a little about architecture, British watercolors, music, theater, and above all people. I felt a freedom in London I've never felt elsewhere. I made lasting friends. The city lends itself to walking, can be intensely exciting at eye level, and is being eaten alive block by block by brutal corporate leg-lifting.

In the 1980s I raised an advance from Donna

Martin, my patient editor at Andrews and McMeel, which paid for a trip to London for Dan and his second wife, Audrey, my girlfriend Ingrid Magan Eng, and my friends John McHugh and Jack Lane, the photographer. We retraced Curley's walk from Belsize Park to Archway and produced *The Perfect London Walk*. One day a few years later when Chaz and I were taking the walk, we arrived at the top of Parliament Hill and saw a couple reading the book.

"Any questions?" I asked.

"Oh! Is this included?"

In the days of my illness, unable to walk, I started walking around this London in my mind. These were enveloping daydreams, enhanced by pain medication and lassitude. I hadn't started again to do any writing or see any movies and had nothing to do but lie in bed with my memories. Mentally I walked out of the Eyrie Mansion and down Jermyn Street to Wiltons. I ordered roast turkey with fresh peaches, and raspberry syllabub for dessert. Then I walked down St. James's and into the park and around the ponds. Admired the view of Westminster from the bridge. Then out of the park toward Victoria and on into Pimlico. Pushing on now, following an instinctive map in my mind, I stop for coffee at that little street (I know just how to find it) with all the shops and street vendors. Then down to the Tate and following the Thames all the way around to Hammersmith, not a short walk, but in my mind it didn't take long. Ahead to where houseboats are moored, and to Chiswick House to nap on the lawn and have tea. But stopping first at the churchyard where Hogarth lies buried. Before that at the pub down from Hammersmith Bridge with the deck overlooking the water. And of course near that bridge is the Gate, London's best vegetarian restaurant. I realized I'd made a mental U-turn at Chiswick and retraced my steps.

Once I started daydreaming, those memories started happening all the time. As I retraced my steps, I remember details I haven't thought of since my visit. I wonder if everything is stored away, every step I took, every street I walked, every window I looked at and wondered, who lives there? At the east end of Pembridge Square there was a high window with a wooden silhouette of a palm tree in it. Whose was it?

I believe that I could pause right now and remember something I saw on a walk that I have never thought of again since that time. I just have. After you leave the Belsize Park Tube stop you angle down through an old churchyard on your way to Keats House. On the corner a blue plaque marks the location of the bookshop where George Orwell once worked, the one that inspired his novel *Keep the Aspidistra Flying*. Some steps up the hill you will find the

Roebuck Pub, and a blue plaque marking the dwelling of one of the Huxleys, perhaps Thomas, "Darwin's bulldog." A door or two away, there used to be a nursery school, and displayed in its windows one day were colorful zoo animals, cut out of construction paper. That was at least thirty-five years ago, and it was still waiting in my mind. My memory was accurate. After I wrote about this in a blog, a reader signing herself Leapy wrote: "The nursery school in Pond Street (above the Orwell pizza shop and the Huxley town house) still exists. I attended it forty-odd years ago and now my own children are pupils." She didn't mention the paper animals, but we both know they were there.

I found many people who liked to walk around London with me, but only one was always ready to walk, no matter how early in the morning. This was my grandson Emil Evans. "There's no such thing for me as getting up too early," he told me. We often walked down into St. James's Park, fed the ducks, and made our way over to Westminster. We walked every morning. Our mission was always the same. We were not walking for health or to educate ourselves. We were walking to find a cup of hot chocolate. We found the cheapest cup in London at Chubby's in Crown Passage and the most expensive at Fortnum & Mason, a thousand steps from each other.

On my imaginary walk I could have turned right at the end of Jermyn and walked up St. James's to Piccadilly, down to Park Lane, up toward Notting Hill, and passed the Mason's Arms on my way to Pembridge Square, nodding while passing the Hyde Park West Hotel, where when I had no money in the 1970s I always asked for the same tiny room, number 310 I believe, with a window I could climb through to stand on a roof overlooking the square. In that hotel I miserably read a Penguin paperback on alcoholism years before I took any action. I could have had lunch at Costas, behind the Gate at Notting Hill, the movie theater. Or I could have walked to the far end of Pembridge Square and had lunch at the Sun in Splendour, which was the *Evening Standard* Pub of the Year in 1968. Why do I remember that?

18   EYRIE MANSION

IN 2009 I learned that they tore down 22 Jermyn Street in London. The whole block went. Bates's hat shop, Trumper the barber, Getti the Italian restaurant, the Jermyn Street Theatre, Sergios café, the lot. Jermyn Street was my street in London. My neighborhood. There, on a corner near the Lower Regent Street end, I found a time capsule where the eccentricity and charm of an earlier time was preserved. It was called the Eyrie Mansion. When I stayed there I considered myself to be living there. I always wanted to live in London, and that was the closest I ever got.

Many years ago I was in London and cramped into a hotel room so small they had to store my empty luggage elsewhere on the premises. I could sit on the bed and rest my forehead against the wall opposite. Fed up, I walked out one fine Sunday morning to find a better hotel, but just as inexpensive. Nostalgically I returned to Russell Square, where I had gone on my first visit to the great city in 1961, steered by *Europe on $5 a Day*. On the first trip I found a room and full English breakfast for £2.50 a night. You might think it a shabby hovel. I was deliriously happy. I stayed up half the night writing a letter to Edna O'Brien, an Irish novelist I had a crush on. "Here I am in a cheap hotel near Russell Square," I wrote, "writing this letter in the middle of the night." Those words alone would convince her of my romantic genius. Alas, that long-ago hotel had been replaced by a monstrosity. I skulked around the square at a loss about where to look next and recalled that Suzanne Craig, a Chicago friend of mine, once informed me, "If you like London so much, you should stay at the Eyrie Mansion in Jermyn Street."

"A haunted house?"

"No, stupid. Spelled like an eagle's nest. And Jermyn isn't spelled like the country, either."

I took the Tube from Russell Square to Piccadilly and surfaced to find backpackers sprawled on the steps of Eros, still asleep after their Saturday night revels. One block down Regent and right on Jermyn and I found a small sign over the sidewalk above a doorway. It opened upon a marble corridor pointing me to a man who regarded me from a horribly scarred face. The gatekeeper of the Eyrie. He disappeared. When I drew abreast I found he was now behind a wooden counter protecting an old-fashioned switchboard, a thick ledger, and a wall of pigeonholes.

"How may I help you, sir?"

"Is this...a hotel?"

"Since 1685, I believe. And you require a room?" He spoke in a Spanish accent.

"How much are your rates?"

He consulted a card tacked to the wall.

"For you, sir, thirty-five pounds. That includes full English breakfast, parlor and bedroom, own gas fire and maid service. Bath en suite."

The rate was half of what I was paying. I asked to be shown a room. He locked the street door. We ascended in an open ironwork elevator and I was let into 3-A. The living room had tall old windows overlooking Jermyn Street, a dark antique sideboard, a desk, a chest of drawers, a sofa facing the fireplace, two low easy chairs, tall mirrors above the fire and the sideboard. He used a wooden match to light the gas under artificial logs.

A short hallway led to a bedroom in which space had been found for two single beds, a bedside table between them, an armoire, a chest, a small vanity table, and another gas fireplace. In the bathroom was enthroned the largest bathtub I had ever seen, even in the movies. The fixtures were not modern; the water closet had an overhead tank with a pull-chain.

"This is larger than I expected," I said. "How many rooms does the hotel have in all?"

"Sixteen."

When I'd moved my luggage in, it was still only ten o'clock and I rang down for the full English breakfast. The Spaniard said he would prepare it himself as soon as possible "because Bob is indisposed." He appeared with two fried eggs, a rasher of bacon, four slices of toast in an upright warmer, butter, strawberry jam, a pot of brewed tea, and orange juice. I sat at my table, regarded my fire, poured my tea, turned on Radio 3, and read my *Sunday Telegraph*. For twenty-five years I was to come to 22 Jermyn Street time and again. Now I can never return. Some obscene architectural extrusion will rise upon the sacred land, some eyesore of retail and condos. Piece by piece, this is how a city dies. How many cities can spare a hotel built in 1685, the year James II took the crown?

I will barely be able to bring myself to return to Jermyn Street, which is, shop for shop, the finest street in London. When I approach it again I will have to enter from Piccadilly by walking down through the Piccadilly Arcade and not from Lower Regent Street.

I can still attend a lunchtime concert at St. James's, or call in at Turnbull & Asser the haberdashers, Paxton & Whitfield the cheesemongers, Wiltons the restaurant, and Waterstone's the bookstore, but I cannot and will not ever again walk past 22 Jermyn Street. The address will be dead.

That first morning I walked down Regent to St. James's Park, strolled around the ponds, came up by Prince Charles's residence, climbed St. James's Street, and returned the full length of Jermyn. I ordered tea. It consisted of tomato, cucumber, and butter sandwiches, which the English are unreasonably fond of; ham and butter sandwiches with Colman's English Mustard; and biscuits. The tea was freshly brewed. I never saw a tea bag on the premises. I'd ordered Lapsang souchong, which has the aroma of a freshly tarred road at one hundred yards. I find this aroma indescribably stirring. When I smell it I am walking through the twilight in Cape Town to visit my friend Brigid Erin Bates.

I had settled in my easy chair when a key turned in the lock and a nattily dressed man in his sixties let himself in. He held a bottle of Teacher's scotch under his arm. He walked to the sideboard, took a glass, poured a shot, and while filling it with soda from the siphon, asked me, "Fancy a spot?"

"I'm afraid I don't drink," I said.

"Oh, my."

This man sat on my sofa, lit a cigarette, and said, "I'm Henry."

"Am I . . . in your room?"

"Oh, no, no, old boy! I'm only the owner. I dropped in to say hello."

This was Henry Togna Sr. He appears in a Dickens novel I haven't yet read. He had a drink in my room almost every afternoon when I stayed at the Eyrie Mansion. It was not difficult to learn his story. Henry and his wife, Doddy, lived in the roof-top flat. He may have been the only man ever to live all of his life within a block of Piccadilly Circus. The Mansion was originally purchased in 1915 by his parents, who came from Italy, and Doddy's parents, who were English. The two children grew up together, married, and fathered Henry Jr., "who keeps his irons in a lot of fires." He asked me how I learned of the Eyrie Mansion. "Oh, yes! Suzanne! A lovely girl!" He discovered I worked for the *Chicago Sun-Times*. "You must be joking. Tom Buck stays here. He's from the *Tribune*, you know." Henry told me that the Spaghetti House on Jermyn served a sole meunière not to be equaled.

I was usually in London three times a year: in midwinter, in May after Cannes, and in summer. Henry was naturally confiding and cheerfully indiscreet.

That first day he lamented that Bob had gone missing when I wanted my breakfast. "Bob is a great trouble to me," he said. "He gets drunk every eighth day. I have implored him to make out a seven-day schedule and stick to it, but no. He will not be content unless he is throwing us off."

"I was well taken care of by the man who checked me in," I said.

"Poor fellow. He was a famous jockey in Spain. His face was burned in a stable fire while he tried to help his horses. He was one of those handsome Spanish boys. He was in a movie once by Buñuel. A film critic like yourself must have heard of him."

"Oh, I have," I said. "I wonder which film?"

"You'll never get that out of him," Henry said. "Nor will he tell you his real name. He says he's hiding out here, working overnights, when there's so little traffic because we lock the street door at midnight. He doesn't want to be seen or allow anyone in Spain to learn where he's gone."

I began to think of Jermyn Street as Ampersand Street. On Jermyn Street you will find Turnbull & Asser, where Saul Bellow bought his shirts. You will find Paxton & Whitfield, with its window stacked with cheeses. Ian Nairn, in his *Nairn's London*, lists only one shop in London, and that is the shop. You will also find Fortnum & Mason, where you can lunch at the Fountain or wander in the food hall, stacked to the ceiling with anchovies, rare coffees, Oxford marmalade, Scottish shortbreads, caviar, Westphalian ham, and tins of inedible imported biscuits. Down the street are Sims, Reed & Fogg, the antiquarian booksellers. And of course Hilditch & Key, Harvie & Hudson, Russell & Bromley, Crockett & Jones, New & Lingwood, Thomas Pink, all shirt sellers. In the UK Jermyn Street is synonymous with shirts and shoes.

There are shops without ampersands as well. Until it was replaced by Waterstone's the booksellers, there was Simpsons of Piccadilly, where they held a sale every January and marked down everything but the umbrellas. Dunhill, where they never have a sale on anything. Church's English shoes. DAKS and the Burberry store, which always had its impeccably restored 1920s delivery truck parked at the curb. Floris the perfumers. Davidoff the tobacconist, where Churchill and James Bond stored their Cubans in the locked humidor. Next door to the hotel, there is Bates Gentlemen's Hatter, with a big top hat hanging over the sidewalk. This was one place where you knew for sure you could find a bowler, a deerstalker, or a collapsible opera topper. They have had the same cat for fifty years (although it has been stuffed and with a cigar in its mouth for most of that time). Next to Bates is Geo. F. Trumper, the men's hairdressers.

I make it a practice to get my hair cut in every city where possible. Near the Eyrie I went first to Georgio's, a one-chair Greek barbershop in a mews off Duke Street. One day I followed the archbishop of Canterbury into his chair. In the basement of Simpsons, I had my hair cut in the chair next to the former prime minister Edward Heath. Jermyn is that kind of street. Finally I graduated to Trumper, a magnificent haven of brass and leather, wood and mirrors, and the aroma of hair tonics with exotic spices. An aged retainer knelt at my feet unbidden to shine my shoes. He discovered I was from Chicago.

"Chicago!" he said. "Do you know Barbra Streisand, sir?"

I said I did not.

"Do you like the way she sings? I do!"

I said I did as well.

"Can you sing like her? Could you? Do you think you would?"

Around the corner from Jermyn on St. James's is D. R. Harris the chemist, the oldest chemist in London, by appointment to H.R.H. the Prince of Wales. Miss Brown has been there for years, and I have always wanted to ask her for tea. There I buy a pot of their Arlington shaving cream, Wilberg's Pine Bath Essence, Eucryl Freshmint Toothpowder, and a transparent bar of Pears soap. I remain suspicious of D. R. Harris's famous Pick-Me-Up, an elixir still prepared from the 1850 recipe.

Long ago I read a book called *The Toys of a Lifetime*, by Arnold Gingrich, the founder of *Esquire*. In it he writes of his acquired tastes in clothing, automobiles, furniture, music, books, gloves, ties, aftershaves, and on and on. He spent a great deal of time on the ritual of shaving. All I had ever used was lime Barbasol from a can and a Gillette blade. But some Gingrichian impulse came stealing forward in Trumper's and Harris's. In their windows were elaborate displays of razors, brushes, and creams. No foam. They sold traditional hard shaving soaps, which my father always used, favoring Mennen. And tubes and pots of soft creams. "You put just a little dab on your hand, wet it, and apply it," Miss Brown explained. "All that foam in a can holds the blade too far off the skin." She had so many flavors to choose from. Rose, lavender, lime, hazelwood, almond, and Harris's signature Arlington. I bought a pot and shaved myself while sitting in the Wilberg's bright green pine water in my tub at the Mansion, with Radio 3 floating in from the living room. Miss Brown had spoken the truth. I'd never had a closer shave. One pot lasted me for months. It came in tubes for traveling. This was the beginning of my life as a toiletries fetishist. I came home with Harris's After Shaving Milk, a proper styptic pencil, a pot of their shampoo, which would do me for weeks, their Scalp Tonic, their bone-handled razors, and their Arlington bar soaps, which came in large, larger, and big enough to break a toe.

A block from the Eyrie was the Red Lion, reckoned by Nairn to be the last pub in London he could do without, with the best pub interior, crystal and cut glass everywhere, thrown back on itself by the mirrored walls. If you turn off Jermyn and stroll down Duke or Old Bond Street, you will be in the heart of a district that has harbored art galleries since the eighteenth century; Spink's is down that way, and Peter Nahum, and the Appleby Bros., and Chris Beetles the watercolor expert with his muttonchops. I especially liked walking down Jermyn Street during cold and rainy January days. In the early dusk the lights from the shop windows reflected on the pavement. If the weather grew too foul, I could step into the Piccadilly Arcade, which runs from Jermyn Street up to Piccadilly. Nearby there was always a welcome at Christopher Wren's St. James's Piccadilly, which has the midday classical music concerts and usually has a jumble sale under way in its courtyard. The Wren at St. James was a coffee shop with excellent soups and breads, baked potatoes, and chocolate cake. It is a most wholesome place, almost next door to Tramp, the infamous private club.

Wiltons was the most elegant place on the street to have lunch. If you came in alone, you could sit at the counter and watch how thinly they could slice the Parma ham. On my first visit I ordered cold turkey and peaches. Cheap food and drink were to be found at Sergios, a hole-in-the-wall in Eagle Court, which served a perfect cappuccino with cinnamon sprinkled on top. Jules' Bar was a popular place for Sloane Rangers and Hooray Henrys, who ordered expensive champagnes with their plates of baked beans on toast or bangers and mash. The bar at the Cavendish Hotel was dark and discreet, as it should be, since the original Cavendish witnessed the indiscretions of Rosa Lewis, the duchess of Duke Street.

"Did you know the duchess?" I asked Henry one day. Chaz and I had been honored by an invitation to have tea with Henry and Doddy, whose top-floor flat had a flowery veranda commanding a view all the way down to Westminster. "Everyone knew the duchess," Henry said. "She was to be seen every day in St. James's Square, walking her dogs, dressed in exquisite Edwardian fashions. Pity about the old Cavendish. The Germans got it with a bomb. During the war, it was well known that the Cavendish was the one place in London where you could find a girl or a drink any hour of the night."

"Henry!" Doddy said. "You make it sound like a brothel!"

"Sex for cash, m'dear. That's m'definition."

Henry was an enthusiast on ribald matters. One day when I was single, he poured himself a drink and said, "Roger, my boy, I have the girl for you! Have you in your comings and goings seen the elegant brunette staying in 1-A, who is usually dressed in red? Rita Hayworth hair? High heels?"

"I don't believe I have," I said.

"Our countess from Argentina," he said. "I want you to ask her out," he said. "Theater, a nice dinner... she's rich as Croesus, you know. You could do worse."

"Is she looking for someone?"

"She must be. She comes here twice a year, always alone, never any company. What she needs is a young man to take her out, show her a good time. Never know what it might lead to. She has masses of time on her hands. She hardly leaves 1-A except to go to Harley Street for her shock treatments."

Sometimes in walking about the area I would happen upon Henry, who knew everyone of any interest, from the maître d' at Wiltons to the man with the *Evening Standard* kiosk behind St. James's Piccadilly. I never saw Henry in a pub, however, and despite the visiting bottle of Teacher's I never saw him tipsy. One day he invited me to lunch. We walked to a cozy French restaurant in a byway near Leicester Square. Customers waiting in line were ignored as we were seated immediately. We were shown to our banquette by a handsome Frenchwoman of a certain age, whose hand, I observed, lingered longer on his shoulder than one might have expected. Henry saw me notice, and his eyes twinkled. He said nothing, but his eyebrows lifted to a minute degree, and if you hadn't been looking for it, you would have missed the almost imperceptible nod of his head.

"Henry!" I said.

"My dear boy," he said, "if you don't flush out the pipes, they'll run brown."

Henry was much concerned about the future of the Mansion. "Our landlady is the queen," he told me. "The Crown Estate agents have always tried to keep the lease terms reasonable, but the price of property is making alarming advances. I've raised my prices as much as I dare. Henry Junior wants to take over and make this a luxury hotel. Well, it's in the blood. But it frightens me. What kinds of loans will he have to take out? How will he make the payments?" He brought Henry Junior around to meet me. This was a pleasant young man, friendly, confiding. He said he hoped to keep the charm of the Eyrie

Mansion. "But at the prices I'll be forced to charge, the public won't stand for this," he said, regarding the carpets frayed at the edges and the nicked furniture and staring balefully at the gas fireplace.

As it happened, the gas fire was one of my favorite features at the Eyrie. In jet-lagged winter mornings before dawn I'd awaken in a bone-cold flat, pull on warm clothes, and walk up to the newsagent on Piccadilly. I'd buy the *Telegraph, Independent, Guardian*, and *Times*, and a large cup of hot coffee from an all-night shop around the corner. With these I would return to the Mansion, tune in Radio 3, sit in my low easy chair before the fire, and dream wistfully that such was my life. The fire was never left to burn when unneeded; the maids saw to that. But it held promise of warmth after a brisk walk. Fires, I decided, were a source of heat, not merely, like central heating, its presence. There must be something deep within our memory as a species that is pleased by being able to look at what is making us warm.

One winter's day I set out to walk across Hyde Park from Kensington Gardens to Hyde Park Corner. It was raining, but that was fine with me; I had my Simpsons umbrella. What I didn't know was that the gates to the park were locked at dusk. This I discovered on a notice inside the gate I'd intended to leave by. I could see the traffic hurrying past up the road from the direction of the Albert Memorial. There were a lot of taxis. Unfortunately, an iron fence topped with spikes stood between me and the road. It began raining harder. I scouted and found a low tree branch that might just allow me to stand atop the railing. That meant climbing a hill slippery with wet grass. I failed twice and became smeared with mud. Digging in the point of my umbrella, I finally made my way up the hill and onto the limb and balanced on the fence, but it was a good leap down to the sidewalk and I could easily imagine myself with a sprained ankle. Or worse: impaled on the fence.

Pedestrians hurried past, apparently not seeing me. I tried calling for help. I was ignored. Well, if you were hurrying through the park in the rain and saw a fat man with a soaked coat smeared with mud, balanced on a fence with a filthy umbrella, what would you do?

"Hey, look, it's Roger Ebert!" an American kid said. He was with a group of friends. "No way! Is that really you?"

"Yes it is," I said. If I had been Prince Charles I would have answered to "Roger Ebert."

"Far out, dude! What are you doing up there?"

"Trying to get down," I observed.

They helped me down and asked for my autograph, which I gladly supplied. I opened my umbrella, hailed a cab, and was at 22 Jermyn Street in ten minutes. That was one of the occasions when I lit the gas fire and treasured it beyond all reason. After warming up, I filled the big tub for a bath. It was deep, and as long as I was tall. I tinted it a bright green with Wilberg's Pine Bath Essence and inhaled warm pine and reflected that you are never warmer than when you have been cold.

Word came in 1990 that Henry Junior had taken over operations and closed the hotel for renovations. In his announcement, he wrote, "I agreed to buy the hotel from my father, famous for his wonderful eccentricity." Chaz and I stopped in to inspect. He was filled with enthusiasm. He was fitting it out elegantly with new rugs and draperies, sofas and chairs, beds, the lot. Of course he removed the gas fires. I was pleased to see he was keeping the old furniture, purchased in 1915 by his grandparents. "After we had it refinished," he said, "it turned out to be very good stuff. You couldn't touch it today."

Henry Junior said the workmen had sorted through the memories of three generations. In the basement, he said, he discovered a cache of naughty French postcards from the 1930s. Inside a walled-over hall closet on the second floor he found his mother's hoarded supply of sugar from the days of rationing in World War II. I realize that never during all those years did I ever figure out where the hotel's kitchen was.

The Eyrie Mansion was renamed 22 Jermyn Street. Perhaps "Eyrie Mansion" was possibly not an ideal name for a hotel. Chaz and I stayed there many times. I liked it, she adored it. When I said I missed the gas fire that you lit with a match, she gave me one of those looks I got when I said I would rather drive a 1957 Studebaker than a new car. As a luxury hotel, 22 Jermyn Street prospered. Croissants and cappuccino were now served as an alternative to full English breakfast. There'd be a flower on the tray. Clients included movie stars and politicians like Gary Hart, who valued its privacy and its absence of a lobby. Doddy and Henry Senior would have been proud. But in autumn 2009 Henry Junior wrote to us: "Sadly the lease has expired and the greater part of the city block in which the hotel is located is to be redeveloped by the Crown Estate as a project named St James's Gateway, over the next two or three years. Like much else in London, it is planned that this very comprehensive and handsome project will be completed in time for the Olympic Games in 2012." Just what Olympic guests will be looking for in London. One more goddamned comprehensive and handsome project.

In the mid-1990s, after Cannes, Chaz and I were

staying at Champneys health farm in Tring, an hour or so outside London. One morning the *Telegraph* carried news of Henry Senior's death. I took an early train to London and arrived in time for the funeral at St. Patrick's Catholic Church in Soho Square, where Henry had served as an usher for decades. So much was made of Henry Senior's devotion to the Church that I could imagine his eyes twinkling. In Catholic churches they don't customarily ask friends of the departed to come forward and share a few words. It's just as well. Had I been called upon, I have no idea how I would have begun, or how long it would have taken me to finish. And I didn't really even know Henry that well. Was there a Dickens quote I might have used? I think only an entire character would have done. Perhaps Mr. Pickwick, with a touch of Mr. Micawber and a dash of David Copperfield's jolly impractical optimist friend Mr. Dick.

19   ALL BY MYSELF ALONE

In Venice there is a small bridge leading over a side canal. Halfway up the steps crossing this bridge there is a landing, and a little café has found a perch there. In front of this café there is one table with two chairs. If you choose the chair with its back to the café, you can overlook the steps you climbed and also the steps leading toward you from the canal path ahead of you. This is an obscure neighborhood crossroads, a good place to sit with a cup of cappuccino and the newspaper you got from the newsstand behind Piazza San Marco. Of course you must have a newspaper, a book, a sketchpad—anything that seems to absorb you. If you are simply sitting there, you will appear to be a Lonely Person and people will look away from you. If you seem preoccupied, you can observe them more closely. In any event, I do not sit there for the purpose of people watching. No, I am engaged in the pastime of Being by Myself in a City Where No One Knows Who I Am and No One Knows Where to Find Me. I have such places in many cities: London, of course. Paris. Rome. Stockholm. Edinburgh. Cape Town. Cannes.

I have another private place in Venice. The night of the day in 1965 when I disembarked from Cape Town, I wandered into a little bar in Piazza San Giacomo, behind San Marco, and was greeted by the exuberant owner, a young man whose wife was minding their son in a corner. Lino, for that was his name, knew the name of everybody who came in. He hurried around the bar and, without asking, deposited a plate of oysters in front of me. They were alive and began to click. I had never eaten a raw oyster. It was the wise Jonathan Swift who told a friend, "It was a brave man who first ate an oyster." I opened the oysters and ate them. I'd never tasted one before except in Uncle Bill's turkey dressing. I returned to Lino's every time I came to Venice, and returning to Venice became a necessity. Once in Lino's an old man who ran a tourist gimcrack shop on the other side of the square personally cooked everyone gnocchi. No charge. Lino always recognized me, or made signs indicating he did. I went once with my friend McHugh. Every subsequent time, Lino used his hands to indicate a man of Falstaffian dimensions and we would agree on my friend's name: "Giovanni."

One year I returned and there was no Lino. I asked inside: "Lino?" I was pointed around the corner to the Trattoria alla Rivetta, with canal steps passing its front window. Lino had moved up in the world to a restaurant with a back room. I walked in. *Giovanni! Giovanni!* He used sign language for Santa Claus. During the 1972 Venice Film Festival, I took everyone I knew there: Dusan Makavejev, Manny Farber and Patricia Patterson, Thomas Quinn Curtiss. Usually I would go alone and sit in the back room, reading during dinner. Lino and I had only one word in common, but we always remembered it.

On our honeymoon in 1982, Chaz and I visited Lino's. I waited for Lino to say "Giovanni!" He did. Chaz was surprised: "I thought you were making that up." Nearly thirty years had passed. In 2004, we took my stepdaughter Sonia and her children to Venice. I looked in at Lino's in the afternoon. There was no Lino. His son, now nearing forty, explained: "Lino, he a little retired. Here only in morning." The next morning I looked in through the window. All the lights were off except those in the kitchen. Lino, now bald and grey, was kneading pasta. I could have knocked on the glass and had his attention and heard *Giovanni!* again, but I didn't. That would have been pushing it.

In *Two Weeks in the Midday Sun*, my book about the Cannes Film Festival, I wrote that I always wake up very early on the morning after I arrive, because of jet lag. I leave Chaz sleeping in our room at the Hotel Splendid and walk down the rue Félix Faure, passing the flower sellers setting out their bouquets, the fish-mongers unloading iced oysters, and the street cleaners hosing down the pavement. I walk through the market, inhale the scents of the melons and the roses, and buy the *International Herald Tribune*. I turn down the hill toward the old harbor, and at a particular café, Le St. Antoine, at a particular table on the sidewalk, I order, in shameful French, a café au lait, a Perrier, and a croissant. This is a ritual. One year I looked up and saw Jeannette Hereniko, the founder of the Hawaii Film Festival, approaching me from the direction of the bus stop. She was in a bit of a crisis. It was six a.m., the airline had lost her carry-on bag, and she had no idea of the name of her hotel. She had been reading my book on the flight over and decided to see if she could find me at that café. Of course she could. I couldn't tell her where she was staying, but she had a cup of coffee.

Of all the words I have written, a brief passage in that out-of-print book is the one most often mentioned to me. People tell me they know exactly what I'm describing. Here it is. It takes place on the other end of town from the old harbor:

I walked out of the Martinez and was made uneasy again by the wind. So I turned inland, away from the Croisette and the beach, and walked up into one of the ordinary commercial streets of Cannes. I cut behind the Carlton, walked past the Hotel Savoy, and before long was at the little fruit and vegetable marketplace, at the other end of town from the big market. I took a table at a cafe, ordered an espresso and a Perrier, and began to sketch.

Suddenly I was filled with an enormous happiness, such a feeling as comes not even once a year, and focused all my attention inward on a momentous feeling of joy, on the sense that in this moment everything is in harmony. I sat very still. I was alone at a table in a square where no one I knew was likely to come, in a land where I did not speak the language, in a place where, for the moment, I could not be found. I was like a spirit returned from another world. All the people around me carried on their lives, sold their strawberries and called for their children, and my presence there made not the slightest difference to them. I was invisible. I would leave no track in this square, except for the few francs I would give to the cafe owner, who would throw them in a dish with hundreds of other coins.

After a time the intensity of my feeling passed, and I sat absolutely still at the table, a blank, taking in the movements before me. There are times when I think it would be possible to lead my life like this, a stranger in a foreign land, sitting in a cafe, drinking espresso, sketching on a pad, sometimes buying a newspaper which would tell me in my own language what was happening in other places to other people. I would see myself in the third person—that anonymous figure in the distance, crossing under the trees. Most of the time I am too busy to entertain such fantasies. I have filled my life so completely that many days there is no time to think about the fact that I am living it. But these still moments, usually in a strange city, give me the illusion that in some sense the person that is really me sits somewhere quietly at a table, watching it all go by.

I've been back to the café several times again, always hoping for the same seat at the same table. Such returns are an important ritual to me. Chaz says it is impossible to get me to do anything the first time, and then impossible to stop me from doing it over and over again. After we were married, we went to Europe on our honeymoon.

"What did you visit?" her best friend Carolyn asked her.

"We visited Roger's previous visits," she said.

It is true. "I always go to Sir John Soane's house," I would tell Chaz. And, "This is my favorite Wren church." And, "This is the oldest restaurant in London. I always order cock-a-leekie soup, toad-in-the-hole, bangers and mash, and, to follow, spotted dick." I always say it exactly that way: "...and, to follow, spotted dick." Chaz studied the menu and told the waiter she would have the lamb chops. "Excellent choice, madam," he said, giving me a look that translated as, *I remember you, all right.*

My new bride was also made to take a particular train from the Liverpool Street station to Cambridge and accompany me on a walk in the meadows above the River Cam to the village of Grantchester to visit the Rupert Brooke memorial and have lunch at the Green Man. And of course we had to walk slowly past the Old Vicarage, as I recited:

Stands the Church clock at ten to three?
And is there honey still for tea?

And we had to ascertain that the church clock indeed still stood at ten to three, the irrefutable evidence cited by generations of Cambridge students who protested it was not yet Closing Time. The villagers have recently raised the money to repair the clock, so that for the first time since before the Great War it keeps accurate time. The repair amounts to vandalism.

I may appear to suffer from some sort of compulsive repetition syndrome, but these rituals are important to me. I have many places where I sit and think, "I have been here before, I am here now, and I will be here again." Sometimes, lost in reverie, I remember myself approaching across the same green, or down the same footpath, in 1962 or 1983, or many other times. Sometimes Chaz comes along on my rituals, but just as often I go alone. Sometimes Chaz will say she's going shopping, or visiting a friend, or just staying in the room and reading in bed. "Why don't you go and touch your bases?" she'll ask me. I know she sympathizes. These secret visits are a way for me to measure the wheel of the years and my passage through life. Sometimes on this voyage through life we need to sit on the deck and regard the waves.

I first visited the Moscow Arms near Pembridge Square in 1970, when the room fee at the Hyde Park West Hotel, now named the Blue Bells, was four pounds a night. I have never met anybody in that pub. I always sit in the same corner. There is a man who comes in every lunchtime, tattooed, bald, and wearing a motorcycle jacket. He is nearly forty years older now, but he is still there, and it appears to be the same jacket. Has he noticed me crossing his field of vision fifty or seventy-five times in his lifetime? Certainly not. But if he still comes at lunchtime every day, it is my duty to bear witness, because by now I have become the only person in the Moscow Arms who knows how long he has been doing this, or cares. I believe this includes him.

I always visit a used bookstore, Keith Fawkes, in Flask Walk, Hampstead. I've found many precious books there. Then I go to the Holly Bush pub, up Heath Street to Holly Mount, where there are snug corners to ensconce myself. A corner is important. It provides privacy and an anchor and lets you exist independently of the room. It was while walking down from the Holly Bush that I first saw the Catto Gallery and made my best friends in London. In the opposite direction there is a pub I have been visiting so long that I remember when Helena Bonham Carter moved in upstairs, and when she moved out. I've had some pleasant interviews with her, going back to 1986, when she made *Lady Jane* and was nineteen. Did I ever ring her bell? Certainly not.

In the years when I was drinking, I drank in these places. I haven't had a drink since 1979, and I still visit them with the same enjoyment—actually more. The thing about a British pub is that you don't have to drink booze. If you don't, nobody looks at you funny. They provide tea, coffee, lunch, atmosphere, a place to sit, a time to think. At the Holly Bush I always have the ploughman's lunch with an extra pickle.

But let me stop place-dropping. These places do not involve only a visit, but a meditation: I have been here before, I am here now, I will be here again. Robert Altman told me he kept track of time not by the years, but by the films he was working on. "I'm always preparing the next film," he said. That is living in a time outside time. Of course everyone's time must run out. But not yet. Not until I'm finished touching a few more bases. I will sit in the corner by the fire in the Holly Bush again, and stand in the wind on top of Parliament Hill, and I know exactly how to find that café in Venice, although I could never describe the way. Oh, yes I do.

20   SUN-TIMES

AFTER RETURNING FROM Cape Town I did another two semesters of graduate school at Illinois. I'd been accepted as a Ph.D. candidate in English by the University of Chicago. I needed a job, and wrote to Herman Kogan, editor of the weekend arts magazine of the *Daily News*. He'd bought some freelance pieces from me, a review of a collection of John O'Hara's short stories and an elegy for Brendan Behan. For O'Hara I tried out the "first-rate second-rate writer" dodge, and Herman told me O'Hara called to thank him for assigning a "smart-ass college punk" to review his book. Kogan forwarded my job application to Jim Hoge, then the city editor of the

Sun-Times, who wrote asking me to come to Chicago for an interview.

Chicago was the great city over the horizon. The typography in the *News-Gazette*'s nameplate and its standard eight-column Railroad Gothic banner headline were copied from the *Trib*. We read Chicago's newspapers and listened to its powerful AM radio stations. Long after midnight I listened to Jack Eigen on WMAQ, broadcasting live from the Chez Paree, chatting with Martin and Lewis or Rosemary Clooney. Thomas Wolfe had taught me that my destiny waited in New York, but Chicago was obviously the first step on my path.

I arrived in Chicago one morning on the Panama and walked up Wabash Avenue to the Sun-Times/Daily News Building, which looked like a snub-nosed ship on the banks of the Chicago River. A boat was moored at its dock, and a crane was offloading huge rolls of newsprint. Hoge and Ken Towers, the city editor, took me out the back way to lunch at Riccardo's and offered me a job. I would work under Dick Takeuchi, the editor of the paper's Sunday magazine. He was a cigar smoker, calm, confiding, tactfully showing a green kid the ropes. He gave me a desk close to his, in the back row of the city room. At lunch I began joining Takeuchi and Jack McPhaul, the magazine's copy editor. McPhaul wrote the 1943 articles that became the movie *Call Northside 777*; his reporting freed Joseph Majczek, the "Stop Me Before I Kill Again Killer," from prison after eleven years. He also wrote *Deadlines and Monkeyshines*, the best account of the Front Page era when the Chicago dailies went at each other with hammer and tongs and hit men. He was my living connection to the Front Page era.

"Tell Roger the one about the atom being split," Dick said.

"After the war," McPhaul said, "they had a ceremony under the grandstands at old Stagg Field to commemorate where the first self-sustaining nuclear reaction took place. Our photographer from the *Times* got down to the U of C late, and a flack rounded up Fermi and his team.

" 'I got a great idea for a series of three photos across the top of page one,' the photographer tells them. 'You're puttin' in the atom, splittin' it, and standing around lookin' at the pieces.' "

When Friday of my first week came around, I joined a general emigration to Riccardo's, where reporters from all four papers gathered to gobble free hors d'oeuvres. I felt a glow of camaraderie. I knew I lacked authenticity in this company. I was young and unseasoned, but I discovered there was nothing like drinking with the crowd to make you a member.

I copied the idealism and cynicism of the reporters I met at Riccardo's and around the corner at the downscale but equally famous Billy Goat's. I spoke like they did, laughed at the same things, felt that I belonged.

At about six p.m. on New Year's Day of 1967, only two lights on the fourth floor were burning—mine and Mike Royko's. It was too early for the graveyard shift to come in. Royko walked over to the *Sun-Times* to see who else was working. A historic snowstorm was beginning. He asked me how I was getting home. I said I'd take the train. He said he had his old man's Checker car and would drop me at the L station. He had to make a stop at a twenty-four-hour drugstore right where the L crossed North Avenue.

Royko at thirty-five was already the city's most famous newspaperman, known for complex emotions evoked with unadorned prose in short paragraphs. Growing up as the son of a saloon keeper, he knew how the city worked from the precinct level up, and had first attracted attention while covering city hall. He was ten years older than me and had started at the old City News Bureau, the cooperative supported by all the dailies that provided front-line coverage of the police and fire departments. Underpaid and overworked kids worked under the hand of its editor, Arnold Dornfeld, who sat beneath a sign reading:

If your mother says she loves you, check it out. When I met him he'd been writing his *Daily News* column for two years. It was his writing about Mayor Richard J. Daley that took the city hall word *clout* and made it national. He chain-smoked Pall Malls and spoke in a gravelly poker player's voice. He drank too much, which to me was an accomplishment.

That snowy night the all-night drugstore was crowded. "Come on, kid," he said. "Let's have a drink at the eye-opener place." He told me what an eye-opener was. "This place opens early. The working guys around here, they stop in for a quick shot on their way to the L." It was a bar under the tracks so tiny the bartender could serve everyone without leaving his stool. "Two blackberry brandies and short beers," he said. He told me, "Blackberry brandy is good for hangovers. You never get charged for a beer chaser." I sipped the brandy, and a warm glow filled my stomach. It may have been the first straight shot of anything I'd ever tasted. I'd been in Chicago four months and I was sitting under the L tracks with Mike Royko in the eye-opener place. I was a newspaperman. A Blackhawks game was playing on WGN radio. The team scored, and again, and again. This at last was life.

"Jeez, they're scoring like crazy!" I said, after the third goal in less than a minute.

"Where you from, kid?"

"Urbana," I said.

"Ever seen a hockey game?"

"No."

"That's what I thought, you asshole. Those are the game highlights."

I began to be welcome in Royko's cubicle. It amused him to explain the obvious to the downstate kid. He wrote on an old manual typewriter—not his own, just one from the office pool, with keys that stuck and ribbons that jammed. His office was filled with newspapers, books, letters, coffee cups, ashtrays, and ties that he had taken off and thrown in the corner. It contained a holy relic: The wooden city room hat stand from the old Daily News Building on Wacker, which was brought along when the paper moved into the new building on the river.

Mike sat in a swivel chair with his back to the river, and there was a straight-backed chair for his visitors. He had a lot of visitors. Mike could have written his column at any time from anywhere and his editors would have been happy to have it, but he spent eight hours a day, sometimes longer, at the paper. He was the soul of the *Daily News* and the honorary soul, by osmosis, of the *Sun-Times*. No journalist in Chicago was more admired. Any time of the day, if you glanced back there, someone would be standing in the door of the cubicle or sitting inside. It might be one of his legmen, who had their own desk just outside. Or a press agent like the boxing promoter Ben Bentley or Danny Newman from the Lyric Opera. Most likely it was a fellow reporter. Mike always had time to talk. Even when he was in the middle of a column, he had time to talk. He was the most prolific of columnists, turning out five a week at such a high level that I never heard anybody look up from the paper and say, "Royko wrote a bad column today."

During that first year I was also a Ph.D. student at the University of Chicago, where I failed French as usual but grew absorbed in a class on Milton taught by George Williamson, who treated *Paradise Lost* as history and once said, "But Satan is clearly wrong, because on the next page, God tells him..." On April 1, 1967, the feature editor, Robert Zonka, told me I would become the paper's film critic. This came without warning, although I'd written some pieces on the movies. I couldn't be the film critic and a graduate student at the same time, and I didn't return to Chicago the next autumn. That was just as well. I loved the life of studying English literature but would never have made a competent academic. During 1967–68, as a means of keeping my draft deferment, I taught freshman English in a Chicago city college on the South Side, at Seventy-Sixth and Pulaski, where I swore my students to secrecy and told them I wouldn't teach the syllabus if they didn't tell anyone. I assigned books I thought would excite them, like *Gatsby*, *In Cold Blood*, *Crime and Punishment*, and E. E. Cummings.

My deferment ran out, and I was drafted in 1968. There was a farewell party at O'Rourke's. Everybody chipped in for the pizzas and beer. Mike wrote a check. I had rented my apartment, sold my car, and put my books in storage. The next day I left for Urbana to report for induction. They put me on the Panama Limited back to Chicago, where I reported to the induction center and flunked the physical. I walked back into O'Rourke's the same night. John McHugh from the *Daily News*, who had organized the farewell party, told me, "Royko heard you were coming back and stopped payment on his check."

When the *Daily News* folded in 1978, Mike worked at the *Sun-Times* until Rupert Murdoch bought the paper in late 1983. Mike had been involved in backstage negotiations that would have allowed Jim Hoge to buy the paper. Marshall Field, who owned half the paper, said he was willing to sell to that group, but Murdoch offered $10 million more than Hoge could raise, and Marshall's brother, the movie producer Ted Field, insisted they take it. This was a crushing blow to Mike. He went home and had a few drinks, and when the local TV stations brought their cameras into his den, he announced that a Murdoch paper was "not fit to wrap fish in."

The next afternoon I sat with him at Billy Goat's.

"I guess I resigned, huh?"

"Murdoch doesn't care what you say about him," I said.

"It's not what I said about him," Mike said. "It's that after describing a Murdoch paper that way, how can I work there?"

Before the *Daily News* was folded, the city rooms of the two papers shared the fourth floor. They had separate but equal facilities, except that the men's room of the *Daily News* had real bars of soap, and the men's room of the *Sun-Times* had liquid soap from a dispenser. Office legend explained the real soap was a concession wrung from Marshall Field IV when he bought the *Daily News* from John S. Knight. The city rooms of the two papers were separated by a glassed-in no-man's-land called the wire room, ruled by copyboys/pot dealers, where Teletypes chattered and printers turned out wirephotos. On either side of the wire room were the copy desks of the two papers, and then the desks of editors and reporters receded into the distance in both directions, until when you got to the far corners there was Royko at the *Daily News* and me at the *Sun-Times*.

The city room was a noisy place to work. Type-writers hammered at carbon-copy books that made an impatient slap-slap-slap. Phones rang the way phones used to ring in the movies. Reporters shouted into them. They called out "Boy!" and held up a story and a copykid ran to snatch it and deliver it to an editor. Reporters would shout out questions on deadline. "Quick! Who was governor before Walker?" There were no cubicles, except for Royko's. We worked at desks democratically lined up next to one another, row after row. Ann Landers (actually Eppie Lederer) had an office full of assistants somewhere else in the building but insisted on sitting in the middle of this chaos, next to the TV-radio critic, Paul Molloy. Once Paul was talking on a telephone headset, tilted back in his chair, and fell to the floor and kept on talking. Eppie reached in a file drawer and handed down her pamphlet *Drinking Problem? Take This Test of Twenty Questions*.

When you went on an interview, you took eight sheets of copy paper, folded them once, and ripped them in half using a pica stick. Then you folded them again. Now you had a notebook of thirty-two pages to slip in your pocket with your ball-point. You had a press card. You were a reporter from the *Chicago Sun-Times*. In the 1990s one of my young editors asked if it was really true they allowed reporters to smoke at their desks in the old days. Yes, and drink too, if they could get away with it. Reporters sent Milton the copyboy out the rear loading dock to Billy Goat's to fetch them a drink in a paper coffee cup. Copyboys were known as wiseass insiders with an angle on everything, but Milton became a legend. He buttonholed reporters on deadline with his opinions about being and nothingness. He had been a University of Chicago student and still lived in Hyde Park. That explained everything. One day an inspector from the Chicago post office came to Ralph Otwell, the managing editor, with a puzzling discovery. Several hundred empty envelopes addressed to Ann Landers had been found in the trash behind an address in Hyde Park. With an eerie certainty, Ralph asked Milton for his address. Milton, whose tasks included distributing mail, had been stealing the quarters sent in for Ann Landers's pamphlet *Petting: When Does It Go Too Far?* Discussing his firing after work at Billy Goat's, Milton was philosophical: "Hundreds of kids can thank me they were even conceived."

Billy Goat's and Riccardo's. Billy Goat's was a dive so subterranean that after you were already on the lower level of Michigan Avenue you had to descend another flight of stairs. There really was a short-order cook like John Belushi's *SNL* character shouting *Chizzbooger! Chizzbooger! Cheeps, no flies!* Riccardo's was a good Italian restaurant at the other end of the block, facing Rush Street, with a bar shaped like an artist's palette and paintings representing the arts, including one by the famous Ivan Albright, who among other distinctions was the father of Jim Hoge's wife, Alice. A tall, mournful guitarist and a short, cheerful accordion player circulated while playing a limited but well-chosen repertoire. Here the front booth harbored such regulars as Bill Mauldin, Studs Terkel, and John Fischetti. It was said that when the original Riccardo's future wife walked into the bar and asked where she should sit, Riccardo told her, "On the floor." His son, an actor, took over the operation and lived above the restaurant. When he sold the restaurant, he was interviewed by our Pulitzer-winning columnist Tom Fitzpatrick. He said that he'd enjoyed running the restaurant, except "on Friday nights, they let the animals out of the zoo." John McHugh studied this and said, "Ebert, he means us." Fitzpatrick possibly saved my life during 1968's Days of Rage (a phrase he coined) before the Democratic Convention. We were watching a crowd of demonstrators run down a narrow street in Old Town. Fitz reached out, grabbed my belt, and hauled me to the ground just before a cop car, speeding in reverse, would have blindsided me.

Jim Hoge ruled a gifted staff that collected six

Pulitzers. He financed an elaborate sting in which the paper opened and operated a bar called the Mirage and was able to develop a thirty-day series of articles about the graft and corruption involved. After Murdoch bought the paper, Hoge became the publisher of the *New York Daily News* and later the editor of *Foreign Affairs* magazine. He was back in Chicago in early 2011 and at a brunch with some survivors of those days, he said, "We were right there on the edge of doing something great." There was still pain in his voice.

The city room was filled with colorful characters. Many years later our columnist Neil Steinberg complained at lunch, "I feel like I missed the boat. There were all these eccentrics on the staff and they all hung out together in bars after work. Now all we do is work and go home." "Neil," I told him, "you did miss the boat."

He missed, for example, Paul Galloway, a handsome man with senatorial hair and an expression that showed him amused by the peculiarities of life. He had a southern accent. His favorite note was puzzlement about the things people do. He was well educated, and that was reflected by the richness of his writing. He worked by seeming to tell a story straight and then sneaking in well-chosen words to set it subtly askew. That reminded me of Mark Twain. He told me, "I was named after my father. Our only difference was, his name was preceded by Bishop, and mine was followed by Junior."

I met him in the early 1970s at the *Sun-Times*, where he was a reporter and feature writer, effortlessly stylish. The most famous story is about the Friday night when Paul went out the back door to Riccardo's and started to brood about some undefined atrocity committed by Jim Hoge. His indignation grew. A statement had to be made. He stalked back to the *Sun-Times*, entered via the freight elevator, emerged on the fourth floor, picked up an office chair, and hurled it at the window of Hoge's office. "Something I had not foreseen," Paul told us back at the bar, "was that the window was made of Plexiglas. The chair bounced back and almost hit me."

The newsroom stood transfixed. Paul walked over to the city desk and said firmly, "Log it." The desk assistant said, "Forget it, Paul." Paul said, "I said log it, damn it." The chair-hurling incident was duly logged. On Monday morning, he was hunched over his desk, trying to keep a low profile. His phone rang. It was Hoge. He got up and walked slowly across the city room. All eyes were on him like a man on his way to death row. Hoge had the city desk log open in front of him. He said, "Paul, I understand you have a problem with the interior decoration." Paul said he replied, "No sir! I find it excellent! Nothing what-soever wrong with it! Enviable, in fact!" Hoge said, "That's a relief. Now get back to work." After the success of the movie *Tootsie*, Paul recruited professionals to costume him and do his wig and makeup like Tootsie. Then he walked down Michigan Avenue, followed by a photographer. "I didn't mind if I wasn't mistaken for a woman," he wrote, "but I was disappointed I wasn't even mistaken for Tootsie."

There was the day Art Petacque and Hugh Hough won the Pulitzer for their coverage of the Valerie Percy murder case. Hough was a superb rewrite man. Petacque was our mob reporter. Nobody ever actually saw him typing. He was priceless for his sources. He was the only Chicago newsman who knew all mob nicknames. It was rumored he invented many of the nicknames himself. Nobody ever complained. What would Joey "the Clown" Lombardo do? Write a letter to the editor? Petacque and Hough were a familiar team in the city room. Petacque would walk in looking like the cat that ate the canary, take a chair next to Hough, pull out a sheaf of notes, and start whispering in his ear. Hough would type, stopping occasionally to remove his cigar and say, "You're kidding!" Then Hough would write up the notes, and the story would appear under a shared byline. The day they won the Pulitzer, Hough was on a golf course. Petacque walked in, got a standing ovation, climbed onto a desk, bowed, and said, "I only wish Hugh Hough was here to tell you how happy I feel."

Bob Zonka became my best friend and father figure. He was a chain-smoker with thinning hair and a gut, and such charm that he was devastatingly successful with women. He was the last editor at the paper who worked himself up from copyboy, a passionate editor and a decent man. When Polish jokes were an epidemic in the 1970s, he refused to listen to them: "When a joke diminishes anyone, it diminishes me." At his funeral, Jon Anderson, a former *Daily News* columnist, said, "I spent more hours talking with Zonka than anyone except my three wives. And more quality time than with anyone."

Zonka's desk was just in front of mine. One day he was leaning back with his feet up, surveying the city room, and said, "Ebert, you're single. Why don't you ask Abra Prentice out on a date?" She was a tall, good-looking brunette, famous because while she was covering the Richard Speck trial, the nurse murderer never took his eyes off of her.

"She's not my type," I said.

"Ebert, Ebert, Ebert," Zonka said. "When you grow up, you'll learn that a Rockefeller is everybody's type."

"Huh?" I said.

Abra married Jon Anderson, and together they wrote a gossip column at the *Daily News* titled *Jon & Abra*. When they left to start *Chicagoan* magazine, the column was renamed *Mort* and inherited by Governor Dan Walker's press secretary, Mort Edelstein. "It makes me feel creepy when our space has been taken over by Death," Jon told me. Yes, Abra was a Rockefeller. Once when Jon and Abra and I were visiting London at the same time, we made a deal: I would buy lunch, they would buy dinner. Lunch would be bangers and mash in a pub. Dinner would be in a place with no prices on the menu. One night after dinner we were riding in a taxi through Soho and passed the famous Raymond Revuebar.

"Jon," said Abra, "I've never seen a strip show. Why can't I see a strip show?"

"Abra," Jon said, "as you know, you can see a strip show."

We found that Raymond's was closed on Mondays. Another taxi was waiting by the curb, with a driver who touted, "Evening, mates! Want to see the best strip show in town?" We did. As we were being carried through dark lanes, Abra said, "We're doing the very thing they warn tourists to avoid. Isn't it exciting?" We entered a lurid doorway and descended two flights of stairs to a neon-lit room with a small stage and a couple of dozen tables. It was explained that this was a private club, and it would cost us five quid to become members. Jon paid up. We were given a table in front of the stage and ordered our drinks.

"Do you have an account?" asked the waiter.

"Oh, we're members," Abra told him. "Jon, show him our card."

"Yes, madam, but we do not sell alcohol by the drink. Members maintain their private stocks."

Jon ordered bottles of scotch, vodka, and champagne. We wondered if we could take them home with us. There was a three-piece band. A stripper materialized and began to disrobe a yard in front of us. Abra's eyes surveyed the shadows of the room.

"Dodger," Abra said, "why are all those men sitting alone at their tables?"

"I think they're lonely," I said, "because they have to buy a girl her own bottle if they want her to sit with them."

"They all seem so sad," Abra said. She took another look around the room. The stripper finished and left the stage to indifferent applause. Abra whispered something to Jon. He was a distinguished Canadian and knew how to handle these things. He rapped smartly on the table with a pound coin. "Waiter!" he said. "Blow jobs for everyone!"

Such, such were the days. There was adrenaline in the city room when a big story broke. The resignation of Nixon. The death of Mayor Richard J. Daley. The time when an L train derailed and we could see it from the office window. The afternoon when Jay McMullen, then the *Daily News* city hall reporter, later married to Mayor Jane Byrne, commandeered the paper's suite at the Executive House across the river and phoned the office to tell us to check out a balcony on the seventeenth floor. There he was, the phone to his ear, waving, standing next to a woman. They were both stark naked.

One day our columnist Bob Greene heard a five bell alert ring on the AP wire and walked over to the machine. I looked up to see if it looked like anything. He walked over with tears in his eyes. "Elvis just died," he said.

21   MY NEW JOB

ONE DAY IN March 1967 Bob Zonka called me into the conference room and told me I was being named the paper's film critic. This came as news to me. He said Eleanor Keen, the current critic, was taking early retirement. When I walked back into the newsroom, Ellie was smiling across from her desk. She said she would finally not be asked five times a day if she'd seen any good movies lately. Actually, what people are more likely to ask is, "How many movies do you see in a week?" They ask as if no one had ever thought of that question before. Gene Siskel told me that as an experiment he tried answering, "Ten." He said people mostly just nodded and said, "Thanks."

I'd written a few reviews for the *Daily Illini,*

but being a movie critic was not my career goal. If I had one at all, it was to become a columnist like Royko. Now I had a title, my photo in the paper, and a twenty-five-dollar-a-week raise. Eleanor Keen and Sam Lesner of the *Daily News* were notable in Chicago for writing under their own names. The *Tribune* had an all-purpose byline, "Mae Tinee," under which any staff number could write. The *New York Daily News* used the pseudonym "Kate Cameron."

I got attention from the start because I was young, part of Hoge's plan to cultivate new talent. I was first-person and often autobiographical from the start, and it's interesting (or depressing) that my reviews from 1967 are written in roughly the same voice as my new ones. I've always written in the same style, which seems to emerge without great pondering.

In those days the Chicago movie business was still centered in the Loop. New movies opened on Fridays in vast palaces altogether seating perhaps fifteen thousand people. To name them is to evoke them: the Chicago, the State-Lake, the Oriental, the Roosevelt, the Woods, the United Artists, the Cinestage, the Michael Todd (then owned by Elizabeth Taylor), the Bismarck Palace, the Loop, the World Playhouse, the McVickers. On the Near North Side, there were the art deco Esquire, the Carnegie, the Cinema. All of the great neighborhood theaters were still open, including the Uptown, said to have more seats than Radio City Music Hall.

Then there was a revival house, the Clark Theater, which showed a different double feature every day. Bruce Trinz, its owner, was a serious movie lover and would show programs of John Ford, Hitchcock, Preston Sturges, or MGM musicals. It was at the Clark that I did some of my catching up, because unlike the acolytes of Doc Films at the University of Chicago, I hadn't grown up seeing every film. The Clark offered a $2.95 special: a double feature, a three-course meal at the Chinese restaurant next door, and free parking. It was open twenty-three hours a day. They advertised "Our Little Gal-ery for Gals Only." It was there one Sunday, while sitting in the balcony watching *Help!* with the Beatles, that I saw a fan run down the aisle, cry out, "I'm coming, John!" and throw himself over the rail. Strangely, there were no serious injuries.

The movie studios started shutting down their regional film exchanges, and Bruce switched the Clark over to first-run art films. His competitor was Oscar Brotman, whose Carnegie was on Rush Street next to the nightclub Mister Kelly's. In my first week on the job, Oscar took me out to lunch and gave me two rules: (1) "If nothing has happened by the end of the first reel, nothing is going to happen," and (2) "The definition of a good movie is, a tuchus on every seat."

Being a movie critic meant interviewing the stars who came through town, and this often meant having lunch or dinner at the Pump Room, where the *Sun-Times* columnist Irv Kupcinet famously had a telephone installed in booth #1. I was by then twenty-five years old, naïve for my age, inexperienced, but representing an important newspaper, so the stars and directors were kind to me. It was so new to me that I took it very seriously indeed—not just my job, but their fame and glamour. Zonka gave me all the space I wanted in the paper, which was gorged with ads.

The big events of that period were the movies like *Bonnie and Clyde*, *The Graduate*, and *2001: A Space Odyssey*. The French New Wave had reached America. *TIME* magazine put "The Film Generation" on its cover. A few months later they did a piece about me in their Press section, headlined "Populist at the Movies." Pauline Kael had started at the *New Yorker*, and movie critics were hot.

It was a honey of a job to have at that age. I had no office hours; it was understood that I would see the movies and meet the deadlines. I loved getting up from my desk and announcing, "I'm going to the movies." A lot of my writing was done at night and on weekends. I saw about half of the movies in theaters with paying audiences, sinking into the gloom to watch John Wayne fighting flaming oil wells in

Hellfighters at the Roosevelt, or Pam Grier inventing blaxploitation at the Chicago. There were also experimental and indie films showing at the Town Underground—John Cassavetes, Andy Warhol, Jonas Mekas, Orson Welles's Falstaff.

Lacking a formal film education, I found that on-the-job training was possibly more useful. Every director I interviewed taught me something, and I don't mean that as a cliché. I mean that when I asked, they actually sketched out shots on a piece of paper and told me what they were trying to do, and why. My teachers included Norman Jewison, Richard Brooks, Peter Collinson, Stanley Kramer, and Otto Preminger. They seemed to have an instinct for teaching, and I soaked it in.

There was more direct contact. Stars were less protected and cocooned, and sets were less private. I spent full days on sound stages during movies like *Camelot* and *Butch Cassidy and the Sundance Kid*, watching a scene being done with a master shot and then broken down into closer shots and angles. I heard lighting and sound being discussed. I didn't always understand what I was hearing, but I absorbed the general idea. I learned to see movies in terms of individual shots, instead of being swept along by the narrative.

I'd read Dwight Macdonald's movie column in *Esquire* starting in high school, and now I studied his book *On Movies*. In the introduction he wrote that when he began writing reviews he made a checklist of the things a good movie should contain and then found it growing shorter as good movies came along that didn't contain them. Finally he did what Pauline Kael once told me she did: "I go into the movie, I watch it, and I ask myself what happened to me."

That was useful, and from another critic I found a talisman. Within a day after Zonka gave me the job, I read *The Immediate Experience* by Robert Warshow. He wrote, "A man watches a movie, and the critic must acknowledge that he is that man." By this he meant that the critic has to set aside theory and ideology, theology and politics, and open himself to—well, the immediate experience. More than once in my early years his words allowed me to find an approach to writing about movies I didn't understand, like Bergman's *Persona* the first time I saw it. I wrote about what happened to me.

All the major studios had their own publicists in Chicago. The legendary figure was Frank Casey, the man from Warner Bros. who told Zonka he should make me the film critic. Casey was a hyperactive ginger-haired guy with a conspiratorial smile who knew the angles. It was said he got his studio job because his family was obscurely connected politically. Mayor Martin Kennelly called him in, said he had a call from Jack Warner, and was recommending Casey for the Chicago studio job.

"I don't know," Casey said.

"You don't know what?"

"I already have a good job at Coca-Cola."

"This is Warner Brothers!"

"Coke provides me with a uniform."

It was said that the richest people in Chicago didn't all know one another, but they all knew Casey. He seemed to have placed himself more or less in charge of distributing new Cadillacs on loan from Hanley Dawson, which had a big showroom near Rush Street. Irv Kupcinet once paid tribute at a roast: "Frank has opened a lot of doors for me, especially on Hanley Dawson Cadillacs."

It was my opinion Casey had never seen a movie all the way through. He was too restless. Unlike other publicists, who mostly used screening rooms, Casey liked to take over a theater like the World Playhouse for the Chicago preview of a big movie like *Batman* and invite all his friends from the worlds of business and politics. Only at a Warner Bros. movie were you likely to see Mayor Daley, several aldermen, and various Pritzkers.

Many Casey stories involved the Warner star Ronald Reagan. Once when Casey picked up Reagan at Midway Airport, it was said, the flight was delayed and they were running late for a schedule of interviews. Casey wanted to pull over and get some gas. "You can make it, Frank," Reagan told him. They ran out of gas. Casey took an empty gasoline can out of the trunk, handed it to Reagan, and said, "There's a station about two blocks up there." It was also Casey who fixed up Reagan on a date with Nancy Davis, the pretty daughter of one of his North Shore physician friends.

The secret of Casey's appeal was perhaps his irreverence. In an industry devoted to ass-kissing, he just didn't care. One morning he called me and said, "Whozis wants to know if you want to talk to Whatzis."

The night of his funeral, friends gathered in an upstairs room at Gene & Georgetti, his favorite steak house, right behind the Merchandise Mart. Rob Friedman, the publicity boss at Warner and later a studio chief, told stories that mostly involved how Casey defrauded the studio. He recalled how Casey convinced his friend Pat Patterson, president of United Airlines, to lend the studio a surplus passenger jet so stars would always be seen with the United logo behind them. Then Casey rented the jet to Warner for $8,000 a month: "We all wondered how he negotiated such a low price."

In the early days, he said, publicity field men were paid tiny salaries and told, "Make it up on your expenses." Few publicists took this encouragement as sincerely as Casey. After the dinner was over, one of the waiters at Gene & Georgetti pulled me aside.

"This is the special credit card machine we used when Casey took you to dinner here," he said.

"When did Casey ever take me to dinner here?"

"Every night. Even on Mondays, when we were closed."

The first film I reviewed for the *Sun-Times* was *Galia*, from France. I watched it from a center seat in the old World Playhouse, bursting with the awareness that I was reviewing it, and then I went back to the office and wrote that it was one more last gasp of the French New Wave, rolling ashore. That made me sound more insightful than I was.

I was more jaded then than I am now. At the time I thought that five years would be enough time to spend on the movie beat. My master plan was to become an op-ed columnist and then eventually, of course, a great and respected novelist. My reveries ended with a deep old wingback chair pulled up close to the fire in a cottage deep in the woods, where a big dog snored while I sank into a volume of Dickens.

There is something unnatural about just...going to the movies. Man has rehearsed for hundreds of thousands of years to learn a certain sense of time. He gets up in the morning and the hours wheel in

My uncles Everett and Bill Stumm are in this group near Taylorville.

My great-grandparents on my mother's side.

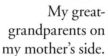

In the living room on Clark Street: My aunt Mame and aunt Hulda, my father, my grandparents, and my aunt Wanda. Possibly my great-grandfather on the wall?

Aunt Martha, Aunt Mary, and my mother.

In the 1940s, all the surviving children. In front: Mary and Annabel. Second row: Martha and Bob. Back row: Bill and Everett. I believe this was taken during a visit to Taylorville.

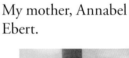
My mother, Annabel Ebert.

My father as a young dude in West Palm Beach.

In my dad's living room chair.

My dad's chair and its bookcases were the center of our home.

With my first cousins Tom Stumm and Marianne Stumm Dull and our grandmother Anna.

With our towels on the way to Crystal Lake Park: Jerry Seilor, Steve Shaw, Hal Holmes, me, Larry Luhtala, and Gary Wikoff.

With my dog Blackie in the Weavers' front yard next door.

The blessing of the candles on St. Blaise's Day. Father J. W. McGinn, Pat Connerty, me, and Bill Miller.

I interview Senator Estes Kefauver for the high school paper, wearing the press badge my father ordered up.

In the backyard with my parents on my high school graduation day. Daddy had three months to live. Hal Holmes took the photo.

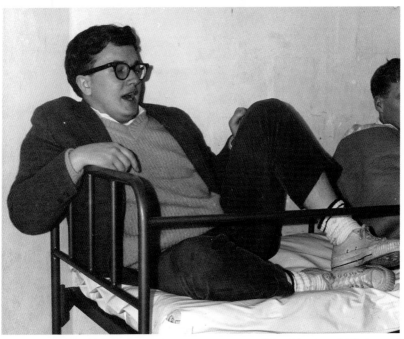

Outside Cape Town in 1965, at a meeting of the National Union of South African Students. I was singing "Union Maid."

En route to Europe with McHugh, who took the photo. Airline rules were more lax in those days.

Circa 1967.

McHugh, me, and Charlie in Leicester Square.

Outside Bates's, next to the Eyrie Mansion, on Jermyn Street in London. Now all gone, gone, gone, replaced by a hideous boil on the face of the city.

With McHugh in Drumcliffe churchyard.

At my desk on the big day in 1975.
Image: The Chicago Sun-Times

With Thea Flaum and Gene Siskel when we won our Chicago Emmy.
Image: Jon Randolph/ WTTW Chicago

With Gene and Thea. We were having an argument.
Image: Jon Randolph/ WTTW Chicago

First season of
Sneak Previews.

A drawing by
Ori Hofmekler.
Image: Ori Hofmekler/
OriHofmekler.com/
Ori@warriordiet.com

REX REED   SIR ALEX WALKER   ROGER EBERT   KATHLEEN CARROLL   CHARLES CHAMPLAIN   MOLLY HASKELL   ANDY SARRIS

BILLY BAXTER

Billy "Silver Dollar" Baxter posing with film critics and a priceless American Express bag at Cannes, 1979. *Image: Billy Baxter*

With Pauline Kael at Cannes, 1977.

With Mitch at the Virginia Festival of American Film, 1993. *Image: Virginia Film Festival, University of Virginia*

With Russ Meyer in 1969.

With Peter O'Toole and Jason Patric at the 2004 Savannah Film Festival. *Image courtesy of SCAD*

Soon after we both started working at the ABC station in Chicago, Oprah and I co-hosted the local Emmys. *Photograph by Paul Natkin/Photo Reserve, Inc., advertisement courtesy of ABC7Chicago*

Ingrid, Monica, and Magan Eng at the house in Michigan.

On our wedding day: Chaz and me with Gene, Marlene, Kate, and Callie Siskel.

My star is dedicated in front of the Chicago Theatre. I'm with Will Siskel, Chaz, Mayor Daley, Marlene Siskel, and Maggie Daley.
Image © Chicago Sun-Times, used with permission.

London's Museum of Natural History. In front: Josibiah's son Joseph Smith, Taylor, Raven, Sonia, and Emil Evans. In back: Chaz and Josibiah.

Chaz and me at a Cubs game with two of our grandchildren, Emil and Taylor Evans.

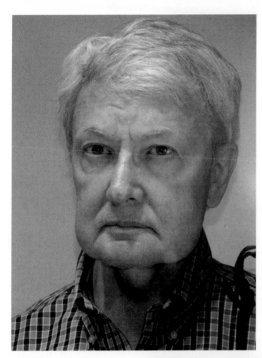

I took this self-portrait
on the night before my
surgery in 2006.

The *Esquire* photo by
Ethan Hill.
*Image: Ethan
Hill/Contour by
Getty Images*

Chaz and me at the presentation of the Directors Guild Honorary Lifetime Membership. *Image: Kevin Winter/Getty Images*

With Chaz and Martin Scorsese as the American Pavilion at Cannes dedicates the Ebert Conference Center. *Image: Carol Iwata*

At home in my office. Bob Zonka bought the smiling lady from its eighty-year-old wood-carver in Michigan. *Image: Ethan Hill/ Contour by Getty Images*

their ancient order across the sky until it grows dark again and he goes to sleep. A movie critic gets up in the morning and in two hours it is dark again, and the passage of time is fractured by editing and dissolves and flashbacks and jump cuts. "Get a life," they say. Sometimes movie critics feel as if they've gotten everybody else's. Siskel described his job as "covering the national dream beat," because if you pay attention to the movies they will tell you what people desire and fear. Movies are hardly ever about what they seem to be about. Look at a movie that a lot of people love, and you will find something profound, no matter how silly the film may seem.

I have seen untold numbers of movies and forgotten most of them, I hope, but I remember those worth remembering, and they are all on the same shelf in my mind. There is no such thing as an old film. There is a sense in which old movies are cut free from time. I look at silent movies sometimes and do not feel I am looking at old films; I feel I am looking at a Now that has been captured. Time in a bottle. When I first looked at silent films, the performers seemed quaint and dated. Now they seem more contemporary. The main thing wrong with a movie that is ten years old is that it isn't thirty years old. After the hairstyles and the costumes stop being dated and start being history, we can tell if the movie itself is timeless.

What kinds of movies do I like the best? If I had to make a generalization, I would say that many of my favorite movies are about Good People. It doesn't matter if the ending is happy or sad. It doesn't matter if the characters win or lose. The only true ending is death. Any other movie ending is arbitrary. If a movie ends with a kiss, we're supposed to be happy. But then if a piano falls on the kissing couple, or a taxi mows them down, we're supposed to be sad. What difference does it make? The best movies aren't about what happens to the characters. They're about the example that they set.

Casablanca is about people who do the right thing. *The Third Man* is about two people who do the right thing and can never speak to each other as a result. The secret of *The Silence of the Lambs* is buried so deeply that you may have to give this some thought, but its secret is that Hannibal Lecter is a Good Person. He is the helpless victim of his unspeakable depravities, yes, but to the limited degree that he can act independently of them, he tries to do the right thing.

Not all good movies are about Good People. I also like movies about Bad People who have a sense of humor. Orson Welles, who does not play either of the Good People in *The Third Man*, has such a winning way, such witty dialogue, that for a scene or two we almost forgive him his crimes. Henry Hill, the hero of *GoodFellas*, is not a good fella, but he has the ability to be honest with us about why he enjoyed being bad. He is not a hypocrite. The heroine of *The Marriage of Maria Braun* does some terrible things, but because we know some of the forces that shaped her, we understand them and can at least admire her resourcefulness.

Of the other movies I love, some are simply about the joy of physical movement. When Gene Kelly splashes through *Singin' in the Rain*, when Judy Garland follows the yellow brick road, when Fred Astaire dances on the ceiling, when John Wayne puts the reins in his teeth and gallops across the mountain meadow, there is a purity and joy that cannot be resisted. In *Equinox Flower*, a Japanese film by the old master Yasujiro Ozu, there is this sequence of shots: a room with a red teapot in the foreground. Another view of the room. The mother folding clothes. A shot down a corridor with the mother crossing it at an angle, and then a daughter crossing at the back. A reverse shot in a hallway as the arriving father is greeted by the mother and daughter. A shot as the father leaves the frame, then the mother, then the daughter. A shot as the mother and father enter the room, as in the background the daughter picks up the red pot and leaves the frame. This sequence of timed movement and cutting is as perfect as any music ever written, any dance, any poem.

I also enjoy being frightened in the movies, but I am bored by the most common way the movies frighten us, which is by loud noises or having something jump unexpectedly into the frame. Such tricks are so old a director has to be shameless to use it. Alfred Hitchcock said that if a bunch of guys were playing cards and there was a bomb under the table and it exploded, that was terror, but he'd rather do a scene where there was a bomb under the table and we kept waiting for it to explode but it didn't. That was suspense. It's the kind of suspense I enjoy.

Love? Romance? I'm not so sure. I don't much care for movies that get all serious about their love affairs, because I think the actors tend to take it too solemnly and end up silly. I like it better when love simply makes the characters very happy, as when Doris Day first falls for Frank Sinatra in *Young at Heart*, or when Lili Taylor thinks River Phoenix really likes her in *Dogfight*.

Many of the greatest directors in the history of the movies were already well known when I started 1967. There was once a time when young people made it their business to catch up on the best works by the best directors, but the death of film societies and repertory theaters has put an end to that, and for today's younger filmgoers, these are not well-known names: Buñuel, Fellini, Bergman, Ford, Kurosawa, Ray, Renoir, Lean, Bresson, Wilder, Welles. Most people still know who Hitchcock was, I guess.

Compared to the great movie stars of the past, modern actors are handicapped by the fact that their films are shot in color. In the long run, that will rob most of them of the immortality that was obtained even by second-tier stars of the black-and-white era. Peter Lorre and Sydney Greenstreet are, and will remain, more memorable than most of today's superstars with their multimillion-dollar paychecks.

Color is sometimes too realistic and distracting. It projects superfluous emotional cues. It reduces actors to inhabitants of the mere world. Black and white (or, more accurately, silver and white) creates a mysterious dream state, a world of form and gesture. Most people do not agree with me. They like color and think a black-and-white film is missing something. Try this. If you have wedding photographs of your parents and grandparents, chances are your parents are in color and your grandparents are in black and white. Put the two photographs side by side and consider them honestly. Your grandparents look timeless. Your parents look goofy.

Go outside at dusk, when the daylight is diffused. Stand on the side of the house away from the sunset.

Shoot some natural-light portraits of a friend in black and white. Ask yourself if this friend, who has always looked ordinary in every color photograph you've ever taken, does not, in black and white, take on an aura of mystery. The same thing happens in the movies.

On the other hand, I am not one of those purists who believe the talkies were perfect and sound ruined everything. To believe that, I would have to be willing to do without Marilyn Monroe singing "Diamonds Are a Girl's Best Friend" and Groucho Marx saying, "This bill is outrageous! I wouldn't pay it if I were you!" Sound and music are essential, but dialogue is not always so. The big difference between today's dialogue and the dialogue of years ago is that the characters have grown stupid. They say what is needed to advance the plot and get their laughs by their delivery of four-letter words. Hollywood dialogue was once witty, intelligent, ironic, poetic, musical. Today it is flat. So flat that when a movie allows its characters to think fast and talk the same way, the result is invigorating, as in *My Dinner with André,* or the first thirty minutes of *White Men Can't Jump.*

Home video is both the best and the worst thing that has happened on the movie beat since I've been a critic. It is good because it allows us to see the movies we want to see, when we want to see them. It provides an economic incentive for the prints of old movies to be preserved and restored. It brings good movies to people seeking them. Viewing via video has destroyed the campus film societies, which were like little shrines to the cinema. If the film society was showing Kurosawa's *Ikiru* for a dollar and there was nothing else playing except the new releases at first-run prices, you went to *Ikiru* and then it was forever inside of you, a great film. Today, students rent videos, stream them online, or watch them on TV, and even if they watch a great movie, they do it alone or with a few friends. There is no sense of audience, and yet an important factor in learning to be literate about movies is to be part of an audience that is sophisticated about them. On the other hand, today every medium-size city has a film festival, where if you are lucky you will see a wonderful film you have never heard of before. And a lot of museums have excellent film centers.

What I miss, though, is the wonder. People my age can remember walking into a movie palace where the ceiling was far overhead, and balconies and mezzanines reached away into the shadows. We remember the sound of a thousand people laughing all at once. And screens the size of billboards, so every seat in the house was a good seat. "I lost it at the movies," Pauline Kael said, and we all knew just what she meant.

When you go to the movies every day, it sometimes

seems as if the movies are more mediocre than ever, more craven and cowardly, more skillfully manufactured to pander to the lowest tastes instead of educating them. Then you see something absolutely miraculous, and on your way out you look distracted, as if you had just experienced some kind of a vision.

22   ZONKA

I BOUGHT MY Smith-Corona ball-bearing typewriter for twenty-five dollars from the *Daily Illini*,
loaded my books and clothes into the family Dodge,
and drove up Route 45 to Chicago on September 3,
1966, a Saturday. I would be sharing a flat with a law
student, Howie Abrams, on the ground floor of a two-
flat on Seventy-Second Place in South Shore, close
to the University of Chicago. On Monday, I went to
work at the *Sun-Times*. On the Friday of that week,
there was a staff party at the home of Ken Towers,
the young city editor, who also lived in South Shore.
That's where I met Bob Zonka, whom I would love
more than any other man since my father died.

People felt a particular quality in Zonka. They

gravitated toward him. You sensed he noticed you—you, particularly you—and was in league with you, and had your back. He had a conspiratorial quality; he and you were in league against the world, and were getting away with it. A little more than twenty years later at his funeral, our friend Jon Anderson stood beside the coffin, looked around the room of mourners, and said, "Most of us here were probably sure we were Zonka's best friend."

Bob was the last editor of the *Sun-Times* who began at the paper as a copyboy and worked his way up. Bob must have gone to college, but he never mentioned it and I never thought to ask. Zonka seemed to have been formed fully educated. The party at Ken Towers's house was to celebrate his promotion to features editor. I stood to one side feeling joy and uncertainty as a new member of this group, the fraternity of Chicago newspapermen, the most desirable club in the world. Zonka materialized next to me. "You're the kid Jim Hoge hired," he said.

He was a large man, balding, not a good complexion, kind of a Karl Malden face. Not lovely, but men and women loved him, and the women I knew him with were beautiful and proud to be at his side. He chain-smoked and drank too much. I was also starting to drink too much and found this quality attractive. I studied him to learn how it was done.

According to my definition, I never saw him drunk, and many nights we drank until long after the chimes at midnight. He said he had never had hangovers. I find that impossible to believe. He became my friend, mentor, father figure, accomplice, and the center of a universe of what seemed to me altogether the most privileged people in Chicago. He loved that word, "altogether." "Ebert, this is altogether the best story you've written today."

Zonka was married and had three children and a home in the suburbs that I never saw. I met his wife Mary Lou and liked her instantly, but something was happening in his marriage that he never discussed and it ended fairly soon after we met. His wife and children told me at various times that he simply pulled out one day and moved into Chicago, and they didn't know why. It was something he wouldn't discuss. It remained an area of silence in our friendship, a Don't Go zone. I often met his children, Lark, Marco, and Laura ("Package"), at his apartment on Belmont in Chicago, and after his death had a brief but heartfelt romance with Lark, which was founded at least in part by our sadness. All three children felt wounded and betrayed; Lark kept the most distance, but all were in frequent communication, and so was Mary Lou, who struck me as nicer than she should have been about the way she and her children had been treated. I was his close friend, his best friend according to the Anderson definition, but I never knew the story of that marriage. It is often that way. How a marriage appears from the outside is not how it seems within a family. Not long before his death Zonka had planned a trip to San Francisco to meet Marco's child, his first grandchild. Marco, a hippie idealist, was involved obscurely in the tofu business. Zonka postponed that trip when I got the advance on my *Perfect London Walk* book that allowed me to buy him a ticket to London. Marco told me, not with anger but with sadness, that he was bitter Zonka put friends above family. I said Zonka had never been to Europe, would otherwise never have the money to go, and had no idea he was soon to die.

Zonka was the center of a wide circle, and his homes were often filled with confidants, strays, and visiting firemen. He was a scout. He collected the brilliant, the charismatic, the characters, the raconteurs. In his company we felt we had admission to a crowd altogether more fascinating than ordinary people were likely to meet.

It was because of Zonka that I met Harry and Irene Bouras, who lived in an Evanston home that contained as many books and works of art as physically possible. Harry was a man of effortless gifts. He was above all a painter, but he commanded literature,

history, drama, architecture, and politics, and once
a week he delivered a talk on WFMT, the fine arts
station that was our sound track in those days. That
station was also the home for decades of Studs Terkel,
who told me about Harry, "He comes in, sits down,
and talks for thirty minutes. Not even a note. I've
never seen anything like it." This coming from Studs,
who could do the same thing.

Zonka also introduced me to Jacob Burck, who
was teamed with Bill Mauldin as one of our two editorial cartoonists. Jake always seemed unimaginably
ancient, another chain-smoker, formal in a twinkling
European manner. He lived in a house he and his
wife had filled with his inexhaustible outpouring of
art. He couldn't pick up a stone without sketching a
few lines on it that turned it into the head of a man or
an animal. Through Zonka I met the Chicago novelist Harry Mark Petrakis, in whose company Bob
seemed to become Greek, and the novelist Father
Andrew Greeley, in whose company Bob became
Irish. And where and how did Bob find Alcibiades
(Al the Greek) Oikonomides, the cheerful giant who
towered over our gatherings in those days? Al presided over our regular Friday night dinners at the
Parthenon in Greektown on Halsted and seemed to
know everyone Zonka knew, and (here is the curious part) no one Zonka didn't know, except for the

Jesuits at Loyola, where he was a professor of antiquity. Did Zonka supply him with a circle of friends?

I came to the *Sun-Times* with a lot of experience from the *News-Gazette* and the *Daily Illini*, but Zonka taught me his newspaper code, which he liked to express as, "When you have to march, march." This included writing a story you lacked all enthusiasm for, meeting a deadline no matter what hours were necessary, getting an interview after you'd been decisively turned down, not falling in love with your deathless prose, remembering you were there to write a story and not have a good time. These were not rules he enforced. They were standards he exuded.

Zonka's desk was in the far southwest corner of the city room, where he propped his feet and observed goings-on. He did not much like the boy editor Jim Hoge, "Baby James." He built a little fiefdom of loyalists back there in the corner and entertained people such as John McMeel, a young Notre Dame graduate who was trying to sell a new comic strip named *Doonesbury*. Zonka and McMeel agreed over an extended period of negotiations in several bars that the *Sun-Times* should buy the strip, but it ended up at the *Tribune*. I never heard the full story, but I'm sure there was one.

Zonka lived as newspapermen did in the Front Page era, and indeed in those days the city room still had writers like Ray Brennan and Jack McPhaul, who dated from those days. Zonka was both on the job and off the job every waking hour. If he was having a long lunch in the upstairs room at Hobson's Oyster Bar he was "making friends for the paper," and that often resulted in good stories. He kept in touch by calling his own desk. One day Jon Anderson picked up the phone. "The Zonker asked if there was any activity around his desk," Anderson told me, "and I said, 'Only Hoge directing the movers.'"

Zonka resigned from the *Sun-Times*. The paper wasn't large enough to accommodate two men who thought they should be its editor, and although Hoge was manifestly better suited to the job, Bob remained in constant rebellion. He had by then married Connie Zonka, a publicist whose clients included Columbia College Chicago in its early days under the educational showman Mike Alexandroff. Connie and Bob established an office and Bob bonded with Mike, another larger than life character, who was then running the school out of a single building on Lake Shore Drive with a combination of promotion and willpower. Both Harry Bouras and I ended up teaching there. That was how it worked. Columbia is now a considerable institution whose buildings, theaters, and dorms sprawl across the South Loop, but in the early days it was held together with smoke and mirrors. Connie's sister was the famous Broadway costume designer Patricia Zipprodt, who helped her find Columbia people upon whom to confer honorary degrees, which is how Bob Fosse one year found himself being honored by a school he had never heard of, and having lunch with Zonka and me in the Greek Taberna in the basement of the Time-Life Building.

Connie had fallen under Zonka's spell while she was married to Richard Harding, owner of the Quiet Knight folk club on North Wells. In the kind of synergy that seemed to unfold naturally in those days, when the Quiet Knight was planning to move from Old Town to New Town, we turned its closing night into a benefit to buy a ticket for John McHugh to fly to Los Angeles for a bit part as the bartender in a bar named O'Rourke's in *Beyond the Valley of the Dolls*. Admission was five dollars and since no booze in open bottles could be moved, the deal was we'd drink the bar dry. Richard lined up some of his acts, including Malvina "Little Boxes" Reynolds and the Chad Mitchell Trio, and McHugh took advantage of Connie's connections with a costume company to appear, for reasons unclear, as Henry VIII.

I believe it might have been that night that Connie and Bob locked eyes, and history was made. I was also present in another bar when Richard Harding discovered by mischance the two of them smooching.

This was handled by all three in a fairly civil manner. Bob was then living in a two-bedroom apartment on Belmont, a block in from the lake, and Connie and Richard on the ground floor of a three-flat a few doors down the street. Richard moved out, Bob moved in, and Alcibiades Oikonomides took over Bob's old flat. That inspired a memorable housewarming to which Al the Greek invited Jesuits from the faculty of Loyola and a crowd of Zonka followers. Al at that time had a mattress on the floor, a kitchen table, and some lamps. He invariably appeared in a dark business suit, a white shirt and tie, and slightly smoked glasses, which for a friendly man with a bullet head made him seem somehow shady.

"I have here everything I need, man!" he told me. "I sleep on the mattress, I eat on the table, I buy new white shirts at Walgreens, and when my collar gets dirty"—he opened the door to his second bedroom—"I throw it in here." He slammed the door before I could get a good look. Al had laid in a good supply of Roditis Greek wine and Johnnie Walker Black Label. There was no music, and the rooms were illuminated by table lamps sitting on the floor. Talk filled the rooms, and later in the evening several earnest conversations developed between Jesuits and sinful newspapermen. I believe the sacrament of penance was performed at least once.

"By all the gods, man!" Al cried at one point. "These Jesuits have had all the whiskey!" He thought he had another half gallon of Johnnie Walker around somewhere, but new supplies had to be ordered in from the corner package store.

At least six weeks later, Al was presiding as usual on a Friday night at the head of a long table at the Parthenon in Greektown.

"By all the gods, I have had an explosion at my apartment," he announced. "I decided for the first time to use my kitchen, and I turned on the oven to heat it for a pizza. I am reading in the other room, and suddenly there is a great explosion and a blast of flame comes out of the kitchen!"

He roared with laughter.

"What do you think had happened? Somebody had hidden that missing bottle of scotch in the oven, and it exploded!"

Across the table from me, John McHugh looked thoughtful.

Connie and Bob's apartment became the scene of one gathering after another. They often invited their clients to dinners with their friends. They represented the suburban Lake Forest Playhouse, the enterprise of a creative producer named Marshall Migatz, and that led to a long evening with Jason Robards Jr. after the premiere of O'Neill's *Hughie*. One Thanksgiving the

Zonkas pushed together two tables and a slab on saw-horses to improvise a dinner table reaching from one room to the next, and Colleen Dewhurst was guest of honor. Clair Huffaker, the author of Western novels, was represented by Bob on a book tour for *One Time, I Saw Morning Come Home* and became a friend after the two of them filled a taxi with helium balloons and set them free over Lake Michigan.

One night there was a historic dinner at Bob and Connie's with the directors Gil Cates and Armando Robles Godoy, who was in Chicago from Peru as the guest of honor of the film festival. Gil, later to serve as president of the Motion Picture Academy, was relaxed and benevolent. Armando was another of the tall, mustached romantics who seemed to fall into Bob's orbit. That night he was seated next to the first wife of our friend Jack Lane, the photographer. The next morning I was awaked in my apartment on West Burton Place by Jack and his friend Ed McCahill, a *Sun-Times* reporter.

"Roger, I need to find Armando," he said. "He has stolen my wife."

"All the festival guests stay at the Ambassador East," I said. "He's probably under his own name."

I went back to sleep. The phone rang. It was Armando.

"Roger," he said, "somebody has slipped a note

under my door, reading *Beware! You are a stranger in a strange land!*"

"That's undoubtedly from Jack Lane," I told him.

"The husband! Aye, yie, yie!"

"He and his friend McCahill are probably downstairs in the lobby," I said. "Here's what you do. Get on the elevator and push the button for the concourse level. There's a passage under State Parkway linking the Ambassador East and West. Walk over to the West, catch a taxi, and get out of Dodge."

About that time the publicist for the film festival, who called herself the Blessed Virgin Mary Sweeney, was arriving at the East. She knew Lane and McCahill from Riccardo's.

"What are you doing here?"

Even in his hour of turmoil, Lane was unable to resist: "Waiting for Godoy."

Gil Cates has never forgotten that dinner. I've seen him many times over the years, on the sets of his movies and as the Academy president and frequent director of the Academy Awards. He invariably asks me if I remember that night. He would ask about Zonka. They sometimes chatted on the phone. They never met again, but he sent flowers to the funeral. "There was something about that man," he would tell me. "I'll always remember that night."

Zonka wasn't happy with life as a publicist. "I

wasn't cut out for stamping envelopes," he told me. What went unsaid was that Connie was better at it. Our friends Herman and Marilou Kogan, in whose Old Town apartment I first met Studs Terkel, had by then retired to New Buffalo, Michigan, a small town just over the Indiana line on the shore of Lake Michigan. He told Bob the weekly *New Buffalo Times* was for sale. Zonka bought the paper, Connie took an apartment on Lake Shore Drive, and together they rented a big old house on a bluff over the lake.

Bob was the editor at last. Also the publisher and owner of the ancient press. He hired a secretary. An old guy came in once a week to operate the press. He had a high school kid deliver bundles of the paper in a pickup. He paid a member of the school's photography club to take photos at a dollar a pop. A prominent citizen died, and Zonka told the kid to put on a tie and shoot a nice respectful photo at the funeral.

"Some of these kids, they just don't have the instinct," Zonka complained later. He showed me what his photographer had handed in. It showed the family lined up at the graveside, seen from behind.

Zonka wrote about local politics and schools, law enforcement and zoning, taxes and lawsuits. Those were subjects you expected in a newspaper. But he also wrote about going fishing with his and Connie's son, Milo. And how sweet it was when spring finally

came. About preserving the area's parks and shore-
lines. About his priceless three-dollar dog named
Spoons. About the day they chopped down the tree
in front of Rosie's Restaurant. And when he obtained
the plans for an antique cider press and convinced
local carpenters and metalsmiths and the kids in the
high school shop class to build him a half-scale model
to his design, in time for a pressing of the first Michigan apples.

When his father died on September 29, 1984, he
wrote, "He was an anxious man, my dad, and anxious
to do the right thing. When I told my father I wanted
to be a newspaperman, he took me to the Sears at
Western and 63rd. There he bought, on time, a Rem-
ington portable typewriter, a *Webster's Collegiate Dictionary* and a *Roget's Thesaurus*. 'That's the best I can
do for you,' he said."

The paper was not making a lot of money. The
first winter, before he and Connie rented the house,
Bob slept on a deck chair in the press room. He traded
ads for dentistry and veterinarian services. He got
to know everyone in town. He bonded with Rosie,
whose restaurant was the breakfast hangout. He
made good friends with Nick and Sophie Fatsoulas,
who had a little restaurant next to Jackson's big fruit
and vegetable stand at the red light on Red Arrow
Highway. Zonka was Serbo-Croatian, drawn to

Greeks. "Sophie's Place," as we called it, became his dinner club, and when Russ Meyer came out for the lake fishing, we took our catch there and Nick prepared the lake trout Greek style.

The house on the bluff became the scene for weekend gatherings of the Chicago crowd, and one by one friends began to settle in Berrien County, which was later renamed "Harbor Country" by Karen Connor, another friend of Zonka's who had relocated and set up as a Realtor. In the early 1970s the area was far from being a fashionable location for second homes of Chicagoans and South Benders. It was blue collar, a little run down, with cheap housing left over from its previous boom in the 1920s. In those days it could be reached by interurban rail and ferry boat from Chicago, which is how Saul Bellow's Augie March once crossed to Michigan. Ethnic and labor groups set up summer camps, and in Union Pier, once a terminus for the Underground Railroad, African Americans including Jesse Owens bought summer homes. The Capone mob owned an inn near there, and when it was being rehabbed around 1980 a hidden room was found in the basement that some people fancied had once held gambling devices. Jumpin' Joe Savoldi, the Notre Dame football star, champion pro wrestler, bottler of Jumpin' Joe's Root Beer, and American spy who parachuted into Sicily, bought land near Carl

Sandburg on the lake and brought his Sicilian brothers over to build a house with sixteen-inch fieldstone walls, and it is in that house that I am writing this sentence. One of the brothers, quite old, was driven over to see the house about fifteen years ago, and said it had held up well.

Everybody's families gathered in New Buffalo. There were lots of kids, including Milo, who was a holy terror in fireworks season, which for him began on Memorial Day and ended on Labor Day and was sometimes celebrated in the middle of the night. May I speak for all of us from those days in saying we are proud and astonished that he is now a family man, investment counselor, and the city manager of a town in Florida.

Bob and Connie were divorced after about fifteen years of marriage but shared custody of Milo and remained good friends. Bob called me in 1980 and said he'd found a duplex in Union Pier with beach path access. This was a small two-bedroom country house from the 1920s, to which an A-frame addition with a sleeping loft had been added. He suggested we buy it together. Including the double lot, the price was $50,000. Jack Lane had given up his high-end business as an advertising photographer and he and his second wife, Sharl, had moved to New Buffalo, where he worked at his first love, country and contracting. Zonka said he wanted a deck built.

"How big?"

"As far as the eye can see. And a fire pit."

"How big?"

"Big enough to roast a goat."

By then many key members of the circle had moved into the area, and the fire pit was the focus of much anecdotage, punctuated by explosions from Milo somewhere in the woods. Announcing a gathering, Zonka always said, "I'll light a candle in the window," and he always did. Dan and Audrey Curley were frequent weekenders. Bob's older brother Lou, a lifelong paraplegic and successful businessman, had died by then. His younger brother Tom and his wife bought a house not far away. It was the summer of 1987 that I got the advance for *The Perfect London Walk*. It was understood that Zonka, who had never been to Europe, would come along.

In London we took rooms at the Eyrie Mansion, and Bob bonded with Henry Togna Sr. He traveled the city hungrily, having imagined it all of his life. McHugh and I noticed something: Bob took a pass on the walk over Hampstead Heath and took taxis whenever possible, even when our destination was in sight. "I'm out of training," he said. "In New Buffalo, you can park right outside of everywhere." McHugh was sharing a room with him and was awakened one night by cigarette smoke. Bob was sitting up in bed. That morning he and I cornered Bob and badgered him that he *had* to give up smoking. "I've been smoking since I was thirteen," he said. "That's just the point," John said.

Back home, Bob announced that he was lighting the candle in the window, and there was a gathering at his place. We began around the fire pit, watching the sparks fly up into the night sky. It was a chill evening, and everybody had sweaters on except Zonka, who wore one of his short-sleeved shirts and explained that he was a hot-blooded Slav who would not require a jacket until the snows fell.

We moved inside. The occasion for the party was the publication of my new *Movie Home Companion*, which was dedicated to Zonka. I sat between McHugh and our friend the best-selling priest Andy Greeley, who owned a lake home nearby in Grand Beach, home of his friends the Daleys. In his house Greeley held frequent salons, and celebrated Mass in the backyard every Saturday, never forgetting the sermon. Seated the other side of John were Grace and Norman Mark, both over six feet with loud merry laughter. Norman had been TV critic of the *Daily News* and a talk show host. Grace had been his big crush in high school, where their eyes must have met over the crowd, and they'd met again and made a second marriage.

Following the Zonka immigration, they'd bought a house in Lakeside and now were having serious problems with dampness in the basement. Grace murmured their troubles in John's ear. She was fairly new to us then and had attracted attention, as tall, elegant blondes in black leather pants are likely to do. During a break, Andy leaned over and asked McHugh, "What is she talking to you about, John?" McHugh lowered his voice. "Female problems, Father. You know."

Greeley nodded and we fell silent. Grace continued, "When they got a good look down there, they told us the walls had been completely softened by mold and would have to be entirely removed." John and Andy exchanged a significant nod.

After the room had cleared, Zonka said, "Ebert, I think this was altogether the best party I've had here. The whole crowd was here." And so they were: my girlfriend Ingrid Eng and her daughters Monica and Magan; Father Greeley, Al the Greek; Jack Lane, McHugh, the Marks; Dennis and Connie Brennan, who ran the bookstore; Terry Truesdell, who had a woodworking shop downtown and whose wife, Judy, would run for Congress; Sophie and Nick; Tom

Zonka; Marilou Kogan, now a widow; and Ivan and Marge Bloom, who had another two-city marriage, Ivan owning a showroom in the Merchandise Mart and Marge owning a spa on Whittaker Street. With a few exceptions, all of them had come to the area following Bob.

The next morning Bob drove down to the Union Pier bakery and brought back apple strudel. We made coffee. We sat around and replayed the party. We told the story of the walls doomed by mold, which showed every sign of becoming a classic. Things had gone very late, and now it was time for Bob to drive Milo to the train station to be met by Connie in Chicago. I was sleepy and went over to my half of the house to have a nap. I vaguely heard Bob return to his half of the house.

I had a vivid dream in which I had awakened, walked over to his side of the house, and found Bob seated at the head of the table, dead. In my dream I wrote a memorial column for the *New Buffalo Times*, word by word, very specific. I didn't like that dream, and it awakened me. I got out of bed, went next door, and called through the screen: "Bob?" At the foot of the lawn, the Engs were sitting in the sun. I walked inside, and Bob was seated at the head of the table, dead, a cigarette having fallen from his hand.

I called out to the yard for the Engs. The girls

telephoned for an ambulance, made difficult because it was hard to describe the address of the house in the woods. It made no difference. Ingrid held a mirror to his lips and we felt for a pulse, but he was clearly dead. We called Andy Greeley, and he hurried over. Bob was a Catholic, long since lapsed. Father Greeley said the last rites and pronounced conditional absolution. The ambulance found the house. We called the family and friends.

I sat down and started to write the story exactly as I had worded it in my dream. It appeared in the next issue of the *New Buffalo Times*, which was edited by McHugh with the help of the secretary and the old guy who came in to run the press. These words had been dictated in my dream: "As I write these words, I am looking out the window at the lawn where Robert Zonka stood last autumn and sowed wildflower seeds into the wind. In the spring, the flowers pushed up through the snow, and Zonka stood on his deck and said that was the way it was supposed to be. No landscape gardener was going to get within a mile of his land, where he encouraged the natural grasses and flowers of the sandy dunes to grow."

The family gathered. A decision had to be made about the newspaper. There'd been a change in management at the NBC 5 News in Chicago, and McHugh had been swept out with the old team. He moved into Bob's house and edited and published the paper for a year, until a buyer was found. He liked the area and decided to stay, teaching himself programming and installing computer systems for small businesses. He and his girlfriend from Chicago, Mary Jo Broderick, bought a house in the village of Three Oaks and live there today.

In Skoob, a used bookstore in London, Bob had purchased a large volume of *Don Quixote* with the illustrations by Gustave Doré. It was on the table before him when he died. When I spoke at the memorial service, I quoted Cervantes' words on the last page:

For if he like a mad man lived,
At least he like a wise one died.

There were more real tears at the funeral than any other I have ever attended. Sherman Wolf and I clung to each other and sobbed. Bob was buried in the New Buffalo cemetery. The next spring when I visited his grave, I saw the stone, on which his children had the words from *Don Quixote* engraved.

When Bob saw or parted with anyone, he invariably said, "God love ya."

23   McHUGH

I MET JOHN McHugh in the autumn of 1966, when I was a cub reporter on the *Sun-Times* and he was a rewrite man, two years my senior, on the *Chicago Daily News*. He worked the overnight shift, and among his duties was taking calls from readers. After midnight, they wanted to settle bets. "And what do you say?" McHugh would ask. He would listen, and then reply, "You're one hundred percent correct. Put the other guy on." Pause. "And what do you say?" Pause. "You're one hundred percent correct." If he was asked for his name, he said, "John T. Greatest, spelled with three T's." He explained, "They can never figure out what that means."

John was one of ten brothers from Sligo, Yeats

country, on the west coast of Ireland. His father, "Trooper," had been a member of the IRA gang that held up the Ulster Bank of Sligo. "They were raising funds for the cause," he explained. "All of the money was never accounted for. Trooper is the only man in Sligo who has a son who graduated from Indiana University." He was entrusted to Indiana under the protection of a cousin in Indianapolis who was a nun. John himself had studied briefly for the priesthood under the Christian Brothers but was expelled at fifteen, charged with smoking.

Late one night at the Old Town Gate, we decided to pay a visit to his homeland. David Lean was filming *Ryan's Daughter* on the Dingle Peninsula, and MGM was flying in film critics to visit the location. We traded one first-class ticket for a couple of cheap ones. Robert Mitchum, my favorite movie star, was living in a rented cottage on the edge of town, and he drank scotch with us one night while he fed peat to the fire and listened to Jim Reeves records with his man Harold, who had been a paramedic with the Coldstream Guards.

On that trip McHugh became the great friend of a lifetime. As young men we sowed wild oats. As middle-aged men we ripened. As old men we harvest, and always we laugh. We flew on to Venice, where

McHugh bonded with Lino, the trattoria owner. Although they did not speak a word of each other's language, McHugh was so successful at communicating that Lino gave him his apron and installed him behind the counter.

Sophia Loren was on the mainland, in Padua, filming *The Priest's Wife* with Marcello Mastroianni. The studio laid on a car to take me over for an interview, and I took along McHugh, "from the *Chicago Daily News*." In those days film critics flew everywhere on the studios' money and with the approval of our papers. We had to rise early in the morning, and I was hungover. On the road, I gave McHugh his instructions: "I've interviewed a lot of these stars and I know the drill. Just keep quiet, let me do the talking, and they won't know any the better." But when Loren glided into the room, I was paralyzed by hangover, drenched with sweat, and speechless. McHugh whipped out his Reporter's Notebook and came to the rescue.

"Miss Loren, is that a tiara you're sportin'?"

"This? It is a hair clip."

"I see." McHugh took notes. "Miss Loren, I understand you recently gave birth. Can you confirm that?"

"Yes, it is true. I had my little Cheepee. When I was pregnant, I had to stay for weeks in a clinic in

Switzerland. Now I feel like a true woman. Carlo visits from Rome on weekends. If I never make another film, it is all right with me. Now I am a mother!"

McHugh nodded and took more notes.

"And in addition to little Cheepee, have you any other hobbies?"

"You call my baby a *hobby*?"

"I meant...like poker, or something?"

In those years I was living in the attic of the house of Paul and Anna Dudak, at 2437 North Burling, and paying $110 a month. Pop was a retired window washer from the Ukraine, where he had been an anarchist playwright. Anna was an Okie from the Dust Bowl, who spent six weeks every winter in what Pop referred to as "Lost Wages." She said it cost her less than at home: "Nine dollars for a motel, $1.95 for the buffet, and I never gamble." When some friends from O'Rourke's Pub came over one night, Jim Hoge looked around and said, "Jesus, Roger, I pay you too much to live in this dump."

An apartment opened up on a floor below, and John moved in. Like me, he had to survive a severe grilling from Pop: "We have here only intellectual gentlemen, who enjoy the luxury of conversation." The Dudaks did no drinking to speak of, but these interviews were always smoothed by Pop's secret recipe cocktail, made of Pepsi and Green Chartreuse.

The front yard of his house, never very popular with the neighbors, was populated by a zoo of colorful little animals, sunk in concrete to prevent theft. In the backyard was a pond with a showerhead to supply a fountain, and in this pond floated a plastic frog with an orange golf ball glued to its head.

One year McHugh and I returned from another trip to Ireland. John entered his apartment, fell in bed without turning on the lights, and awoke at dawn to see snakes crawling all over the walls. He called me and I hurried downstairs. He'd not been imagining things. The snakes were there. Pop had painted them in florescent greens and yellows. "I am working in my capacity as a room decorator," he explained. "For trendy young gentleman, I have created psychedelic wall paintings."

He had also improved my attic apartment, where the roof leaned at low angles over the rooms.

"Ebert!" he said, greeting me in front of the house. "Does your mirror steam up when you shave after a shower?"

"Yes," I said.

"Working in my capacity as an inventor, I have solved the problem!"

He led me upstairs and proudly showed me that he had cut a square hole through the roof and installed a sliding pane of glass in it, directly above the bathtub.

"Prop open the window when you shower," he explained, "and steam escapes to outer atmosphere, leaving mirror ready for shaving!"

This innovation proved flawed. Even on summer days, the outside breeze blew chilly into the shower. On rainy days, twigs and leaves would wash past the sliding glass into the bathtub. When I lay soaking, I would find myself being regarded by squirrels' beady little eyes. They found the glass warm in wintertime, and my tub began to collect squirrel shit.

John was popular with the ladies, although his girlfriend in the 1970s, Mary Ulrich, who was a banker, once told me: "John's idea of being charming on a date is to look up from the bar, notice me sitting next to him, and say, *Mary, me old flower! How long have you been sittin' there?*" Miss Mary, for so she was known, was a perfect lady. Skirts instead of pants. Nylons. Heels. Business suits. Every hair in place. She loved the guy. Nobody could figure it out. She cooked for him, mended his shirts, took naughty Polaroids that no one was allowed to see. She hardly drank.

Mary eventually fell in love with a lawyer, but thanks to John's influence, he was a colorful one. John, in the meantime, had left the *Daily News* to become a feature writer for *Chicago Today*, the former

Chicago's American. "The best job in town," he told me. "It's what I dreamed of when I was down in Bloomington that last summer. I had just graduated and had my degree in my pocket. I got a job with the Arab Pest Control, crawling under houses and spraying around bug poison. One day it was about ninety-eight degrees, and a trap door opened above my head. It was the lady of the house.

" 'It must be hot down there,' she says. 'Wouldn't you like some nice cold lemonade?'

"I tell her I would. I stand up through the trap door but don't climb into the kitchen because I'm all covered with sweat, dust, and cobwebs. She pours me out a nice big glass from a pitcher from the icebox. Then she calls her little boy into the room.

" 'Junior,' she says, 'you take a good look at that man. If you don't study hard and go to college, that's what will happen to you.' "

After *Chicago Today* folded, John went to work for the news division of NBC Chicago as the assignment manager. At one time his two principal anchors were Maury Povich and the legendary Ron Hunter, who was possibly the model for every character in the movie *Anchorman*. John liked Maury but found Ron unendurable: "He's so vain that instead of wearing glasses, he has a prescription windshield on his

Jaguar." Anchormen value stories when they can go on the street and be seen in the midst of the action. One day McHugh came up with a juicy assignment for Povich. "The next day," he told me, "Ron Hunter comes into my office, puts his feet up on my desk, and says, 'John, that was a good story you had for Maury yesterday. What do you have for me today?' I tell him, 'Contempt.'"

At NBC, John met the sunny Mary Jo Broderick, with whom he has lived happily now for many years. Our friend Zonka died a few years after buying the *New Buffalo Times* across the lake in southwest Michigan. John took over editing and publishing the paper for a year. By then he had come to like the area, and he and Mary Jo purchased a little white frame two-story in Three Oaks, the home of a dandy Fourth of July parade where Shriners circle in formation on their power lawnmowers. Three Oaks, with barely three thousand souls, has an excellent downtown art theater, the Vickers, which Mary Jo faithfully attends every week. McHugh never goes. When he was a child, once a year he was delegated to take all of his brothers to the movies. "It was always the same show: *How Green Was My Valley.* Every time I saw it, nine months later I'd have another brother."

I lived at 2437 North Burling for most of the years between 1967 and 1977. Then I bought a coach house behind the Four Farthings Tavern on Lincoln Avenue. I held a housewarming, at which one of the guests was my friend the press agent Sherman Wolf, a really nice man, which helps explain this story. Sherman found me in the kitchen and said, "Congratulations on your new house! You've worked hard and you deserve it. It's a real step up from that pigpen you used to live in."

"Sherman," I said, "I don't believe you've met my landlady from Burling Street, Mrs. Dudak."

Sherman turned red. "Oh my God!" he said. "Oh, Mrs. Dudak, actually it was a very nice place on Burling, the rent was low, Roger was happy there, I was just trying to think of something nice to say to Roger."

"Now, Sherman, don't you apologize for a thing. It was time Roger found something better, and we're happy for him."

Sherman fled to the deck outside the kitchen door. McHugh was sitting out there.

"How are you, Sherman?"

"God, John, I'm so embarrassed I could crawl into a hole. I just told Roger this place was a lot better than that pigpen he used to live in, and who was standing right there but Mrs. Dudak!"

"I'll bet that made you feel awful," John said.

"It's one of those things you can never take back," Sherman said.

"Sherman," John said, "I don't believe you've ever met Mr. Dudak, who is sitting right here next to me."

"Good...lord!"

"And Sherman? When Roger moved out of the pigpen, I moved in."

24   O'ROURKE'S

O'ROURKE'S WAS OUR stage, and we displayed
our personas there nightly. It was a shabby street-
corner tavern on a dicey stretch of North Avenue,
a block after Chicago's Old Town stopped being
a tourist haven. In its early days it was heated by a
wood-burning potbellied stove, and ice formed on
the insides of the windows. One night a kid from
the street barged in, whacked a customer in the front
booth with a baseball bat, and ran out again. When
a roomer who lived upstairs died, his body was discovered when maggots started to drop through the
ceiling. A man nobody knew was shot dead one night
out back. From the day it opened on December 30,
1966, until the day I stopped drinking in 1979, I

drank there more or less every night when I was in town. So did a lot of people.

The Front Page era had a halfway rebirth in the 1970s, centering on O'Rourke's and the two other nightly stops in the "Bermuda Triangle," Riccardo's and the Old Town Ale House. The triangle got its name, it was said, because newspaper reporters crashed there and were never seen again. Riccardo's, equidistant from the daily newspapers, was for after work. The Ale House had a late-night license and was for after O'Rourke's. Few lasted through the whole ten hours. People would ride awhile and jump off. Billy Goat's was for when you wanted to drink with Royko, who had been eighty-sixed from Riccardo's after calling Bruno, the maître d', a Nazi.

The regulars mostly knew one another. There were maybe a hundred members of the "O'Rourke's crowd," perhaps fifty or sixty of them lasting the whole duration at that address and many following the bar when it moved to Halsted Street, across from the Steppenwolf Theatre. It was driven west by rising real estate prices, the victim of the gentrification it introduced. Jay Kovar, the manager from day one, the co-owner in later years, received a loan from the actor Brian Dennehy to finance the move. Actors had always been part of the mix, many of them from the nearby Second City. And folk singers from the Earl of Old Town: Larry Rand, John Prine, Ed and Fred Holstein, not so much Steve Goodman. I was invited for opening night in 1966 by Nan Lundberg, an editor of the *Daily Illini*, who'd married Will Kilkeary, its owner. Will was a friendly little guy who sometimes late on St. Patrick's Day would climb onto the shelf above the door for a nap. A call from McHugh woke me one March 17: "Ebert, I think Willie is in the slammer. On the news they said a man in a leprechaun costume was arrested while trying to paint a green stripe down North Avenue."

On a good night you might see Mike Royko, Studs Terkel, Nelson Algren, and such visiting firemen as Robert Novak, Pat Conroy, and Tom Wolfe. Nelson had an unrequited crush on Jeanette Sullivan, the Japanese-American co-owner, and was friendly enough but didn't come primarily to hang out with the crowd. During a disagreement with Tom Fitzpatrick, he and Fitz pelted each other with shot glasses. Royko appeared one night after midnight, supported by two volunteers, his trench coat a shambles. He was scheduled to appear the following morning on the *Phil Donahue Show*. I made it a point to watch. He was lucid and didn't seem hungover.

Few of the regulars often seemed hungover, although many must have been on some mornings. Michaela Tuohy, "Mike," accounted for that by the practice of "recovery drinking," which was how you got your act together enough to be taken onstage at O'Rourke's. As a general rule, most of the people in the bar were having a good time. There was a lot of laughter. Groups formed and shifted.

The bar's Sydney Greenstreet was Alcibiades Oikonomides (Al the Greek), a mountainous man who would head-butt friends as a gesture of solidarity, chanting, "To the ten thousand years we will drink together." Hank Oettinger, the most-published letter-to-the-editor writer in Chicago, would turn up night after night with his pockets stuffed with letters that either had just been published or were about to be published. These he would read to us. Hank was a retired Linotype operator, then in his seventies, a fervent leftist, a regular at every protest march, a confidant of Dick Gregory's. His black hair slicked back over his big German-American head, he always wore a jacket and tie and ordered a beer. One beer. He had been making his rounds, sometimes composing his letters on a bar, since midday stops in the Loop. But only sipping beer. Making his way nightly through the mean streets.

Years prior to his present position as a professor of antiquities at Loyola University, Al the Greek said, he had been an aide-de-camp for Haile Selassie in the Ethiopian-Somalian border wars, and he had a much-creased photograph of himself in uniform, standing next to a horse, to prove it. He claimed to be a member of an ancient Greco-Venetian trading family that still owned a palazzo on the Grand Canal and also a partner in a bookshop on Shaftesbury Avenue. About Selassie I was not sure, but I met the cousin in the palazzo and stood under a Tiepolo ceiling, and when he took me to the bookshop his name was on the door.

What brought Al the Greek night after night to this obscure corner of Chicago? O'Rourke's was not boring and embraced eccentricity. Ordinary yuppies, those who frequented the bars on Rush Street and in Old Town, did not blend in. For one thing, they were unimpressed by the booths and tables, knocked together from plywood, shellacked, caked by smoke and sweat. For years the bar no more had air-conditioning than central heating. O'Rourke's was the ultimate singles bar, it was said. You went there with a date and came home alone. Cabaret could break out at any moment. Bagpipers drank free. Everybody knew the words to all of the songs on the jukebox, some of which had been on the machine when it was new. When Jerry Lewis would sing "Come Rain or Come Shine," it was not unknown for a customer to climb up on the bar and sing along. The songs of the Clancy Brothers and Tommy

Makem played again and again, and customers would sing with them: *And always remember the longer you live, the sooner you bloody well die.* Press agents would bring visiting movie stars to view the local color, and they were good sports, Charlton Heston one night autographing Natalie Nudlemann's bra while she was wearing it.

Many of us at O'Rourke's became fake Irishmen, swayed by the Clancy Brothers and the big blown-up photographs of Behan, O'Casey, Shaw, and Joyce. I was one-quarter Irish but submerged the other three-quarters and assured strangers, "Your blood's worth bottling." Fund-raisers allegedly from the IRA would visit and we would naïvely give five bucks to the cause, probably not funding any terrorism because they were con artists preying on boozing Irish wannabes. Above all we drank. It is not advisable, perhaps not possible, to spend very many evenings in a place like O'Rourke's while drinking Cokes and club soda. Sometimes I attempted to cut back by adopting drinks whose taste I hated (Fernet-Branca) or those with low alcohol content (white wine and soda). Night after night I found these substitutes relaxed me enough to switch to scotch and soda. For a time I experimented with vodka and tonic. I asked Jay Kovar what he knew about vodka as a drink. He told me, "Sooner or later, all the heavy hitters get to vodka."

I studied Jay as he worked behind the bar, trying to figure out how he did it. A saturnine, compact
man, fit, looking a little like Jason Patric, he steadily
drank half shots of whiskey and smoked Pall Malls.
I never saw him clearly appear to be drunk. Indeed
I saw relatively few of the regulars when they were
drunk, although that could happen after hours at the
Ale House. Some people, like Al the Greek, could
drink terrifying mixtures of drinks to little apparent effect. Others were more reasonable drinkers, but
steady.

We had our own *Sun-Times* delivery truck. Red
Connolly would make O'Rourke's his last stop of the
night. Red, whose brother was the Hollywood columnist Mike Connelly, would deliver bundles of the
early editions for us to study. The day's Royko column might be read aloud. Editors were libeled and
publishers despised. Red sometimes used the *Sun-
Times* truck to ferry us from one bar to another. One
night Cliff Robertson was in the bar and had fallen
under its spell. Red offered to give us all a lift to the
Oxford Pub on Lincoln Avenue, which was a late-
night joint. We piled into the back of his big red *Sun-
Times* truck: Robertson, McHugh, a bagpipe player,
assorted other regulars, and Good Sydney Harris.
Good Sydney Harris was a Spanish Civil War veteran, not to be confused with the Bad Sydney Harris,

the *Daily News* columnist. Good Sydney had fallen into conversation with a dominatrix named Jake, who joined us.

We tied the canvas flaps closed on the back of the truck, because of Red's theory that what we were doing was not technically legal. Jake took off her belt and began to flog Good Sydney. We passed around the Dew. The bagpipe player began "My Bonnie Lassie." We heard the *whoop! whoop!* of a police prowler, and Red pulled over to the curb.

"Top o' the mornin', Sergeant!" he said, and handed down copies of the *Sun-Times* and the *Wall Street Journal.* The prowler pulled away.

"My last delivery," Red said.

"Chicago," said Cliff Robertson.

A few of the regulars, I suspect, had little identity other than the one conferred by O'Rourke's. John the Garbage Man was a regular, displaying his sculptures made from objects discovered in the garbage. He would take discarded silverware and melt it down into jewelry that looked like blobs of melted silverware. These were sold to be worn around the neck. Jon Anderson wrote a column about him and he enjoyed a little run on business. I bought a chess set from him, but it was not a success because the pieces looked interchangeable. These I tried to use only once, while playing in an O'Rourke's chess tournament that sprang up during the Bobby Fischer fever in Iceland. The winner, who played chess for money at the North Avenue Beach Chess Pavilion, was Andre, a stringy hippie, tie dyed and ponytailed, who explained he had been the armorer of the Luxembourg army before fleeing to America as a political refugee.

We regulars knew one another. We dated one another. We slept with one another. We went to Greektown together, with Al presiding at the head of a long table. We met on Saturday mornings at Oxford's for "recovery drunch," named by Mike Tuohy, who believed peppermint schnapps and Coke would snap you out of it. Tom Butkovich would pull up behind O'Rourke's in his old Volvo station wagon and unload the equipment to barbeque a lamb. His mother, from the far Southwest Side, would bring in covered dishes of macaroni and cheese and potato salad, while his stepdad, a steelworker, would dance with his T-shirt pulled above his belly, singing *It must be jelly, 'cause jam don't shake like that*. We went to one another's weddings and funerals and observed holidays together. We took collections for bail money, or helped the Jim and Mike Tuohy family to move, which they did frequently, Mike once complaining to McHugh that he had failed to move her kitchen garbage.

The 1968 Days of Rage demonstrations passed

through Old Town, and Jimmy Breslin and Norman Mailer came in. We watched the moon landing and the fires after Martin Luther King Jr. was killed. We watched after Nixon resigned. We sang, laughed, and cried. We rehearsed the same stories over and over. I said we knew one another. We knew who we said we were, who we wanted to appear to be, and who O'Rourke's thought we were, and that was knowing one another well enough.

Now Studs Terkel, Mike Royko, and Nelson Algren are dead, and so are John Belushi, Steve Goodman, Tom Fitzpatrick, Mike Tuohy, Hank Oettinger, Al the Greek, and John the Garbage Man. Will Kilkeary sobered up and became a poet. Jeannette Sullivan married a nice guy she met in O'Rourke's, who became a police officer. Jay Kovar sold the location across the street from Steppenwolf and walks his dogs.

25   LEISURE OF THE THEORY CLASS

I LIVED MORE than nine months of my life in Boulder, Colorado, one week at a time. There more than anywhere else I heard for the first time about more new things, met more fascinating people who have nothing to do with the movies, learned more about debate, and trained under fire to think on my feet. It all happened at the sleep-inducingly named "Conference on World Affairs."

For sixty-six years, this annual meeting at the University of Colorado has persuaded a very mixed bag of people to travel to Boulder at their own expense, appear with one another on panels not of their choosing, lodge with local hosts who volunteer their spare rooms, speak spontaneously on topics they learn about only after they arrive, be driven around town by volunteers, be fed at lunch by the university and in the evening by such as the chairman, Jane Butcher, in her own home. For years the conference founder Howard Higman personally cooked roast beef on Tuesday night. The hundreds of panels, demonstrations, concerts, polemics, poetry readings, political discussions, and performances are and always have been free and open to the public.

In springtime in the Rockies, which some years didn't preclude two feet of snow, the birds were singing in the trees, and I strolled beside the bubbling brook and looked upon the bridge where Jimmy Stewart kissed June Allyson in *The Glenn Miller Story*. In every place like this I have sacred places where I touch base in order to preserve the illusion of continuity. In April 2009, I paid what turned out to be a final ritual visit to Daddy Bruce's Bar-B-Que, where I was greeted by Daddy Bruce Junior and purchased the Three Meats Platter to take away for Chaz. After untold decades in business, Daddy Bruce's still lacks a refrigerator. All meats are fresh today, hickory smoked over real logs. Cold drinks are kept in a big picnic cooler filled with ice. The interior is large enough for a few counter stools, two tables for two, and Daddy Bruce Junior's piano, on which he claims he can teach you to play in one day. I go back so far

I remember Daddy Bruce Senior, famous in Denver for his free Thanksgiving feeds. Bruce Junior is eighty-two years old. At least Daddy Bruce's is still here. These touchstones reassure me that I am, too.

"You know Tom passed?" Bruce asked me. "You always liked Tom's." Yes, I did. Tom's Tavern is no more, replaced by—I can't bear to tell you. There Howie Movshovitz the film critic and I would make an annual pilgrimage without fail, to talk about how we had been eating Tom's hamburgers since 1969 and our "real" lives were a Platonic illusion separated by visits to Tom's Tavern. Maybe that was more my theory than Howie's.

Two doors down, the Stage House II is also no more. I walked into this vast used bookstore and art gallery when a thirtysomething man was unpacking cardboard cartons to open up shop. This was Richard Schwartz, an example of the sort of person a college town will attract: well read, intellectual, funny, setting down roots and making a difference, because a college town without good used bookstores is not worthy of the name. It was Dick who sold me my first Edward Lear watercolor. Let me tell you how engaging he could be. Telephoning me in Chicago, he started chatting with Diane Doe, my secretary at the *Sun-Times*, and something traveled through the phone wires and into their hearts. They were married for twenty-five years before Dick passed away. Now the site of the Stage House II is occupied by—I can't bear to tell you.

Boulder is my hometown in an alternate universe. I have walked its streets by day and night, in rain, snow, and sunshine. I have made lifelong friends there. I grew up there. I was in my twenties when I first came to the Conference on World Affairs. I returned the next year and was greeted by Howard Higman, its choleric founder, with "Who invited you back?" Since then I have appeared on countless panels where I have learned and rehearsed debatemanship, the art of talking to anybody about anything. "Ask questions," advised Studs Terkel, who gave the keynote one year. "If you don't know anything, just respond by asking questions. It's not how much you know."

There are world-famous scientists there, filmmakers, senators, astronauts, poets, nuns, surgeons, addicts, yogis, Indian chiefs. One year Chief Fortunate Eagle, who led the sit-in at Alcatraz, was astonished to be picketed by a cadre of topless lesbians, who objected to—I dunno, the exploitation of Pocahontas, maybe. At Boulder I discussed masturbation with the Greek ambassador to the United Nations. I analyzed dirty jokes with Molly Ivins, the cabaret artist David Finkle, and the London parliamentary correspondent Simon Hoggart. I heard the one about the four-hundred-pound budgie from Andrew Neil, later editor of the *Sunday Times*. I found that the poet laureate, Howard Nemerov, had no interest at all in discussing his sister, Diane Arbus. I was on a panel about the Establishment with Henry Fairlie, who coined the term. Fairlie boarded at Higman's house and eventually holed up in Boulder for a time; he was famous and successful but always out of pocket and held his eyeglasses together with Scotch tape. There Margot Adler, the famed Wiccan, drew down the moon for me. There I met Betty Dodson, the sexual adventurer, who arrived one year wearing a sculpted brass belt buckle in the form of a vagina. There I asked Ted Turner how he got so much else right, and colorization wrong. There Patch Adams turned up wearing a psychedelic suit and floppy red clown shoes. I rather avoided him until he chased me across a room and announced, "I agreed with every word of your review of that loathsome film about me." From the basement of Macky Auditorium, I participated in Colorado's first live webcast, although I'm fairly certain no one was watching. It was in Boulder that I bought my first real computer, the DEC Rainbow 100. And in Boulder that I fell quickly in love or lust several times, as is the way with conferences.

The local people fed and feted the guests. The

opening-night party was held for many years in a home downhill from the campus on Boulder Creek by Betty Weems, a much-married rich liberal with the manner of a southern belle. One year she introduced a new husband, a Texas oil man named Manro Oberwetter, who was a good sport but unused to Boulder. One night he interrupted a hootenanny in the living room by striking a large gong and announcing, "I don't care if you all smoke weed. I don't care if you all go skinny dipping with your dirty dingus magee flapping in the wind. But which one is the son of a bitch who left a turd floating in my pool?"

I stayed for many years in the home of Betty Brandenburg, Howard's long-suffering assistant, and got a private glimpse behind the scenes. "Take your shower tonight," she told me. "In the morning we need the bathtub to wash the romaine."

I wrote about such events in a diary one year for *Slate*. "You give the wrong impression!" Chaz told me. "It's not all witches and topless lesbians. It's mostly serious." Quite true, and improvisational, and surprising. In this lockstep world of sound bites, how refreshing to witness intelligent people actually in spontaneous conversation. It is unusual to listen to people in the act of having new ideas occur to them.

I could tell you about the Irish storyteller. The blind New Orleans pianist. The fire-walking astrophysicist.

The SETI guy. But I want to be impressionistic. I want to describe a week when bright, articulate people think on their feet. No, not all pointy-headed elites. Over the years, Temple Grandin, who is autistic and the designer of most of the world's livestock-handling chutes. Buckminster Fuller, who, when I said, "Hello," responded, "I see you." Dave Grusin, the Oscar-winning composer. A bricklayer. A monk. Designers of solar energy systems.

Ramin Bahrani, who won a Guggenheim while he was there, joined me for a week in 2009 to discuss his *Chop Shop* in minute detail. It was astonishing. The smallest details of the film reflected the vision of Bahrani and his cinematographer, Michael Simmonds. He explained why each shot was chosen. How each was choreographed. How the plot, which seems to some to unfold in a documentary fashion, has a three-act structure, a character arc, and deliberate turning points. Why there was a soccer sticker on the back of a pickup truck. How every visual detail, including the placement and colorization of junk in the far background, was consciously planned. How certain shots were influenced by Bresson, Antonioni, Alexander Mackendrick, Godard. How the colors were controlled. How he worked in real situations by backing off and using long shots. How he worked with nonactors for months. How twenty-five takes of a shot were not uncommon. How he had prepared on the location for six months. How the film was anything but improvised.

"I'd do anything to meet Werner Herzog," he told me. We conspired to lure Werner to Boulder in 2010, where he joined Ramin in a shot-by shot analysis of *Aguirre, the Wrath of God*. Herzog's famous accent is a work of art. It could make E. E. Cummings sound like the wrath of God.

I'd been doing the shot-by-shot approach at the CWA every year since about 1970. After watching Herzog and Bahrani do it together, I decided to call it a day. I won't return to the conference. It is fueled by speech, and I'm out of gas. Why go to Daddy Bruce's if I can't eat? But I went there for my adult lifetime and had a hell of a good time.

Every year there is a jazz concert featuring world-class professional musicians, performing for free, convened by the Grusin brothers, Dave and Don. I heard a set of bongo drums played by Rony Barrak more rapidly and with more precision than I have ever heard before. I heard the flautist Nestor Torres playing Bach with all his heart and then segueing into Latin jazz, with songs he composed especially for the conference.

During one song, the charismatic jazz vocalist Lillian Boutté, from Germany out of New Orleans, was so happy that people started dancing in the aisles. People, to my knowledge, ranging from sixteen to eighty. You know these days how people when they're dancing sometimes look intensely serious about how cool they are? Their arm movements look inspired by seizures and the hammering of sheet metal. These aisle dancers weren't like that. They were feeling elevation. They weren't smiling. They were grinning like kids. On the stage, the musicians were grinning, too. There was a happiness storm in old Macky Auditorium. After all their paid gigs in studio recording sessions, how often do fourteen gifted improvisational jazz and Latin artists get to jam together just for fun? All free, all open to the public. And a few blocks away, Daddy Bruce Junior ready to teach me the piano.

26   ALCOHOLISM

IN AUGUST 1979, I took my last drink. It was about four o'clock on a Saturday afternoon, the hot sun streaming through the windows of my little carriage house behind the Four Farthings on Dickens. I put a glass of scotch and soda down on the living room table, went to bed, and pulled the blankets over my head. I couldn't take it anymore. I visited old Dr. Jakub Schlichter, recommended by Zonka, because when I discussed drinking with my previous doctor he said unhelpfully, "I know what you mean. With me, it's martinis." Schlichter, a refugee from Nazism, advised me to go to "AAA," which is what he called it. I said I didn't need to go to any meetings. I would stop drinking on my own. He told me, "Go right ahead. Check in with me every month."

The problem with using willpower was that it lasted only until my will persuaded me I could take another drink. At about this time I was reading *The Art of Eating* by M. F. K. Fisher, who wrote: "One martini is just right. Two martinis are too many. Three martinis are never enough." The problem with making resolutions is that you're sober when you take the first drink, have had a drink when you take the second one, and so on. I found it almost impossible, once I started, to stop after one or two. If I could, I would continue until I decided I was finished. The next day I paid a price in hangovers. I've known a couple of heavy drinkers who claimed they never had hangovers. I didn't believe them. Without hangovers, it is possible that I would still be drinking. I would also be unemployed, unmarried, and probably dead. Most alcoholics continue to drink as long as they can. Unlike most drugs, alcohol allows you to continue for what remains of your life, barring an accident. The lucky ones find their bottom and surrender.

That afternoon after I pulled the covers over my head, I stayed in bed for thirteen hours. On the Sunday I poured out the rest of the drink, which at the time I had no idea would be my last. I sat around the house not making any vows to myself but somehow just waiting. On Monday, I went to see Dr. Schlichter. He nodded as if he had been expecting this and said, "I want you to talk to a man at Grant Hospital. They have an excellent program." He picked up his phone and an hour later I was in the man's office. He asked me the usual questions, said the important thing was that I thought I had a problem, and asked me if I had packed and was ready to move into their rehab program.

"Hold on a second," I said. "I didn't come here to check into anything. I just came to talk to you."

He said they were strictly inpatient.

"I have a job," I said. "I can't leave it." He doubted that, but asked me to meet with one of their counselors.

This woman, I will call her Susan, had an office on Lincoln Avenue in a medical building across the street from Somebody Else's Troubles, which was well known to me. She said few people stayed sober for long without AA. I said the meetings didn't fit with my schedule and I didn't know where any were. She looked in a booklet. "Here's one at 401 North Wabash," she said. "Do you know where that is?" I confessed it was the *Chicago Sun-Times* building. "They have a meeting in the fourth-floor auditorium," she said. It was ten steps from my desk. "There's one today, starting in an hour. Can you be there?"

She had me.

Once in the building, I was very nervous. I stopped in the men's room across the hall to splash water on my face and walked into the room. Maybe thirty people were seated around a table. I knew one of them. I sat and listened. The guy next to me got applause when he said he'd been sober for a month. Another guy said five years. I believed the guy next to me. They gave me the same list of meetings Susan had consulted. Two day later I flew to Toronto for the film festival. At least here no one knew me. I looked up AA in the phone book and they told me there was a meeting in a church hall across Bloor Street from my hotel. I went to so many Toronto meetings in the next week that when I returned to Chicago, I considered myself a member.

Susan was unconvinced that I was fully a member, however, and told me she'd seen too many relapses after an early glow of victory. I'd never before stopped for long. She required me to begin taking a daily dose of Antabuse, a drug said to cause great distress when combined with drinking. Perhaps it was a similar drug that my mother slipped to my father before I was born, when Aunt Martha remembered him being too sick to move. Whatever it was, he never drank again. There were rules involving Antabuse. I was not allowed to take it myself. I had to find a Helping

Person to hold the bottle of pills, give me one every day, and call Susan the first day I missed one. Part of this policy, she said, was designed to help me admit my alcoholism to another person and be willing to ask for help.

It was no use asking drinking friends. They're a lot friendlier late at night than after awaking in the morning. I went to see Sue Gin, the Chinese-American woman who owned the Four Farthings and had sold me the coach house. Sue had been born above a Chinese restaurant in Aurora, became one of the first Playboy bunnies at eighteen, used the money to put herself through college, got a real estate license, and at the time I met her owned and managed a lot of rental properties in the Lincoln Park area, as well as the bar, Café Bernard on Halsted, and a bakery. These she managed more or less by herself.

When she started buying real estate along Halsted, it was a no-go area plagued by gangs and drug dealers. She was a barely drinking honorary member of the O'Rourke's crowd, and we all went to the opening of the French bistro she opened with a chef named Bernard LeCoq. This was the first outpost of gentrification on a rough stretch of Halsted, Tom Fitzpatrick distinguishing himself by getting into a fight. A lesser woman would have been furious that her opening had been disrupted. Sue had an instinctive feel for people. She told me, "I filled it with a freebie for newspaper people and a few radio and TV. Not the food critics, not the straight arrows, but you guys who all hang out together. So Fitz got in a fight. I didn't like it, but tomorrow that will be all over town. How else will anybody hear about a French restaurant in the middle of nowhere?" This was true enough, and although I can no longer eat, Café Bernard is still there, almost forty years later. Sue has an instinct for synergy.

One day she took me along to buy a tuckpointing company a few doors down from Bernard. We entered the shabby old building with its garage opening onto the galley, and she heard the elderly owner's story about his life in tuckpointing. She cross-examined him, saying she thought there was a future in tuck-pointing. He sold her his building and business for what must have been close to its market value. "Are you really going into tuckpointing?" I asked her. "I sure am. I'm starting Monday." On Monday, the Four Farthings building, a four-floor structure containing eight large flats, was surrounded by the tuckpoint-ers of her new company. Within a year the former garage was a storefront for one of the early stores of the Gap. When she bought the old bakery on Armit-age, however, she kept it in business, supplied res-taurants, and used it as the base for a company she named Flying Food Fare, which supplied in-flight meals to Midwest Airlines. She met one of its owners, Bill McGowan, who was to found MCI, one of the first competitors to AT&T. They fell in love. Sue had never been married, and I knew her well enough to see this was the real thing. They began to shuttle between Chicago and Washington. A few times she brought him along to dinner with some of her newspaper pals, who'd started favoring the Farthings as a fourth angle in the Bermuda Triangle. They invited a planeload of friends on a trip to Ireland, and at a dinner there McGowan's brother, a priest, announced that a year earlier he had married them. Some years later McGowan became an early recipient of a heart transplant, and Sue Gin became an expert on the procedure and its leading practitioners. All this time running her little empire, as nearly as anyone could tell, out of her head. She rehabilitated a few white-collar drinkers from the Farthings and put them back to work for her as architects or accountants.

All of this was still ahead on the morning I walked across my yard to the Farthings building and climbed four flights to Sue's sunny kitchen to receive my first Antabuse pill. She had coffee waiting, and pastries from her bakery. Every morning we repeated this ritual. If I overslept she woke me on the phone: "Rog! Time for your medicine!" She reported back to my counselor at the end of every week. Sue was brash and direct, analytical, always networking. She quizzed me on alcoholism, went to a meeting with me, and started working on some of her rescue cases in the bar downstairs. She drank, but very sparingly. She was comfortable in bars. When she looked at a customer and told him he was drunk, the customer believed her. Eventually I told Susan the counselor I wanted to get off Antabuse because I was in love with AA and it made me feel like a fraud at meetings. I have a feeling Sue kept an eye on me for my counselor.

Sue was possibly the only person I could have asked at that time to help me. At a bad time in my life, she was very helpful to me. She helped a lot of people. We occasionally see each other, more rarely these days, maybe at a benefit. "How you doing, Rog?" she asks, smiling, and we know what she means.

An AA meeting usually begins with a recovering alcoholic telling his "drunkalog," the story of his drinking days and how he eventually hit bottom. What's said in the room stays in the room. You may be wondering, in fact, why I'm violating the AA policy of anonymity and outing myself. AA is anonymous not because of shame but because of prudence; people who go public with their newly found sobriety have an alarming tendency to relapse. Consider those pathetic celebrities who check into rehab and hold a press conference. Anonymity encourages humility. People who tell everyone they've gone two weeks without a drink are on thin ice. When I decided to out myself as a recovering alcoholic, I hadn't taken a drink for thirty-one years, and since my first AA meeting I attended, I have never wanted to. Since surgery in July of 2006 I haven't been able to drink at all, or eat or speak. Unless I go insane and start pouring booze into my G-tube, I believe I'm reasonably safe.

I have seen that AA works. It is free, everywhere, and has no one in charge. It consists of the people gathered in that room at that time, many often unknown to one another. The rooms are arranged by volunteers. I have attended meetings in church basements, schoolrooms, a courtroom, a hospital, a jail, banks, beaches, living rooms, the back rooms of restaurants, and on board the *Queen Elizabeth II*. There's usually coffee. Sometimes someone brings cookies. We sit around, we hear the speaker, and then those who want to comment do. Nobody has to speak. Rules are, you don't interrupt anyone, and you don't look for arguments. We say, "Don't take someone else's inventory." There are some who have problems with Alcoholics Anonymous. They don't like the spiritual side, or they think it's a "cult," or feel they'll do fine on their own, thank you very much. The last thing I want to do is start an argument about AA. I tell people, don't go if you don't want to. It's there if you need it. In most cities, there's a meeting starting in an hour fairly close to you. It works for me. That's all I know. I don't want to argue about it.

What a good doctor and good man Jakub Schlichter was. He was in one of those classic office buildings in the Loop, filled with dentists and jewelers. He was a gifted general practitioner. An appointment lasted an hour. The first half hour was devoted to conversation. He had a thick *Physicians' Desk Reference* on his desk and liked to pat it. "There are twelve drugs in there," he said, "that we know work for sure. The best one is aspirin." One day, after a month of sobriety, I went to see him because I feared I had grown too elated with the realization that I need not drink again. I had started needing only a few hours of sleep a night, began to see coincidences everywhere, started to find hidden AA messages in Johnny Cash songs. I was continually in heat.

"Maybe I'm manic-depressive," I told him. "Maybe I need lithium."

"Alcohol is a depressant," he told me. "When you hold the balloon under the water and suddenly release it, it is eager to pop up quickly." I nodded.

"Yes," I said, "but I'm too excited. I'm in constant motion. I'd give anything just to feel a little bored."

"Lois, will you be so kind as to come in here?"

he called to his wife. She appeared, an elegant Jewish mother.

"Lois, I want you to open a little can of grapefruit segments for Roger. I know you have a bowl and a spoon." His wife came back with the grapefruit. I ate the segments. He watched me closely. "You still have your appetite," he said. "When you feel restless, take a good walk in the park. Call me if it doesn't work." It worked. I knew walking was a treatment for depression, but I didn't know it also worked the other way.

That was the beginning of a long adventure. I came to love the program and the friends I was making through meetings, some of whom are close friends to this day. I made friends at meetings in London, Edinburgh, Paris, New York, Cannes, Park City, Telluride, Cape Town, and Los Angeles. It was the best thing that ever happened to me. What I hadn't expected was that AA was virtual theater. As we went around the room with our comments, I was able to see into lives I had never glimpsed before. The Mustard Seed, the lower floor of a two-flat near Rush Street, had meetings from seven a.m. to ten p.m., and all-nighters on Christmas and New Years' eves. There I met people from every walk of life, and we all talked easily with one another because we were all there for the same reason, and that cut through the bullshit. One was Humble Howard, who liked to perform a dramatic reading from his driver's license—name, address, age, color of hair and eyes. He explained, "That's because I didn't have an address for five years."

When I mention Humble Howard, you're possibly thinking you wouldn't be caught dead at a meeting where someone did dramatic readings from his driver's license. He was as funny as a stand-up comedian. I realized that I'd tended to avoid people because of superficial judgments about who they were and what they would have to say. AA members who looked like bag ladies would relate what their lives used to be like, what happened, and what they were like now. Such people were often more eloquent than slick young professionals. I discovered that everyone, speaking honestly and openly, had important things to tell me. The program was bottom-line democracy.

Yes, I heard some amazing drunkalogs. A native American who crawled out from under an abandoned car one morning after years on the street, and without premeditation walked up to a cop and asked where he could find an AA meeting. And the cop said, "Follow those people going in over there?" A 1960s hippie whose VW van broke down on a remote road in Alaska. She started walking down a frozen riverbed, thought she heard bells ringing, and sat down to freeze to death. The bells were on a sleigh. The couple on the sleigh took her home with them, and then to an AA meeting. A priest who eavesdropped on his first meeting by hiding in the janitor's closet of his own church hall. Lots of people who had come to AA after rehab. Lots who just walked in through the door. No one who had been "sent by the judge," because in Chicago, AA didn't play that game: "If you don't want to be here, don't come."

Funny things happened. In those days I was the movie critic for a 10:00 p.m. newscast on one of the local stations. The anchor was an AA member. So was one of the reporters. After we got off work, we went to the 11:00 p.m. meeting at the Mustard Seed. There were maybe a dozen others there. The anchor took the chair and asked if anyone was attending his or her first meeting. A guy said, "I am. But instead I should be in a psych ward. I was just watching the news, and right now I'm hallucinating that two of those people are in this room."

AA has "open meetings" to which you can bring friends or relatives, but most meetings are closed: "Who you see here, what you hear here, let it stay here." By closed, I mean closed. I told Eppie Lederer that I was now in the program. She said, "I haven't been to one of those meetings in a long time. I want you to take me to one." Her limousine picked me up at home, and we were driven to the Old Town meeting, a closed meeting. I went in first, to ask permission to bring in Ann Landers. I was voted down. I went back to the limo and broke the news to her.

"Now I've heard everything!" Eppie said. "Ann Landers can't get into an AA meeting!"

Alcoholism is a family disease. My father had a drinking problem before I was born, and my mother began to drink for the first time in her life during her marriage to George Michael. I was by then living in Chicago and drinking too much myself, and at times I welcomed this, because we drank together. This led to conversations of unprecedented frankness and occasional recriminations. Whatever was said, she simply dismissed it the next day. I came to dread her visits to Chicago. I didn't want her to see me drunk, although she did.

After joining AA, I understand alcoholism better and realize that my father was an alcoholic who stopped before I was born, my mother was after he died, and I was from the time I took my first drink. The disease caused deep wounds, driving me into a personal life of evasion, denial, and concealment, and keeping me unmarried for an unnatural length of time. Did I know drinking made me unmarriageable, or did I simply put drinking ahead of marriage?

27 BOOKS DO FURNISH A ROOM

CHAZ AND I have lived for twenty years in a commodious Chicago town house. This house is not empty. Chaz and I have added, I dunno, maybe three or four thousand books, untold numbers of movies and albums, lots of art, rows of photographs, rooms full of comfortable furniture, a Buddha from Thailand, exercise equipment, carved elephants from India, African chairs and statues, and who knows what else. Of course I cannot do without a single one of these possessions, including more or else every book I have owned since I was seven, starting with *Huckleberry Finn*. I still have all the Penrod books, and every time I look at them, I'm reminded of Tarkington's inventory of the contents of Penrod's pants pockets. After reading it a third time, as a boy, I jammed my pockets with a pocketknife, a Yo-Yo, marbles, a compass, a stapler, an oddly shaped rock, a hardball, a ball of rubber bands, and three jawbreakers. These, in an ostensible search for a nickel, I emptied out on the counter of Harry Rusk's grocery, so that Harry Rusk could see that I was a Real Boy.

My books are a subject of much discussion. They pour from shelves onto tables, chairs, and the floor, and Chaz observes that I haven't read many of them and I never will. You just never know. One day I may need to read *Finnegans Wake*, the Icelandic sagas, Churchill's history of the Second World War, the complete Tintin in French, forty-seven novels by Simenon, and *By Love Possessed*. That 1957 best seller by James Gould Cozzens was eviscerated in a famous essay by Dwight Macdonald, who read through that year's list of fiction best sellers and surfaced with a scowl. I remember reading the novel late into the night when I was fourteen, stirring restlessly with the desire to be possessed by love.

I cannot throw out these books. Some are enchanted because I have personally turned all their pages and read every word. They're shrines to my past hours. Perhaps half were new when they came to my life, but most were used, and I remember where I found every one. The set of Kipling at the Book

Nook on Green Street in Champaign. The scandalous *The English Governess* in a shady bookstore on the Left Bank in 1965 (two dollars, today ninety-one). The Shaw plays from Cranford's on Long Street in Cape Town, where Irving Freeman claimed he had half a million books. Like an alcoholic trying to walk past a bar, you should see me trying to walk past a used bookstore. Other books I can't throw away because, well, they're books, and you can't throw away a book. Not even a cookbook from which we have prepared only a single recipe, for it is a meal preserved, in printed form. The very sight of *Quick and Easy Chinese Cooking* by Kenneth H. C. Lo quickens my pulse. Its pages are stained by broth, sherry, soy sauce, and chicken fat, and so thoroughly did I master it that I once sought out Ken Lo's *Memories of China* on Ebury Street in London and laid eyes on the great man himself, dining alone in a little room near the entrance. A book like that, you're not gonna throw away.

I can't throw out anything. I possibly don't require half the shirts I have ever owned. But look at this faded chamois cloth shirt from L. L. Bean, purchased through the mail in about 1973 from a two-inch ad in the back of the *New Yorker*: *The longer you wear it, the more it feels like chamois!* I've been wearing it a long, long time. I can't say it feels like chamois, but I want to work on it some more. I also need this tea mug from Keats House in Hampstead, even though its handle is broken off. I need it to hold these ball-point pens I had printed with the words *No good movie is too long. No bad movie is short enough.* They were one hundred for thirty-nine dollars, I think. The ink has dried up over the years, but I still need them in order to provide a purpose for the mug.

And here are my thick reference books. Not only the *Shorter Oxford English Dictionary,* but the small tiny-type edition of the complete *OED,* which came with its own magnifying glass. And *Bartlett's Familiar Quotations,* the *Halliwell's Filmgoer's Companion,* a hardbound *London A to Z* from 1975, and two dozen books on the occult, including the *I Ching* and *The Confessions of Aleister Crowley,* who was a flywheel but surely wrote one of the best of Edwardian autobiographies (Crowley explained that he invented modern British mountain climbing in the Himalayas after his predecessors "had themselves carried up by Sherpas"). In idle hours I like to leaf through my well-worn leather-bound 1970 edition of *Brewer's Dictionary of Phrase and Fable,* which offers entries not to be found elsewhere:

- *Giotto's O.* The old story goes that the Pope, wishing to employ artists from all over Italy, sent a messenger to collect specimen of their work. When the man approached Giotto (c. 1267–1337), the artist paused for a moment from the picture he was working on and with his brush drew a perfect circle on a piece of paper. In surprise the man returned to the Pope, who, appreciating the perfection of Giotto's artistry and skill by his unerring circle, employed Giotto forthwith.

- *October Club.* In the reign of Queen Anne, a group of High Tory MPs who met at tavern near Parliament to drink October Ale and abuse the Whigs.

Now here is the Penguin paperback of Apsley Cherry-Garrard's *The Worst Journey in the World*, the story of his agonizing trek through the darkness of the Antarctic winter to investigate the eggs of the penguin. The book is as long as the walk. I may not read it a second time. Do I require two later editions? Of course I do. You just never know. And both the second and third editions of the *Columbia Encyclopedia*? You bet.

Chaz gave me this facsimile of Shakespeare's First Folio. Will I ever read it? Not with that spelling and typography. But I will always treasure it. I look at it and wonder at the genius of the man. Do I need, for that matter, all of my other editions of Shakespeare?

The little blue volumes of the Yale Shakespeare, and the editions by Oxford, the Easton Press, and the Folio Society? Handsome books, finely made. But I read only my battered and underlined old Riverside Shakespeare from college, because it was edited by G. Blakemore Evans, and he was my professor, you see.

My possessions are getting away from me. We have an agreement. My office is my office. Chaz has her own book-filled office and takes care that the rest of the house is clean and orderly. My office has a glass door with this gilt lettering:

The Ebert Company, Ltd.
Fine Film Criticism since 1967

I have not been able to get into the storage closet of my office for four years. What? You expect me to throw out my first Tandy 100? And there's a forty-year run of *Sight and Sound* in there somewhere. I have a book named *Rodinsky's Room*, by Rachel Lichtenstein and Iain Sinclair, about a mysterious London cabalistic scholar named David Rodinsky who in 1969 disappeared from his attic above a synagogue on Princelet Street in the East End. His flat was strangely left undisturbed for years, and when it was opened all was exactly as he left it—his books, papers, possessions, even a pot of porridge on the stove.

That's what I should do. Just turn the key and walk away, and move into 150 square feet. Get me a little electric coil to boil the coffee water. Just my Shakespeare, some Henry James, and of course Willa Cather, Colette, and Simenon. Two hundred books, tops. But no, there wouldn't be room for Chaz, and I would miss her terribly. That I could never abide.

RUSS MEYER

A MOVIE NAMED *The Immoral Mr. Teas* opened in 1959 at the little Illini Theater, across from the Illinois Central station and the *News-Gazette*, wedged in between Vriner's and a pool hall. It ran for something like two years and became a rite of passage for the Illinois students, particularly popular during exam weeks. In 1961 I parked my car in the *News-Gazette* lot and, exact admission counted out in my hand, hurried across the street hoping to slip in unwitnessed. Similar figures materialized out of the shadows of Main Street. Once inside, guys in groups joked nervously and the rest of us sat very still, intent on the screen, avoiding eye contact.

The plot was not complex. A delivery man for false

teeth pedals a bicycle on his rounds. This unassuming man finds himself encountering voluptuous women, who appear completely nude in his daydreams. There is no physical contact, they seem unaware they're naked, and Mr. Teas seems primarily puzzled. A narrator comments on his dilemma and the sound track evokes bucolic wonderments. The film's sixty-one-minute running time allowed the Illini to schedule as many as ten screenings in a day, and students rotated in and out.

I'd never seen anything like it, certainly not in nudist camp "documentaries," which centered largely on the difficulties of playing volleyball with the ball constantly shielding the genitals. Meyer's women looked healthy and wholesome, unlike the carnal strippers in such films as *French Peep Show*, which I had also attended while "studying at the library." In the glossy *Show* magazine, no less than Leslie Fiedler described *Mr. Teas* as "the best American comedy of the 1950s."

One day in the spring of 1967, I noticed *Faster, Pussycat! Kill! Kill!* playing at the Biograph on Lincoln Avenue. The posters displayed improbably buxom women, and I was inside in a flash. That was when it first registered that there was a filmmaker named Russ Meyer, and he was the same man who made *The Immoral Mr. Teas*. I'd never seen anything like this black-and-white film. *Pussycat* was photographed in a jazzy style, all tilt shots and oblique angles, with intercuts of incongruous close-ups. The story was told inside a hermetic world. Nothing existed except three buxom hellions in fetishwear, the hero and his family in an isolated cabin, and the desire of the women to exploit the situation. The dialogue was ornate parody, the narration was strangely disconnected, the images popped out of the screen; the effect was surreal. Here, I felt, was a filmmaker. A couple of years later Meyer had a breakthrough hit with *Vixen!*, which cost $26,500 and grossed more than $6 million. The *Wall Street Journal* ran a front-page article headlined "King of the Nudies," observing that was a 40-to-1 return, allegedly second in film history only to *Gone With the Wind*. I wrote a letter to the editor, I received a letter from Russ Meyer, and one of the great friendships of my life began.

Russ was flying to Chicago to screen *Finders Keepers, Lovers Weepers!* for exhibitors. He invited me to the screening. I noted in my review: "Meyer edits by juxtaposing his sex scenes with incongruous cutaways to something else. For example, his heroine has just finished shaving the hero's chest. The hero, aroused, advances on her. 'But can't we wait?' she asks. 'I want to go to that symphony tonight. Erich Leinsdorf is conducting Maxim Gorky's Prelude in D Major.'

Then Meyer cuts to shots of a stock car destruction race."

After the screening we went to a rib place for an interview. Our conversation inevitably turned to large breasts, which we were both in favor of. Ever since I became aware of them, which was undoubtedly long before I can remember, I've considered full and pendulous breasts the most appealing visual of the human anatomy. Russ saw them differently, somehow considering a woman's breasts part of her musculature. In the maniacal lyricism of his advertising copy, jacket covers, and everyday speech, he referred to them as instruments of erotic aggression. They were bra busters, man grabbers, awesome configurations, the Guns of Navarone. His mind contained an endless thesaurus of synonyms, none of them referring to gentle, comforting qualities. His ideal women were cantilevered, top-heavy, awesomely endowed. These qualities were described without the least suggestion of lust or desire, but rather with apprehension. He seemed to live in fear or anticipation of being overwhelmed by a woman who was, as he wrote in a copy line for *Lorna*, "too much for one man." Of June Mack and Ann Marie, two of the stars of *Beneath the Valley of the Ultra-Vixens*, he said, "They required brassieres built along the lines that made the Sydney Opera House possible."

In 1969 the Twentieth Century–Fox studio was going through hard times, having lost millions on unsuccessful productions such as *Star!* and *Doctor Doolittle*. The studio heads Richard D. Zanuck and David Brown, noting the *Journal* article, invited Meyer to the lot for an interview. They owned the rights to the title *Beyond the Valley of the Dolls* and had turned down three screenplays proposed by Jacqueline Susann. They offered him the title, unattached to any story. Meyer offered me the screenwriting job, Jim Hoge gave me a six weeks' leave of absence, and I fell into a delirious adventure.

Meyer was a tall, solidly built man with a Victor McLaglen mustache and a man-to-man manner. He enlisted in the army before his eighteenth birthday and learned cinematography as a Signal Corps cameraman during World War II. His war years created a template that he spent the rest of his life trying to duplicate; he said, and I believed him, that they were the happiest years of his life. He never told a lie to my knowledge, and his stories seemed to check out. When he told me he lost his virginity to a big-bosomed whore in a French bordello where he had been taken by Ernest Hemingway, I doubted it. "No, that's true," Jim Ryan told me. "I was there with them." Ryan was Meyer's lifelong Sancho Panza, the star of his second film and a crew member or technician on almost all of the others. Meyer set himself up as the liaison for all the survivors of his Signal Corps unit, presiding at quarterly lunches at Nicodell's outside the Paramount gates and acting as the organizer of annual reunions, sending tickets to those who couldn't afford them. "Russ is still fighting the war," Jim Ryan told me once. "He gets us all together, we go off to some god-forsaken location and we work our butts off, bunk down in some motel that reminds him of a barracks, and chow down together. He's never happier than when he's waking everybody up in the morning." I saw this myself when I worked on the location of *Supervixens* in the Arizona desert, and one night at Dan Tana's one of the supervixens, Haji, told me that on the *Pussycat* location Russ nailed shut the windows of Tura Satana's motel room because he feared she was slipping out at night for rendezvous that would deplete her sexual energy. Like a football coach, he banned sex from the job. Tura was one of Russ's most improbable discoveries. That was her real name, and she was half Japanese, half Apache.

The *Supervixens* location took over the Green Gables Motel, which had nothing green about it and cringed under the sun in the high desert. Rooms were assigned two roommates. The furnishings were rudimentary; the closet was a broomstick hanging from the ceiling on wires, and the water from the shower ran directly out a slot in the wall to the desert outside, so that the vegetation behind the hotel thrived while cacti held on elsewhere. Meals were at the lunch counter, which offered hot dogs, microwave Tombstone pizza, hamburgers, and Tecate beer. Fred Owens, another Signal Corps buddy who was production manager, engaged the cook: "Have you ever made meat loaf here? What you do is, you take you some ground beef…" Within a day Owens had established himself at the grill and was acting as mess officer.

There was an intern from the UCLA film school on the production, who was assigned one day to dig a posthole in front of the Green Gables. A scene required Meyer's frequent actor Charles Napier to drive his pickup to the motel, skid to a stop, leap out, and grab a pay phone. I commiserated with the intern, who was wearing a big tourist sombrero. "I'm a senior in cinema, and all I'm learning to do is use a fucking posthole digger."

In midafternoon Owens returned from the nearest town with an Arizona Bell pay phone and a cooler filled with groceries. Meyer asked him if he'd had trouble finding the telephone. "I requisitioned it," he explained. The light was failing, and there was no time for rehearsal. Napier drove the truck down the highway while the kid inserted the pole into his hole and arranged stones around the base. Meyer peered through the viewfinder to frame the highway shot. He shouted, "Action!" Owens waved a bandana over his head, and Napier sped down the highway and into the motel lot, skidded to a stop, leaped out, and grabbed the telephone, which was only four feet above the ground. The pole was proportioned to stand on a paved surface.

Everybody started laughing. Meyer walked over to the kid. "UCLA film school my ass," he said. "Dig up the telephone and fill in your hole."

One morning before dawn Meyer took me for a walk in the desert. "Need your help on this. Edy has refused to play SuperVixen." Edy Williams was the Twentieth Century–Fox starlet I'd introduced to Russ in the commissary one day. They married and moved into a house on Mulholland Drive with a kidney-shaped indoor-outdoor pool.

"I gave her the best role of her life in *Dolls*," he said, "and now she thinks she's too big for *Supervixens*. She doesn't want to appear naked. This is a girl selling a poster of herself floating spread-eagled on her back in a pool. This is a hell of a time for her to develop scruples. It's for SuperAngel in the last sequence in the film. I don't have time to find another girl. What should I do?"

The story involved a series of supervixens, each

named after the heroine of a Meyer movie: Super-Lorna, SuperCherry, SuperSoul, SuperEula, Super-Haji, and so on. The solution was clear. "You have to circle back to the beginning," I told him. "You started with SuperVixen, and now you have to end with SuperVixen. Fly Shari Eubank back in." Shari was a beautiful farm girl from Farmer City, Illinois, who had moved to Los Angeles with hopes of being discovered.

"I see a problem with that," Meyer said. "In the opening sequence she is shot, stabbed, drowned, and electrocuted. How is the audience going to buy her as still alive?"

"Resurrection," I explained. "When they last saw her, she was dead in the bathtub. Now it's dawn." I pointed to the top of a small nearby peak. "The bathtub is on the mountaintop. The sun is rising. We play *Thus Spake Zarathustra*. Now she's SuperAngel. We see her rising out of the bathtub wearing a see-through diaphanous gown. She is alive."

Russ liked it. "All we have to do is get the bathtub up there," he said. He discussed the logistics at breakfast. Napier's part-time job was as a columnist for *Overdrive: The Voice of the American Trucker*. He drove to the interstate and walked into a truck stop on the route bringing fresh vegetables from Arizona to New York. He was recognized, possibly for his column but more likely for playing one of the title roles in Meyer's *Cherry, Harry and Raquel*. "Any of you good old boys like a day's work on Russ Meyer's new picture?" he said. "The beer is free and the girls are great looking, but it's strictly look, don't touch."

Before the next day six truckers carried a bathtub to the top of the nearby peak. Meyer focused a tele-photo lens. Haji, who was doing all the makeup in addition to playing SuperHaji, crouched out of sight, poised to retouch Shari Eubank's body makeup and hair styling. As the sun rose, Fred Owens waved his bandana, and SuperAngel rose from the tub. Russ got several good takes. Russ held a preview of the film in Chicago. Our scene was missing. I asked what hap-pened. "I tried it in and I tried it out," he said. "It just didn't make any sense. This way, I just cut to Super-Angel. She's so good-looking the audience doesn't ask any questions." The scene didn't go to waste. In *Up!* (1976), a sex scene is intercut with shots of six men carrying a bathtub up a mountainside.

In the late summer of 1969, we wrote the screen-play for *Beyond the Valley of the Dolls* in six weeks flat. Meyer and I had a three-room office suite in the Fox director's building, across the hall from Martin Ritt. Our offices were separated by the office of June, a veteran from the secretarial pool. As we interviewed actresses, June confided she had seen a few of them before, also visiting directors, but not to audition for a role. Meyer in fact hired none of the cold auditions. He cast two Playboy Playmates (Cynthia Myers and Dolly Read) and an African-American woman (Marcia McBroom) who had the innocent quality he was looking for, although she lacked the standard RM measurements. Other roles were filled by veterans from his earlier films (Napier; Erica Gavin, the original Vixen; Haji; Henry Rowland, his stock Nazi). For the key role of Ronnie (Z-Man) Barzell, we found John LaZar, who was to become a cult figure.

It was not long after the Manson Family murders, and Hollywood was in the grip of paranoia. Meyer and I shopped for a place for me to live and settled on the Sunset Marquis, near Sunset Boulevard. In those days it was an inexpensive motel, inhabited by semipermanent guests such as Van Heflin and Tiny Tim. When I called room service, a voice answered, "Greenblatt's Deli." Meyer specified a second-floor room: "I don't want you being murdered by any of these Satan worshippers."

We fell into a routine. At nights we would dine like trenchermen, Russ insisting on large cuts of beef to keep my strength up. On yellow legal pads we made up the story day by day. I would write from ten to six. Russ kept all the office doors open. He equated writing with typing. When my typewriter fell silent, he would call, "What's wrong?" One day, at about page 122 of the screenplay, an inspiration struck. I entered Russ's office dramatically.

"I've got news for you," I said. "Z-Man is a woman. He's been a woman all along."

"I like it," Meyer said.

Although Meyer had been signed to a three-picture deal by Fox, I wonder whether he didn't suspect that *BVD* might be his only shot at employing the resources of a studio at the service of his pop universe of libidinous, simplistic creatures. Meyer wanted everything in the screenplay except the kitchen sink. The movie, he explained, should simultaneously be a satire, a serious melodrama, a rock musical, a comedy, a violent exploitation picture, a skin flick, and a moralistic exposé of what the opening crawl called "the oft-times nightmarish world of Show Business."

What was the correct acting style for such a hybrid? Meyer directed the actors with dead seriousness, discussing the motivations behind each scene. "I know Russ treats this like Shakespeare," Chuck Napier told me, "but it reads to me like a comedy." The uncertainty of the cast led to a curious tone; the actors were directed at a right angle to the material. "If the actors seem to know they have funny lines, it won't work," Meyer said. The movie was inspired in title only by *Valley of the Dolls*. Neither Meyer nor I ever read Jacqueline Susann's book, but we did screen the Mark Robson film, and we lifted the same formula: Three young girls come to Hollywood, find fame and fortune, are threatened by sex, violence, and drugs, and either do or do not win redemption. Susann's novel was a roman à clef, and so was *BVD*, with a difference: We wanted the movie to seem like a fictionalized exposé of real people, but we personally possessed no real information to use as our inspiration for the characters. The character of teenage rock tycoon Z-Man Barzell, for example, was supposed to be "inspired" by Phil Spector, but neither Meyer nor I had ever met Spector. It was eerie when many years later the tragedy of his own life played out like Z-Man's. There was a happier coincidence: Joan Jett said the film's all-girl rock trio was one of the inspirations for her band the Runaways.

In late June of 1977, I got a call from Meyer, who said the Sex Pistols, the most notorious British punk rock band, were among the fans of *BVD*. He'd received a call from Malcolm McLaren, their Svengali, explaining that he, Johnny Rotten, and Sid Vicious had visited the Electric Cinema on Portobello Road, where *Beyond the Valley* played at midnight on weekends. They wanted Meyer to direct them in their own film. Meyer asked me if I wanted to return as screenwriter.

"What sort of picture will it be?" I asked.

"McLaren says he wants to do the flip side of *Beyond the Valley of the Dolls*," Meyer said.

"But *Beyond* itself was the flip side of *Valley of the Dolls*," I said.

"You figure it out," Meyer said. "McLaren is flying out here to Los Angeles next week."

I met with Meyer and McLaren. I established headquarters at the Sunset Marquis, and Meyer hauled in card tables, typewriters, and yellow legal pads. McLaren briefed us on the Pistols. He showed us press clippings, describing the Pistols being thrown out of clubs, attacked by fans, arrested in front of Buckingham Palace, and saying "fuck" on the BBC. We looked at videotapes of the Pistols on TV and in concert. We listened to all of their records. McLaren talked and talked and talked. McLaren himself would have made a good subject for a movie. He was an educated Londoner, of average appearance except for the bondage pants he wore—leather pants equipped with straps and buckles, so that he could be rendered immobile at the drop of a whip. The pants were a best-selling item at Sex, the punk boutique McLaren ran with Vivienne Westwood on King's Road. The buckles and straps saw action in restaurants, where he'd sometimes get his restraints tangled and overturn his chair.

McLaren's notion was that the Sex Pistols stood for the total rejection of modern British society, and especially of the millionaire rock establishment symbolized by Mick Jagger. "These guys are all in their thirties and drive around in Rolls-Royces," McLaren said. "What do they have in common with the typical sixteen-year-old school-leaver who has no job, no money, no prospects, and no hope?" The Sex Pistols' music spoke for these disenfranchised, he said, and the movie should be a statement of anarchic revolt against the rock millionaires, and the whole British establishment.

Within a week, I had a rough treatment ready. It included an opening scene in which a millionaire rock star leaps from his chauffeured Rolls and kills a deer with a bow and arrow. He is witnessed committing this act by a young girl who reappears at the end of the film to assassinate the star and shout the immortal line, "That's for Bambi!" McLaren's working title was *Anarchy in the UK*, but now I suggested *Who Killed Bambi?* The action included such passages as Vicious fighting a dog named Ringo and Johnny Rotten demolishing a street-corner Scientology-style testing center.

After we finished two drafts in Los Angeles, Meyer and I flew to London, where we met the Sex Pistols themselves. McLaren's idea was that they would go over their dialogue with us, making suggestions. I assumed they would reject everything I had written, but they seemed completely uninterested; I suspected it was McLaren, not the Pistols, who was the Russ Meyer fan. Paul Cook and Steve Jones were hardly seen during the days we spent in London. McLaren came to the flat every day and took a lively interest in the process of auditioning possible actors for the movie. (Among the actors cast were Marianne Faithfull, who would play Vicious's mother, and fallen rock idol P. J. Proby, who would more or less play himself.) One day McLaren, Rotten, Meyer, and I went out for lunch. Rotten seemed to enjoy intimidating waiters by playing dumb and asking the same questions over and over again, until Meyer lost patience and ordered for him. If the film had ever been made, there would have been warfare between the two, because Meyer was emphatically unimpressed by Rotten's aggressive rudeness. But this day, mellowed by beer, Rotten relaxed and even showed some glimmers of the person he would eventually metamorphose into— John Lydon (his real name), leader of Public Image Ltd. and radio personality. We were talking about Sid Vicious, and Rotten observed that Sid had become like a new man since he had fallen in love. I do not know if the woman Sid had fallen for was Nancy Spungen, the eventual heroine of *Sid & Nancy*, but I assume so. I remember Rotten observing with wonderment that romance had inspired Sid: "He changed his underwear for the first time in two years."

Sid Vicious was angry most of the time about something, but one night he was particularly mad because he was a fucking star and Malcolm McLaren had him on rations of eight quid a week. We were in Russ Meyer's rented car, driving down the Cromwell Road in London, and Vicious told Meyer to pull over in front of a late-night grocery so he could purchase some provisions. Meyer and I watched as he skulked into the store, wearing leather pants, a ripped T-shirt, and Doc Martens, the shoes favored by punks because they were ideal for kicking people. Sid's hair was spiky and his eyes were bloodshot. Through the window we saw the store owners exchange uneasy glances before Sid checked out with his supper, which consisted of two six-packs of beer and a big can of pork and beans. Then we dropped Sid off at an anonymous brick building on an anonymous brick road. It was the last time I would see Sid Vicious, but it would not be the last time I would hear about him.

After the *BVD* experience, I saw Russ every time I went to L.A. and joined in tributes to his work at Yale, the National Film Center in London, the Museum of Modern Art, and UCLA. He came to my housewarming, he flew all the way to Urbana for my mother's funeral, we went fishing on Lake Michigan, and I sat with him the night his own mother died and saw him completely depleted, blank eyed, barely able to talk. He was a Rabelaisian workaholic, demanding total dedication and loyalty. He was the general and the movie was the war. He would travel anywhere to promote his films or appear at events and talk shows, and interviewers liked him because he was good copy and fun to be around. He could have taken advantage of the Hollywood casting couch ritual, but didn't. Of all his actresses, the only ones I know for sure he slept with were his wife and producing partner Eve, Edy Williams, and his frequent star and later companion Kitten Natividad. He was close with Haji, a Canadian actress and stripper who appeared in six of his films and did makeup and crew work on most of them, but I never heard them refer to sex. He and Uschi Digard, a Swedish stripper/model who appeared in four of his films, were good friends; she later married a European diamond merchant and became a gemologist. Kitten, a Mexican-American, was introduced to Russ by Uschi. She was warm and funny, and they liked each other. I went along with them for dinner one night at her grandmother's apartment, jammed with antique furniture. They were a couple on and off for fifteen years.

One night Russ convened a gathering of the Signal

Corps buddies at a prime-rib house he'd found in the Valley. By this time I'd met them all several times. Midway through dinner Russ related a story, paused, and repeated it again, almost word for word. Our eyes all met around the table. In the 1980s he began to exhibit gathering dementia. He completed *Beneath the Valley of the Ultra-Vixens* in 1979, and it was his last film, although he announced others. He began to work on his autobiography, originally titled *Russ Meyer: The Rural Fellini*. I suggested *A Clean Breast*, and he liked that more. This project grew and grew like a book in a fantasy.

Writing on legal pads, he drew from fifty years of leather-bound scrapbooks on shelves dividing his living room. RM Films was being run by Janice Cowart, whom he met as the manager of his favorite video store, and she feared it would never end. He consulted printers about paper that would not deteriorate after five hundred years. It would be leather bound. It would contain countless illustrations, repeat many interviews, copy many documents. It would have photographs of every important woman in his life. When he couldn't find a photograph, he would shoot a body double with a paper bag over her head. Yes. Janice typed, and his long-suffering graphic and advertising man, George Carl, assembled the manuscript. Russ was proud that all of the lines were the same width but asked why there was a little more space between the words in some lines than others. George explained justification. Russ holed up with a thesaurus in his second home in Palm Springs and substituted longer or shorter words as needed. He found a printer in Hong Kong.

"Three volumes," he told me. "Eighteen pounds. One-hundred-pound stock. A hundred and ninety-nine dollars." He was publishing it himself.

"When will it be in stores?" I asked.

"No stores. I'm selling it personally. If they want it, they can call here."

"But your number is unlisted."

"It's out there. I was in a bookstore once and I saw Olivia de Havilland's autobiography marked down to half price. I worked with her once. A great lady. That will never happen to my life."

As his illness progressed, Janice took away his car keys, and Kitten, who was fighting cancer, did his driving. The time came when he required around-the-clock caregivers. He died in 2004. He was eighty-two. Chaz and I attended the funeral at Forest Lawn. The night before, there had been a gathering of the friends. All the surviving army buddies. All the crew members, collaborators, lawyers, distributors. Janice, Jim Ryan, and Chuck Napier, of course. And Erica Gavin, Kitten, Tura Satana, Haji, Marcia McBroom,

Cynthia Myers, Sue Bernard. Kitten told me Uschi would have been there but was having eye treatments. This was the family. Russ had a son, he told me, whose mother had never told him who his father was. "I've seen him from a distance." The stories went long into the night. The women cried. In the cruel world of X-rated films, Russ had treated them with respect, paid them moderately well, photographed them lovingly, required them to act and not simply be naked, never did hard-core sex, worked their asses off climbing mountains and fighting in mud, and stayed in constant touch forever after.

The sermon was a dreary affair by a Forest Lawn rent-a-preacher, who uncanned the usual boilerplate about Russ being in a better place now, in the bosom of Jesus. "He'd rather be in the bosom of Mary Magdalene," Napier whispered. Chaz told me, "If you don't go up there and say something Russ will come out of his coffin and strangle you." I walked up to the altar. The hired man droned on about heavenly rewards, looked at me uncertainly, and asked if I wanted to speak. "Thank you," I said. "The family has asked me to say a few words." I spoke of Russ's friendship, loyalty, and lifelong efforts to stay in touch and keep us all in touch.

It was so sad seeing him in the final decade, this vital man. Chaz and I would visit him at his home on Arrowhead in the hills. On our last visit he didn't know who we were, or who he was. "Sometimes he has a flash of memory," Janice said. A nurse came in to give him pills and a glass of milk. He looked after her as she walked away. "No tits," he said.

29　　　　　　　　　　THE INTERVIEWER

My SECRET AS an interviewer was that I was actually impressed by the people I interviewed: not only by Bill Clinton, John Wayne, or Sophia Loren, but by Sandra Dee, Stella Stevens, and George Peppard. I am beneath everything else a fan. I was fixed in this mode as a young boy and am awed by people who take the risks of performance. I become their advocate and find myself in sympathy. I can employ scorched-earth tactics in writing about a bad movie, but I rarely write sharp criticism of actors themselves. If they're good in a movie, they must have done something right. If they're bad, it may have been the fault of filming conditions or editing choices. Perhaps they may simply have been bad. I feel reluctant to write in a hurtful way; not always, but usually. I feel repugnance for the critic John Simon, who made it a specialty to attack the way actors look. They can't help how they look, any more than John Simon can help looking like a rat.

My job involved doing a great many interviews. I was always a little excited by the presence of the subject. As a teenager covering the Champaign County Fair, I stood behind the bandstand in the racetrack infield and interviewed the teenage country singer Brenda Lee, and was terrified. That established my pattern of low-key interviews. I tend not to confront or challenge, and my best technique has been to listen. This turns out to have been a useful strategy, because when you allow people to keep on talking they are likely to say anything.

The best interview I ever wrote was one about Lee Marvin, in *Esquire* in 1970. I sat in his beach house in Malibu for a long afternoon of drinking, and he said exactly what came into his mind. There was no press agent present and no mental censor at work. He didn't give a damn. I was a kid he'd never heard of, but that afternoon he gave me the opportunity to write accurately about exactly what it was like to join Lee Marvin for an afternoon of desultory drinking. I took notes. Later, typing them up, they came to resemble dialogue. They weren't interrupted by questions, because I realized quickly that questions and answers were not going to be happening. Lee was passing time in public.

I took this dialogue, added a spare minimum of exposition, and submitted it to Harold Hayes, who printed it in *Esquire*. The piece contains no background on Marvin. No autobiography. It isn't hooked to his latest movie. There is no apparent occasion for it. It is his voice. Some years later, I was rather surprised to be invited to his house outside Tucson for another interview. He was by then married to the high school sweetheart he'd left behind forty years earlier to join the Marines. I wondered why he wanted to see me again. It may have been because he had been giving a performance in Malibu that day of the *Esquire* interview and my article recognized that and got out of his way. I mentioned the earlier article, saying I was relieved he didn't "mind" it. His wife said, "Well, I wasn't there, but it was all true."

In those days movie stars didn't move within a cocoon of publicists and "security." Today's stars are as well protected as the president. Then it was possible for stars like Charlton Heston, Cliff Robertson, and Clint Eastwood to walk into a place like O'Rourke's Pub and have a drink and not give a damn. The master of that was Robert Mitchum, who had never given a damn about anything. The "bad publicity" he got for posing at Cannes with a topless actress or being busted for pot only enhanced his aura, because he'd spent no effort in trying to be someone he wasn't.

The routine in those days was usually for a star to fly into town and meet with the local press. Movies opened differently then. The premiere might be in New York or Los Angeles, and then a film would gradually "go wide," market by market, with the star traveling a week ahead of it. Then in the 1970s studios started advertising on national television, and it made sense for many movies to open nationally on the same day. The junket was born: The journalists would be flown in to meet the stars.

Early junkets were bacchanals of largesse, and none was ever larger than one in 1970 when Warner Bros. flew planeloads of interviewers to the Bahamas for a week to attend premieres of five of their films. We stayed in luxury, ate and drank like pigs, and were platooned at Sam Peckinpah, Katharine Hepburn, and Kim Novak. Francis and Eleanor Coppola were there with his *The Rain People*, an art film that was greeted with some bafflement. I sat at an ice cream counter with Coppola and he wondered if he had a future in the business. One great film was shown, Peckinpah's *The Wild Bunch*. I thought it was an important act of filmmaking. The general reaction to the film was disbelief and disgust. "I have only one question," said the lady from *Reader's Digest*. "Why was this film ever made?"

Later the studio junket developed into a way of life for "junket whores," who appeared more or less weekly at luxury hotels. They all knew one another and exchanged family photos. When one had a birthday, there was likely to be a cake or a little celebration arranged by their "friends" the studio publicists. Minor eccentricities were indulged. During one junket a bathroom door flew open in a hospitality suite and revealed two junketeers having sex on the floor.

Junket guests were given swag bags containing the press release, a baseball cap, and a bottle of cheap wine. Soon a Swag Industry came into being, and the swag bag itself might be by Louis Vuitton. Companies lobbied to have their products given to famous people, or even lowly journalists; a new electronic device like the Flip, for example, might be well placed in the hands of a junket whore. High-priced swag was reserved for "talent" (not interviewers). I qualified as "talent" once, at a Friars Club roast of Whoopi Goldberg, and was invited into a backstage swag room and offered resort holidays, designer chocolate, TV sets, cases of wine, computers. A tailor with a measuring tape was eager to size me for a new suit.

The rules for junket whores were informal but well understood. You flew into Vegas, or New York, or London. You saw the movie at a premiere or private screening. If you were "print," you sat at a round table while publicists rotated stars and filmmakers. Each new occupant of an empty chair was greeted by cries of affection and familiarity. Difficult questions were rare. Everyone was asked, "What did it feel like working with (name of another star in the same movie)?"

Television interviewers found themselves cycled through interview rooms strung along a hotel corridor and connected by umbilicals of cables. Companies sprang up that specialized in doing the AV for junkets. The interviewers, camera operators, and "room directors" would greet one another happily. The stars would come and go; the crews remained. The stars would be perfectly lighted and made up and seated in front of a poster for their movie. Talent would take a chair, also after TV makeup. Questions were limited to three minutes, five in the case of "major markets." A star could cover six markets in an hour.

Appearing at such junkets was a species of hell for them but was often mandated by their contracts. We all had more fun in the days when TV was disregarded and stars came into town and actually spent time with the newspaper people. Off the top of my head I can tell you of eight times when a movie star and I got more or less drunk together. One night as

Peter Cook left with my date, I called after him, "I knew she was a star fucker, but I thought I was the star!"

I flew on the junkets. It was understood to be a part of the newspaper job, "bringing back a star" for the Sunday paper, not unlike the old TV show *Bring 'Em Back Alive*. In Dallas for the premiere of *9 to 5*, I had an uncanny experience, and on the plane home to Chicago I confessed it to Siskel: I had been granted a private half hour with Dolly Parton, and as we spoke I was filled with a strange ethereal grace. This was not spiritual, nor was it sexual. It was healing or comforting. Gene listened, and said, "Roger, I felt the exact same thing during my interview with her." We looked at each other. What did this mean? Neither one of us ever felt that feeling again. From time to time we would refer to it in wonder.

Was accepting a junket a conflict of interest? Was it a form of bribe, to assure a kind interview and a more positive review? Of course it was. In the early days the ethical question didn't arise because newspapers were eager to get celebrity interviews into print and couldn't afford to send their writers flying somewhere every weekend. I never gave a bad movie a good review just because I'd been on the junket, and I tried to choose junkets only to movies I thought I might like: *Close Encounters of the Third Kind*, for example.

One day Siskel told me, "Our show has gotten too big for us to go on junkets anymore." "But the paper wants the stories," I told him. "Let the paper pay its own way. That's what the *Tribune* is doing." Of course he was right. I took no junkets after about 1980, but when I was at the Toronto or Cannes festivals the junkets would come to me, and I did TV for the ABC station in Chicago and wrote pieces for the paper. If I accepted a junket, I split my expenses between the *Sun-Times* and the TV station. Sometime in the 1990s interviewers started being asked to sign agreements promising to ask no questions in certain areas (politics, marriage, religion, past flops). I refused to sign anything. Since they weren't paying my expenses, they had no leverage. Curiously, I found I got better interviews that way. Warned that I hadn't signed an agreement, stars sometimes seemed almost compelled to bring up their forbidden subjects. I got the impression the agreements hadn't originated with the stars but from the protective publicists.

What the interviewer has to understand is that he is not a friend or a confidant. He has engaged in a superficial process for mutual benefit. In a few cases I have become, if not friends, at least very friendly with actors or directors. I felt bonds with Werner Herzog, Martin Scorsese, Robert Altman, Paul Cox, Ramin Bahrani, Errol Morris, Jack Lemmon, Walter

Matthau, Shirley MacLaine, Clint Eastwood, William Friedkin, Mike Leigh, Sissy Spacek, Michael Caine, Atom Egoyan, Paul Schrader, Brian De Palma, Francis Coppola, Jason Reitman. I am a good friend of Gregory Nava and Anna Thomas, whom I met at the Chicago International Film Festival in 1975 and whose *El Norte* (1983) was the first epic of the American indie film movement. I felt a meeting of the minds with Robert Mitchum, but that was because of who he was, not because of who we were together.

Losing the ability to speak ended my freedom to interview. There are new stars and directors coming up now whom I will never get to know that way. Tilda Swinton, Sofia Coppola, Ellen Page, David Fincher, Colin Firth, Jennifer Lawrence. I've never even had a proper conversation with Philip Seymour Hoffman, Marisa Tomei, Edward Norton, Darren Aronofsky, Catherine Keener, or George Clooney. I tried a few interviews using the voice in my computer while tape-recording the answers. I got some good answers, but you couldn't call those conversations. I tried sending questions by e-mail, but that isn't conversation, either. I've felt better about one other approach: I ask prepared questions and take digital video of the responses, finding that being on camera inspires more conversational frankness. During those interviews I pause to type up follow-through questions. All the same, my last real interview was at Cannes in May 2006, when I talked with William Friedkin, Tracy Letts, and Michael Shannon, the director, writer, and star of *Bug*. That was a movie I was eager to discuss. Now that is all in the past.

30   LEE MARVIN

ONE DAY IN 1967 I was at Paramount to visit the set of Josh Logan's troubled musical *Paint Your Wagon*, in which Lee Marvin and Clint Eastwood were to sing with such undeniable results. Logan was setting up a shot and Marvin went with some friends to a bar outside the studio gate. I went along, because in those days stars were self-confident and didn't give a damn and would take a pee on the sidewalk if it was called for. I took notes.

Returning to my room at the Hollywood Roosevelt I typed them up on my sky blue Olympia portable from high school, read them, and realized I essentially had the article right there. That's how I discovered a method that would carry me through all my later articles for *Esquire* and many other interviews, until it became unusable because stars grew too timid to allow access. I was a deadpan witness, apparently simply recording what happened. No or few questions. Just the star observed. There was more contrivance involved than it seemed, as any writer would know, but that was the apparent method. It proved a godsend, particularly with actors like Marvin and Mitchum, who rejected linear Q & A's and free-associated. I simply wrote it all down and got some of the best interviews I would ever be able to do.

I typed up that Marvin interview and mailed it over the transom to the Sunday *New York Times*, which was then the venue of the newly celebrated Rex Reed. I took a minimalist approach, the opposite to him. The *Times* bought it and later took similar pieces from me about Groucho, John Wayne, and Bob and Ray.

I don't intend to make this book an anthology of my best newspaper pieces, but I think I'll print that interview from December 1968 because it has some interest as my breakthrough into national print, and my discovery of what would become my frequent method.

"Well, here we are at the Paramount commissary and Lee Marvin is facing straight into the corner," Lee Marvin said. "It is what Lee Marvin should expect, because Lee Marvin was late getting to lunch, and he got the only chair left. Pauline? Could you get me a Heineken's?"

"Only the Heineken's?" the waitress said.

"Whaddya mean, only the Heineken's?"

"I mean, you won't be eating?"

"Oh, yeah. Yeah, I'm only having the Heineken's."

Marvin was in costume for some studio scenes on "Paint Your Wagon," and he had silver locks down to his shoulders and whiskers and a moustache-sideburn combination, and he looked hairy. He was wearing an old blue blazer. This was Monday and his call had been for 7:30 a.m. and now here it was past noon and he'd been waiting all morning and had worked himself into an interesting condition. He twisted around in his seat and saw John Wayne three tables down. Wayne was in Western costume for "True Grit."

"He wears his gun to lunch," Marvin said.

The beer came. "You ever hear me sing an Armenian song?" Marvin sang an Armenian song. "What else? Let's see. Did you see that article in Life? By that Peace Corps kid, about the picture I was making with the Jap, Toshiro Mifune? 'Hell in the Pacific'? That article was written by a kid 21 years old, and he already has his Ph.D." He pointed his finger like a pistol and made a noise that began with a whistle and ended with a pop. "Twenty-one." Whistle-pop. "I'll give it to you straight, I liked the picture. Here I am—me, the combat veteran—20 years later and having bad dreams at night about the Pacific. The dreams go away, and where am I? Back on that island. Back in the goddamned Pacific. It was a rough picture. It was hotter than hell out there. I was hot, Lee Marvin was hot, we were all hot. The Jap was great.

"My next picture after 'Paint Your Wagon'—which of course we all remember is *this* picture—is going to be called 'Diehard.' About older men confronted by younger men and all those obvious phrases. Phrases. I mean I could go on, but—" Whistle, ascending to a suggestive note. "I mean I could, but—" Pop! Significant wink. "I was in the Pacific. I was young and tough at the time. But I got it whipped: Now I'm old and tough. Tough as nails. Mean. All those words. You know all those words. Save time."

Marvin poured his beer into a glass, drank, looked at the glass, drained it, held it up to the light and said: "Well I'll be good goddamned. Look at this. D.S.C. Who the hell's D.S.C.?"

"D.S.C.?" asked the studio press agent.

"Yeah, right here. Damnedest thing you ever did see. The initials on this glass spell D.S.C. First time I ever heard of coming into the Paramount commissary and they give you a monogrammed glass. Now who could it be? Darryl S. . . . hmmm.

"But let's talk about 'Paint Your Wagon.' That's why we're here, isn't it? The way I see it, the picture has seven saving factors: Josh Logan, Clint Eastwood, Jean Seberg and, of course, me. I'm established, right? I mean, I *am* established, right?"

"That's only four, Lee," the press agent said.

"Four what?" Whistle-pop. "Pauline? Hey, Pauline? Look at this glass. Funniest thing you ever saw. Look here. D.S.C. Dudley S. Conover? Might be, could be... trouble of it is, nobody around here *by* that name."

"I'll check on it," Pauline said. "That really *is* something."

"No hurry about it," Marvin said. "Think of D.S.C. having lunch right now, thinking, where's my monogrammed glass? Let him cool his heels, what I say. Teach him the value."

A woman at another table came over with a photograph of Marvin and asked him to autograph it for her daughter. Marvin wrote his name in the shape of a tattoo on the arm. The woman said she'd liked Marvin in "The Dirty Dozen."

"I really don't care about it, 'The Dirty Dozen,'" Marvin said when the woman had left. "The D.D. was a dummy money-maker, and baby, if you want a money-maker, get a dummy. 'Hell in the Pacific,' now, that's a rough movie. I think it'll be a failure. If you say it'll be a success, who listens? Say it's a failure, they listen—because it *sounds as if you're saying some-thing*. Interviews like this, after a while you try to get beneath them. Things happening on all kinds of levels. See what I mean? Tunnel under the situation, come up behind the guards, and—"

His hand made an airplane dive. "Pow! It's the only way to do an interview, take my word. Hit them straight on, and the s.o.b.'s will clobber you every time. Of course, I'm in a very raunchy mood this morning."

A long pause. "So the Algonquin Hotel is dead... they *think!* Pack up the old round table. Zappo! When things started getting better for me financially, I went to the Algonquin. I was drinking Jack Daniels and water, reading the label. Elliott Nugent, a writer, had a typewriter, sitting there, took him 25 minutes to type 'and.' Bartender said... Never mind what the bartender said.

"That of course was during my righteous period. I was married at the time, and so... I ordered breakfast. The room service guy kept his head down. Subservience, and I'm an American. Can't stand it. So I said, it's O.K., sweetheart, we're married. *Still* kept his head down. And my mother of course loved the Algonquin. The dear, dear old Algonquin... Pauline?"

"Right, Mr. Marvin, we checked and you know who that glass belongs to? Douglas Cramer, one of the TV executives next door."

"Well," Marvin said, "send it back with my compliments. Cramer? With a C? Must have chickened out."

He lit a cigarette. "Come on now, ask me questions," he said. "Is it true? Ask me something is it true?"

Is it true you're the highest-paid actor in Hollywood?

"That's it. Not a great question, but a good question. No, it isn't true. No, Paul Newman makes more money, a million two, I think it is. But what you gonna do?" Conspiratorial wink. Pause.

"Listen, stop me. I'm rambling. I'd go on like this all day. It's up to you. I never rise above *any* situation."

Is it true you and Josh Logan have been at each other's throats during the filming of "Paint Your Wagon"?

"Logan and me, I'll tell you the truth, we're so simpatico we refuse to accept the other person. That's beautiful. I mean, *he's* so right, and *I'm* so right...we're *both* so right...well, what you gonna do?"

Marvin's agent, Meyer Mishkin, arrived at the table and suggested that everybody walk on over to the set. Everybody got up and, on the way out, there were two women at the commissary door selling raffle tickets for a charity. Marvin pulled some money out of his pocket. "Meyer, I told you, never give me anything smaller than hundreds," he said. He put a $20 bill on the table and said, "Here, baby, buy yourself a drink." As he walked away, he grumbled under his breath: "Big shot movie star, throwing money around."

"This isn't the way to the set," the studio press agent said.

"Nope, going to my D.R. first," Marvin said. "To save you all embarrassment, we'll go in the back door." He led everyone to the back door of his dressing room, but the key didn't fit. "Well," he said, "to save you all embarrassment, we'll go in the front door. What the hell, the whole world knows anyway..."

"He started out rough," the press agent said, "but you know why he's bringing you along to his dressing room? He likes you. This is one great guy..."

Marvin decided not to stop at his dressing room after all, and he walked on down the studio street. Three doors down was Barbra Streisand's dressing room. Marvin took a nickel out of his pocket and left it on her door mat.

"She's a good broad," he said.

A few yards farther down the street, he was stopped by a young Negro woman who said: "Mr. Marvin, do you remember when you embarrassed me the other morning in Alan Jay Lerner's office?"

She was smiling.

"What?" Marvin said. "Me? I mean, *me*?"

The girl laughed. "You came in and...remember? You tried to rub the color off my skin. Like this."

"Well," Marvin said, "did I win?"

"I...don't know," the girl said. "Well, goodbye."

"Goodbye," Marvin said. He walked along the street in silence. Finally he said, "Did you hear that? She was stuck for an answer. She brought up the subject, and then she didn't know how to get out of it. Stuck! And I even gave her the straight line. If it was my daughter, baby..."

The set was across the street from the main Paramount lot, and along the way was a lounge, the Playboy's Buffet. One moment Marvin was walking straight ahead and the next he had made a sudden left turn and was inside the lounge.

Mishkin hurried in after him. The studio press agent walked on toward the set. Inside, Marvin ordered a beer. Mishkin sat at the bar next to him, a short, apple-cheeked man in a business suit next to Marvin's hairy bulk. Nobody said much. The press agent came back with Michelle Triola, Marvin's girl friend. Marvin and Miss Triola spoke quietly for a few minutes, jokingly, and then Marvin said he'd be right back and he walked alone toward the dining room section in the next room. Before long, laughter and rumblings floated back into the bar.

"Listen to him," Mishkin said, shaking his head wonderingly. "I'm telling you, this man is loved every place he goes. The only thing is, if they would only get him in the morning and *get him set*. But when he has to wait around all day..."

"I'm going to see what he's doing," Miss Triola said. She went into the other room.

"I've been with Lee Marvin for 17 years," Mishkin said. "We've gone from scale to a million dollars a picture. You know what scale was in those days? We were getting $175 a week. That was $17.50 for me, and now look where he is. Paul Newman gets more a picture, but he committed on that deal at Universal. We have freedom. We never sign a multiple picture deal. We sign one picture at a time. We won't even sign a two picture deal unless we know what the second picture is. And we won't sign a deal for a picture to be made two, three years from now. Who knows? The market might change."

Another wave of laughter floated in from the dining room. Marvin's voice could be heard saying something undecipherable in a rhythm which suggested it was a joke.

"Now will you listen to that?" Mishkin said, inclining his head toward the dining room. "There's something about that man, when he's in a room, people just naturally look at him, they admire him. He's got some quality, I don't know what it is. Let me put it this way, have you ever seen Lee Marvin in a picture that wasn't right for him? Where he didn't look good? Sure, we could go to Universal, sign the contract, get the extra two, three hundred thousand a picture, but when you're making the money Lee Marvin's making, who needs it? I mean, who *needs* it? And Paul Newman...let me put it this way. Think back. Has Lee Marvin ever done a 'Harry Frigg'? Go right ahead, think back. Has Lee Marvin ever done a 'Secret War of Harry Frigg'? That's what it gets you into..."

His head was inclined more anxiously now toward the dining room, where the noises indicated some change of mood, although there was still laughter. In a moment Michelle Triola came back out of the dining room and sat on her stool at the bar again.

"No, I won't have anything," she told the bartender. She is a pretty girl, very soft-spoken.

"What's going on in there?" Mishkin asked.

"Oh, you know," she said.

"Well, they haven't come looking for him," Mishkin said. "They know where he is."

"Look what time it is," Miss Triola said. "Almost 2:30. He comes to work at 7:30 in the morning, *ready* to work, and they make him wait. And you know how that drives him up the wall. I'm sure he doesn't *mean* to be rude, but..."

"He hasn't been rude," the studio press agent said.

"Well," she said, "he just was to me."

31   ROBERT MITCHUM

ROBERT MITCHUM DIDN'T give a damn what anybody thought about him. He never seemed to be making the slightest effort to be a movie star. But of the stars I met in my early years on the job, he was the most iconic, the most fascinating. That fits into my theory that true movie stars must be established in our minds well before we reach a certain age, perhaps seventeen. Mitchum was embedded in my mind from an early age when one night in the basement I came across a copy of my father's *Confidential* magazine and electricity ran through me when I saw a photo of the topless starlet Simone Silva at Cannes, embracing Mitch. He looked pleased but not excited. Perhaps it was his composure that made such an impression.

I met Mitchum for the first time in autumn 1969 in a stone cottage on the Dingle Peninsula in Ireland, where he was filming *Ryan's Daughter* for David Lean. I walked up to the cottage one afternoon with John McHugh and John's brother Eugene. Mitchum was utterly relaxed. His voice played the famous low laconic melody. His eyes were hooded, his manner lazy. It was his day off. He stretched his legs out long under the coffee table, whirled the ice in his glass, and whistled *My heart knows what the wild goose knows*. I sensed that Mitchum would not be patient with standard questions. He spoke in streams of consciousness, and that's how I quoted him. That afternoon and evening, he taught me as Lee Marvin had how I would write interviews in the future. I would not ask formal questions and write down the replies. I would drift with the occasion and observe whatever happened. Because that's what I did with Mitchum, I think he grew to tolerate me. He didn't mind me being around, even during unrehearsed moments as when he smoked pot while being driven through Pennsylvania and parts of Ohio in search of a movie location. During a day like that, he never made the slightest suggestion that I shouldn't quote him in full or mention the pot. He didn't care.

At some point that first time in Dingle I asked him, "How long you figure you got to live?" His answer was like free verse: "About...oh, about three weeks. I have this rash that grows on my back every twenty-eight days. I was bitten by a rowboat when I was thirteen, in a park in Cleveland, Ohio, and every twenty-eight days a rash appears on my back. I've offered my body for science. Meanwhile, I sit here in Dingle and vegetate. I was a young man of twenty-six when I arrived here last month. The days are punctuated by the sighs of my man, Harold, as he waits for the pubs to open. But don't get me wrong. Usually I'm gay with laughter, fairy footed, dancing about and rejoicing. But this afternoon, well, I just woke up. So I sit here and weep. Finally everyone staggers into town to Tom Ashe's pub and leaves me here alone weeping. That's my day."

Mitchum's attention drifted. Outside the window, children played in the road. They called to each other in Gaelic. We began talking about some recent movies. "I never saw *The Sand Pebbles*," he said. "Of course that was a problem picture out in front, with Steve McQueen in it. You've got to realize a Steve McQueen performance just naturally lends itself to monotony." A melancholy shake of the head. "Steve doesn't bring too much to the party."

A silence fell. Mitchum yawned and let his head drop back. He stared up at the ceiling. "No way," he said. "There's just no way." Drawing out the no. "Noooo way."

He emptied his glass.

"I've put away more fucking scotch since I got to Dingle than I've put away in my whole life," he said. "No, there was Vietnam . . . one day we were out there in the boondocks and I must have had fourteen, no, sixteen cans of beer and the greater part of a bottle of whiskey. And that was at lunch. Then they took me back to base in a helicopter and all the clubs—the officer's club, the noncom's club, the enlisted-men's club—they all said, 'Come on, Bob, have a drink.' 'No way,' I said. 'No way. I'm a Mormon bishop. Sure, Bob, we know.' "

Mitchum took a fresh glass from his man, Harold. "No way," he sighed. "I've looked into it, and there's just noooo way. My father was killed when I was three, so I was principally shipped around to relatives. I finally left when I was fourteen. Jumped on a train, came back, left again when I was fifteen, wound up on a chain gang in Savannah, came back, went to California. My first break was working for Hopalong Cassidy, falling off horses. So now I support my favorite charity: myself. That's where the money goes. My wife, my kids. I have a brother, weighs about 280 pounds. Two sisters, a mother, a stepfather. I think my sisters are religious mystics. They belong to that Baha'i faith. Somebody asked my wife once, What's your idea of your husband? And she answered: He's a masturbation image. Well, that's what we all are. Up there on the screen, our goddamn eyeball is six feet high, the poor bastards who buy tickets think we really amount to something."

Mitchum stood up and walked over to the window. "Let's take a walk around the house," he said.

It was nearly dark outside, cold and damp, the lights of Dingle on the hill across the river. "It's going to be a good picture," he said. "I trust Lean. He's a good director. He'd better be. This is eight goddamn months out of my life. I'll be here until the last dog dies." He kicked at the grass, his hands in his pockets, his face neutral.

"Any more questions?" he said.

Are all the rumors about you true?

"Oh, sure, every one. Where there's smoke there's fire. Make up some more if you want to. They're all true. Booze, broads, all true."

What about pot?

"I don't have any," he said. "I sit and weep and wait for the weather to change, waiting for my crop to grow." He leaned over and picked up a flowerpot that was leaning against the side of his cottage. A sickly spindle of twig grew in it. "My crop," he said. "I'm waiting for my crop to grow. In my hands I hold the hopes of the Dingle Botanical Society."

The following year, Mitchum and the movie's publicist, Bailey Selig, came through Chicago to promote the Lean picture. I told him his co-star Trevor Howard had been through town not long before on the same assignment.

"What was he saying?" Mitchum said.

"Something about his wife falling off a mountain," I said.

Mitchum and Bailey laughed together. "That was Trevor for you," Mitchum said. "I'll tell you what really happened. It wasn't a mountain, it was a ledge. Helen was walking up to my cottage one night. The road turned, and she went straight. We were having a bit of a party at my place. A few drinks, a few laughs. Trevor was in the kitchen making love to a bottle of Chivas Regal. Harold, my stand-in, walked out front of the cottage and came in white as a sheet. He said there was a woman outside with a bloody head and only one shoe. We went out and it was Helen Howard. We got her on the couch and fanned her back to witness, and she said she'd fallen off the ledge. Dead sober she was. Harold had been a medic with the Coldstream Guards. He ascertained Helen had broken her coccyx."

Mitchum sipped his Pernod. "I went into the

kitchen to tell Trevor. 'Nonsense!' Trevor said. 'Pay no attention! I'm the only one who has a coccyx in this family! She pulls these stunts all the time. It's her way of attracting attention.' Then Trevor poured himself another Chivas."

Mitchum shrugged. "Well, as it turned out, for poor Helen it meant a twenty-five-mile ride over the mountains in a Land Rover to the nearest hospital, at Tralee. So I went back into the kitchen and broke the news to Trevor."

"Right you are, sport," Trevor said. "Bloody unpleasant trip over the mountain on a rocky road to Tralee in a Land Rover."

"It's going to be awfully painful," Mitchum told Howard. "Poor Helen sitting up in a Land Rover with her injured tailbone."

"Yes indeed," Trevor said. "Bloody difficult trip. Sure to be goddamned uncomfortable. No sense in my going!"

The next year, in the autumn of 1971, Mitchum was in McKeesport, Pennsylvania, to film *Going Home*. I was to meet him outside the Sheraton Motor Inn. The sky hung low and wet, and Mitchum hunched his shoulders against it and scooted around to the passenger side of the car. He'd dismissed his union driver and would be driven by his friend Tim Lawless, who claimed he knew where the location was. Tim started the car and guided it down a ramp and onto a highway, turning left, which was, as it turned out, a fateful decision.

"Jesus, what a lousy, crummy day," Tim said.

"And here it is only two in the afternoon," Mitchum said. "Reflect on the hours still before us. What time is the call for?"

"They're looking for you around two thirty, quarter to three," Tim said. "You got it made."

"You know the way?" Mitchum said.

"Hell, yes, I know the way," Tim said. "I was out here yesterday. Sons of bitches, picking locations way the hell the other side of hell and gone."

"What do we gotta shoot this afternoon? We gotta jam our asses into those little cells again?"

"Those are the smallest cells I've ever seen," Tim said. "Can you imagine pulling solitary in one of those?"

"I did five days of solitary once, when I was a kid," Mitchum said. "In Texas. Of course, in Texas you might as well be in as out."

"You did solitary?" Tim said.

"I liked it," Mitchum said. "You read about Alvin Karpis, up in Canada? They finally let him out after forty years. Son of a bitch walks free, and the guy who put him inside is still sitting there. J. Edgar. Son of a bitch does forty years, the least we could do for him is not have J. Edgar still sitting there when he gets out a lifetime later."

"Karpis?" Tim said.

"I guess he was a real mean mother at one time," Mitchum said.

The wipers beat back and forth against the windshield, and on the sidewalks people put their heads down and made short dashes between dry places. We were in Pittsburgh now, and the smoke and fog brought visibility down to maybe a couple of blocks.

"I'm glad we're shooting inside today," Tim said.

Mitchum whistled under his breath, and then began to sing softly to himself: "*Seventy-six trombones led the big parade...*"

"With a hundred and ten cornets in the rear," Tim sang, banging time against the steering wheel.

"'A hundred and ten'? Is that right?" Tim said after a while.

"All I know is the seventy-six trombones," Mitchum said. "I don't have time to keep pace with all the latest developments."

"How long you been in Pittsburgh?" I asked.

"I was born here," Mitchum said, "and I intend to make it my home long after U.S. Steel has died and been forgotten. I intend to remain after steel itself has been forgotten. I shall remain, here on the banks of the Yakahoopee River, a greyed eminence. I used to come through here during the Depression. I don't think the place has ever really and truly recovered."

He reached in his pocket for a pipe, filled it carefully, and lit up.

"I don't think we went through a tunnel yesterday," Tim said.

"Well, we're going through a tunnel now," Mitchum said.

"Are you sure we're supposed to be on Seventy-Nine and not Seventy-Six?" Tim said.

"I think I'm sure," Mitchum said. "We were either supposed to sing 'Seventy-Six Trombones' to remind us to take Seventy-Six or to remind us not to. I'm not sure which."

"You're not leading me down the garden path, are you, Bob?" Tim said.

"Route Seventy-Nine," Mitchum said. "Maybe it was Seventy-Six. Or . . . Route Thirty?"

"This is the goddamn airport road," Tim said. "Look there."

"Steubenville, Ohio," Mitchum said. "Jesus Christ, Tim, we're going to Steubenville, Ohio. Maybe it's just as well. Make a left turn at Steubenville and come back in on the Pennsylvania Turnpike . . ."

"Ohio's around here somewhere," Tim said.

"I've always wanted to make a picture in Ohio,"

Mitchum said. "Maybe I have. I was bitten by a rowboat once in Cleveland."

There were three lanes of traffic in both directions, and Tim held grimly to the wheel, trying to spot a sign or an exit or a clue.

"The Vesuvius Crucible," Mitchum said. "Pull off here, and we'll ask at the Vesuvius Crucible. If anybody ought to know where they are, the Vesuvius Crucible ought to."

Tim took the next exit and drove into the parking lot of the Vesuvius Crucible. Mitchum rolled down the window on his side and called to a man inside the office: "Hey, can you tell us how to get to the Allegheny County Workhouse?"

"The what?" the man said.

"The Allegheny County Workhouse," Mitchum said.

"Hell, they closed that down back here about six months ago," the man said. "It's empty now."

"We just want to visit," Mitchum said. "Old times' sake."

The man came out into the yard, scratching himself thoughtfully. "The Allegheny County Workhouse," he repeated. "Well, buster, you're real lost. You turn around here and go right back to downtown Pittsburgh. Take the underpass. When you get to downtown Pittsburgh, ask for directions there."

"How wide are we off the mark?" Mitchum said.

"Buster," the man said, "you're thirty-eight or forty miles away from where you should be."

"Holy shit," Mitchum said.

"I'm telling you," the man said, "they shut the workhouse down back here six, seven months ago. You won't find anybody there."

"Thanks just the same," Mitchum said.

Tim drove back up to the expressway overpass and came down pointed toward Pittsburgh. "We should have taken Route Eight," he said.

"Sorry about that," Mitchum said. "There's the road to Monroeville. Ohio's around here somewhere."

"Nice countryside," Tim said. "You ought to buy it and build yourself a ranch."

"I could be the biggest rancher in Pittsburgh," Mitchum said. "Get up in the morning and eat ham and eggs in my embroidered pajamas. Some girl broke into the motel; did you hear about that? With a pair of embroidered PJs?"

"Embroidered?"

"A great big red heart right over the rosette area," Mitchum said. "I've got an idea. Maybe we should hire a cab and have it lead us to the Allegheny County Workhouse."

"I don't even think we're in Allegheny County," Tim said.

Mitchum hummed "Seventy-Six Trombones" under his breath and filled his pipe again.

"There's a funny thing about this picture," Mitchum said. "At the same time I was reading this script, I was also reading a script about a jazz musician in San Francisco. So I ask myself, do I want to play a jazz musician in San Francisco, or do I want to go on location in some god-forsaken corner of McKeesport, Pennsylvania, and live in a motel for two months? No way. Noooo way. So these two guys come in, and we have a drink or two, and I sign the contract. On their way out, I say I'll see them in San Francisco. They looked at me a little funny. Do you know what I did? I signed up for the wrong fucking movie."

"Here's Route Eight right now," Tim said.

"That's Exit Eight, not Route Eight," Mitchum said.

"We're going to be real late," Tim said.

"They can rehearse," Mitchum said. "They can practice falling off stairs, tripping over lights, and shouting at each other in the middle of a take."

The car was back in the tunnel again now. Tim came down through a series of cloverleafs and found himself back on Route 79, headed for the airport.

"I'm lost," he said. "Baby, I am lost."

In desperation, he made a U-turn across six lanes

of traffic and found himself on an up ramp going in the wrong direction with a cop walking slowly across the street toward him.

Mitchum rolled down his window. "Roll down your window," he told Tim. "Let's get a breeze in here." He shouted to the cop: "Hey, chief! We're lost! We been forty miles out in the country, and here we are headed right back the same way again."

"What are you doing making a U-turn against all that traffic?" the cop said. "You could go to jail for that."

"Hell, chief," Mitchum said, "that's where we're trying to go. We been looking for the Allegheny County Workhouse for the last two hours."

"They closed that down back here six months ago," the policeman said.

"We're shooting a movie out there," Mitchum said.

"Hey, you're Robert Mitchum, aren't you?" the cop said.

Mitchum pulled his dark glasses down on his nose so the cop could see more of his face and said, "We are so lost."

"I tell you what you do, Bob," the cop said. "You take this underpass and follow the road that curves off on your left before you get to the bridge."

"Thanks, chief," Mitchum said.

Tim drove onto the underpass, followed the road that curved off on the left before he got to the bridge, and groaned.

"We're back on Route Seventy-Nine heading for the airport," he said.

"Jesus Christ," Mitchum said. "Screw that cop. Screw that cop and the boat that brought him."

"Now we gotta go back through the tunnel," Tim said. "I'm upset. I am really upset."

On the other side of the tunnel, Tim pulled over next to a state highway department parking lot and backed into it down the exit ramp. A state employee came slowly out of a shed, wiping his hands on a rag and watching Tim's unorthodox entry.

"Ask that guy," Mitchum said. "Offer him a certain amount to lead us there with a snowplow."

Tim got out and received some instructions from the state employee. The instructions required a great deal of arm waving, and their essence seemed to be: Go back that way.

Tim tried it again, back through the tunnel, across the bridge, down the overpass to a red light where a police squad car was stopped in front of their Mercury. Mitchum jumped out of the car and hurried up to the squad car for instructions. He got back just as the light turned green.

"You'll see a sign up here that says Blawnox," he said. "That's what we need. Blawnox."

"I'm out of gas," Tim said.

"I got a letter from John Brison today," Mitchum said. "John's in Dingle, in Ireland. Where we shot *Ryan's Daughter.*"

"I am really upset," Tim said.

"According to John," Mitchum said, "they've formed a Robert Mitchum Fan Club in Dingle. The membership is largely composed of unwed mothers and their brothers."

"Where the hell are we?" said Tim.

"That's what happens when you shoot on location," Mitchum said. "It's nothing but a pain in the ass."

In 1975, I went to talk with Mitchum in his office on Sunset Strip. He had just finished playing Philip Marlowe, a role he was born for, in *Farewell, My Lovely.*

"They were gonna make *Farewell, My Lovely* last year," Mitchum said. "They wanted Richard Burton. He was doing something else. The producer, Elliott Kastner, comes by with Sir Lew Grade, the British tycoon. He has a black suit, a black tie, a white shirt, and a whiter face. 'I know nothing about motion pictures,' Sir Lew says. 'What I know is entertainment: Ferris wheels, pony rides.' I suggested we buy up the rights to *Murder, My Sweet* with Dick Powell, rerelease it, and go to the beach.

"But, no, they hired a director, Dick Richards, so nervous he can't hold his legs still. They have all the hide rubbed off them. He started doing TV commercials. He was accustomed to, you know, start the camera, expose a hundred and twenty feet of film, and tell somebody to move the beer bottle half an inch clockwise. He does the same thing with people."

Mitchum inhaled, exhaled slowly, leaned forward to see into his outer office. "Bring me a Miltown, sweetheart," he said to his secretary. "Christ, I can't keep up during this mad, merry social season. Comes the rites of spring, there's nothing but elections, premieres...why they continue to send all these invitations to me is...thanks, sweetheart...

"The girl on the picture was Charlotte Rampling. She was the chick who dug S and M in *The Night Porter.* She arrived with an odd entourage, two husbands or something. Or they were friends and she married one of them and he grew a mustache and butched up. She kept exercising her mouth like she was trying to swallow her ear. I played her on the right side because she had two great big blackheads on her left ear, and I was afraid they'd spring out and lodge on my lip."

It was a lucky chance that got Mitchum into *Farewell, My Lovely* in the first place. He was on Corsica to play the lead in Preminger's *Rosebud* when he was fired, or quit, and came back to Hollywood just as the Marlowe role opened up.

"I might have been able to give Otto some advice on that picture," Mitchum mused. "I was out there at five thirty one morning, looking at the raw eggs they were describing as breakfast and doing my Otto Preminger imitation, and Otto comes up behind me and starts bellowing."

The exchange, as Mitchum remembered it, went like this:

Preminger: "You have been drinking with the Corsicans!"

Mitchum: "Who the hell else is there around here to drink with, Otto?"

Preminger: "By the end of the day, you are hopelessly drunk!"

Mitchum: "It's the end of the day, isn't it?"

Preminger: "You are drunk now!"

Mitchum: "Now, Otto, how in hell can I be drunk at five thirty in the morning?"

Preminger: "You are *through*!"

Mitchum: "Taxi!"

The last time I saw Mitchum was in Charlottesville at the 1993 Virginia Film Festival, four years before his death. They were honoring him, they said, "because he embodies the soul of film noir." That was true, but Mitchum only smiled at it. "We called them B pictures," he said. "We didn't have the money, we didn't have the sets, we didn't have the lights, we didn't have the time. What we did have were some pretty good stories." It was my job to be onstage with Mitchum and question him after the screening of Jacques Tourneur's *Out of the Past* (1947), one of the greatest of all film noirs, the one where Jane Greer tells Mitchum, "You're no good and neither am I. We were meant for each other." And where Mitchum, informed that everybody dies sooner or later, replies, "Yes, but if I have to, I'm going to die last."

Instead of attending the screening we had dinner at a local restaurant, where I learned his wife prudently instructed the bartenders to water his martinis. On the stage after the screening, he lit a Pall Mall to loud applause, blew out smoke, and sighed.

"Making faces and speaking someone else's lines is not really a cure for cancer, you know. If you can do it with some grace, that's good luck, but it isn't an individual triumph; it is about as individual as putting one foot before the other. One of the greatest movie stars was Rin Tin Tin. What the hell. It can't be too much of a trick."

"In *Out of the Past*, you co-starred with Kirk

Douglas," I said. You've always been laid back. He was more...laid forward."

"Well, Kirk was very serious about it. Just before *Out of the Past*, Bettejane Greer and I saw a picture that came over from Paramount called *The Strange Love of Martha Ivers* and Kirk was very interesting in it. So we said, 'Let's get him,' and the studio got him and he's quite serious about his profession, while I personally take or leave it, you know. I have a come-what-may attitude. And he spent most of his time on the set with a pencil on his chin...which kind of tickled the hell out of Bettejane. But I saw that he was very serious about it. He came to Janie and said, 'How can I underplay Mitchum?' She said, 'Forget it, man. He ain't playing it; he's just doing it.'"

He wanted to get underneath you somehow? Underact you?

"Yeah. He was an actor. I was a hired man."

Out of the Past is perhaps the greatest cigarette-smoking movie ever made, with Mitchum and Douglas standing face-to-face and smoking at each other. There's a scene where Douglas offers Mitchum a smoke and Mitchum holds up his cigarette and says, "Smoking." It always gets a laugh.

Did you guys have any idea of doing a running gag involving cigarette smoking? I asked.

"No, no."

Because there's more cigarette smoking in this movie than in any other movie I've ever seen.

"We never thought about it. We just smoked. And I'm not impressed by that because I don't, honest to God, know that I've ever actually seen the film."

You've never seen it?

"I'm sure I have, but it's been so long that I don't know."

I asked him about *Night of the Hunter* (1955), the great film directed by Charles Laughton, in which he played the sinister preacher with "LOVE" tattooed on the knuckles of one hand and "HATE" on the other.

"Charles called me up," Mitchum recalled, "and he said, 'Robert? Charles here. I have had before me since yesterday a script that is a totally unremitting, completely unforgivable, flat-out, total, piece of shit.' I replied, 'Present!' So, we made a date and we went out to dinner and that was it. I wanted to shoot it in West Virginia or Ohio, where it was laid. I knew that sort of country, but the budget made it out of the question. And he cast Shelley Winters and I thought that was a bit odd because she was sort of an urbanite from St. Louis or Kansas City or someplace, and I asked, 'Why Shelley Winters?' 'Because we can get her for twenty-five thousand dollars.' I said, 'Okay, man.' And so we went into it and Charles, along with the scenic designer, had stylized all the scenery. For instance, there's one shot where the kids are up in the barn loft and they hear him singing, and they look out and across the horizon they see him riding against the sky. Well, that was done on the sound stage with a miniature pony and a midget."

Are you kidding?

"The scenic design was really incomparable, and Charles was an enormous appreciator, if you understand what I mean. He was like John Huston or people like that. He didn't tell you what to do or what you're thinking. Somebody like Cukor would say, 'Now, he's thinking this, and this...' And I would say, 'Really?' But Charles would just nerve you up and he would be so appreciative that you did it to please him. Honest to God, you know, you did your really best to try to enchant him and of course it was effective. People always want to know why he never directed another picture. He died, that's why."

Mitchum by now had the audience in the palm of his hand. If he had affection for Laughton, there were many film icons he took with a grain of salt. David Lean, for example: "David would sit there in his chair, thinking. Thinking. Sitting. Thinking. For hours. Once on *Lawrence of Arabia* he was shooting in Jordan and they had to pick up the chair and carry him off in a pickup truck. A war had broken out."

He wasn't a spin doctor, turning memories into public relations. Asked how he would compare his work in the 1962 version of *Cape Fear* with Robert De Niro's performance in the same role in Martin Scorsese's 1991 remake, he said, "I've never seen it."

The Scorsese version?

"Neither one, as a matter of fact."

Somebody in the audience asked him about Marilyn Monroe, and his face softened.

"I loved her," he said. "I had known her since she was about fifteen or sixteen years old. My partner on the line at the Lockheed plant in Long Beach was her first husband. That's when I first met her. And I knew her all the way through. And she was a lovely girl; very, very shy. She had what is now recognized as agoraphobia. She was terrified of going out among people. At that time they just thought she was being difficult. But she had that psychological, psychic fear of appearing among people. That's why when she appeared in public, she always burlesqued herself. She appeared as you would hope that she would appear. She was a very sweet, loving and loyal, unfortunately loyal, girl. Loyal to people who used her, and a lot who misused her."

And what about Humphrey Bogart? someone asked. Did you know him?

"Yes, I knew him. Bogey and I were pretty good

friends. One time he said to me, 'You know, the difference between you and me and those other guys is,
we're funny.'"

There were a lot of academic types from the University of Virginia in the audience, and one of them
asked, "Ah, Mr. Mitchum, given your casual attitude
toward film, what do you think of a festival like this
that studies film critically and analytically?"

"My what?"

"Your casual attitude…"

"Yeah, yeah, I got the casual part. What was the
other part?"

"What do you think of film festivals?"

"They're freak shows. In any community, if somebody notifies the local TV stations that there's a
giraffe loose in their backyard, the whole populace
turns up."

Mitchum exhaled and looked at the audience as if
they were looking at a giraffe.

32   BIG JOHN WAYNE

THE FIRST TIME I saw John Wayne, he was striding toward me out of the Georgia sun as helicopters landed behind him. His face was a deep brown. He was wearing a combat helmet, an ammo belt, had a canteen on his hip, was carrying a rifle, and stood six feet four inches. He stuck out his hand and said, "John Wayne." That was not necessary.

John Wayne. When I was a kid, we said it as one word: Johnwayne. Like Marilynmonroe. His name was shorthand for heroism. All of his movies could have been titled *Walking Tall*. He wasn't a cruel and violent action hero. He was almost always a man doing his job. Sometimes he was other than that, and he could be gentle, as in *The Quiet Man*, or vulnerable, as in *The Shootist*, or lonely and obsessed, as in *The Searchers*, or tender with a baby, as in *3 Godfathers*.

He had an effect on people that few other actors ever had. Gene Siskel was interviewing him in the middle of the night during a Chicago location shoot. The Duke had been doing some drinking, to keep warm. At three a.m. he wanted something to eat. "We walked into an all-night greasy spoon," Gene told me. "He threw an arm over my shoulder. I felt protected. We sat down in a booth. The waitress came over, took one look at him, and made the sign of the cross. She was trembling when she asked him what he'd like to have. 'Eggs! And plenty of 'em!' How would he like them? 'Starin' at me!'"

He smoked until he had a lung removed and didn't shy clear of booze. He told me: "Tequila makes your head hurt. Not from your hangover. From falling over and hitting your head." People had this idea he was a reactionary Neanderthal. What they didn't understand is that he could be funny about his politics. Once I was on location for *Chisum* in Durango, Mexico. Clive Hirschhorn of London's *Daily Express* was there, too.

"Duke," he asked, "what do you think about Nixon's policy in Vietnam?"

Wayne sized him up as one of those goddamned hippies.

"I think the president is conducting himself with honor," Wayne said, "and there's only one thing better than honor."

"What's that?"

"In her."

He explained that he was a liberal. "Hell yes, I'm a liberal. I listen to both sides before I make up my mind. Doesn't that make you a liberal? Not in today's terms, it doesn't. These days, you have to be a fucking left-wing radical to be a liberal. Politically, though... I've mellowed."

On that same set, we were playing a chess game, both of us bending over the board on an upended apple crate. Wayne, slouched in his old stitched leather director's chair, had a crowd of kibitzers: wranglers, extras, old cronies, drinking buddies, a couple of Mexican stuntmen. He studied the board, roared with laughter, and said, "God...damn it! "You've trapped my queen!"

We studied the board. I made a decisive move.

"Why the *hell* did I just say that?" he asked. "If I hadn't-a...said it, you wouldn't-a...seen it."

That's how he talked, with pauses in the middle of a sentence. In his documentary *Directed by John Ford*, Peter Bogdanovich quotes him: "I started in silent pictures. One of my teachers was the old character actor Harry Carey. He told me, 'John, the talkies are coming in, and that's a fact of life. Those Broadway playwrights are going to be selling the studios all of their plays. What they don't know is, people can't listen that fast! My theory is, we should stop halfway through a sentence and give the audience a chance to catch up.'"

He was utterly without affectation. He was at home. He could talk to anyone. You couldn't catch him acting. He was lucky to start early, in the mid-1920s, and become at ease on camera years before his first speaking role. He sounded the way he looked. He was a small-town Iowa boy, a college football player. He worked with great directors. He listened to them. He wasn't a sex symbol. He didn't perform, he embodied.

I met him three times officially, on the sets of *The Green Berets* and *Chisum*, and at his home in Newport Beach. And one other time. "Duke is in town to visit a sick friend at the hospital," the Warner Bros. press agent Frank Casey told me one day in 1976. "He wants me to invite over all the movie critics to have a drink. He's got the Presidential Suite at the Conrad Hilton." At a time when movie stars employ security with black belts to keep the press away, how does that sound? We all gathered at the Hilton— Siskel, David Elliott of the *Chicago Daily News*, Mary Knoblauch of *Chicago's American*, and me. "I've been visiting Stepin Fetchit down at Illinois Central Hospital," Wayne told us. "We worked together for the first time in 1929. But I don't want that in the paper. I don't want a goddamned death watch on him. Don't tell Kup! He'll run it in his column!"

What did we discuss? None of us took notes. I recall we discussed some politics. Wayne supported the war in Vietnam. ("I've been over there and I believe what we're doing is necessary.") He was a defender of Nixon. He was a born conservative, but in an old-fashioned, simple, and patriotic way. He would have had contempt for the latter-day weirdos of today's Right.

His big, masculine, leather-brass-and-wood hilltop home in Newport Beach stood guard over his yacht, a converted navy minesweeper. One end of the room was occupied by Wayne's big wooden desk, piled with books, papers, letters, and scripts. There was an antique army campaign table with a bronze sculpture of cowboys on it. The walls were lined with cabinets, bookcases, an antique firearm collection, and a display of trophies and awards. Wayne went in the kitchen, brought out tequila and ice, and gave me a tour. He pointed out autographed photos of Eisenhower, Nixon, Goldwater, and J. Edgar Hoover. I said I had to take a pee. On the wall of the bathroom opening off the den, he had a photo of Hubert Humphrey, inscribed "With warm appreciation for your continued support."

Waiting on the other side of the room, he showed me his firearm collection. "This is my rifle from *Stagecoach*," he said. "I always kept it. In *True Grit*, I spun it like this."

He took the rifle in his right hand and spun it. Pain crossed his face.

"Jesus Christ!" he said. He replaced the rifle on its rack and massaged his shoulder. "Jesus, I wrecked that shoulder. Down in Baton Rouge, when I was making *The Undefeated*, I twisted around in the saddle and the damn stirrup was completely loose. I fell right under that goddamned horse; I'm lucky I didn't kill myself."

He took another rifle for inspection. "And this," he said, "is the weapon the Russians are sending to kill our boys in Vietnam. People just won't see we're at war over there. Win or lose. Look at that—isn't that a mean-looking rifle? It's a good one, too. And this is the piece of shit we're giving our boys to shoot back with. But people just won't realize. I heard a poem the other day. How did it go? 'Every day I pray, I won't go my complacent way...' Hell, I can't remember it all. Something to the effect of, I'll never let those kids down.

"Jesus, that was a terrible thing about Gloria and Jimmy Stewart's kid getting killed over there. It makes you want to cry. At least Jimmy was over there to see the kid a few months ago. That's something. But it makes you want to cry. And Bob Taylor's going was terrible. He was terminal since they opened him up. I know what he went through. They ripped a lung out of me. I thank God I'm still here.

"All the real motion picture people have always made family pictures. But the deadbeats and the so-called intelligentsia got in when the government stupidly split up the production companies and the theaters. The old giants—Mayer, Thalberg, even Harry Cohn, despite the fact that personally I couldn't stand him—were good for this industry. Now the goddamned stock manipulators have taken over. They don't know a goddamned thing about making movies. They make something dirty, and it makes money, and they say, 'Jesus, let's make one a little dirtier, maybe it'll make more money.' And now even the bankers are getting their noses into it. I'll give you an example. Take that girl Julie Andrews, a sweet, openhearted girl, a wonderful performer. Her stint was *Mary Poppins* and *The Sound of Music*. But she wanted to be a Theda Bara. And they went along with her, and the picture fell flat on its ass. A Goldwyn would have told her, 'Look, my dear, you can't change your sweet and lovely image...'"

An eager white puppy hurried into the room. Wayne snapped his fingers and the puppy ran to him. "Hey, little fella." The puppy growled and rolled over on its back. "His name's Frosty," Wayne said. "Belongs to my daughter Aissa." He played with the puppy.

"But you know," he said, "I'm very conscious that people criticize Hollywood. Yet we've created a form, the Western, that can be understood in every country. The good guys against the bad guys. No nuances. And the horse is the best vehicle of action in our medium. You take action, a scene, and scenery and cut them together, and you never miss. Action, scene, scenery. And a horse."

Frosty began to chew on the carpet. "Hey, you, get away from there!" Wayne said. The puppy looked up inquisitively and resumed chewing.

"I ought to get him some rawhide to keep him busy," Wayne said. "But when you think about the Western, it's an American art form. It represents what this country is about. In *True Grit*, for example, that scene where Rooster shoots the rat. That was a kind of reference to today's problems. Oh, not that *True Grit* has a message or anything. But that scene was about less accommodation and more justice. They keep bringing up the fact that America's for the downtrodden. But this new thing of genuflecting to the downtrodden, I don't go along with that. We ought to go back to praising the kids who get good grades, instead of making excuses for the ones who shoot the neighborhood grocery man. But, hell, I don't want to get started on that— Hey, you!"

The puppy looked up from a sofa leg. Wayne captured it and shooed it out through the sliding glass doors onto the patio. "The little fella was smelling around the wrong way there. But back to *True Grit*. Henry Hathaway used the backgrounds in such a way that it became a fantasy. Remember that scene where old Rooster is facing those four men across the meadow, and he takes the reins in his teeth and charges? 'Fill your hands, you son of a bitch!' That's Henry at work. It's a real meadow, but it looks almost dreamlike. Henry made it a fantasy and yet he kept it an honest Western."

Wayne sipped at his tequila absentmindedly. "You get something of that in the character of Rooster," he said. "Well, they say he's not like what I've done before. Even I say that, but he does have facets of the John Wayne character, huh? I think he does. Of course, they give me that John Wayne stuff so much. They claim I always play the same role. Seems like nobody remembers how different the fellas were in *The Quiet Man*, or *Iwo Jima*, or *Yellow Ribbon*, where I was thirty-five playing a man of sixty-five. To stay a star, you have to bring along some of your own personality. Thousands of good actors can carry a scene, but a star has to carry the scene and still allow some of his character into it. What do you think?"

It was uncanny being asked by John Wayne what I thought about the John Wayne image. What came to mind was a scene in *True Grit* where Wayne and Kim Darby are waiting all night up on a hill for the bad guys to come back to the cabin. And Wayne gets to talking about how he was married once, to a grass widow back in Cairo, Illinois, and how she took off one day. And how he didn't care much, how he missed her some, but he'd rather lose a wife than his independence. And how he took off alone, glad to be alone, and stuck up a bank or two, just to stake himself, back in the days before he took up marshaling. And Darby asks him about those old days, about how he got to where he was now. It's a scene that echoes back to Howard Hawks's *El Dorado*, in which old hand Wayne teaches young James Caan how to hold a gun and shoot it. But the *True Grit* scene is even more nostalgic. It's a summation of the dozens of Western characters played by Wayne. That's what I told him, anyway.

"Well," Wayne said. "Well, maybe so. I guess that scene in *True Grit* is about the best scene I ever did." He sprawled on a cracked leather sofa. "And that ending," he said, pouring a few more drops of tequila, "I liked that. You know, in the book Mattie loses her hand from the snakebite, and I die, and the last scene in the book has her looking at my grave. But the way Marguerite Roberts wrote the screenplay, she gave it an uplift. Mattie and Rooster both go to visit her family plot, after she gets cured of the snakebite. By now it's winter. She offers to let Rooster be buried there someday, seeing as how he has no family of his own. Rooster's happy to accept, long as he doesn't have to take her up on it any too quick. So then he gets on his horse and says, 'Come and see a fat old man some time.' And then he spurs the horse and jumps a fence, just to show he still can."

He was a totally nontheoretical actor. He never studied his craft. He became good at it because he went out into Monument Valley a great many times with Ford, and they made some of the greatest American movies without giving it much more thought than the whiskey and the poker games and the campfires with which they occupied their evenings. Those were Wayne's great days, when Pappy and his wagon train camped out in the desert, far from Hollywood and its agents and moguls, and made what they used to call cowboy pictures.

On-screen he held so much authority so that he was not being ironic when he explained his theory of acting: "Don't act. React." John Wayne could react. Other actors had to strain the limits of their craft to hold the screen with him. There is this test for an actor who, for a moment, is just standing there in a scene: Does he seem to be just standing there? Or does he, as John Wayne did, seem to be deciding when, why, and how to take the situation under his control?

His last picture was called *The Shootist*, in 1976. He played an old gunfighter who had fought his way through the West for a lifetime and had finally come to a small town and was filled with the fear of dying. He went to the doctor, played by James Stewart, learned that he had weeks to live, and conducted himself during those days with strength and dignity. There was one other movie he wanted to make, and never made, that he talked about once. It didn't have a title and it didn't need a title, not in Wayne's mind. It would simply have been one last movie directed by John Ford, who died in 1973 with Wayne at his bedside.

"God, that was a loss to me when Pappy died," Wayne told me. "Up until the very last years of his life, Pappy could have directed another picture, and a damned good one. But they said Pappy was too old. Hell, he was never too old. In Hollywood these days, they don't stand behind a fella. They'd rather make a goddamned legend out of him and be done with him."

John Wayne died on June 11, 1979. He had lived for quite a while on one lung, and then the Big C came back. He was near death and he knew it when he walked out onstage at the 1979 Academy Awards to present Best Picture to *The Deer Hunter*, a film he wouldn't have made. He looked frail, but he planted himself there and sounded like John Wayne.

33   "IRVING! BRANG 'EM ON!"

IT'S BEEN MANY years since Billy "Silver Dollar" Baxter last graced the Cannes Film Festival, and yet I never go there without imagining him beckoning to me across the bar of the Hotel Majestic. Billy created an alternate reality at Cannes, and such was the force of his personality that those who came within earshot were seduced.

Billy was a loudmouth operator from the pages of Damon Runyon. His gift was creating scenarios to entertain us. He didn't want our money, he didn't want publicity, he didn't want a free lunch, he only wanted to know that we would pass around the latest "Billy Baxter story." We are still passing them around. Billy is still alive, and we are in touch. He lives not far from Broadway, which is to Billy as the stream is to the trout, and posts countless New York photos on his Facebook page, but all of my stories about him will be set at Cannes, because that was his stage, and he was the player on it.

I was never sure what Billy did, or even how he earned a living, although there were many, many stories. I will tell you that he was never short of funds and never committed any crimes that I heard about, and if Billy had committed any crimes, we would have heard about it from him. The closest he came to describing his occupation was informing me, "The president of American Express is an old buddy-boy of mine." I met him the first time I went to Cannes, in the mid-1970s. I walked into the American Bar of the Hotel Majestic and heard my name resounding in the air: *Ro-jay Eggplant! Get over here! Irving! Brang 'em on! Johnnie Walker! Black Label! Generous portion! Clean glass! Pas de soda! Pas de ice! And clear off this shit and bring us some of those little olives! And some better peanuts!*

A pink-faced man with an Irish pompadour was patting the chair next to him. I had never seen him before. "Sit down right here, Monsieur Eeebair! You know the sexy Miss Carroll, dontcha?" I did. He was seated next to Kathleen Carroll, the film critic of the *New York Daily News*. He never introduced her as his girlfriend. That would have been too mundane. She was described only in compliments: *The love of my life. The most beautiful woman in France. She makes me the envy of every guy in Cannes. Catherine Denouveau, get outta of town!* It was Billy's opinion that every man in Cannes and everywhere else lusted for Kathleen, who was protected from their predations only by his vigilance. Kathleen was indeed lovely, soft-spoken, smart, conservatively dressed. It amazed us that she had taken up with the closest thing to Nathan Detroit that any of us would ever meet. When Billy was in the Majestic bar, he owned it. It was his headquarters. All the top stars and producers visited there, and he kept an eagle eye on the arrivals, grandly introducing mispronounced people he had never met. *Lord Low Grade, meet John Weisenheimer! Boop-a-doop!* He did this with such confidence that these strangers felt strangely pleased to be assigned supporting roles in his act.

Silver Dollar Baxter got his nickname because he arrived at Cannes every year with countless American silver dollars, which he bestowed as tips. "You think this is something?" he told me. "You shoulda seen what I paid in air freight. I gotta ship them in advance, because you try to get through customs with silver dollars, you're gonna be explaining things for hours. My banker handles it."

"Do you call your banker Irving?"

"Yeah. Irving Trust."

Billy had decided some years earlier that all waiters in every saloon in the world were named Irving, and every establishment he entered became a saloon: the Majestic, the Hotel Carlton, Félix, Le Moulin de Mougins, the Grand Hotel du Cap d'Antibes, the Casino des Fleurs, La Pizza, every single one. The Hotel du Cap, or *Hotel du Cap Gun*, was so exclusive in those days it refused all credit cards and personal checks. Only payment in cash was accepted. Movie moguls arrived with their valets padlocked to briefcases. Madonna once had the pool cleared for her morning dip. Prince Albert of Monaco was said to run a tab. Billy reduced this splendor to its essence: *Irving! Brang 'em on!* He never asked someone if he could buy them a drink. He announced it from across the room. *Irving! Take care of Francis Ford Chrysler over there! And set 'em up for Prince Albert in a can! Whatever he's having. Doo-blays!*

Did this cause offense? Did security men in tuxedos form a human wall and walk him out of the room? Not at all. The waiters snapped to attention. Everyone in the room grinned. Billy got away with it by daring to do it at all. It took confidence, timing, nerve, and above all style. So great was Billy's generosity that other customers began to take his hospitality for granted and would sign his room number to their own bar bills. To stop such fraud, Billy appeared at the 1982 festival with a small rubber stamp that reproduced his signature and added underneath, "None genuine without this mark."

Billy had a genius for sweeping up people who had no idea who he was and introducing them to other people he wanted to meet. "Sir Lord!" he boomed one night to Lord Grade, the millionaire head of England's largest film company. "I want you to meet Miss Boop-a-Doop-a-Dee from Venezuela." Instead of remembering names, he often simply improvised them, along with identities, credits, and national origin. "She directed the winning film in last year's festival. That's why she gets to come to the bar in her underwear." Miss Boop-a-Doop-a-Dee was, in fact, Edy Williams, Russ Meyer's ex-wife who posed wearing a bikini while standing in the town's public fountains. Lord Grade looked prepared to believe that she was a director from Venezuela. He looked prepared to believe almost anything about her.

One morning around eleven, Billy was in the Majestic bar reading that day's Cannes edition of *Screen International*. "I see here that Lord Low Grade is back in town," he announced. "He's taking delivery on his new yacht." He looked up to see Lord Grade entering the room at that moment.

Uncharacteristically, Billy did not order him a drink or introduce him to Gérard Belowpardieu. "Irving! Hotel stationery! Fountain pen! On the doo-blay! Hup, hup, hup!" The embossed stationery was produced, and Billy composed a letter:

Dear Lord Lew, All arrangements are in order for the maiden voyage of your lordship's yacht. I have been successful in inviting the top film critics of England and America to join you. They are eager to learn about your legendary show business career.

As of today, I have confirmations from Kathleen Carroll and Rex Reed of the <u>New York Daily News</u>, *Charles Champlin of the* <u>Los Angeles Times</u>, *George Anthony of the* <u>Toronto Sun</u>, *Alexander Walker of the* <u>London Evening Standard</u>, *Richard and Mary Corliss of* <u>Time</u> *magazine, Andrew Sarris of the* <u>Village Voice</u>, *Molly Haskell of* <u>Vogue</u>, *and Roger Ebert of the* <u>Chicago Sun-Times</u>. *I have told them to keep tomorrow morning free for embarkation. Please have your office send cars to the front entrance of the Majestic at about 10.*

He signed the letter, called for a candle, dripped wax on the flap, and sealed it with his ring.

"Billy, this is the most insane stunt you've ever pulled," Rex Reed said.

"Be in front of the hotel on time, sexy Rexy, or the ship sails without you."

The next morning, Lord Grade's Mercedes limos arrived on time, and we lined up and piled in, ready for our audience with the man who made *Raise the Titanic*, of which it was said, it would have been cheaper to lower the ocean. We motored down the Croisette and twenty miles along the coast, past the Hotel du Cap, toward the yacht harbor at Antibes. The limos pulled up to the harbor, and there was Grade, pacing nervously by his gangplank, wearing grey flannel trousers, a blue blazer, and a Panama hat. In his hand was one of the twenty-five-dollar cigars he stored in the vaults of Davidoff on Jermyn Street.

"I was growing nervous," Grade said. "I thought perhaps you hadn't been able to find the yacht."

"You kidding?" Baxter asked. "A yacht this size, you could fire off a machine gun."

Baxter led his parade of film critics aboard, held an inspection of the ship's crew, which was standing at attention, and passed out flight bags that said American Express on them. These bags, Billy explained, were priceless. They were a limited edition, authorized personally by his old buddy-boy the president of American Express. They would become invaluable collector's items. He had been authorized to place them in the hands of people with the highest prestige, so that simply by carrying them, they would lend luster to the reputation of American Express.

The yacht crew politely accepted their bags. Grade looked on balefully. Billy hesitated, then gave him one. For three or four hours, we sailed offshore from Antibes to Cannes. Far away across the blue waters of the Côte d'Azur, the hapless tenants of the Hotel du Cap shaded their eyes on the verandas of their thousand-dollar rooms and squinted at us rocking at anchor.

"I have been thinking," Grade told us, "of writing my autobiography. My life has been filled with coincidences. When I began in London, for example, I had an office across from the Palladium. Now I own the Palladium."

"What an amazing coincidence," Rex Reed said.

"I began as a dancer," Grade said. "I did a double act with my brother, Lord Delfont. I was a natural at the Charleston, but for the others I had to finesse. It was called 'eccentric dancing.' Like this."

He stood up, clasped his hands above his head, and bumped to an imaginary rhythm.

"We played Paris, Germany...we were always broke. Those were the days. I remember I was in love with twins. Two lovely girls. Dancers. I couldn't make up my mind between them."

Luncheon drew to a leisurely close. I sat in a deck chair next to Alex Walker, dozed off in the midday sun, and was awakened by a quickening tempo in Lord Grade's voice.

"Television—television!" he was saying. "What an impact. With one successful program, we reach ten times as many people as with a hit movie. My most successful television program was, of course, *Jesus of Nazareth*, directed for me by Franco Zeffirelli. Do you know that a survey was taken of 6,525 people? Forty percent of them said they had learned the most about Jesus from my program. Twenty-one percent named the Bible. Thirty percent named the church."

"That leaves nine percent undecided," Rex Reed said.

"Some of them saw it twice."

Billy's method was to boldly cut through bureaucracy. One year he issued his own credentials to the festival. This was in connection with a television special he had convinced Lord Grade to bankroll. "These Frenchies are hung up on anything that looks official," he said. "They issue you a permit to take a shit. But half the guards can't read, and besides, they don't have time, because there's always a commie riot going on." Billy printed up official-looking credentials for the "World International Television Network." He attached the photographs of his friends to the cards, had them laminated, and we wore them around our necks. Every one of Billy's friends was exactly the same height, weight, and age, and had the same hair and eye color. "What this document certifies," he explained to us, "is that it is worn by the bearer."

Every year the Marché issues a little booklet with the names of key industry figures, their hotels, and the words "buying" or "selling." I decided to do a story about a Seller and a Buyer. I knew one of each, and they agreed to allow me to observe, as long as I agreed to keep all dollar amounts "symbolic." The Seller was Dusty Cohl, a friend from Toronto whom I'd met at Cannes 1977. He presided on the Carlton terrace in much the same way that Billy ran the Majestic. Ambassadors were exchanged between the two fiefdoms, and Billy and Dusty exchanged signing privileges on each other's tabs. Dusty was selling a Canadian film named *Outrageous!*, which starred Craig Russell as a drag performer who befriends a helpless waif. The Buyer was Baxter, partnered with a kindly older man named Herb Steinman, who had made his money in aspirin, and whose wife, Anna, was Jack Nicholson's psychoanalyst.

"Herb is my buddy-boy back home," Baxter

explained. "I bring him here, he smiles at the dollies, he takes his wife out to dinner."

On the morning when Billy was to welcome Dusty in the Majestic bar, I sat with Herb beside the Majestic's pool. A starlet approached and stood beside Herb's deck chair. She was topless. Herb turned his head and found that he was staring directly at a nipple. "I'll take the one with the pink nose," he said. Billy materialized and took Herb into the bar for a conference of war.

"Herb, you know and I know that this is a hot film. But does Dusty know that? This is his first time up against experienced operators like ourselves. Okay. What do we use for openers? We say, when we bought Lina Wisenheimer's *Love and Anarchy*, we paid two hundred thousand dollars for the U.S. rights, and we cleaned up. So we gotta tell Dusty we will only pay him half of what we paid for *Love and Anarchy*, right?"

"Sounds okay to me, Billy," said Steinman.

"Only get this. What we tell him is, we only paid *half* of what we did pay for *Love and Anarchy*—so that in offering him half, we're really offering him a *quarter*, right? Fifty thousand?"

"In other words," said Steinman, "twenty-five percent. That's very simple, Billy."

"You got it," said Billy. "We tell him half, but we

tell him half of half. Okay. We're all set. Here he comes now."

Dusty Cohl walked into the bar and sat down. He was dressed for business, with a grey summer suit, a black cowboy hat, and a Dudley Do-Right T-shirt. He passed around cigars.

"Irving! Brang 'em on!" Baxter shouted. "Bring Mr. Cohl here whatever he wants and doop-a-dop-a-doo for everybody else."

Dusty opened by pleading innocence: "I'm a guy who is new to this, I'm feeling my way, I'm learning as I go along, and maybe we can make a deal that will make everyone happy."

"Cut the crap," Baxter said. "You got a piece of shit here about a Canadian pricksickle aficionado, and nobody wants it. You're talking to the guys who put Lina Boop-a-doop on the map. How much you want for this movie?"

"I was thinking fifty grand up front, against some guarantees and percentages," Cohl said.

Baxter was stunned. Cohl had opened by asking for what Baxter was prepared to open with. In his mind, his $50,000 opener should instantly be reduced by another 50 percent, to $25,000.

Steinman spoke: "Dusty, we can only give you half of *Love and Anarchy*."

Baxter's face turned pink. "Irving!" he cried.

416

"On the double!" This was a diversionary tactic. He turned to his partner. "Herb," he said intensely. "Think. Think! We can only give *half* of *Love and Anarchy*. Do you see what I mean?"

"That's right, Billy, half of *Love and Anarchy*."

"Not half, Herb—*half*!"

"Like I say, half."

Dusty Cohl sat patiently.

"*HALF!* Of *Love and Anarchy*!" Baxter repeated, desperately trying to get Steinman to read his mind.

I did the mental arithmetic. Billy was trying to get Steinman to make a two-stage transition: (1) To think, not half of the real original price, which would have been $100,000, or half of that price, which would have been $50,000, but (2) half of that, which would have been $25,000—one-eighth of the actual price of *Love and Anarchy*. Then, presumably, Cohl would make a counteroffer, and they would negotiate from there. But could Steinman make the mental leap?

"Right, Billy," said Steinman. "I know what you're saying. Half of *Love and Anarchy*."

"But are you talking half," Billy asked urgently, "or are you talking *half*? Think real hard, Herb."

"I'm talking half of half, aren't I?"

"No! Not half of half! *Half of half of half!*"

"This is not sounding good," said Cohl.

Baxter leaned forward, trying to project his thoughts into Steinman's mind.

"The original half?" asked Steinman.

"The revised original half," said Baxter.

"Half of that?"

"Herb! Think! Half of *Love and Anarchy*. Do you know what I'm thinking when I say the word 'half'?"

"That's not the problem," Steinman said.

"Then what's the problem?"

"Billy," Herb said slowly, "I know what you mean when you say the word 'half.' But suddenly, I don't know what you mean when you say the word 'all.'"

Near the end of that year's festival, Edy Williams had to worry about how to ship herself home. She'd received a publicity bonanza by taking off her clothes while standing on a roulette table at the Casino des Fleurs, but her appearances were pro bono, and she was broke. She had been flown to Cannes by a Japanese syndicate hopeful that an Edy Williams poster would run up sales to equal Farrah Fawcett's best seller, but the poster proved too racy for the teenage boy market, and the Japanese fled town. Billy got wind of this development. "She's a sweet kid," he said. "I told her to meet me at Félix and we'd have a little chat." I went along, having known Edy since the fateful day in 1969 when I introduced her to Russ Meyer in the Twentieth Century–Fox commissary. Billy commandeered booth #1 in the window at the cost of a silver dollar, and greeted Edy when she arrived in full starlet regalia.

"Hi, handsome," she said to Billy.

"Sit down right here and tell me about your problems," Billy said. "I got you sitting in the window, you might be discovered."

"Oooooh, Billy!" she said, running her long red nails up the sleeve of his blazer and teasing the nape of his neck. Edy not only spoke like a starlet in the movies, she had been a starlet in the movies. She was now being profiled as the Last Hollywood Starlet, which was true. There was a time when Hollywood studios had dozens of starlets under contract. Fox was the last studio to continue that tradition, and Edy had been their last starlet.

"Irving," said Baxter, "brang Miss Boop-a-Doop here some champagne. None of that French crap. Look at this joint. Last year, you couldn't fight your way in here, with all the Iranians. Now they're at home with the Allhetoldya Cockamamie. Irving! And the menu! What do you recommend, apart from another restaurant?"

"Oh, Billy, you always know what to say," Edy said.

"Always thinking of you, sweetheart," said Baxter. "What'd you spill all over your boobs?"

"Gold sparkle. It's the latest thing. But, Billy, I was thinking. You know, I'm not in my twenties anymore. I was wondering if maybe my bikini routine is getting a little dated."

"What bikini routine? You mean where you walk outside and take off your bikini?"

"I was thinking of a new image for my thirties."

"I can't believe my ears," Billy said. "We're talking about the girl who jumped into the ring before the Ali-Spinks fight and took off her clothes in front of seventy thousand people in the Superdome."

"They were caught completely by surprise," Edy said.

"What did it feel like?" asked Baxter. "I'll bet you are the only person in history to take off her clothes in front of seventy thousand people. At the same time, anyway."

"The worst part was right before I did it," Edy said. "I was standing at ringside, and I was scared. What if they didn't like it? What if everybody booed? Or didn't pay any attention!"

"That's gotta be every girl's nightmare," said Baxter.

"But it was the most unbelievable sensation, when I was in the ring and they were all cheering," she said. "I knew what Ali must feel like."

"Irving," said Silver Dollar Baxter, "look at these flowers on the table. It looks like you picked them up off of the street."

Edy brushed at her glitter absentmindedly. "I'm stranded and heartbroken," she said. "When the Japanese left, they took my airplane ticket with them. What am I gonna doooo, Billy?"

"You're gonna hold a sale."

"A sale? Of what?"

"Answer me this. How much you need to fly home?"

"There's a cheap fare for nine hundred dollars."

"You got any posters left?"

"Almost all of them."

"Okay. You had a sale. You marked them down to one dollar, and you sold me nine hundred of them."

"Ooooo, Billy!"

The next morning, the phone in my room rang. "Ro-jay Eggplant! Get over here to the Majestic lobby. I'm holding my ceremonial departure."

Half an hour later, I found Billy waiting in the American Bar.

"Irving! Talk to the concerturdgie. Tell him I want the staff all lined up in the lobby so I can leave them with a little forget-me-not."

He went upstairs to his room. A line of waiters, barmen, cooks, and doormen formed. The elevator doors opened. A bellboy emerged with a luggage cart, followed by Billy Baxter, who presented every one of them with an Edy Williams poster.

34 INGMAR BERGMAN

WHEN I WAS finally home for good from the hospital, I recalled Norman Cousins's famous account of how he was healed by laughing at Marx Brothers movies. I found I was cheered by the existential dread of Ingmar Bergman. My shoulder hurt too much for me to sit at my desktop computer, and Chaz found me a "zero gravity" chair where I could sit effortlessly for hours. I rested a thin wooden lap desk on the arms, and it became my workstation and still is.

I began to watch Bergman movies. I began with the Death of God trilogy (*Through a Glass Darkly*, *The Silence*, *Winter Light*) and continued through *The Passion of Anna* and *Hour of the Wolf*. These were on DVDs from the Criterion Collection, playing on an HD television, and although I'd seen them all at least two or three times, I had never seen such a clear picture. I knew what the stories contained and how they were told, but the startling clarity of the black-and-white images caused me to admire more than ever the cinematography of Sven Nykvist, Bergman's longtime collaborator.

I froze frames, advanced slowly, noticed the care with which he controlled the light on human faces to a precision of fractions of an inch. The films of the trilogy were more than ever things of beauty. To see them in color would be unthinkable. Although he later made many color films, I wondered if Bergman would have been perceived as a master if he had started that way. The same might be said of Fellini. By losing the choice of black and white, modern directors have been forced to surrender half their palette.

I felt a kinship with Bergman. In his compulsion to ask fundamental questions I sensed the intensity I struggled with in my childhood debates with Catholicism. His father had been a Lutheran pastor, his childhood apparently spare and forbidding, his guilt deep. As an adult he sought completion through women but was not long faithful. Women were like a sacrament he turned to in his state of sin.

Recently hauled back from the jaws of death, I was immune to laughter as a medicine and found some solace in his desperate seekers who confronted profound matters. This was a new stage in my relationship with Bergman. In college I went to the Art Theater to see *The Virgin Spring* and the trilogy in their first runs. I wasn't a prodigy raised on the Internet and DVDs; I learned about film mostly from the reviews in *TIME* magazine and Dwight Macdonald's column in *Esquire* and watched Bergman's films in solemn half comprehension, sure he was asking important questions, unsure exactly what they were. Perhaps they were versions of mankind's original question: *Why?*

In 1967, new in my job at the *Sun-Times*, I walked into the Clark Theater and saw *Persona*. I didn't have a clue how to write about it. I began with a simple description: "At first the screen is black. Then, very slowly, an area of dark grey transforms itself into blinding white. This is light projected through film onto the screen, the first basic principle of the movies. The light flickers and jumps around, finally resolving itself into a crude cartoon of a fat lady." And so on. I was discovering a method that would work with impenetrable films: Focus on what you saw and how it affected you. Don't fake it.

Bergman produced a film a year, writing every winter, filming every summer, working always with the same close-knit family of collaborators. I heard about him firsthand from Ernie Anderson, an old-style publicist who worked only for the clients of Paul Kohner, the legendary independent agent. I met Ernie on a frigid New York location for *Death Wish*, after *Esquire* assigned me to write a profile on Charles Bronson. Curiously, Ernie spent most of two days talking to me about Bergman. Both Bergman and Bronson were Kohner clients, as were Liv Ullmann, John Huston, Nykvist, Max von Sydow, Bronson's wife Jill Ireland, Huston's daughter Anjelica, and so on.

"Ingmar would like to meet you," Ernie said—unlikely because he had probably never heard of me. Ernie, who established Burl Ives as "the most popular folk singer in history," was an expert in creating factoids. On his word the media learned that Bronson was the biggest movie star on earth, and there was a billboard with him on it that stretched for two blocks in Tokyo. Remove "biggest" and "two" and who could argue? Ernie was middle-aged, conservatively dressed, a gentleman, a press agent suitable for the clients of the courtly Kohner from Vienna, who would not subject his clients to the vulgarities of studio publicists. He was old world. He represented John Huston on the basis of a handshake.

Bergman was in the news after he fell into conflict with Sweden's tax laws. I don't recall the details. As the greatest living Swede he was outraged by threats of criminal prosecution, and he went into exile, appearing at a press conference in Rome with Fellini to announce they would make a film together. What I would have given to witness one of their story conferences. Then I read that Bergman was making his first trip to America, and would visit Hollywood.

Ernie called me one day. "You can't repeat this," he said. "Ingmar wanted to visit a working set. Charlie is out here shooting *Breakheart Pass*, and I got Tom Gries to invite him onto the lot. I introduce him to Charlie. They both know I work for them through Kohner. Charlie says, 'This is just an action picture, Mr. Bergman. Nothing like what you make.' Ingmar says, 'No, no! I am fascinated! Tell me what you are doing today.' Charlie says, 'Well, I get shot.' He takes off his shirt and shows his trick vest. 'This vest has these little squibs that explode and release fake blood. But you know all this stuff. You make movies.' Ingmar says, 'No, no! I've never seen this before.' Charlie says, 'You mean...you don't use machine guns in your pictures?'"

Bergman returned to Sweden, the tax business was settled, and in the summer of 1975 Ernie called me from Stockholm with an invitation to visit the set of *Face to Face*. I watched Bergman at work with Nykvist, I spoke to him and Liv Ullmann in their "cells" at the Swedish Film Institute's Film House, and those alone were experiences for a lifetime. But it was Ernie who elevated my trip to another level. He was a priest in the church of Bergman. He pumped me full of observations: How Ingmar had used the same carpenter on every film, how the same woman served tea and biscuits every afternoon on the set, where he lived in Stockholm when he wasn't on his island home of Fårö, how his annual routine was inviolable, how he also directed for the stage, what he ate, how he liked his coffee.

When he is in Stockholm, Ernie lectured me, Bergman lives in an apartment he considers not a home but a dormitory to sleep in while he's making a film. His wife, Ingrid, prepares meals there, but if the Bergmans entertain it is more likely to be at his table in the Theater Grill, a restaurant directly across the street from the back door of the Royal Dramatic Theatre. The table is not easily seen; Ernie took me for lunch there and revealed it behind a large mirrored post, so that Bergman, who could see everyone in the room, would be all but invisible.

During the eight or ten weeks it takes him to direct a film, Ernie said, Bergman awakens around eight and drives to Film House, five minutes' drive from the center of Stockholm. The building is always filled with discussion and activity, much of it centered on the bar of the Laurel and Hardy Pub on the second level, but when Bergman is in residence a certain self-consciousness seems to descend on Film House. It's the same, Ernie said, as when the pope is in the Vatican.

Bergman joins his actors and technicians for breakfast. It is served in a cluttered little room presided over by the hostess, whose job is to make coffee and serve afternoon tea and fuss over people in a motherly sort of way. When you are making a picture about the silence of God, it helps if everyone feels right at home and there's a pot of coffee brewing.

Bergman that summer had directed a production of Mozart's *The Magic Flute* at the Drottningholm Court Theatre, a restored two-hundred-year-old jewel box. We took a steamer through the archipelago to the royal palace, embarking from the pier in front of the Grand Hôtel, dining on what Ernie explained was "the famous steamer steak," also famous for being the only thing on the menu except for herring. What I saw was essentially what Bergman shot for his 1976 film, right down to the wooden waves and the rotating boxes filled with stones to make the sound of thunder.

The next day I visited the set. *Face to Face* was about an attempted suicide by a tormented psychiatrist, played by Liv Ullmann. "For some time now,"

Bergman wrote in a letter to his cast and crew, just before production began, "I have been living with an anxiety which has had no tangible cause." His attempt to work it out led to the screenplay for *Face to Face*, in which the woman faces her terrible dread (common enough in Bergman), attempted to surrender to it (also nothing new), but then transcended it in a small victory over her darker nature. "Ingmar had grown more hopeful lately," Ernie said. "His friends all speculate about it."

The company joined him for coffee. Liv Ullmann was dressed in an old cotton shirt and a full blue denim skirt; she wore no makeup and her hair was tossed back from her forehead as if to make the declaration that she'd been asleep until fifteen minutes earlier. Bergman had met her on a street corner talking to her friend Bibi Andersson, just at the moment he was casting *Persona*. He liked the way the two women fit together and cast them both, on the spot. He and Liv also had a daughter, Linn. That morning she was friendly and plainspoken, more like a mother than a star.

Gunnar Björnstrand, tall and stately in his sixties, gravely considered the room and leafed through his script. He was the squire in *The Seventh Seal* and the father in *Through a Glass Darkly* and was one of the familiar figures in Bergman's repertory company.

"He's been ill," Ernie whispered, "but he came out of retirement to play Ullmann's grandfather. He's responded so well that Bergman has expanded his role."

Katinka Farago, the production manager, a robust woman in her thirties, had no time for coffee; she wanted a moment to speak with Bergman about the next week's production schedule. Katinka came to Stockholm from Hungary in 1956, a refugee, and got a job as Bergman's script girl. He made her production manager a few years later, in charge of all the logistics of time, space, and money. "This is her seventeenth film with Ingmar," Ernie said.

Sven Nykvist was a tall, strong fifty-two, with a beard and a quick smile. He was better dressed than Bergman, but then everyone was. "His friends say Ingmar doesn't spend a hundred dollars a year for personal haberdashery," his publicist Ernie Anderson told me. Nykvist first worked for Bergman on *The Naked Night* in 1953 and had been with him steadily since *The Virgin Spring* in 1959. The two of them together engineered Bergman's long-delayed transition from black and white to color, unhappily in *All These Women* and then triumphantly in *The Passion of Anna* and *Cries and Whispers*.

Nykvist was in demand all over the world, but he always left his schedule open for Bergman. "We've already discussed the new film the year before," he told me, "and then Ingmar goes to his island and writes the screenplay. The next year, we start to shoot, usually about the fifteenth of April. Usually we are the same eighteen people working with him, year after year, one film a year. At the Cannes Film Festival one year, Ingmar was talking with David Lean. 'What kind of crew do you use?' Lean asked him. 'I make my films with eighteen good friends,' said Ingmar. 'That's interesting,' said Lean. 'I make mine with one hundred and fifty enemies.' "

It is rare for Bergman to invite outsiders to one of his sets. It is much more common, during a difficult scene, for him to send one technician after another out to wait in the hall, until the actors are alone with Bergman, Nykvist, a sound man, an electrician, and the scene. "When we were making *Cries and Whispers*," Liv Ullmann told me, "none of the rest of us knew what Harriet Andersson was doing in those scenes of suffering and death. Ingmar would send away everyone except just those few who must be there. When we saw the completed film, we were overwhelmed. It was almost as if those great scenes had been Harriet's secret—which, in a way, they were supposed to be, since in the film she died so much alone."

There was a lunch break precisely at noon. The

director retired to his tiny cell across from the sound stage to eat fresh fruit and think about the afternoon's filming. Liv Ullmann had lunch brought to her dressing room. It was like a co-ed's dorm, with paperback novels turned down to mark the place, letters meant to be answered, and her award as best actress from the New York film critics. She'd ordered open-faced sandwiches and fresh radishes.

"We must close the door and not talk very loudly," she said, "because Ingmar has been edgy this morning. He doesn't want his leading lady talking to some writer during the lunch hour. It's a terrible scene today. It's a scene in which my character has just tried to commit suicide. Now she must face her child. The girl who plays my daughter is so trusting, so sensitive, she reminds me of my daughter. It's hell to get through, this scene.

"The film goes a long way down. It goes to the very bottom, she really does think she's killed herself, and then it comes back up again. It ends with real hope. That's something that Ingmar had hardly ever shown in his films, until quite recently. He was always such a pessimist, and now he begins to see a little light. In the last scene of *Scenes from a Marriage*, for example, when the two people cling to each other in the middle of the night, maybe that's not much, but it's something."

Ullmann, who lived with him for several years, said he didn't look the same on the set these days: "He's mellowed, in a nice way. He's sweeter. Isn't that a funny thing to say about Ingmar Bergman! He's more tolerant. We've all been through some rough times with him, we've had some fights on the set, but if he was wrong, he apologizes. And if one has been wrong oneself, he takes one's hand. Ingmar, they give him a tough time in Sweden. Some of the younger critics, they're so political, they won't praise any film that doesn't reflect their politics. Ingmar is hardly political at all; he's more interested in the insides of people. When we go abroad, we hear all the praise and recognition for his films, and he hardly receives it at all here. We eat the cake and he sits here reading the Swedish papers."

Ernie knocked softly on the door, poked in his head, and said, "Ingmar has a little time."

Ullmann made a face. "His highness!"

Bergman had an army cot, a table and a chair, a bar of chocolate and an apple. He told me he'd been watching television the night before. They had been interviewing Antonioni. He couldn't take his eyes off Antonioni's face. "The most important subject of the cinema is the human face," he said.

35 MARTIN SCORSESE

IN THE AUTUMN of 1967 I had been a film critic for seven months. I walked into "the submarine," the long, narrow, dark screening room knocked together out of plywood by the Chicago International Film Festival. I was twenty-five. The festival's founder, Michael Kutza, was under thirty. Everything was still at the beginning. I saw a movie named *I Call First*, later to be retitled *Who's That Knocking at My Door*. If I was sure of anything, it was that it was the work of a natural director. I wrote a review suggesting he would become "the American Fellini" and a few days later received a call from its director, Martin Scorsese. What I'd seen had started as a short film he made as a student at NYU and then lengthened into a feature on a shoestring. The term "indie" hadn't come into its present use, and there was no category to assign; Scorsese was another of the children of John Cassavetes who found that you could make your own film in your own way for very little money.

I looked him up not long after when I was in New York. We were the same age but I realized his understanding of movies was much deeper than my own. A daily critic tends to go wide. A director like Scorsese tends to go deep. There would never be a time we met when I didn't learn something useful and true about the cinema. He was filled with enthusiasm. He had a joy about directing that was much more than simple ambition. He didn't seem concerned with money. He defined success as being able to make the films he wanted to make. Scorsese was part of that generation that began immediately after Cassavetes and the French New Wave demonstrated that films could be made outside the studio system. They wanted to make the Great American Movie; too soon they were joined by a generation that wanted to make the Great Weekend Hit.

He was slight and filled with energy. He was funny. He was a creature of New York. The first time I went to his house, he was living in a high-rise next to the Russian Tea Room and his living room was jammed with video equipment I had never seen before, allowing him to project on a big screen. Of course there was also a 16 mm projector. To some degree his house was a screening room with sleeping and kitchen accommodations.

That first time we met in New York, he took me to visit his job, as an assistant director and editor on Michael Wadleigh's *Woodstock*. The footage from Woodstock was being edited by a team headed by Thelma Schoonmaker, later to become the editor of Scorsese's features, and Walter Murch, a tall young man with a mustache who would later reinvent the strategy of sound design. In a top-floor loft in Soho, reached by a freight elevator, a headquarters had been cobbled together with a skylight and a lot of little rooms off the big one. "You know what picture was cut in this loft?" Scorsese asked me. "They made *Greetings* in this loft." That was the De Palma movie with Robert De Niro in his first role. So much was still ahead. The loft was a crazy, jumbled place, with earnest young editors bending over their Kellers. "The Keller Editing Machine," I was told. "The finest editing machine in the world, and the only one you can use to cut three-screen footage with eight-track synch sound, with thirty-five-millimeter and sixteen-millimeter film on the same machine at the same time."

There was a stir at the elevator door. Bill Graham,

proprietor of the Fillmore East and West rock venues, had arrived. Graham was then the biggest rock promoter in the country. He'd come to see rushes from the movie, rough cuts of acts he managed. Everybody went into the projection room, which was lined with sheets of soundproofing, with a big screen on the wall and speakers underneath it. They had three projectors lined up and synchronized, so that from the rushes Graham could see how the movie would look with the split screen technique. The soundproofing in the doorway was cut out in the shape of Mike Wadleigh with his hat on, which I figured out when Wadleigh walked through it and fit. Graham's people sat on the sofa, the rest on the floor. The lights went out and the first rushes were of Richie Havens.

On my next trip to New York, Marty took me down to Little Italy, the neighborhood where he had been born. We pushed our way through streets crowded for the feast of San Gennaro and into an Italian restaurant where he was known, although for being a neighborhood kid, not a director. His first film, now retitled *Who's That Knocking at My Door*, hadn't yet found distribution. He gave me a briefing on some of the other customers. I found out what it meant to be a "made man." I sensed an alertness in the air, as if some of these diners at their tables were aware of one another in a special way involving offstage roles.

Marty mailed me screenplays titled *Jerusalem, Jerusalem* and *Season of the Witch*, which was later to become *Mean Streets*. One night during the New York Film Festival he and I and Pauline Kael ended up in my hotel room, drinking and talking, and his passion was equaled by hers. Pauline became urgent in her support of those filmmakers she believed deserved it. She sensed something in Scorsese. Her review in the *New Yorker* of *Mean Streets* would put him once and for all on the map.

Her connections were crucial. One night we met in the lobby of the Algonquin and went out to eat with Brian De Palma, Robert De Niro, and Paul Schrader. De Palma and De Niro had made two low-budget films. Did Marty, De Palma, De Niro, and Schrader know one another at that time? Certainly. Did anyone guess *Raging Bull* would result? Pauline must have sensed the mixture was volatile. We went to an Italian restaurant. Pauline was then between her jobs at *McCall's* and the *New Yorker*; De Niro and De Palma were unemployed; and Schrader was a hopeful screenwriter. Thinking I was the only person at the table with a paycheck, I picked up the tab. "You dummy," Pauline told me. "Paul just sold *The Yakuza* for $450,000." She always knew about the deals.

Scorsese and I were born five months apart in 1942, into worlds that could not have differed more, but in important ways we had similar childhoods. We were children of working-class parents well aware of their ethnic origins. We attended Roman Catholic schools and churches that, in those pre–Vatican II days, would have been substantially similar. We memorized the Latin of the Mass, we were drilled on mortal sins, venial sins, sanctifying grace, the fires of hell; we memorized great swaths of the Baltimore Catechism. We were baffled by the concept of Forever and asked how it was that God could have no beginning and no end. We were indoors children, not gifted at sports: "That boy always has his nose buried in a book."

We went to the movies all the time, in my case because television came unusually late to my hometown, in Scorsese's because to begin with his father took him, and then he went on his own, sometimes daily, watching anything and learning from it, watching WOR-TV when the Movie of the Week was repeated all week and he watched every screening. He became fascinated by the details. He told me about a single shot of Deborah Kerr in Powell and Pressburger's *Black Narcissus* that arrested his attention. It was a close-up of Kerr, but mysteriously more than a close-up. Something had happened there, and he couldn't see what it was or how it was done, but he could sense it. Years later, he was to enlist Michael

Powell as a consultant and discover the answer to his question. Powell told him he had told Kerr to stand up into the shot and then had edited to start the shot one frame before she arrived, so there was an invisible urgency in her appearance. Powell and Thelma Schoonmaker of course met each other, and to general delight began a happy marriage. All ahead on that night in the loft.

When I saw Marty's first film, why did it have such an emotional impact on me? I wasn't reacting to its greatness, but to something more fundamental and personal. I had so much in common with J.R., its hero, played by Harvey Keitel. I, too, idealized women but shied away from sexuality. In high school there were some girls I dated and some girls I furtively "made out" with, and they were not the same girls. I associated sex with mortal sin. I understood why J.R. could have nothing more to do with a young woman after he discovered she had been raped. She had been touched in a way that meant J.R. could not touch her, and he blamed her. By the late 1960s I identified with the camaraderie of the friends J.R. ran with. Drinking had melted my solitary shyness and replaced it with shallow bravado. I identified with the movie's rock and roll, and indeed *I Call First* was the first movie I recall seeing with a sound track that was not a composed score, but cobbled together from

45 rpm records. The energy of the cutting grabbed me with the opening shots when the fight broke out and the handheld camera followed it down the sidewalk. Everything about that movie touched me, heart and soul. I had seen great films, I had in truth seen *greater* films, but never one that so grabbed me. Perhaps it was because of that experience that I *became* a film critic, instead of simply working as one.

Every time I've met Marty, the conversation has come around sooner or later to Catholicism and sin. At a time when he had been married twice, he told me he knew he was living in a state of mortal sin. "You believe you will go to hell?" "Absolutely." Scenes such as the one in *Mean Streets*, with Keitel holding his hand in the flame of a candle and imagining the fires of hell, were not mere character behavior but came from a well deep inside Scorsese. *Jerusalem, Jerusalem*, that early screenplay he sent me, had contained a scene involving a sermon like the one all Catholic schoolchildren seem to have heard, the one about the endless torments of sin.

His greatest film is *Raging Bull*, and it is an act of self-redemption. In a period before it, he'd become addicted to cocaine and told me that after an overdose he was pronounced dead in an emergency room and then resuscitated. "That, for me, was hitting bottom," he said flatly. He's been clean since. One day in the hospital, De Niro walked in and threw a book about Jake LaMotta on his bed. "I think maybe we should do this," he said. Certainly there is more of LaMotta in Scorsese than some will realize, including the same Madonna-whore complex that obsessed the hero of his first film.

In 1983, we had a long talk about his film *The King of Comedy*, a movie the studio was ready to give up on until some good reviews started coming in. For Scorsese, the making of the film coincided with a painful period of his life, a time when he fell in love with Isabella Rossellini, married her, and was divorced. Although it is easy to see *The King of Comedy* as the most barren and unemotional of all Scorsese's films, that wasn't the way he saw it.

"The amount of rejection in this film is horrifying," he told me. "There are scenes I almost can't look at. There's a scene where De Niro is told, *I hate you!* and he nods and responds, *Oh, I see, right, you don't want to see me again*. I made the movie during a very painful period in my life. I was going through the Poor Me routine. And I'm still very lonely. Another relationship has broken up."

Since Isabella?

"Since. I'm spending a lot of time by myself now. I go home and watch movies on video and stay up all night and sleep all day. If I didn't have to work I'd sleep all the time. I've never had such a long period when I've been alone."

Toward the end of our dinner I discovered by accident how deeply he was hurt. I mentioned a new film named *Exposed*, by James Toback, starring Nastassja Kinski. I said I thought Kinski possessed whatever rare magic Marilyn Monroe had; that whatever Kinski appeared in, good or bad, she commanded the screen.

"I can't bear to see Kinski in anything," Scorsese said. "She reminds me too much of Isabella. It tears me apart. I can't even go to see a film by the Taviani brothers, because Isabella and I had a little courtship on the set of one of their films. I can't ever go back to the island of Salina, where Visconti's *The Leopard* was shot, because we were there. In fact, I can hardly even watch a film by Visconti without growing depressed."

"By memories of Isabella?"

"By memories of a period when I thought I was happy. I'll put it that way. A period when I really thought I had the answers."

"Okay, then," I said, "I've got a new movie that can't possibly depress you or bring up any old associations. It's called *Say Amen, Somebody*, and it's this wonderful documentary about gospel music."

"Can't see it." Scorsese was grinning, but he was serious.

"Why not?"

"It's distributed by United Artists Classics."

"You mean you can't see a film that is distributed by a company that is connected to a woman you once loved?"

He smiled. "I'd see the United Artists logo and it would ruin the movie for me."

"Maybe you could come in after the logo had left the screen?"

"I'd know."

In the spring of 1988, Marty got into hot water with elements of the Church for making *The Last Temptation of Christ*, which contained scenes they found blasphemous. William Donohue, the self-appointed leader of the Catholic League, was at the head of the pack. Universal Pictures had been threatened with a boycott and to its credit refused to back down. Tensions rose after Scorsese began to receive death threats.

I was in Cannes when I got a call asking if I'd be able to see the film in a screening room in London and then talk to Marty about it in New York. I was sworn to secrecy; it wasn't known that a print even existed in London. I was given a time and address for a screening room on Wardour Street, passed through security guards, and saw the film all by myself.

In New York, I was given a number and asked to

call it from a pay booth on the Upper East Side. Scorsese described his address in words, not using a street number. I was admitted by two security guards and taken upstairs to his living room, and we discussed the film in terms mostly theological, not cinematic. Setting aside the question of whether it was good, we agreed that it was devout. Scorsese fell naturally into that kind of conversation. The physical making of a film was by then well within his abilities; it was the moral challenge that consumed him.

His living room was appointed in a style suited to an upper-class New York family of the vintage of the nineteenth-century town house itself. I had no doubt there was a screening room, but this room had deep sofas, a fireplace, and floor-to-ceiling bookshelves.

"I've been trying to catch up on great literature," he said. "I subscribed to the Folio Society." Five years later, he was to release *The Age of Innocence*, based on the novel by Edith Wharton. I suspect after he moved into that house he began to imagine the people who had built it and inevitably made a film about their time and class.

Since his first work, Scorsese has never disappointed me by making an unworthy film. He has made a few films that, he confided, he "needed" to do to get other films made, but if it is true, for example, that *After Hours* was done simply to distract him after the heartbreak of the first cancellation of *The Last Temptation of Christ*, it is also true that *After Hours* is one of his best films.

One of Scorsese's strengths is a technical mastery of the medium. Like Orson Welles long before him (who allegedly watched Ford's *Stagecoach* one hundred times before directing *Citizen Kane*) he learned his art not only in classrooms at New York University but by the intense scrutiny of other directors' films. Once when I told him I had seen his personal print of Renoir's *The River* at the Virginia Film Festival, he told me he watches it at least three times a year. When Gene Siskel visited him during a low time in the 1970s, he took him into a screening room (in a basement, as I recall) and said he spent most of every day down there, watching movies. He does not copy other directors, he does not do homage, but he absorbs and transmutes.

We have never become close friends. It is best that way. We talk whenever he has a new film coming out, or at tributes, industry events, or a special evening after a retrospective at the Wexner Center for the Arts at Ohio State University. We did a Q & A onstage for perhaps two hours, maybe longer, but even so I was astonished to see that the transcript amounted to more than twenty thousand words, which came pouring out of Marty in the full flood of memory and enthusiasm. He isn't guarded like members of subsequent film generations, cannot be limited to sound bites, will answer just about any question he is asked, including some he should really not answer. His long-serving publicist, Marion Billings, is not the type of person who rehearses "sound bites" with her clients, but more of a supporter and a friend. His personality could not abide one of today's rigidly controlling publicists. The Billings philosophy: If Marty said it, that's what he said.

I only have one story left to tell. Siskel and I were asked to host a series of career tributes at the Toronto International Film Festival. Our first choice was Scorsese, whom Gene admired no less than I do. On the afternoon of the tribute, we ran into Marty and his ebullient mother, Catherine, in the lobby of the hotel.

"What's the dress code tonight?" he asked.

"We are the presenters, and so of course we'll have to wear tuxedos," Gene said. "But you are the guest, and you can wear anything."

"Maybe I'll just wear my jeans," he said.

"*Martin!*" Catherine said, her voice in italics. "You will wear your tuxedo!"

"Right, Mom," he said. And he did.

36 "FIDDLE ON THE CORNER WHERE THE QUARTERS ARE"

IN MAY 1996, Chaz and I had lunch with Robert and Kathryn Altman at the Grand Hotel in Cannes. I was shocked by how frail he looked. Here was a man who had seemed indestructible, and now he was thin and walked with a cane and his voice was weak. He was at the festival for the premiere of *Kansas City*, his film about the early jazz scene in his hometown.

The film opened that June and received some harsh reviews, especially by Richard Schickel in *TIME* magazine, who wrote (I'm quoting from memory) that if you seek a definition for unethical, look no farther than Robert Altman.

My phone rang, and it was Harvey Weinstein, who was releasing the film at Miramax.

"Did you see what that fucker Schickel wrote about Bob Altman?" he asked. I said I had. I said Altman had been called many things, but never unethical.

"Roger, you saw him at Cannes. Robert Altman is a dying man. That review may kill him. If he doesn't get some support for his movie, I'm telling you he will die."

This was the first (and remains the only) call I received from a distributor asking for a favorable review. I admired Harvey's spirit in fighting for the film. I didn't believe for one second he made the call because of financial considerations. He cared more about Bob than box office. I didn't consider *Kansas City* one of Altman's best films, but I found it ambitious and honorable and gave it three stars in the paper, and a degree of praise.

The next time I saw Altman, he had gained weight and wasn't using a cane; it would turn out he had ten years of films ahead of him. But how poignantly I remembered the night in 2006 when he was given an honorary Oscar and revealed to the Academy that he had received a heart transplant ten years earlier. Now it all made sense. In an industry where rumors of bad health can end careers, it was a statement of unusual courage, typical of Altman. Perhaps he suspected his death was near; he died on November 20, 2006, five months after the release of *A Prairie Home*

Companion, which is, I believe, a knowingly auto-biographical film. Along with his previous film, *The Company*, it is about the way he worked.

The night before the Oscars, there was a little gathering in a room off a restaurant of the Beverly Hills Hotel. This wasn't a promotional event, and no publicists were attached. It was just Bob and Kathryn and some of their friends and family. I remember Lauren Hutton, Shelley Duvall, Keith Carradine, Henry Gibson, Virginia Madsen. I talked for a while with Lily Tomlin, who had just finished making *A Prairie Home Companion*. She looked across the room and said, "I love that man." Madsen had played a guardian angel in the film and said Altman had wanted her on the set even when she wasn't needed; perhaps as an angel, perhaps because she floated in the background of many shots, or perhaps simply because with Altman you never knew when an actor might be needed.

Altman was a collaborator. Many directors are private and dictatorial. He involved everyone. He and Kathryn moved in a crowd, and actors became like family. He directed in a conspiratorial style, as if he and the actors were putting something over on absent enemies. I spent an unusual amount of time with him over the years. A lot of people did. His sets were open, and he even invited outsiders to his screenings of daily rushes.

I sat once in his screening room at Lionsgate in Westwood and watched the dailies of a film with maybe twenty others; the sweetness of marijuana floated forward from his chair. He made no attempt to conceal his use of pot. When he was shooting *The Company* in Chicago, Chaz and I had dinner twice with the Altmans and Mayor Daley and his wife, Maggie. Daley and I arrived at the restaurant early one night and sat at the bar awaiting the others. Bob came in from the winter cold, bringing with him a cloud of marijuana smoke. Daley raised his eyebrows at me and smiled. In 1999, when Altman premiered *Cookie's Fortune*, he sat in the middle of the opening night reception and made no attempt to conceal what he was smoking. It occurs to me now that it may have been medical marijuana, obtained by prescription.

There may not have been a director who liked actors more. He had a temper, and I saw him angry with cinematographers, Teamsters, prop men, lighting guys, critics, and people making noise during a shot, but actors were his darlings and they could do no wrong. When he asked for another take, there was the implication that he enjoyed the last one so much he wanted to see the actors do it again simply for his personal pleasure.

I met him properly for the first time in 1974, in Iowa City, where we had both agreed to attend a film festival because we were promised Pauline Kael would be there. There we were, sitting cross-legged on a table in front of a room jammed with students, before a screening of his movie *Thieves Like Us*. After high praise from Kael and others, the movie had failed at the box office. "I blame United Artists," he said. "All the ad campaign said is that the movie's a masterpiece. Would you go to a movie that was hailed as a masterpiece? Already it sounds like hard work."

He spoke in a cheerful voice, youthful, as if savoring the fun of being a director. I met him again at Cannes in 1977, where he was premiering his masterpiece *3 Women*, which won the Best Actress award for Shelley Duvall—a waitress he saw in a Houston diner and made into a star. That day he was sitting on a rented yacht in the Cannes harbor, talking about how in a month he would begin shooting *A Wedding* in Chicago with forty-eight actors, every one of whom would have their dialogue separately recorded with his pet project, Lionsgate Sound. So much of a democrat was he that he didn't believe in isolated foreground sound, and starting with *McCabe & Mrs. Miller* (1971) key lines were sometimes delivered by supporting actors only vaguely present in the background.

In those days he seemed to engender new films from inspired whims. "I'll tell you how *3 Women* got started," he said. "I dreamed it. I dreamed of the desert, and these three women, and I remember every once in a while I'd dream that I was waking up and sending out people to scout locations and cast the thing. And when I woke up in the morning, it was like I'd done the picture. What's more, I liked it. So, what the hell, I decided to do it."

I asked him about a story I'd heard about how he got the idea for *A Wedding*.

"Yeah, it's close. We were shooting *3 Women* out in the desert, and it was a really hot day and we were in a hotel room that was like a furnace, and I wasn't feeling too well on account of having felt too well the night before, and this girl was down from L.A. to do some in-depth gossip and asked me what my next movie was going to be. At that moment, I didn't even feel like doing this movie, so I told her I was gonna shoot a wedding next. A wedding? Yeah, a wedding.

"So a few moments later my production assistant comes up and she says, 'Bob, did you hear yourself just then?' Yeah, I say, I did. 'That's not a bad idea, is it?' she says. Not a bad idea at all, I said, and that night we started on the outline."

He regarded a crowd of photographers two yachts over. "This place is a zoo," he said. "The purpose of a yacht is to pull up the gangplank. I had this lady interviewer following me around. She was convinced that life with Altman was a never-ending round of orgies and excess. She was even snooping around in my bathroom, for Christ's sake, and she found this jar of funny white powder in the medicine cabinet. Aha! she thinks. Cocaine! So she snorts some. Unfortunately, what she didn't know was that I'm allergic to commercial toothpaste because it makes me break out in a rash. So my wife mixes up baking soda and salt for me, and—Poor girl."

Two years later, in 1979, I found myself in the Don CeSar Beach Resort in St. Petersburg Beach, Florida, where he was filming his little-seen *HealtH*. He said he wanted me to meet someone. We walked outside to a line of cars and he introduced me to the Teamsters captain on the shoot. "This man," he said, "is being paid more than anyone else on the film, except for the stars, the cameraman, and me." The man smiled at him.

At the box office, *HealtH* and *A Wedding* were not successes. *Popeye*, made next, turned a nice profit but was perceived as a flop. The next year, I visited him during rehearsals for a Broadway play, *Come Back to the 5 & Dime Jimmy Dean, Jimmy Dean*, which he was staging with his own money. It starred Cher, Sandy Dennis, Karen Black, and Kathy Bates, among others. He then used the stage set to film it as a feature.

Some directors lie fallow when they can't find a

studio project. Altman was essentially unable to find funding for a studio film for a decade after *Popeye* but worked unceasingly on ten marginal independent projects, including the TV miniseries *Tanner '88* he made during the 1988 presidential elections. "You fiddle on the corner where the quarters are," he explained. For him, the actual production of a film or play seemed to be necessary to life, and he was incapable of not working.

37   "I WASN'T POPULAR WHEN PEOPLE *THOUGHT* I WAS POPULAR"

WOODY ALLEN IS the most open and articulate of directors, but interviews with him involved conditions. There was always the stipulation that the piece be embargoed in New York. During some of the 1980s and 1990s I was syndicated in the *New York Daily News* or the *New York Post*, and that meant they couldn't run the interview, possibly because he was giving an exclusive to the *New York Times*. I was happy to talk with him at all, especially since our conversations seemed to stray from the movie at hand into the larger realms of life, death, and the meaning of it all. "I don't care about my lifework for a second," he told me once. "When I die, I don't care what they do with it. They can flush it down the toilet. There's that delusion that it's going to have some meaning to you when, in fact, you'll be a nonexistent thing; there'll be not a trace of consciousness. So it becomes completely irrelevant, what happens after your death. Totally. It doesn't mean a thing."

That was in 1994, when he had made *Bullets Over Broadway.* In 2011, when he was at Cannes with *Midnight in Paris*, he was still saying he didn't expect any of his films to be remembered. The first time I spoke with him, in 1971, he told me there wasn't a day when he didn't give serious thought to suicide. I asked him again every time I saw him, until 2000, if that was still true. It always was.

To talk with Woody was like catching up with your smart college roommate every time you went to New York, and he reminded you that he had gone ahead and accomplished all the things you had talked about in school. He has averaged a film a year for more than forty years. Some were great, all were intelligent, none were shabby. He compared his work habits to those of Ingmar Bergman, whom he admired above all other directors. Like Bergman, he wrote his own screenplays. Like Bergman, he worked over and again with many of the same collaborators. Like Bergman, he could persuade pretty much any actor to work for him at far below their going rate. Like Bergman, he usually had distribution lined up before shooting even began. And they both worked with small budgets that gave them artistic freedom.

He thought of Bergman as a genius. He told me the American cinema had produced only one genius, Orson Welles. "Godard is supposed to be a genius," he told me dubiously one day. I told him I had witnessed the table napkin at Cannes upon which the producer Menahem Golan wrote out a contract with Godard, misspelling Godard's name while promising him a script by Norman Mailer and a cast including Orson Welles as Lear and Woody Allen as the Fool.

"Norman Mailer wrote the screenplay?" Allen asked. "Well, there was no screenplay at all the day Godard shot me. I worked for half a day. I completely put myself into his hands. He shot over in the Brill Building, working very sparsely, just Godard and a cameraman, and he asked me to do foolish things, which I did because it was Godard. It was one of the most foolish experiences I've ever had. I'd be amazed if I was anything but consummately insipid.

"He was very elusive about the subject of the film. First he said it was going to be about a Learjet that crashes on an island. Then he said he wanted to interview everyone who had done *King Lear*, from Kurosawa to the Royal Shakespeare. Then he said I could say whatever I wanted to say. He plays the French intellectual very well, with the five o'clock shadow and a certain vagueness. Meanwhile, when I got there for the shoot, he was wearing pajamas—tops and bottoms—and a bathrobe and slippers, and smoking a big cigar. I had the uncanny feeling that I was being directed by Rufus T. Firefly.

"Do you know how Bergman spends his day, now that he's in retirement? He wakes up early in the morning, he sits quietly for a time and listens to the ocean, he has breakfast, he works, he has an early lunch, he screens a different movie for himself each and every day, he has an early dinner, and then he reads the newspaper, which would be too depressing for him to read in the morning."

There were differences between Bergman and Allen. Bergman lived most of the year on the Swedish island of Fårö. Allen has a horror of leaving Manhattan. He told me once about spending the Fourth of July in New York although Mia Farrow had a house in Connecticut. "The country has insects and animals and ominously alarms me," he said. "I loved having the neighborhood to myself." Only a New Yorker could think of having New York to himself.

"In my movies in the country, I wanted to portray the country the way I want it to be, with golden vistas, and flowers, animals, moon, stars, a perfect setting to deal with problems of love and romance. I saw it as a chance to get in some of my philosophy, that there's more to life than meets the eye, that an intellectual rationalist is also an animal who lusts after women and is not above drawing blood in the throes of passion. He can explain the cosmos, and his friend the doctor can play God and watch people die, but all of these men are...wistful. Wistful, because they haven't met the right woman yet.

"But I hate the country! This Fourth of July weekend, when everybody else has gone out to the country, I worked. I went to see *Poltergeist* at Eighty-Sixth and Third Avenue and I walked around the empty streets. The country is great as it appears in one's fantasies, in Shakespeare's *Midsummer Night's Dream*, with all the little forest spirits, but when I go to the country to shoot a movie, we have to have a nurse for snakebites and poison ivy. They have gnats and mosquitoes. It's awful."

But when you were making *A Midsummer Night's Sex Comedy*, I said, you had to put up with the country?

"Not at all. I drove back to New York every night and stayed in my own bed. Oh, I can take a little of the country. Sometimes I reluctantly visit Mia in Connecticut, but I always come back the same day. I would never think of staying overnight."

In other words, your view of Central Park is about as sylvan as you like to get?

"I like the view just from the window, through glass. I like it best in the winter. I'm not crazy about the green of leaves. At the beginning of our film, when we shot the montage of the leaves and the ponds and the little deer running past, I was hiding behind the camera."

When you were a kid, you never went to the beach?

"I got sun poisoning. It was terrible. I preferred staying home in Brooklyn and playing baseball in the streets. I was a very good athlete, good at baseball, football, from growing up in the streets, but I didn't get to like nature that way. I think we all miss the point that when Shakespeare was talking about summer, he was writing from a land where summer was a lot more like spring is here. He didn't know about dust and ticks. I personally prefer grey, overcast days to sunny ones. That's one reason I don't like it in Los Angeles. I really can't stand the climate.

"Mia's country house is a real Chekhovian setting: a little cottage, a little lake, very Russian. For a long time I've wanted to write a little Russian family drama to set there. I finally did it, but by the time the screenplay was ready the weather had changed, and so we had to build the sets in Astoria Studios here in New York. *Hannah and Her Sisters*, that was the perfect setup. We shot a lot of it in Mia's apartment, and all I had to do was cross Central Park every day.

Bergman shoots right in his own house, and on his island. I'd shoot in my house, but I live in a co-op apartment, and it's against the rules.

"Shooting in Mia's house led to a very strange experience for Mia. She told me she was in bed in her bedroom, looking at *Hannah and Her Sisters* on the TV set at the end of the bed. She realized she was looking at a scene in the movie that showed the same bed and the same TV set, in the same room."

That would have been in the 1980s. In the mid-1990s, it became known that he and Farrow's adopted daughter Soon-Yi Previn were in love. There was a scandal. "The heart has its reasons," he said, using the words of Pascal. In 1994, I met him in his screening room but avoided mentioning the scandal. There are times when I think I must be a lousy journalist, an anachronism in the age of relentless gossip. I avoid asking interview subjects about their private lives. If they bring up a subject, I'm interested, but I dislike gossip. He brought it up himself.

"I thought the whole business was foolish," he told me. "I thought it was going to blow over in two days; I never even took it seriously when it first happened. Apart from the horribleness of not being able to see my children, those of us in the inner circle—myself, my sister, my close friends—found it almost amusing.

"But from a total nonevent, a multimillion-dollar

industry grew. I mean, magazines all over the world, newspapers, television—lawyers were hired, private detectives were hired, more lawyers were brought in, psychiatrists were brought in. It was incredible. And *nothing had happened.* I certainly wasn't going to participate in the craziness. I worked, I never missed an evening with my jazz band, and I conducted my life normally. For me, one thing had nothing to do with the other. The legal battles I've been in were basically fought by my lawyers. There was nothing I could do about it."

I was afraid at the beginning, I told him, that maybe it would turn out like the Fatty Arbuckle case—where whether he was guilty or not, people simply couldn't find him funny anymore. I wondered if after all the controversy people would never be able to laugh at a Woody Allen picture again.

"Yes, people said to me, 'Are you worried about this having an impact in your career?' But from where I sat, it *couldn't* have an impact. Am I going to be less popular? I wasn't popular when people *thought* I was popular. I never had a big audience to begin with. And it never mattered to me. If people said to me tomorrow that I couldn't make a movie again because no one would come, it wouldn't bother me in the slightest."

He was looking into the middle distance, seeing

possibilities that had perhaps occurred to him more than once.

"I almost had a secret hope that maybe this would change my life in a way I didn't have the nerve to do. They'd say I could never make a film again. And I could wake up in the morning and think, 'Oh, great, that option is closed to me. I don't have to think about it. I don't have to feel guilty that I'm not making films.' And I could write for the theater, which is something I like, or even stay home and write a novel.

"But I never thought I was in the position of Fatty Arbuckle. I mean, he was a tremendous star. When you're a writer, you have control over your own fate. I mean, it would not bother me in the slightest if I'd awakened this morning and stayed in my apartment and was working on my typewriter or lying on the bed writing a book."

In 1998, Barbara Kopple made the documentary *Wild Man Blues*, about Allen touring Europe with his jazz group. Soon-Yi was always at his side. The movie wasn't about their relationship, but it helped me to understand it. In life, Woody played his usual role of the dubious neurotic, and Soon-Yi was calm and authoritative, a combination of wife, mother, and manager. She seemed to be good for him. She seemed more like the adult in the partnership. At one point, she advised him to be more animated when he appeared onstage with his band. "I'm not gonna bob my head or tap my feet," he says. "They want to see you bob a little," she says, and he gets defensive: "I'm appropriately animated for a human being in the context in which I appear." But at the next concert, he bobs a little.

In 2000, he came to speak at the University of Chicago. They were by then married. He said: "Soon-Yi bought me this sweater. This marriage has been great for me. If anyone had told me I would wind up married to a much younger Asian woman, with no interest in show business, I'd have told them they were crazy. All I would go out with were little blond actresses, or women who did something in show business. Suddenly I find myself with a woman whose interest in life is teaching learning-disabled children, who is not interested in show business, who is much my junior and doesn't know many of the references from my life experience. She's a wonderful person and makes me very very happy. It's interesting how little you know about yourself as you go through life. I think, my God, why didn't I meet her sooner, I would have had so many more years of happiness."

There was something poignant in that. It reminded me of a time years earlier when we had met in his apartment on the Upper East Side, overlooking Central Park. We talked and drank tea. When we were finished he said he wanted to show me something. He took me into a room with books on the walls and a simple desk and chair facing the window. On the desk was an old portable typewriter.

"My parents bought me that," he said. "It's the only typewriter I've ever had. I'm used to it. I sit down there and write every movie. I could never use an electric typewriter. The thought makes me shudder."

Personal computers were unknown in those days. I don't really want to know if Woody Allen uses one now. When I think of him and his typewriter, I remember a story McHugh told me once about an old Irishman who bought new shoes. He wore them down to the pub and his friends asked him what he was sporting on his feet. "A fine new pair," he said. "These will see me out."

38   WERNER HERZOG

ONE NIGHT IN October 1968, at my first New York
Film Festival, I was invited to a party at the Washington Square apartment of Bob Shaye, who had purchased the distribution rights to a new German film
named *Signs of Life*, by Werner Herzog. Shaye was to
build that first film into New Line Cinema, but all
he had that night was a first feature by an unknown
twenty-six-year-old. There weren't many people at
the party; Herzog and Shaye together didn't add up
to a hot invitation. Maybe it wasn't even actually a
party and we'd simply all ended up there. I'd seen
the film. I was attracted to its strange intensity. It was
about a wounded German soldier sent to an island
with his new wife to convalesce and pretend to guard

a fortress. At one point, going mad from lack of purpose, he shot at windmills, which I suppose is as good a way as any for Herzog to have started out.

All of this was long ago. Herzog and I were the same age. He had a bushy haircut in the 1960s style, but he was not then, and probably never had been, a "kid." I can't remember what we talked about. I keenly remember how I felt, sitting on the floor next to his chair. Here was a young man unlike any I had ever met. He spoke clearly and directly of unusual ideas. I didn't get the impression of an enlarged ego. There was no boasting. He wasn't pitching or promoting. It was clear to him what his mission was. It was to film the world through the personalities of exalted eccentrics who defied all ordinary categories and sought a transcendent vision. Every one of his films has followed that same mission. Every one, I believe, is autobiographical—reflecting not the facts of his life, but his spirit. He is in the medieval sense a mystic.

Herzog took residence in my mind. I had met an important person. I felt a spiritual connection. I didn't know what to make of his *Fata Morgana* in 1971, with its endlessly repeated images of a jet plane landing in the desert through air simmering with heat. He made *Aguirre, the Wrath of God* in 1972, but it was not until 1977 that it came to America and Milos Stehlik showed it to me in the desanctified Lutheran church where he opened the first Facets Cinematheque. "Bring a pillow," he said. "The pews are hard."

By then I'd seen *The Enigma of Kaspar Hauser* in the Chicago International Film Festival, and I felt a connection with Herzog's work that went beyond critic and film. We shared an obsession. He engaged with the infuriating relationship between the human will and the intractable universe. Each film, in a new way, dealt with the fundamental dilemma of consciousness: We know we are here, we know what we see, we learn what we can, we try to do more than is possible, we fail, but we have glimpsed a vision of the infinite. That sounds goofy and New Age, but there is no more grounded filmmaker than Herzog. He founds his work on the everyday realities of people who, crazy or sane, real or fictional, are all equally alive to him.

Later in the 1970s, Milos asked me to do a Q & A with Herzog at Facets, and that night Herzog said that modern man was starving for images. "Television and advertising have pounded us into insensate passivity." His work is alive with images. A man on a raft with chattering monkeys. A man on a mountaintop swept by rivers of clouds. An endlessly circling mechanical chicken. A crypt of negligible human artifacts buried in the Antarctic ice. A boat hauled across land. A ski jumper who flies too far. A man who must be sure he is not locked in. Figures creeping on ice to glimpse a city at the bottom of a lake. A human chain reaching across African hillsides. A boy's palm print left from the distant past. A man and an iguana staring sideways at each other. A man listening to the sound of another man being killed by a grizzly bear. A man from nowhere who appears one day to stand in a village square. Herzog's characters are almost always men; his women characters have supporting roles. One reason for this, perhaps, is that his men are all Man, and represent everyone.

I've seen pretty much every film Herzog has made, and there's not a single one made for simply commercial reasons. Each film has proceeded from an idea of a unique character approaching reality at an oblique angle. Each film has embedded somewhere the idea that we are mortal, that death is our destination, but we can stave off that certainty with divine madness. I instinctively identify with his work. I don't expect it to conform to any popular norm or commercial formula. When he uses movie stars, it is for their oddness, not for their fame. But he doesn't make freak shows. His characters are more human than the grotesque fabrications I see in many romantic comedies or violent action movies.

Herzog seems unable to make an easy film. Does

he seek dangerous and difficult locations? The stories told from his shoots are harrowing. He mentioned once the "voodoo of location." His films have plunged beneath the ice caps and floated over the rain forest in a teardrop-shaped balloon. He has filmed in the jungles of three continents, the deserts of four, the mountains of five. Curiously, the director he reminds me of in this respect is Russ Meyer. What I understand about both of them is a single-minded focus on the work of filmmaking. For Meyer, a new production was like a military mission, an evocation of his teenage years in the Signal Corps. For Herzog, it is more complex: a physical and mental challenge containing the possibility of destruction. When he dies, it will not be in bed, I expect, but in a plunge from an experimental aircraft into a volcano.

I believe it's unwise for a film critic to become friendly with those he writes about. I'm not concerned with a "conflict of interest" so much as with my own ability to see a film at arm's length. I don't want to read a screenplay. I don't want to see a rough cut. I don't want to get involved. That was a flaw of Pauline Kael's: She issued instructions to those she adopted. Perhaps it wasn't a flaw but only a fact, to be taken into account. Certainly she didn't conceal her partisanship. Nor did the *auteur* critics. Every writer must go at things in his own way.

But I have made friends. These friendships weren't sought, but they happened. Russ Meyer became a friend for a lifetime. Gregory Nava and Anna Thomas became good friends after I met them in the 1970s at the Chicago festival. With others, like Martin Scorsese, Paul Cox, Robert Altman, Ramin Bahrani, Errol Morris, Norman Jewison, and Atom Egoyan, I'd say we've been friendly for a long time but not in a close personal sense. And then there is Herzog. With him I sense a bond. I'd call it "spiritual," but the word has confusing theological undertones. I learn from the way he sees things and I admire how he leads his life. I feel an instinctive sympathy for how he regards the subjects of his films. His physical and moral courage inspire me. When I see one of his films, I feel we're walking through it together.

In 1999, the Walker Art Center screened a month of Herzog's films and then scheduled a Q & A for the final night. I think we were onstage two and a half hours. He's a spellbinding speaker. He speaks with a naked sincerity that is sort of entrancing. He says extraordinary things in a matter-of-fact way. That night he read out his "Minnesota Declaration," which he had written for the occasion. Subtitled "Lessons of Darkness" after one of his films, it consisted of twelve points, some of which were funny. ("The moon is dull. Mother Nature doesn't call, doesn't speak to you, although a glacier eventually farts. And don't you listen to the Song of Life.") Some were bleak. ("We ought to be grateful that the Universe out there knows no smile.") The last one remorseless. ("Life in the oceans must be sheer hell. A vast, merciless hell of permanent and immediate danger. So much of a hell that during evolution some species—including man—crawled, fled onto some small continents of solid land, where the Lessons of Darkness continue.")

He said the point of the declaration was to define "ecstatic truth," by which he meant a truth above the mundane. Cinema verité, he said, "confounds fact and truth, and thus plows only stones." He explained: "There are deeper strata of truth in cinema, and there is such a thing as poetic, ecstatic truth. It is mysterious and elusive, and can be reached only through fabrication and imagination and stylization." This was consistent with his lifelong practice of ignoring the boundaries between his fiction films and documentaries.

He goes to the Telluride Film Festival every year, and one year he invited me to his room in the Sheridan Hotel to see tapes of his two new documentaries. One was about men in Russia who walk about in sandals proclaiming they are Jesus Christ. Some have followers who believe them. The other film involved a village in Russia on the shore of a deep lake. Some of the townspeople believe there is a city of angels on the bottom of the lake, and it can be seen through the ice before the ice grows too thick. They creep out on it, the ice sometimes cracking alarmingly beneath them, and Herzog, of course, creeps out with them.

After we discussed these films for a while, he confessed they were both complete fictions. But they were ecstatically true. It was the same with his fiction film *Where the Green Ants Dream*, about Aboriginal peoples in Australia. When he was asked at the Cannes 1984 press conference for the source of his knowledge about Aboriginal beliefs and green ants, he said, "I made it all up. I'm not even certain if green ants exist." He would have made the film during a period I was told about by our friend Paul Cox, when Herzog washed up broke in Melbourne and lived for a time in a tent in Paul's backyard. How he found the financing to make a film like *Where the Green Ants Dream* is a good question, but Herzog has found the financing for one of the most prolific careers of modern directors, always for films with questionable commercial prospects, perhaps because of the singular intensity of his vision.

He came to Ebertfest twice, the second time after my illness. That would have been the festival in 2007, when he explained he had started his journey to Urbana from the top of a South American plateau, had himself lowered by rope to its foot, trekked through the rain forest and then floated down a river, found a steamer to the coast, and then come the rest of the way by air. I suspect there was something about the sheer impracticality of this journey that compelled Herzog to make it.

In 2009, Ramin Bahrani joined me in Boulder to go through his *Chop Shop* in the Interruptus session at the Conference on World Affairs. "I would give anything to meet Herzog," he told me. I introduced them by e-mail and Werner ended up being recruited as the voice of the bag in Ramin's celebrated short film *Plastic Bag*. We persuaded Werner to come to Boulder in 2010 to join Ramin in a shot-by-shot examination of *Aguirre, the Wrath of God*. Although I couldn't speak, it was an inspiring experience for me, bringing these two men together in the act of watching a great film.

I walked around the campus, I sat on panels, I was deeply satisfied every afternoon by the Interruptus sessions, and at some point that week I realized it would be my last trip to Boulder. I had come the first time forty years earlier. As I watched a great director whose career I'd admired from 1968, and another who had emerged in the last few years, I thought that was symbolism enough. I gave Interruptus a push and knew it could sail on its own. I felt good that

Herzog had been in my life close to the beginning and now probably close to the end and had never made an unworthy film. I don't think Bahrani will make one, either. Artists like them bring meaning to my life, which has been devoted in such large part to films of worthlessness.

39   BILL NACK

SOMETIMES IN LIFE you meet someone whose soul seems in tune with your own. Almost from the moment I met Bill Nack at Illinois, we were leaning over our coffee cups in the basement of the student union and exchanging earnest opinions about life and literature. Fifty years have passed since that day and there have been many more conversations, but at this moment I have no idea of his politics and couldn't tell you if he believes in God. When we get together we're like two old stamp collectors, but instead of discussing the Penny Black we discuss Nabokov.

Bill loves good writing with a voluptuous intensity. He commits great chunks of it to memory and isn't shy about reciting it. His own prose is elegant and pure, some of the best sportswriting ever created. Like all great sportswriters, he isn't really writing about sports but about athletes—which is to say, men and women, and horses. He has a mesmerizing effect on his listeners. He doesn't monopolize a conversation; he listens well, but when he speaks people want to listen. Mike Royko was like that. You always wanted a tape recorder.

Nack was sports editor of the *Daily Illini* the year I was editor. He was the editor the next year. He married Mary Scott, an Urbana girl I dated in high school. I'd never made it to first base. By the time we met, I think he may have been able to slide into second and was taking a risky lead and keeping an eye on the pitcher. We had a lot of fun on the *Daily Illini*. It was in the days before ripping stuff off the Web. He insisted on running stories about every major horse race. We had only one photo of a horse, and used it for every winner. If it was a filly, we flipped it. Of this as his editor I approved.

After college, Nack went to Vietnam and ended up writing news releases for Westmoreland's staff. Then he got a job at *Newsday*. On Long Island, he and Mary raised three girls and a boy. One year at the paper's holiday party he stood up on a desk and recited the names and years of every single winner of the Kentucky Derby. Dave Laventhol, the editor, asked him, "Why do you know that?" Bill said he'd been studying it since he was a kid and loved the racetrack. Laventhol said if he wanted to be the paper's turf writer, he should write a memo. Nack wrote to him: "After covering politicians for four years, I would like the chance to cover the whole horse."

From *Newsday* Bill moved to *Sports Illustrated* and came into full flower. He wasn't the kind of writer who covered a particular beat. He was a great prose stylist. At a signing for his book *My Turf,* he read a story and made a woman cry. Then he read another story and there wasn't a dry eye in the house. One was about the death of Secretariat. The other was about a filly breaking down and being destroyed on the track. He wrote long articles I could only envy, because I've spent my career writing shorter pieces on deadline.

Bill was part of the story of Secretariat from before the great horse was born, or maybe a few days later, I forget the details. Discovering the greatest horse in history became the central event in his professional life, as seeing Scorsese's first film became mine. Bill saw the stallion for the last time very shortly before his death. "After the autopsy, the vet said he had a heart twice as big as the average horse," Bill told me. "There was nothing wrong with it. It was simply a great heart." He wrote about this in the best seller

Secretariat: The Making of a Champion, which was made into a movie.

Bill was the writer who exposed the scandal of how owners and vets conspired to use cortisone in order to race horses who were not ready to be raced. "I started seeing horses breaking down all the time," he said. "You hardly ever used to see that." No one at the tracks would give him the time of day for a couple of years. It was a rotten business.

Our friendship has endured despite the inescapable fact that I don't care very much about horse racing and Bill doesn't seem to go to many movies. Our bond is reading, and our subject is often not far removed from the Meaning of It All. We are puzzled that we are now nearly seventy. How did that happen? Our conversations all take place in the present tense. We are always meeting for the first time. When you're young you don't realize that at every age you are always in the present, and in that sense no older; when I look at Bill I see the same man I met at Illinois. He's one of the lucky ones whose lifelong work didn't change him but only confirmed the person he was all along.

One night in Chicago he asked me to drive him past the Old Town Gardens, an apartment complex built in the 1930s where he lived as a boy with his family. I parked, he got out and walked up the front steps and then stepped out carefully onto a ledge and reached for something as far as he could. He climbed down and returned to the car.

"It's still there," he said.

"What?"

"A quarter I wedged between the bricks when I was a kid. That was my bedroom window. I left it there."

We didn't need to discuss the meaning of this. We send messages to ourselves in the future and receive them from the past. We're both conscious of the passage of time, of its flow slipping through our fingers like a long silk scarf, until it runs out and flutters away in the wind. Every time I see Bill, I asked him to recite for me from memory the closing words of *The Great Gatsby*, and every time he does. He did it when Chaz and I were married, and at his own second marriage to Carolyne Starek, whom I love for many reasons, one of them that she has an infinite patience for listening to *Gatsby*. This recitation is not merely a ritual. It is an observance in defiance of time. In some way we are still sitting over coffee in the 1960s, and he is still reciting it to me for the first time.

"I was talking with Jim Carey today," he told me that first time. Carey was the young journalism professor we admired. "I told him I was going to start memorizing passages from books. He asked me what

I was going to start with. I said, 'The end of *Gatsby.*' He said he thought that was an excellent place to start."

Bill told me his friend Hunter S. Thompson once warmed up by copying out every word of *The Great Gatsby* on his typewriter. Not that you can immediately see Fitzgerald's influence in Hunter's style, although perhaps Fitzgerald's words "compelled into an aesthetic contemplation he neither understood nor desired" is the best possible description of Thompson's life's work.

Bill and I conspired to meet a couple of times a year, at the Conference on World Affairs in Boulder and at Rancho La Puerta in Tecate, Mexico. I appointed myself as Bill's impresario. I persuaded Rancho to schedule a program titled "A Concert in Words with William Nack." The room was pretty full, because I'd been working the dining room at mealtimes, flogging the great event. Bill dimmed the lights a little and recited for an hour, standing in front of the lectern without a book.

Bill devours books. When he finds something good he's like a kid. Of all writers he loves Nabokov the most. He'll give you the opening page of *Lolita* or passages from *Speak, Memory.* "There's something I want you to hear," he told me one morning during a hike at Rancho. "It's from Nabokov's *Pnin.* Have you read it? About a university professor. I think this might be the most profound metaphor I've ever found."

It may not seem to belong in a book of this sort, but it expresses a leap of thought that I find magnificent:

> With the help of the janitor he screwed onto the side of the desk a pencil sharpener—that highly satisfying, highly philosophical instrument that goes ticonderoga-ticonderoga, feeding on the yellow finish and sweet wood, and ends up in a kind of soundlessly spinning ethereal void as we all must.

40 THE SWEETEST SET OF WHEELS IN TOWN

IT IS THINKABLE that within a few years there may be no more new Chevys to drive to the levee. The manufacture of Postum has been discontinued. Meccano sets are made of plastic. Piece by piece, the American superstructure is being dismantled. Will the pulse of teenage boys quicken at the sight of the new Kia or Hyundai? Will they envy their pal because his dad drives a Camaro? That's all over with. There will be a void in our national imagination. Let me tell you about how it used to be.

In my opinion, the narrator of "American Pie" drove a Studebaker. It's only that "Chevy" was an easier rhyme. Since the 1950s Chevy we think of first is the '57 Bel Air, it is reasonable to conclude that the ride of Miss Pie's friend on the day the music died was a 1957 Studebaker Golden Hawk—the sexiest American car ever manufactured, although there are those who praise the 1950s Thunderbirds and Corvettes, however slower than the Hawks they may have been.

They say that when a man reaches forty and finds some spare change in his pocket, his thoughts turn to the car he desired with all his heart in the years before he got his driver's license. In 1955, I took a part-time job at Johnston's Sport Shop in Champaign-Urbana. I was not a stock boy. I was a salesclerk. I got an hour for lunch. I stopped first at the Shell station across the street, run by a man who operated jukeboxes and sold his old 45s for a nickel apiece. Marty Robbins. Elvis. Teresa Brewer. Then I'd walk a block down Neil Street to the Chuck Wagon Diner, one of the first restaurants to feature Colonel Harland Sanders's chicken on its menu. This was before the colonel had his own restaurants. I met him in person the day they started serving his chicken, and he asked me how I liked his spices. At age six I was given a penny by old J. C. Penney, so now I had met two titans of marketing.

Between the gas station and the Chuck Wagon was Maxey Motors, a Studebaker-Packard dealer. I didn't pay it much heed. All I knew about Studebakers was that kids joked about how they looked like they were going in both directions at once. Many years later I discovered that Raymond Loewy's design for the 1953 Starliner was proclaimed a work of art by the Museum of Modern Art. One winter day in 1956 as I bent into a chill wind on Neil Street, something caught the corner of my eye. I turned and stood transfixed. It was the new 1957 Golden Hawk. I forgot the rain. I forgot the chicken. I wanted that car. I walked inside the dealership and circled it. My eyes hungered. Before that day, cars were ordinary things like my dad's boxy '50 Plymouth or my mom's '55 Olds, designed along the lines that made a comparison to a loaf of bread seem inevitable. Now here was a Hawk that sprang from a lofty crag and circled the firmament with fierce beauty. It was supercharged and had a grille that breathed great gulps of air.

That year I got my driver's license and was able to buy a 1954 Ford. But I was not faithful in my heart. I lusted for the Golden Hawk. I became expert at sketching it from memory. In profile, the graceful fenders curving down to the headlights. The windshield raked back in harmonious counterbalance. The slant of the roof, leading down to the uprising of the bold fins. Musical. You could sing it.

When I was forty and had a little change in my pocket, my thoughts turned again to the 1957 Golden Hawk. One day I was at Book Soup on Sunset in Los

Angeles, paging through *Hemmings Motor News*, and found an ad for a '57 Hawk being restored out in Santa Monica. I went to look at it, and the deal was sealed. Two months later it was dropped off six blocks from my home by an auto carrier. It was gold with white fins and its engine was mighty.

The year was 1982. I was a syndicated columnist for the *Chicago Sun-Times*. I had won a Pulitzer Prize. I was co-host of a national TV show. These credits were pleasing, but there was something missing, a hollow in my ego waiting to be filled. I turned the key in the ignition, rolled down the window, turned the radio to rock 'n' roll on an AM oldies station, hooked my elbow out the window, and purred out of the parking lot. I was only six blocks from home, but somehow my route took me through Old Town, up and down Rush Street, and slowly through Lincoln Park. I was aware that every male I passed gave it a long look. Not so much the women. Evolution teaches us women are looking for a good provider, not an aesthete. A Volvo driver, not a Hawk man.

Inside of me, intense joy rose. It had nothing do with what I had accomplished in life. It was entirely fueled by what I drove. This is a pure joy known to teenage boys from the golden age of hot rods, who had nothing else to excite envy except their ride. Even if they were all-staters on the football team, it didn't mean much if they were driving their dad's 1940s Olds. What pleasure that Hawk gave me. I kept it at our summer place in Michigan, off of Red Arrow Highway, the old hard road to Detroit. The road had been built in the 1920s and looked retro. There was a roadhouse used by Capone, with a secret gambling room in the basement. A classic brick Shell station. Fruit stands. A sign for the annual Milk Bottle Show. A Frank Lloyd Wright lookalike motel. Reader, on Red Arrow I was envied. I frequented Mikey's in Bridgman because they had carhops and I could roll down my window to hold up a tray with a burger and a shake, and Chaz could roll down her window and have her own separate tray. Life was good.

Searching my old movie reviews for the word "Studebaker," I found these words from my review of *Heavy Petting* in 1989: *There are a lot of adults around today who will tell you that their peak sexual experiences took place in cars, and that beds will never be the same. Not long ago, for example, I took a woman in her 40s for a drive in my 1957 Studebaker, and after sliding across the vinyl upholstery, inhaling the aroma of gasoline and oil, listening to tires spinning on the gravel and waiting for the radio tubes to warm up, she reported that all of these physical associations made her feel exactly as if someone was going to try to take her bra off.*

The following summer, we participated in the

annual Ride of La Porte, Indiana. In its simplicity this is an auto event superior to any other in Indiana, including the Indy 500. What you do is, you park your pre-1960 automobile in a lot at the county fairgrounds, drink a Coke, eat a hot dog, and walk around looking at the other cars. I parked my Golden Hawk next to an immaculate 1949 Hudson of the sort Miss Daisy was driven in. Now there was a car. You could raise a family in the backseat. It had less horsepower, but with such a low center of gravity it would cream them on the turns. At 1:00 p.m., "The Stars and Stripes Forever" blared from the loudspeakers, and we pulled into line and paraded out of the fairgrounds. A state cop with a whistle was directing traffic onto the street. As we passed her, she said, "Sharp car!"

"Did you hear that?" I asked Chaz.

"Yeah. Sharp car."

"Sharp car!" I said. "She called it a sharp car! This is a sharp car!"

"Sharp car, all right," Chaz said. She later told this story about a thousand times, apparently because it meant something special to her.

We drove up and down the streets of La Porte and people sat in lawn chairs and looked at us. No floats. No marching bands. No Sheriff Sid on his horse. Just cars. The citizens of La Porte sat and nodded pleasantly, waved a little, and poured their iced tea. The Golden Hawk was greeted with applause. Perhaps there was a sentimental connection. The Studebaker had been manufactured in South Bend, thirty miles away. Some of these people or their relatives may have worked there.

One weekend we took the car on a pilgrimage to South Bend, where I expected to see Studebakers lining the streets and backed up at traffic lights, like in a *Twilight Zone* episode. I saw one rusted President up on blocks in a vacant lot. We drove down by the St. Joseph River, turned right, and there before us was the Studebaker National Museum. We pulled the Hawk into a parking space right next to the entrance, posted "Studebakers Only." My license plate read FAUCON, French for "hawk."

The museum occupied what once had been the largest Studebaker dealership in the world. It was across the street from the original Studebaker plant, now standing forlorn. Inside were cars, fire engines, school buses, troop transports, armored cars. The station wagon with the roof that would slide back so you could bring home a totem pole standing upright. The nifty Lark. Taxis. Ambulances. Touring sedans from the 1930s. Classic Packards like Gatsby drove. Champion trucks. Conestoga wagons, because Studebaker was the only wagon maker that made the transition to cars; their wagons floated downstream to St. Louis and then journeyed overland toward John Wayne movies.

The museum had the carriage built by Studebaker in which Abraham Lincoln drove to Ford's Theatre. The last Packard ever made, a show car from the year the Packard died. And postcards, T-shirts, visors, books, scarves, hats, jackets, signs, sweatshirts, scale models, books, mugs, jigsaw puzzles, Studebaker medallions, belt buckles, cuff links, videos, key rings, and place mats. If there was one place in the nation that understands the Studebaker, it is South Bend, Indiana. They also have a university there.

Our Michigan guests loved to drive to Mikey's and get the super-thick shakes. One summer our good friends Gillian and Peter Catto and their children visited from London. He drove a Bentley. I took them for a spin in my Studebaker. I startled them by stepping on the gas.

"Now this is something like it," Peter said from the backseat.

"Now tell the story," Chaz said.

"When these cars were new," I said, "they were a lot faster than Corvettes or T-Birds. The salesmen would put a client on the backseat, put a hundred-dollar bill on the front seat, and tell the client he could keep the money if he could overcome the force of the acceleration and lean forward and pick it up while the Hawk was doing zero to sixty."

I treasured the Golden Hawk, but I could not give it the care it deserved. I knew nothing about auto mechanics. When it was built, everybody did. When a car stopped and you looked under the hood, you were actually looking for something, not simply performing a roadside pantomime with a car that required a computer programmer. I found the golden honey a good home with Dan Jedlicka, the automotive editor of the *Sun-Times*, who confessed that he must have driven half the cars in history and the '57 Hawk was the only one he had ever wanted to own.

41   GENE SISKEL

GENE SISKEL AND I were like tuning forks. Strike one, and the other would vibrate at the same frequency. In a group together, we were always intensely aware of each other. Sometimes this took the form of camaraderie, sometimes mutual support, sometimes hostility. We were aware. If something happened that we both thought was funny but weren't supposed to, God help us if one caught the other's eye. We usually thought the same things were funny. That may be a sign of intellectual communion.

Gene died on February 20, 1999. He's in my mind almost every day. He became less like a friend than like a brother. In 1977 we were on a talk show with Buddy Rogers, once Mary Pickford's husband, and he said, "You guys have a sibling rivalry. Your problem is, you both think you're the older brother." Our image was of a state of permanent feud, but our feelings had nothing to do with image. We knew the buttons to push on each other, and we both made little effort to hide our feelings, warm or cold.

Once Gene and I were involved in a joint appearance with another Chicago media couple, Steve Dahl and Garry Meier. It was a tribute to them. They were pioneers of free-form radio, even influencing the young Howard Stern. Gene and I were known for our rages against each other, and Steve and Garry were known for their accord. They gave us advice about how to work together as a successful team. Soon afterward Steve and Garry had an angry public falling-out that has lasted until this day.

Gene and I would never have had that happen to us. In our darkest brooding moments, when competitiveness, resentment, and indignation were at a roiling boil, we never considered it. We were linked in a bond beyond all disputing. "You may be an asshole," Gene would say, "but you're my asshole." If we were fighting, get out of the room. But if we were teamed up against a common target, we were lethal. Our first time on his show, Howard Stern never knew what hit him. He picked on one of us, and we were both at his throat.

We both thought of ourselves as full-service, one-stop film critics. We didn't see why the other one was necessary. We had been linked in a Faustian television format that brought us success at the price of autonomy. No sooner had I expressed a verdict on a movie, my verdict, then here came Siskel with the arrogance to say I was wrong, or, for that matter, the condescension to agree with me. It really felt like that. It was not an act. When we disagreed, there was incredulity; when we agreed, there was a kind of relief. In the television biz, they talk about "chemistry." Not a thought was given to our chemistry. We just had it, because from the day the *Chicago Tribune* made Gene its film critic, we were professional enemies. We never had a single meaningful conversation before we started to work on our TV program. Alone together in an elevator, we would study the numbers changing above the door.

Making this rivalry even worse was the tension of our early tapings. They were held together with baling wire by Thea Flaum, the PBS producer who created the original format. She dealt with us like children. Once when we got fresh coffee and were told we couldn't take it into the studio, we ganged up and told her we wanted to drink it first. She had a mother's diplomacy. "Start drinking it now and walk down to the studio slowly." It would take eight hours to get one show in the can, with breaks for lunch, dinner, and fights. I would break down, or he would break down, or one of us would do something unexpected and throw the other off, or the accumulating angst would make our exchanges seem simply bizarre. There are many witnesses to the terror of those days. Only when we threw away our clipboards and three-by-five cards did we get anything done. We started ad-libbing and the show began to work. We found we could tape a show in under an hour.

At first the show was once a month, on the Chicago PBS station WTTW, and it was called *Opening Soon at a Theater Near You*. We sat stiffly in director's chairs, holding clipboards, and seemed to have slipped onto TV from a local access channel. We had no chemistry. We barely had a relationship. Working to reinvent this stiff format, Thea threw out the chairs, put us in the balcony, and worked with us over her dining room table on Sunday nights. The show moved up to twice a month for its second year, and then become weekly. By the end at PBS, after raises negotiated by Thea, we were making $325 a program. At the time we left PBS for Tribune Entertainment, I think we would have stayed for $1,000, but PBS then, and even more now, didn't have money like that.

As recently as this year, Thea observed, "Gene was

a natural, but Roger was really bad at first." If she'd told me that at the time, I would have collapsed. I had stage fright, I was alert to every disapproving nuance from Siskel, I could be thrown off by any distraction, I would dry up in the middle of a thought. I slowly got better. By the time the show went weekly, I had eased up, and then eventually it got to be easy, and a pleasure, and Siskel and I lowered our guards when we realized we'd gotten ourselves into something good.

People started recognizing us when we went out of town. "You boys will have no idea," Thea told us after a few months. In 1980, we were contacted by Joe Antelo, a producer with a syndication arm of Tribune Entertainment, which had just started. He thought we had possibilities in commercial television. Gene told me we would need an agent and suggested his own, a Chicago lawyer named Donald Ephraim. I resisted the notion of signing with his agent. "If we don't have the same agent," he said, "it will be a disaster." He was right in most business matters and very correct about that. He was also right to believe we should both always be paid the same salaries; different agents and salaries would have been impossible.

Don Ephraim, and later his firm Ephraim and Associates, including his sons Eliot and David, Joe Coyne, and the accountant John Foy, represented us from then on. Don, we found, was legendary for his attention to detail and once sent back a contract to Disney after finding that they had taken two-thirds of a cent and rounded it down instead of up. "It's the principle of the thing," he said, with an indignation I sometimes thought was acting. "If they go to the trouble of rounding it down, we can go to the trouble of rounding it up again."

WTTW itself had decided to take us into commercial syndication. Don Ephraim went to talk to them and found the station viewed this move as primarily a way to make money for itself. They were unwilling to discuss salaries and profit participation. "In syndication you could be off the air in a few months," Ephraim advised. "If you're taking the chances, you should share the rewards." WTTW made us a final offer. They hadn't budged. We signed with Joe Antelo and Tribune and went up to WTTW to inform the station president, William McCarter. It was an incredible meeting. After Ephraim explained our decision, McCarter didn't seem to understand we were really leaving. He began to suggest other salary possibilities. Ephraim interrupted: "You didn't hear me, Bill. You gave us a take-it-or-leave-it offer, and we've left it. The negotiations are over. We're gone." McCarter seemed momentarily stunned, and there was a loud silence. He was a good man and an important figure in PBS nationally in those days, and we remained friendly; it wasn't that he was stingy, I think, so much as that he couldn't envision us daring to actually leave the PBS cocoon.

Gene and I received a lot of criticism for "betraying" PBS and selling out to commercial syndication. What few people understood was that WTTW had already decided to move us to syndication, and we simply did the same thing on better terms. McCarter saw clearly in those days that PBS needed more sources of funds than a trickle from the Corporation for Public Broadcasting and pledge drives. He was the station executive who helped bring about the system of program sponsorship and underwriting, with its chaste announcements at the beginnings and ends of shows that were not supposed to feel like commercials. What most viewers probably have never understood is that most PBS programming is paid for by underwriting; pledge dollars go mostly toward running each station, and those who bring a program to PBS are expected to finance it themselves.

Now the future was in Joe Antelo's hands. It was by then two months after the annual NATPE convention, at which syndicated television programs are bought and sold. Presumably there were no time periods still available. He knew he could bank on time slots in the markets where Tribune owned stations:

Chicago, New York, Los Angeles, Denver, and others. Could he sell ads on this show? A handsome Cuban American who had once been a singer in Manhattan nightclubs, Joe was a born producer and salesman. He called us to a meeting at Ephraim's office. "I walked next door from Tribune Tower to Leo Burnett," he announced, "and they knew the show from PBS and liked it. I sold out all our time in one afternoon."

We went into syndication that fall, after Joe lined up sixty or seventy markets to join the Tribune stations (except for their New York outlet, which wouldn't stoop to carry a show from Chicago). The next January, he took us to NATPE to get more complete national market coverage. Joe forbade us to walk the floor unless we were together. "Together, you're an advertisement," he explained. "Apart, you're shit." People would ask, "Aren't you those two guys?" Once when we were on an elevator, some people started whispering to each other and when we got off, Gene looked back and said, "We're those two guys."

Both of us were obsessed with our newspaper jobs. That was our identity. TV was part-time. We were competitive, but not equally competitive. Gene was the most competitive man I have ever met. Everything was an opportunity. At PBS, the camera crew played one of those gambling games where you throw little metal pigs on the floor and bet on how many of them land on their feet. I never understood it. They gambled for nickel stakes. One day Gene said, "Let's make it more interesting" and suggested raising the stakes to a quarter. Then he started to win every game. There was no way he was cheating. Gene had taken the pigs home with him and mastered the game. Another time on an airline flight, we were sitting next to each other playing gin rummy, and for once I succeeded in making the right play and Gene threw his cards down on his tray table so hard they flew all over the aisle. We never played gin again.

We went to Vegas a lot for conventions and speeches (Steve Wynn even paid us to review twelve employee-of-the-month films for the Mirage). Gene had scorn for games of chance. I never saw him play one. He would gamble only on poker and horse racing. He didn't believe in spending his money on luck. The belief was deeply ingrained that he could figure things out and outsmart the odds. He claimed he was a lifetime net winner. I found that unlikely. His horse-betting buddy was Johnny Morris, the Chicago Bears star who worked with him at Channel 2. Morris was also said to be a gifted bettor. I was told by a third party that they were both, in truth, successful. I asked Gene what his rules were. "There is only one rule: Never play a hunch."

In Vegas, I played the five-dollar poker tables but

Gene was in the more expensive section of the room. At his bachelor party, he swept the tables with his winnings. At my bachelor party, he was a big loser. I asked him what went wrong. "Your friends don't know how to play poker. A good player can never win against someone who makes a bet just for fun."

He had season tickets for the Bulls going back to the late 1970s, when he told me they were a "good young team." When Michael Jordan joined the team in 1984, Gene began to follow Jordan and the Bulls with a passionate intensity. He even bought front-row tickets—not cheap, but more important to Gene than a new car. He was a fan, but not a mindless fan. He became a student of the game. He looked in basketball for the kinds of "tells" a poker player looks for. He said Jordan was better at reading another player's tells than anybody else in the game.

He asked Coach Phil Jackson, "Why does Dennis Rodman almost always miss the first free throw?"

Jackson said, "Why do you think?"

Gene said, "For some reason, he thinks he has to."

Jackson nodded thoughtfully.

"He didn't tell me what he thought," Gene said. "A good coach would never do that."

We left Tribune because of an oversight and a coincidence. We went to NATPE in New Orleans that year without our new contracts having been offered by Tribune—not Joe Antelo's doing. "Technically," Ephraim told us, "they shouldn't be selling you next year if they don't have you under contract." Gene printed a little card that read WORKING WITHOUT A CONTRACT and pinned it inside the lapel of his jacket. He did it to kid Antelo and the Tribune guys.

That first evening, walking out of our hotel ("always together!") we ran into Jamie Bennett, a program executive Gene had known at CBS/Channel 2 in Chicago. He flashed his joke card to Jamie, who said, "You boys ever been to Brennan's?" He took us to dinner, questioned us about our contract situation, and said he was working for Disney to start a new syndication division, Buena Vista Television. At that dinner a deal was discussed, Ephraim firmed up the details, and we left Tribune for Disney and its powerful base of owned and operated stations. "I would have done the same thing," Joe told us.

We kept leaving titles behind. *Sneak Previews* stayed at PBS. *At the Movies* stayed at Tribune when we went to ABC's Buena Vista. Gene had the idea of renaming it *Siskel & Ebert* so it couldn't be recycled without us. At one point all three shows were coming out of Chicago, making it improbably the TV film criticism capital of the world. We were at Disney the rest of Gene's life, and I worked there with Richard Roeper until 2006.

Gene was formidably well informed. It was a sort of armor. He made it his business. He knew the best restaurants, but that was child's play. He knew fine art and antiques. He knew things like the best tuna-salad sandwich in Los Angeles (the Apple Pan) or the best Italian beef sandwich in Chicago (Mr. Beef). We agreed that Father & Son made the best thin-crust pizza in Chicago. We agreed that deep-pan "Chicago style" pizza wasn't worth the time of day. Gene knew the safest family cars, and those were the only ones he drove. He knew the best school for his children. I never thought of buying a place to live without asking his advice.

When Chaz and I were looking at a house, we asked him to check it out. He walked through the house briefly and said, too quickly I thought, "Don't buy it."

We asked why not. "I don't like the skylight," he said.

What's wrong with it? "From their windows," he said, "your neighbors can see you walking to the bathroom."

He was a bachelor when I first met him, living in an apartment that was said to resemble a resale shop. I never saw it. Few did. McHugh played poker there once, but when I asked him if it was a mess, he said he didn't notice. Gene once won a TV set from

Johnny Morris on a bet. Morris bought the largest and heaviest radio-TV-phonograph he could find and had it delivered. The moving men dumped it inside the door, and I learned it was never moved. The door would only open halfway, and visitors had to squeeze through.

Gene began to appear at screenings with a young woman, which filled us with curiosity because he was not known for bringing dates to screenings. This was Marlene Iglitzen. She was working for CBS in New York, but I learned they'd met when she was a producer on the CBS Chicago evening news, and Gene was doing their movie reviews.

Marlene was smart, funny, and pretty. It became clear Gene was serious. Although they'd met a few years before, they'd never dated until after she moved to New York. Now it became clear he would sooner or later have to invite her to his bachelor's pad, and he asked his sister to clean it up "just enough so I can have a cleaning person come in." I gather it wasn't filled with rotting Kentucky Fried Chicken or anything. It was simply filled with everything he had ever brought home and put down, still there wherever he first put it, and never dusted.

There was always a little of the Yale undergraduate in Gene. Tim Weigel, his roommate there and later a CBS Chicago sportscaster, told me Gene was known for wearing a Batman costume and dropping out of trees. He studied philosophy, considered law school, decided to take some time off first. "I told my dad I thought I'd like to try a job in newspapers," Gene said. "He said he'd give me a ride downtown. We had always been a *Sun-Times* family. For some reason, I never knew why, he dropped me off in front of Tribune Tower." Less than a year after walking in the door, he was the *Tribune's* film critic.

He got his second job, as the movie critic of the CBS Chicago news, because the newscast was bring reformatted to resemble a newspaper city room. Van Gordon Sauter from the old Chicago *Daily News* became the executive producer and recruited Gene on the theory "Don't hire someone because they look good on TV; hire them because they cover a beat and are the masters of it." Gene said that was the reason for the success of our show: We didn't look great on TV, but we sounded as if we might know what we were talking about.

When Gene first met Marlene Iglitzen, "we fought like cats and dogs," she told me. She moved to CBS in New York. He started to see her in New York, and when she was visiting her family in Chicago he would bring her to screenings. I don't recall him ever bringing any other dates to screenings. I sensed she was the one. Once we were all in a car in New York and Gene said he wanted to show me the holy place where he had proposed marriage to Marlene. This was on Second Avenue.

"There it is, right on the corner," Gene said, taking Marlene's hand tenderly.

"The Pizza-Fotomat?" I said.

"My darling Gene," Marlene said.

He had discovered the right woman. Thea Flaum said to me not so long ago, "Gene could sometimes be difficult to deal with. Well, you both were. Marlene is a smart woman. She worked in TV news. I wondered how it would work for her being married to Gene. Rog, after I saw them together for a while, I came to the realization that in the most important ways they were the same person."

Miss Iglitzen kept her name. "When I introduced Marlene to Mel Brooks," Gene said, "Mel asked her, 'What was it before you changed it?'" They had two daughters, Kate and Callie, and a son, Will. The girls were flower girls at our wedding. They followed Gene to Yale, and Will seems to be headed there. The Siskels threw a party for us before Chaz and I were married. We remember the party before Gene and Marlene were married. There was a mentalist who told me everything in my own wallet. This was astonishing; I knew my wallet had been in my pants during the whole party.

"How does he do that?" I asked Gene.

"I don't know, but I'll tell you one thing," Gene said. "He couldn't tell me what was in my wallet."

Once we were invited to speak to the Harvard Law School Film Society. We walked into their mock trial courtroom armed with all sorts of notes, but somehow we got started on a funny note, and the whole appearance became stand-up comedy. Separately or together, we were never funnier. Even the audience questions were funny. Roars of laughter for ninety minutes. I'm not making this up. I don't know what happened. Afterward Gene said, "We could do this in Vegas. No, I'm serious." He was always serious about things like that.

The night after that appearance we had dinner together in a hotel in Cambridge and had our longest and deepest philosophical discussion. We talked about life and death, the cosmos, our place in the grand scheme of things, the meaning of it all. He spoke about his Judaism, which he took very seriously. His parents had started one of the early synagogues on the North Shore after World War II. "I had a lot of long talks with my father about our religion," Gene told me. "He said it wasn't necessary to think too much about an afterlife. What was important was this life, how we live it, what we contribute, our families, and the memories we leave. The importance of Judaism isn't simply theological or, in the minds of some Jews, necessarily theological at all. It is that we have stayed together and respected these things for thousands of years, and so it is important that we continue." This was one of the most touching descriptions of Judaism I had ever heard.

In early 1998, I began to notice that Gene sometimes got things out of order; strange, for a man who was always alert and precise. We emceed an awards show with a dozen categories, and Gene asked me to brief him every time we went onstage. In April of that year, we were the guests of honor at a benefit gala for Chicago's Museum of Broadcast Communications. It marked the twenty-third anniversary of the show. "Why the twenty-third?" I asked Chaz. "Why not the twenty-fifth?" We decided maybe the museum needed the money.

That night, Gene addressed a lot of his remarks to his family, seated at a table right in front of the stage. He told them things they should be sure to tell Will when he grew older. He mentioned some of his values. He spoke of their education, and the importance of finding a job you love. I took quiet notice of that.

Not long after, Jay Leno brought his show to Chicago and we were booked to appear. In the limo going out to the Rosemont Horizon, Gene said he had an unbelievable headache. Backstage, they found a darkened room and a cool cloth for his eyes and gave him some Advil. We were supposed to judge a contest of Jay look-alikes. "My headache is too bad to focus on it," he told me. "You do it and I'll agree with everything you say. You can looked amazed. We can make it a shtick."

After the show, Stuart Cleland, our executive producer, said, "Gene, I'm taking you to a hospital." Gene refused. "Nothing doing. I'm going to the Bulls game." His team was in the playoffs. Chaz and I watched the game on TV and saw Gene in his usual seat on the floor. A day or two later, we heard that Gene had gone into Northwestern Memorial Hospital for some tests. We flew to the Cannes festival, and Stuart called us in France: "Gene is having surgery." We wanted to call and send him flowers. "I don't know where he is," Stuart said. "He didn't tell me."

We later found out it was Sloan-Kettering in New York. There was a statement that Gene had undergone tests and was recovering after a procedure. Gene took some time off (together we chose Tom Shales of the *Washington Post* to sit in for him). When he returned to the show, he was obviously ill, but we never discussed his health, except to agree that he was recovering—recovering from what was never said.

I understood this at the time, and understand it better now. Gene was a competitor. He knew all about odds, and they were against him. But from that summer through the following February, he continued to attend screenings and do the show. He was often in his seat at Bulls games. What he went through, only Marlene knew. He spoke to his family about his illness, but to no one else, not even his best friends. He was unhappy when the *Tribune* ran an item saying his recovery was "on schedule." He asked, "What schedule? Whose schedule?"

Before his final shows, the studio was cleared so that his nephew could help him walk onto the set and take his seat. No mention was made of his illness. He taped his last program a week or two before his death. His pain must have been unimaginable. But he continued to do his job, and I never admired him more. Our eyes would meet, unspoken words were between us, but we never discussed openly his problems or his prognosis. That's how he wanted it, and that was his right. In a way, we had our talk that night in Cambridge. We talked about what mattered.

We once spoke with Disney and CBS about a sitcom to be titled *Best Enemies*. It would be about two movie critics joined in a love/hate relationship. It never went anywhere, but we both believed it was a good idea. Maybe the problem was that no one else could possibly understand how meaningless was the hate, how deep was the love.

42 JUGULAR

ONE OF THE things I miss about Gene Siskel is that he's not around to make jokes about my current condition. He would instinctively know that at this point I wouldn't be sensitive, having accepted and grown comfortable with my maimed appearance. He wouldn't have started joking too soon. His jokes would have the saving grace of being funny. Here's one I'm pretty sure he would have come up with: "Well, there's one good thing about Roger's surgery. At least he no longer needs a bookmark to find his chin."

I've never concerned myself overmuch anyway about the way I looked. I got a lot of practice at indifference during my years as the Michelin Man. Before

I acquired my present problems, I was not merely fat but was universally known as "the fat one," to distinguish me from "the thin one," who was Gene Siskel, who was not all that thin, but try telling that to Gene. On the set of the show, between actually taping segments, we had a rule that there could be no discussion of the movies under review. So we attacked each other with one-liners. Buzz Hannan, our floor director, was our straight man, and the cameramen supplied our audience. For example:

Me: "Don't you think you went a little over the top in that last review?"

Gene: "Spoken like the gifted Haystacks Calhoun tribute artist that you are."

"Haystacks was loved by his fans as a charming country boy."

"Six hundred and forty pounds of rompin' stompin' charm. Oh, Rog? Are those two-tone suedes, or did you step in some chicken shit?"

"You can borrow them whenever you wear your white John Travolta disco suit from *Saturday Night Fever*."

Buzz: "Yeah, when are you gonna wear it on the show?"

"He wanted to wear it today, but it's still at the tailor shop having the crotch taken in."

Buzz: "Ba-ba-ba-boom!"

"Here's an item that will interest you, Roger," Gene told me one day, paging through the *Sun-Times*, his favorite paper, during a lull in the taping of our show. We taped in CBS Chicago's Studio One, home of the Kennedy-Nixon debate. "It says here, the Michelin Man has been arrested in a fast food court in Hawaii for attempting to impersonate the Pillsbury Doughboy."

"Yeah," I said. "I read the paper over breakfast. There was an item in Kup's column saying your forehead was named as America's biggest zip code. (*Glancing at the studio monitor.*) Oh...my...God! CNN has just reported that your hairline is receding so rapidly the rising sea level is threatening coastal cities."

"Ba-boom!" Buzz would say.

Yes, I was fat, but I dealt with it by simply never thinking about it. It is useful, when you are fat, to have a lot of other things to think about. If you obsess about fat, it will not make you any thinner, but it will make you miserable. If you try any diet you have read about in a magazine or heard about from a celebrity, it will make you even more miserable. I maintained tip-top mental health during all the years of my obesity. When Chaz dragged me kicking and screaming to the Pritikin Longevity Center, I lost a lot of weight in a healthy way, and I enjoyed it. I kicked and screamed all the way toward anything that might do me any good. It is a proud trait of the American male.

I never looked all that fat to me. I wore a navy blue pullover vest on top of my L. L. Bean oxford-cloth shirt, and when I glanced down it contained every-thing in an attractive convexity merging serenely with my khakis.

"Phone for you, Rog," Gene said, handing me his cell. "Your shoes are calling."

I favored blue sweater-vests, because whenever I wore brown Gene said, "Buzz, the usual offer of ten silver dollars to any cameraman who doesn't make Mr. Ebert look like a mudslide."

"Is the offer limited to close-ups?"

"Twenty coins for any cameraman who can *not* take a close-up of Mr. Ebert."

"Don't worry, Roger," Buzz said. "I'll write a note to management about expanding Studio One so the cameras can pull back a little more."

"Now you're playing on the same side as Mr. Tact," I complained.

"That's why they call me Mr. Thumb Tact," Gene said.

"I heard you were severely lacerated while trying not to thumbtack a note to your forehead," I said.

"Ka-boom!"

When I wore a green blazer on St. Patrick's Day,

Gene congratulated me on my Master's win. For this and other reasons I invariably wore the blue blazer, blue oxford shirt, blue pullover sweater-vest, and khakis. This look was original with me. No other fat man ever thought of it.

Now I look like the Phantom of the Opera. This is so much fun I almost forgot my subject today. There are a lot of Phantom fans who wouldn't think that was such a terrible thing. Some of them have been waiting in line on the sidewalk outside Her Majesty's Theatre in London for more than thirty years. Indeed, that musical was the inspiration for my only published novel, *Behind the Phantom's Mask*, which was written as a newspaper serial.

"The first book in history," Gene said, "that placed *below* Amazon's sales ranking."

"I tried to carry all Gene's books home from the store," I told Buzz, "but it was too much for me."

"Why was that, Roger?"

"Because there weren't any."

"Ka-boom!"

One day in London I was cruelly made aware of my fat. I was walking through Sir John Soane's Museum at 13 Lincoln's Inn Fields for maybe the tenth time. This has been called "the most eccentric house in London." It was the home of the great eighteenth-century architect, who bequeathed it to a grateful nation. ("Now let them dust the bloody man's rubbish," Mrs. Soane said.) Sir John had filled every nook and cranny with an accumulation of books, furniture, oils, watercolors, drawings, mirrors, statuary, writing implements, rifles, pistols, brass buttons, coins, swords, rugs, etchings, tapestries, stuffed heads, and even the Monk's Tomb, engraved "Alas, poor Fanny!" Here rested Mrs. Soane's beloved lap dog, which could never remember which marble bases it was not to pee on. Those must have included the supports for Soane's beloved Egyptian sarcophagus.

Of Sir John's breakfast room, Ian Nairn wrote: "If man does not blow himself up, he might in the end act at all times and on all levels with the complete understanding of this room." I would stand in a corner and try to understand it. Among its features were concave mirrors at the corners of the ceiling, and outside views in parallel windows, one seemingly transparent, the other seemingly a mirror.

In this house is a wondrous art room which contains, I don't know, let's say eighty paintings, including even the original *Rake's Progress* by Hogarth. This room is occupied by a guard with a peculiarly knowing smile. He is sure you will look again at your leaflet and say, "I don't see eighty paintings."

The guard: "Quite right, sir! A complaint we often hear from visitors." Then he pauses and leans forward a little, as if waiting for you to take the bait, which you do, because almost any conceivable question will be the wrong one. The most obvious would be, "You mean there *aren't* eighty paintings in this room?"

"There most certainly are, sir!" He explains that the walls hang on hinges, and the room actually contains three times as many paintings as are on view. Faced with this unfolding display one winter afternoon, my eye fell on a handsome seventeenth-century chair, which had a little card behind it on the wall, saying (as no museum chair ever does) "Have a seat on me!"

My eyes lit up and I advanced on it, until I felt the guard's gentle touch.

"Oh, no, no, no, no, no, sir!" he said, paraphrasing the saddest line in all of Shakespeare.

"But it says to have a seat," I said.

"And so it does. But it's not for the likes of you!"

I turned away mute from this crushing warning and wandered lonely as a cloud 'neath lowering skies in Lincoln's Inn Fields. A slight mist became a light rain. It was January and chilly. I opened my umbrella, for I love London most when I am strolling at twilight under a slight rain with a big brolly. I began to cheer up, and reflected that dinner hours had commenced.

Over the years, people almost never discussed my weight, at least to my face. Perhaps they were being tactful. Perhaps they were blind. I preferred to believe they simply did not notice it, as I never did. I avoided reading blogs, where it was deemed sufficient reason to discredit my reviews: "Why should I believe that fat slob about anything?"

There was only one other disturbing incident. This was in Bangkok, Thailand. Chaz and I were visiting Thailand because at a charity auction she had obtained two weeks, two spas, and a luxury Bangkok hotel at a shamefully low price. "This was a steal!" she exalted. "These people are all so busy they don't have time to take off for Thailand." A bargain indeed, although its value diminished when we discovered the luxury package did not include air travel.

Bangkok was a shopper's paradise. Chaz visited a custom tailor's and ordered four $10,000 designer outfits for $102 each from the pages of *Vogue*. One day while strolling, I saw a little tailor shop with a three-piece white summer suit displayed in the window. Sydney Greenstreet would have been proud to wear it. There was a sign: "Fine Linen Summer Suit Made to Measure—$80!"

I went inside. The tailor and his assistant explained the procedure. "We measure you, quick-quick! Then we make suit, hurry-hurry to hotel! Then we try on, make alterations as needed! Then we hurry deliver suit, your room, eight p.m."

They stood me on a pedestal and the tailor barked out measurements while his assistant wrote them down.

"Your sign says this is eighty dollars," I said. "I thought the Thai currency unit was the baht."

"You are only American tourist who think that," he said. "We do dollar for your convenience."

"But you're sure this suit is really eighty dollars?"

The tailor looked thoughtful.

"Well...it eighty-dollar suit, sure enough. But you...hundred-dollar man!"

But back to the Phantom of the Opera. What is it like to resemble him, since I have lost most of my lower jaw and am what is now described as having Facial Differences? To begin with, I must make this clear: Many people have problems much worse than mine, and at a much younger age, and sometimes joined with other disabilities. I may seem tragic to you, but I seem fortunate to myself. Don't lose any sleep over me. I am so much a movie lover that I can imagine a certain small pleasure in looking like the Phantom. It is better than looking like the Elephant Man. I would describe my condition as falling about 72 percent of the way along a timeline between how I looked in 2004 and the thing that jumps out of that guy's intestines in *Alien*.

The problem is that no one seems to settle on

what the Phantom should look like. I don't look at all like the modern Phantom, played by Gerard Butler in Joel Schumacher's 2004 film. He's handsome as he punts along the sewers. The Phantom I resemble, the real Phantom, is the one played by Lon Chaney in Rupert Julian's classic 1925 version. The 2004 Phantom doesn't skulk about in a clammy subterranean grotto. He inhabits a spacious dockside room in a sewer marina. His disfigurement is picturesque. As his sleek off-white mask covers his right temple, eye, and upper cheek, and curves gently to meet his nose, it looks like a fashion accessory. Everybody will want one.

In the 1925 version, the Phantom wears a full face mask. When Christine Daaé removes it, there is one of the great smash cuts in cinema, showing the Phantom full face with his mouth gaping open. Although his complexion is far from untroubled, his real problems involve his mouth, teeth, and jaw—nothing to do with his right temple. If the Phantom looked as he did in 1925, he could no more sing in a musical than I can. Both the wound and the mask were relocated by Andrew Lloyd Webber. Now the Phantom is clean-cut, square jawed, and looks like the cover illustration of a romance novel.

I rather avoid mirrors. I do not dwell on my appearance. I wear a black turtleneck when I think I might have my picture taken. I usually decline when people want me to pose for a photo with them: I imagine their friends peering at my peculiarities.

"Do I look okay, Gene?" I asked him one night when we were waiting backstage to go on the Leno show. As usual, I was wearing the sweater–sports coat–khakis combo.

"Roger, when I need to amuse myself, I stroll down the sidewalk reflecting that every person I pass thought they looked just great when they walked out of their house that morning."

THE TALK SHOWS

GENE AND I were invited to appear on a noon hour TV show in Milwaukee named *Dialing for Dollars*. We weren't so sure. This would be our first joint appearance since beginning the show on PBS, and we were beset with ethical questions: Could serious film critics appear on such a show? How would it make us look?

"Boys, boys, boys," Thea Flaum said. "Do you think the audience for *Dialing for Dollars* is going to be thinking about things like that?" She put us through a dry run. She spun an imaginary drum and plucked out a three-by-five card on which she had written her own name. "And the winner is Thea Flaum," Gene read. "Congratulations, Thea. You won a dollar."

As the show slowly became better known, we got other invitations. This was known as "station relations." We'd fly to a market, do TV to help the show, and have lunch with the local station executives. The day came when we were invited to Baltimore to appear on a morning show hosted by a young woman named Oprah Winfrey. "She's very big in Baltimore," we were assured by Joe Antelo, who was by now producing the show for Tribune. TV producers seem to be plugged into an extrasensory network informing them of who is very big.

Oprah, who was not yet OPRAH, breezed into the green room to chat. I liked her. She was surprisingly young and warm. She explained we would appear after a segment with a vegetarian chef and before the wrap-up segment, which would be the Chipmunks performing with Hula-Hoops. The show did not go smoothly. While pureeing zucchini, the vegetarian chef knocked over the blender and zucchini sprayed all over the interview sofa. During the commercial break, Oprah covered the sofa with pages of the *Baltimore Sun* and told us to sit quietly and not rustle. In the wings, we could see the Chipmunks waiting with their Hula-Hoops. "Roger," Gene said, "if our eyes meet, we are lost." This was true. Gene and I had a pattern of catching each other's eyes and starting to giggle, especially when we weren't supposed to.

Oprah moved to Chicago not long after, joining the same ABC station where I'd just been hired to do movies on the news. Its new station manager was Dennis Swanson, a tall extrovert whom I had known at Illinois when he ran WPGU, the student radio station. He has since moved on to management at ABC and Fox, but the hire of Oprah was his decision of genius. Morning shows in those days invariably had co-hosts, and he caught a lot of criticism for risking the Channel 7 slot on an unknown young African-American woman, especially when she would be going up against Phil Donahue, then at the height of his popularity. His response: "I'm right."

So forlorn was the *AM Chicago* slot between the death of its former host Bob Kennedy and the advent of Oprah that in the week before Oprah's premiere I was actually the substitute host. I remember in particular interviewing Sophia Loren about a new perfume she was introducing. "What is the perfume made from?" I asked innocently, and then realized she had no idea. I believe she replied, "Oh...flowers, you know, and...scents."

Although some strange stories have gone around, it is not true to say Oprah and I ever dated. We went to the movies once, but that's what it was: We went to the movies. Gene and I were guests on her new show, which had already passed Donahue in the ratings.

She asked me if I went to movies all the time, and when I said I went at least five times a week, she said, "Why don't you take me sometime?" So I did.

It was after that first movie that we had our historic dinner. She told me she was being courted by both King World and the ABC station group to go into syndication, but she had her doubts about King: "If you fail in syndication, you're off the air. It's merciless. If I go with ABC, they own stations in major markets, so I'm more protected."

We were at Hamburger Hamlet on Rush Street. I took a napkin. "Here's what I'm making right now," I said, writing down an amount. "Gene makes the same. So figure twice that. We're on half an hour, you're on an hour. Times two. You're on five days a week, we're on once. Times five. You're in prime daytime, we're in fringe weekends. Worth at least twice as much. My salary times two, times two, times five, times two." Oprah studied the napkin and said, "I'm going with King." She would eventually make much more.

Gene and I were on with Oprah many times, starting at the studio Channel 7 built for her at 190 North State, and later at the Harpo Studios she built for herself on Washington. There was a reason for her popularity. She was gifted and had good producers. She warmed up the show beforehand and stayed afterward for photos and autographs. She wasn't phony. She was generous with her money. Both of us have had weight problems over the years, mine worse than hers, but we never discussed them. There was one moment in particular when for once I had the good sense to keep my mouth shut. Dennis Swanson had teamed us up to co-host the Chicago Emmy Awards, which would be carried by Channel 7. On cue we entered from opposite sides of the stage and met at the lectern. Great applause. "I feel like Diana Ross," Oprah said. It was a straight line. The next line jumped into my mind: "...and the Supremes!" I'm gifted at blurting out the wrong things at the wrong times, but some instinct stopped me in time.

I never thought Oprah was really all that fat. I thought she was sexy. I did ask her out one other time, when the Count Basie Orchestra was at the Park West, but it wasn't precisely a date. She had to leave early to be at work before dawn and left in her own car. Did I have some half-formed romantic notion in mind? Oprah tactfully and subtly communicated that whatever I had in mind, it wasn't happening. What's important to this day, I think, is that she must have sensed what I was wordlessly thinking. We tend to like people when they like us. She liked me too, but never remotely in that way. When Chaz and I were married, she was one of the guests, and I was moved by how happy she was for us.

Chicago was a hub for syndicated talk shows in those days. Oprah was queen of the genre. Phil Donahue, unfailingly intelligent, had a long run. Jerry Springer, Jenny Jones. Jerry was nothing if not honest. Every time we saw him, he said, "I'm going to hell for doing this show." There was one thing to be said for his show: When I was surfing and came across it, I invariably watched. Overweight married transsexuals cheating with their genders of destination. How can you beat that?

Joan Rivers got Gene and me into late night TV. She was the regular guest host when Johnny Carson was on vacation. She invited us onto the *Tonight Show*, perhaps as a tryout for Johnny. I have a memory of backstage chaos, and of her husband, Edgar, nervously trying to keep the lid on a disorganized staff. Joan came up with a stunt where Gene and I wore soundproofing earphones and could hear her but not each other. It was sort of the Dating Game, tweaked to exploit our rivalry. We both spoke very seriously, ever mindful that we were Serious Film Critics and not bozos. We could see people laughing a lot, but we didn't know what they were laughing about.

In the fullness of time, Johnny Carson himself invited us on. We'd done some TV by this time, but we were both terrified. I'd been watching Johnny since his first night on the program. He was an idol.

Gene and I were given separate dressing rooms, but we sat in the same one for moral support. The door opened and it was...Johnny Carson. Alive. In the same room. We bolted to our feet. He wanted to welcome us on the show. He disappeared. On the TV monitor, the Doc Severinsen orchestra began the famous *Tonight Show* theme. "Roger," said Gene. "You and I do not belong here. We belong at home in Chicago, watching this on TV." The door opened, and it was one of Johnny's writers: "Johnny may ask you for some of your favorite movies so far this year," he said. He left. Gene and I looked at each other and an unspoken fact hung in the air between us. Our minds were blank. "Name a movie you like," Gene said. "*Gone With the Wind,*" I said. Gene telephoned Nancy De Los Santos, our producer. "Name some movies we like," he said.

When Johnny retired and Leno famously won the late night war between himself and David Letterman, there was speculation that Dave would jump networks rather than follow Jay on NBC. It happened that Gene and I were guests on the Letterman show the very evening that was scheduled to be announced. There was much talk backstage, among writers, assistant producers, makeup artists, and stagehands (including the friendly Biff), but no solid information. After the show Gene and I headed for the scheduled press conference, where Letterman appeared with CBS president Howard Stringer to announce his move. But we didn't discuss it with him.

Indeed, we never discussed anything with him, apart from two occasions. Leno routinely circulated among dressing rooms, chatting with all his guests before a show, but Letterman never did. That wasn't because he didn't like us. Before Gene's death, we briefly held the record for most appearances on his show. My guess is, Dave coiled in wait for the starting gun at the beginning of every show and didn't believe in dissipating his energy before the red light went on. We understood that. Gene and I never discussed a movie before taping a show; you can only discuss something for the first time once. Dave enjoyed a certain tension, which perhaps built excitement, and one of the veteran members of Paul Shaffer's band told me the band members didn't really know Dave either. I suppose Paul did, but I can't say.

Leno, on the other hand, liked to be everybody's friend. He genuinely did like the movies—was obsessed by them, in fact, and in the dressing room before the show he would debate our latest reviews and very often find fault with them. It's well known that talk show guests are pre-interviewed by a writer, and the host is armed with note cards suggesting questions and the expected answers. "You guys are the ideal guests," Leno's writer Steve Ridgeway told Richard Roeper and me once. That wasn't because we were so great. It was because Leno always knew what he wanted to ask us and always knew what the right answer was, whether or not we agreed. "Your segments always run long," he said, "because Jay won't shut up about the movies."

That was our advantage. We always had a topic: the summer movies, the fall movies, the Christmas movies, the Oscar nominations. "We have enormous studios spending millions of dollars every week to supply us with subject matter," Gene said. Only occasionally was a host surprised.

Gene and I were on the Carson show once, following Chevy Chase, who had just promoted his Christmas release, *¡Three Amigos!* We chatted a little, and then Johnny said, "Roger, what's your *least* favorite Christmas picture?" We were looking directly at each other when he said that, and I noticed an almost invisible expression flash across his face. I knew what the answer was, and I believe in that second Johnny did, too. I paused. "*¡Three Amigos!*" I said.

There was an uneasy audience reaction. Audiences expect guests on talk shows to always be nice. Chevy saved the moment by cracking, "Looking forward to *your* next picture." Carson did one of his double takes and said, "Gee, I wished I hadn't said that." "Me too," I said. After the show, Chevy appeared in the door of my dressing room with a poker face. I was at a loss for words. "I don't think it's so hot either," he said.

One of the reasons for the success of our show, and our interest as talk show guests, is that like the victims of some curse in a fairy tale, Gene and I were compelled to tell the truth. We were critics. We couldn't tell diplomatic lies. We had each other to keep us honest. There might be a temptation to say something diplomatic, but the other guy would call you on it. If I'd tried to talk around Johnny's question, Gene would have jumped like a wolf: "Gee, Rog, you were saying just the other day how much you hated Chevy's movie." Neither one of us could pass up an opening. If Johnny had asked Gene the question, he would also certainly have said, "¡Three Amigos!"

I mentioned that against all odds we had two private conversations with David Letterman. One of them was spread across a balmy autumn day when we went with a *Late Show* camera crew to shoot a video piece in New Jersey. A residential block had been chosen. The gag was, David would knock on a door, and when it was opened, would say, "Good afternoon. I'm Dave Letterman. I have Siskel and Ebert here in case you want to ask them any questions about the movies."

It was a good idea, but in reality it transcended any possible expectation, because there is no telling whom you'll meet when you knock on a door. As the people we met grew more and more curious, a certain bond formed among us, because the experience was becoming surreal. One man introduced his wife, whom he'd had a crush on since high school. They had both married others, but now their first spouses had passed on, and they were together at last. The living room was a shrine to this woman when she had been a high school beauty queen. Big photo blow-ups of her prom night, her senior picture, her decorating a float, her at a sock hop, bordering on idolatry. What we talked about I have no idea.

At another house, a man and his adult son came to the door, both wearing flamboyant mustaches. They said they never went to the movies. What was the last movie they had seen? They couldn't think of one. How about on TV? No, they watched sports. The camera was rolling. Dave took a beat, and spoke to the son: "I'll give you a hundred dollars if you shave off the mustache."

"Who's gonna do it? You?"

"Oh no. We have a makeup artist."

We taped the mustache being shaved.

At another house our visit turned into a basketball game, two on two, in a driveway. Then there was the woman who said she couldn't talk now because she was going to a funeral.

"Oh, I'm terribly sorry to hear that, ma'am," Dave said. "Roger can tap the *William Tell Overture* with his fingernails, and Gene can name all twenty-two of the helping adverbs."

"Well, all right," the woman said. I tapped the *William Tell Overture* on her aluminum storm door, and Gene named the helping adverbs.

The woman regarded us patiently.

"All right," she said. "Now I have to be going."

"Is there anything the boys can do for you while you're gone?"

"The gutters need cleaning."

Dave and his crew found a ladder in the garage and Gene and I climbed up and cleaned her gutters.

This resulted in a very funny video, but it also led to some downtime with Letterman, as we stood in the shade and waited for the crew to set up shots. Our only previous interaction with him had been during those moments when a segment is ending and the host leans over to say something private to the guest. On that afternoon Dave said nothing much of consequence. He and Gene exchanged detailed analysis of the play of Michael Jordan and the Bulls, a subject on which Gene was not afraid to give advice at length to Phil Jackson. Dave and I discussed the genius of

Bob and Ray. My impression was that when he winds down, Letterman is a nice guy from the Midwest, and that the Letterman people see on show days is in hyperdrive. I think he regards the show with great seriousness and aims himself at the opening monologue with a lasered intensity.

Leno, on the other hand, likes to be seen as a regular guy. When I had to leave *Ebert & Roeper* for surgery in 2006, never to return, he sat in as Roeper's co-host on the first show afterward. That seems like an extraordinary kindness unless you realize he'd been watching since the early days with Siskel, and telling himself during every show, "I could do that better than those guys." There might have been a little to that. Sometimes I watch him glancing at his cards in desperation as a guest seems mired in redundancy and inarticulate truisms. What he should do is ask the guests what they think about a new movie, and then answer his own question.

The other time Gene and I talked privately with Letterman broke all precedent. "Dave would like to talk to you in his office after the show," a producer told us. Gene got all wound up. "Roger," he said, "this can only mean one thing! He wants us to do a talk show for his company Worldwide Pants."

As it happened, that was the night when I experienced the biggest genuine, spontaneous laugh I've ever witnessed on a talk show. Gene was telling his story about the time he and John Wayne went into a greasy spoon at three a.m. and the waitress came over, saw him, and crossed herself.

"What was the name of the movie he was making?" Dave asked.

"*Chisum*," Gene said, pronouncing it "jism."

There was a moment of silence. I was sitting in the chair next to Letterman. My head swiveled. Our eyes met. Ba-boom. He, and I, and the audience, and after a while Gene, broke into uncontrolled laughter.

This was a good omen for our new talk show. "They'll probably want us to move to New York," Gene was fretting. After the show a producer took us upstairs to Dave's surprisingly modest office in Worldwide Pants. We sat in two chairs facing him.

"I've got a problem, and I think you boys might be able to help me."

Gene smiled confidently.

"You guys were both on the show we did from the Chicago theater," Dave said. "Oprah was on the same show. Remember that night?"

We did.

"Something happened that night. I don't know what it was, but Oprah has never come back on the show again, and she won't even talk to me. You know Oprah. Has she ever said anything?"

She never said a word to us, we said. People often seemed to assume that since we were from Chicago, we all hung out together. The truth is, if you have access to Oprah, you respect it. You don't ask for a lot of favors. You don't assume. If you are my grandchild, I might be able to call one of her producers and get you a ticket to a taping of her show on your birthday, but that's about it.

"Okay, that doesn't surprise me," Dave said. "But now Michael Jordan also won't come on my show. I have no idea why. Is it because Oprah said something to him?"

Gene and I looked at each other. Gene was actually close to Michael, in the way a journalist can be close to a superstar. You wouldn't call them confidants. The question of whether Oprah had said something to Michael about Dave would be unlikely to come up. We didn't have a clue.

"Right," said Dave, cracking his knuckles. "That's what I expected. Well, thanks for your time. Great show tonight."

When people asked Letterman why he had two interview chairs, his stock answer was, "Siskel and Ebert." After Gene's death in 1999, he had me as a guest one more time, to promote my first *Great Movies* book, and then never again. He didn't get mad at me or anything. Gene and I were a double act. As Joe

Antelo had assured us long ago, "Individually, you're nothing. Together, you're stars."

Leno continued to invite me back, and when Richard Roeper joined me on the show, he was invited, and is still a guest on a regular basis, because Jay loves to talk about movies. It's not often you see Letterman needing the second chair. I thought of it as Gene's chair. He thought of it as mine. We kept meticulous track of whose turn it was to sit next to Dave.

44   WHEN I LAUGHED IN STUDY HALL

I AM AN American who was born before the schools were integrated in the South. I am a midwesterner who went with his mother on a trip to Washington, D.C., and my cousin's company driver showed us the sights, but when we stopped for lunch at Howard Johnson's he explained he couldn't go inside because they didn't serve colored people. "But you're with us!" I said. "I know," he said, smiling over my head at my mother, "but they don't know who you are." Inside, I asked my mother why they wouldn't serve him. "They have their own nice places to eat," she said. I don't believe she was particularly upset on his behalf.

The first time I noticed that people had different

colors of skin I was a very small boy. Our family laundry was done by a colored woman on Champaign's north side. She was our "warsherwoman." Downstate you pronounced an invisible "r," so we lived on Warshington Street. I sat down on the floor to play with her son, who was about my age, and he showed me his palm and said it was as white as my palm. I noticed for the first time that the rest of him wasn't.

In Catholic grade school, there was a colored boy named Donald in my class—that was the word we used, "colored," although "Negro" was more formal. I remember the class being informed by a nun that he was "just as precious as the rest of you in the eyes of God." I believed most of what the nuns told us, and I believed that. It made sense. Some years later it occurred to me to wonder how he felt when he was singled out. He lived in a house across the street from our playground and got to go home for lunch. Donald studied with us, played with us, and I gave him rides on the handlebars of my bike. Only slowly did his color become more—important? is that the word?—to me.

There were Negro students at Urbana High School, and I knew the athletes because I covered sports for the local newspaper. I didn't know them, you understand, in the sense of going to their homes or hanging out at the Steak 'n Shake, and I don't recall any of them at the Tigers' Den, the city's teen hangout in downtown Urbana. They did attend our school dances. There was a kid who wasn't an athlete, whom I liked, and we talked and kidded around, but in those days, well, that was about that.

Strangely, during this time the "idea" of Negroes was on a wholly different track in my mind. I read incessantly during high school, and I met them in the novels of Thomas Wolfe and William Faulkner. I read Richard Wright's *Black Boy* and *Native Son* and Ralph Ellison's *Invisible Man*. So I had this concept shaping in my mind that bore no relationship to what was going on in my life. It was theoretical.

This is not a record of my reading but of my understanding. Racism was ingrained in daily life in those days. It wasn't the overt racism of the South, but more like the pervading background against which we lived. We were here and they were there and, well, we wished them well, but that was how it was. At this time it was becoming clear to me that I was not merely a Democrat, as I had been raised, but a liberal. When Eisenhower sent the National Guard to Arkansas, I defended him against some who said the federal government had no right interfering. So that was my political position. But where were my feelings centered? Theory will only take you so far.

In college, my understanding shifted. I attended the

National Student Congress every summer, and during one held at Ohio State, two things happened. I gave a dollar to Tom Hayden and he handed me my membership card in Students for a Democratic Society. And one night during a party at Rosa Luxemburg House, I met a Negro girl and we went outside and sat in the backseat of a car and we talked and kissed and she was sweet and gentle and she smelled of Ivory soap. We fell asleep in each other's arms. We met again maybe ten years later in New York City, recognizing each other on the street, and had a drink and talked about how young we had been. In my inner development, I had been younger than she knew.

Those were the days of the civil rights movement. We linked hands and sang "We Shall Overcome." We protested. We demonstrated. Among the students I met at those student congresses were Stokely Carmichael, Julian Bond—and, for that matter, Barney Frank. They were born to be who they became. I was still in the process of changing. My emotional life was catching up to my intellectual and political life.

Later in the 1960s Negros became blacks. As a movie critic, I could watch that happening. The new usage first appears in my reviews around 1967 or 1968. Afros. Angela Davis. Black exploitation movies. Black is beautiful. Long interviews with Ossie Davis, Brock Peters, Sidney Poitier, Abbey Lincoln,

Yaphet Kotto. What point am I making? None. It's not as if I sat at their feet and learned about race. It's more that the whole climate was changing, growing more free and open, and the movies were changing, too.

At some time during the years after the day I sat on the floor and looked at that little boy's palm, something happened inside me and I saw black people more clearly—and brown people and Asians as well. I made friends, I dated, I worked with them, I drank with them, we cooked, we partied, we laughed, sometimes we loved. This is as it should have been from the start of my life, but I was born into a different America and was a child of my times until I learned enough to grow up. I do not propose myself as an example, because I was carried along with my society as it awkwardly felt and fought its way out of racism.

When I proposed marriage to Chaz, it was for the best possible reason: I wanted to be married to this woman. Howard Stern asked me on the radio one day if I thought of Chaz as being black every time I looked at her. I didn't resent the question. Howard Stern's gift is the nerve to ask personal questions. I told him, honestly, that when I looked at her I saw Chaz. Chaz. A fact. A person of enormous importance to me. Chaz. A history. Memories. Love. Passion. Laughter. Her Chaz-ness filled my field of vision. Yes, I see that she is black, and she sees that I am white, but how sad it would be if that were in the foreground. Now, with so many of my own family dead, her family gives me a family, an emotional home I need. Before our first trip out of town, she took me home to meet her mother.

I believe at some point in the development of healthy people there must come a time when we instinctively try to understand how others feel. We may not succeed. There are many people in this world today who remain enigmas to me, and some who are offensive. But that is not because of their race. It is usually because of their beliefs.

One day in high school study hall, a Negro girl walked in who had dyed her hair a light brown. Laughter spread through the room. We had never, ever, seen that done before. It was unexpected, a surprise, and our laughter was partly an expression of nervousness and uncertainty. I don't think we wanted to be cruel. But we had our ideas about Negroes, and her hair didn't fit.

Think of that girl. She wanted to try her hair a lighter brown, and perhaps her mother and sisters helped her, and she was told she looked pretty, and then she went to school and we laughed at her. I wonder if she has ever forgotten that day. I never have. It shames me.

45   MY ROMANCES

FROM THE EARLIEST days of my adolescence, my love life was conducted in secrecy. My behavior centered on a paralyzing reluctance to engage my mother's anger. Her conviction that I was destined for the Church led to hostility toward any expression of my sexuality. Late one night after an orgasmic session in the front seat of my car in front of one of the university residence halls, I hung my blue jeans in back of my closet, planning to wash them later. With an uncanny sixth sense, she found them there the next morning and waved the proof of my sin before me, accusing me of having "wasted a baby." I felt humiliated. I began to keep as much of my life as possible a secret from her. If my father had been alive it would have been different, I believe, but he was not alive.

My early social life was conventional. My first date was for an official graduation dance at the Thelma Leah Ritter Dance School, above the Princess Theater. Here I was enrolled after failing to master the fox-trot, the samba, the mambo, and the waltz while practicing with my aunt Martha in the living room of my grandmother's house on Clark Street. My grandmother, my mother, my father, Martha's friend Jean, and my uncle Bob, who had never danced a step in his life, sat around offering suggestions.

For that first dance I invited a St. Mary's classmate I was good friends with, but her name is gone from my memory. We were dropped off at the corner and walked up to the steps, only to find the door locked. I had the wrong night. The evening was saved and much improved when we went instead to see *Bridge on the River Kwai* at the Princess. Here I enacted the ages-old ritual of casually resting my arm on the back of her seat and then advancing it so slowly that had it not been a long movie it might never have reached her shoulder. When the bombs went off my arm made the final decisive leap.

In high school and the full flood of adolescence, I had powerful crushes and even what I took for the time as love. At some point I made it clear I would

not be going into the priesthood—I had no "vocation"—but my mother warned against liaisons with
non-Catholic girls. "There's no future in it. You can't
ever marry them. It's not fair to the girl." When I got
the euphoric freedom of a driver's license, she could
no longer be sure who I was seeing, and I began a
pattern of denying I was seeing anyone at all. I was
out with the gang. Or "working over at the *News-
Gazette*." Or "just down at the Tigers' Den," our
chaperoned Urbana hangout. Or "I went to the movies." Eventually I did acknowledge the reality of some
of my high school romances: Mary Scott, Marty
McCloy, Judi Irle, my senior prom date Carol Zim-
mer. My mother approved of my high school dates,
they were very nice, they came from good families,
but I was reminded that I could never marry one.
"Why don't you date a nice Catholic girl?" If I had,
my life might have turned out differently. But somehow I had known all of the St. Mary's girls too well
for eight years, and when I reached ninth grade the
public school girls seemed, well, women and not playmates. I pointed out that my mother herself, after all,
had married a non-Catholic. "Yes, I did. We had to
be married in the rectory. I don't want you making
the same mistake." Apparently a church wedding was
more important than my happiness.

The roots of my hesitation began before I even

dreamed of romance, much less sex. They involved a fear of my mother's emotionalism. My parents didn't have many domestic quarrels, but they left deep wounds as I curled under my blankets and heard angry voices raised and footfalls up and down the little hallway, between the bedroom and the kitchen, and the slamming of doors. Many children grow up with unspeakable abuse. My parents were always loving and kind. Perhaps that made this anger seem more shocking. In my memory, it is my mother's voice, raised and hysterical, that comes through the bedroom door, and my father's voice sounds lower, placating, reasoning. What was really going on I cannot say, although I had the impression the arguments always began over money and their two families and then escalated into denunciations, "you don't love me," and so on.

I felt a deep aversion to my mother's anger. I began to avoid confrontation by deception. This pattern deepened in college, and I began a double life. During those years I was drawn eagerly into the campus world of beatniks, bohemians, liberals, writers, artists, theater people, the Campus Folksong Club, and hangouts like the Turk's Head Coffee House, the Capitol Bar, and certain tables in the basement of the Illini Union frequented by students who seemed thrillingly nonconformist. I began as an enthusiastic

Phi Delt and even moved into the house for a semester. What began to change me was a growing liberalism, in those years before the upheavals in the late 1960s. Representing the *Daily Illini*, I starting attending the summer congresses of the National Student Association. Judy Johnson, the news editor of the *DI*, brought back from her first one the Port Huron Statement of the new Students for a Democratic Society, and in reading it I found a powerful appeal to my developing feelings. SDS was still then "the Student Department of the League for Industrial Democracy," an element of the Socialist Party USA, the Norman Thomas group of democratic socialists. The card carried an anti-communist statement on its back. I read Thomas's books, and as editor of the *DI* began to run his syndicated column. By "syndicated," I mean that he wrote it for *New America*, the party newspaper, and mailed us a carbon copy from his typewriter for two dollars a week.

At a congress at Indiana University, I met not only Hayden but Stokely Carmichael, H. Rap Brown, Julian Bond, Andrea Dworkin, Barney Frank, Jonty Driver, the famously exiled president of the National Union of South African Students, and others who were about to become famous. Their politics were far more advanced than my own. With "We Shall Overcome" ringing in my ears, I returned to live in the

Phi Delt house, and I became uncomfortably aware that it was an all-white house. When my semester in residence had ended, I moved back home and never returned to the house for the rest of my undergraduate years. Again I avoided a confrontation. Many of the brothers were my close friends, and I explained, "It takes all of my time to edit the paper." This was cowardly, but consistent. My life as a liberal bohemian, the labor union songs I learned at the Campus Folksong Club, the women I dated, my handful of black friends, my fellow faux beatniks were all in a separate compartment. I had schooled myself to avoid confrontation through separating the categories of my life. Not many people ever saw me whole.

Sexually, I was incredibly naïve. After childhood as a Catholic only child and high school in a more innocent time, I remained a virgin until the summer of 1962, when I accompanied a team of the university's wheelchair athletes on a tour of South Africa. I was twenty and acutely aware of my virginity. At a time before the Pill, middle-class sex was more rare than it soon became, but all the same I feared I was missing the boat and was determined to swim out to it.

One night in Durban a group of us went to a nightclub and my inquisitive gaze was returned by a woman on the dance floor. I asked her to dance. Her name was Mary. As our bodies pressed together, it became clear she was not shy. I had a quick erection. "Friendly chap, aren't you?" she said. I drew back but she pulled me close again. "Want to become better friends?" she asked. The next afternoon I called her number and visited her in a beachfront apartment. She was clearly naked under a shift. She was also friendly and tactful. "Let's get the business out of the way," she said, but after I handed over my money I lost my nerve and said, "I don't have a whole lot of experience. Maybe we could just talk."

"Stand up here," she said, and put her arms around me. She laid her head on my chest. She moved against me. She took my hands and pressed them against her breasts under the shift. These were the first breasts I had touched that were not encased in a brassiere. They were full and indescribably gratifying. "Now you're friendly again," she said.

Afterward I walked out into the Durban sunlight and my heart sang. I was a man. My head was held a little higher, I put my hands in my pockets and scuffed my feet. This was what it was all about. I went into an Indian restaurant and ordered a curry.

"Mild?" said the counterman.

"Hot," I said.

"Maybe you like to try medium?" he said.

"Hot. I know what I'm doing."

My lips burned for twenty-four hours.

Returning to Illinois, I didn't find sexual inter-course any more easily available, but once I had experienced the delight of orgasm I discovered that girls also knew of such things, and then began a time of adventures made possible because I owned a car. At the National Student Congress at the University of Minnesota in 1964 I. finally performed intercourse with a female undergraduate for the first time. I had good luck in 1965 at the University of Cape Town, but it was not until the early winter of 1966, when I was in graduate school, that I finally experienced intercourse with a student in Champaign-Urbana for the first time. I was twenty-three.

My delayed sexual initiation was perhaps not as unusual as it seemed to me. Sex was problematical in everyday undergraduate life. The likelihood was that you might get nowhere—or if you did, you could be disciplined, arrested, or expelled. The university took aggressive steps to prevent sex among undergraduates. They weren't allowed to live in their own apartments. In women's dormitories, a strict curfew was enforced, and too many "late minutes" in a semester would get you hauled up before a disciplinary committee. Campus cops patrolled the parking lots of motels, looking for student stickers. It was assumed that by locking down the women, you would prevent sex. If a couple returned to a woman's dorm early, they could share a sofa in the lounge, monitored by matrons who enforced the Three Foot Rule: three of their four feet had to be on the floor, if you follow me. Car crashes were blamed on speeding toward women's dorms to meet the curfew.

In 1960, Leo Koch, an assistant professor of biology, wrote a letter to the editor of the *Daily Illini* that led to a furor over academic freedom:

> With modern contraceptives and medical advice readily available at the nearest drugstore, or at least a family physician, there is no valid reason why sexual intercourse should not be condoned among those sufficiently mature to engage in it without social consequences and without violating their own codes of morality and ethics. A mutually satisfactory sexual experience would eliminate the need for many hours of frustrating petting and lead to happier and longer lasting marriages among our young men and women.

How innocuous that seems today. There was an uproar. Outraged citizens' groups and the *Chicago Tribune* called for the university to take action. President David Dodds Henry directed Koch's dean to relieve the biologist "immediately" of his duties. The

American Association of University Professors, while not siding with Koch's views, said he had a right to express them and noted he had been summarily fired without a hearing. The AAUP imposed censure on the university, which lasted until 1964. In that year Illinois redeemed itself by *not* dismissing the classics professor Revilo P. Oliver after he wrote an article for the John Birch Society magazine charging that John F. Kennedy was a communist agent murdered by other communists because he "was about to turn American."

Believing I was far behind the curve in my sex life, I hid that from friends who seemed more experienced. I thought I must be one of the last to get on board. I knew many graduate students who were living together. Others were "going to Chicago for the weekend." I was a member of the Capitol Crowd, the graduate students who drank in a beloved Green Street bar and eatery. I met most Fridays after classes for the $1.15 perch dinner with Chuck Mullins, a math student whose laugh had an influence on my own; Claire and Alex Gaydasch, who brought along shoe boxes filled with computer punch cards; Mike Bobis, a self-proclaimed universal authority; and Jerry Sullivan, an English major who perpetually seemed to be reading *Tom Jones*. We were the local bohemians, such as the town possessed, and the bar was equidistant from an art theater and the Turk's Head Coffee House, where students declaimed their poetry. The Capitol's atmosphere was relaxed. One Friday night an assistant journalism professor took off his clothes and madly ran about. On Monday morning, he met his class. The incident, as they say, "didn't get back to anyone."

It was one night in the Capitol that I saw for the first time one man, an actor named Lara Maraviglia, kiss another man full on the lips. We all fell silent, our eyes evading one another's, and none of us bold bohemians could utter a single word. Something like a mild electric shock ran through my body. No, I didn't "discover I was gay." I discovered that other people surely were. Until then homosexuality had been known to me only in novels, poetry, vague scenes in films, and rumor. I knew lots of "queers," by which I meant "effeminate men," but my imagination stopped more or less with them laughing about the same things.

Yet I had an active sex life. In the words of the good professor Koch, I petted, although I never heard anyone use that word. The privacy of the photo library at the *Daily Illini* was a godsend. On the desk of the editor's office I did some intense proofreading. In the front seat of my father's '55 Ford I experienced delights made all the more exciting because they were restricted. We kissed. I fondled breasts. My hands strayed to her netherlands. My own movables were rummaged. Orgasms in the case of both parties were far from unheard of, although you had to know the girl pretty well, and you might pretend they came by surprise. Eventually I progressed to the point where "Oops!" became a word of delight, but that took a while.

Part of the game was to get...right...up... almost...to the Oops! Point. If you helplessly hurtled past it, well, as Dean of Men Fred Turner used to warn, "Always remember, boys! A stiff prick has no conscience." So he was widely quoted, anyway. I never heard him say it. It was always someone else who had heard him.

As an undergraduate, these evenings were explained to my censorious mother under "working at the *DI*" or "studying at the Undergraduate Library." In the spring of 1964, there was a sudden blowup between my mother and her second husband, George, who was accused of treasuring possessions that reminded him of his first wife, Berenice. I walked out and rented a fifty-five-dollar attic room on Green Street, providentially across from the Steak 'n Shake. One afternoon there I was being visited by Lyn Cole, an editor of the Roosevelt University's *Torch*. She answered the telephone. It was my mother calling. When I picked up the receiver, I heard her fury. I was living with a woman. I was lying to her. I had forgotten my Catholic training. Now she knew why I'd really moved out. At this time she had never met a single girl I dated in university. Did she think I was celibate? I have no idea what she thought. From that day forward, she met very few of the women I dated, and they were allegedly just "good friends." Believe me, I know this is pathetic. I've never discussed most of it, except with Chaz. It shows a sad emotional obstruction. I am writing about it here because I'll write these memoirs once, and if I were to suppress such an embarrassing area there is no point in writing them at all.

In Chicago, my first serious girlfriend was Tal Gilat, a young architect from Israel with Asian Jewish eyes, and we grew very close. She was a woman who seemed to fit naturally under my arm. She lectured me on architecture; Mies was her God. She took me to my first Japanese restaurant. She slept with me in my attic flat at the Dudaks' house on Burling, and I would wake in the morning to find her up on an elbow regarding me. "I don't know what I'm going to do with you," she said. Some months passed before I found out what she meant by this: "You have to make a choice, between me and O'Rourke's." The pub had by then become the center not so much of my drinking as of my life. I told her I chose her, but she decided

I had chosen O'Rourke's, and in a few weeks she was gone. We remained friends. In her late thirties she inexplicably began smoking, and a few years later she was dead of lung cancer.

In O'Rourke's one night I met Sarah Nance, a divorced nurse who was the mother of three children, and I felt a quick chemistry. She had a loud, natural laugh, and we shared a sense of humor. She was a little taller than I, a Czech American whose father was a doctor. She'd had an unlucky first marriage and was divorced before her oldest child was five. We were together almost instantly. We shared expenses (I was far from an upper bracket). I loved her children, Rita Marie, Gregory, and Britt. I loved being fatherly. I loved telling them bedtime stories, and we went to the circus, Great America, movies, museums. The cat had kittens and we all lay on our stomachs and watched them under the bed, nursing.

With Sarah I played house. We cooked together night after night, undisciplined gargantuan feasts fueled with horrible wines. Friends would drop in, especially her sister Mary Therese, John McHugh from the *Daily News*, and Scott Jacobs from the *Sun-Times*. Also Jim and Mike Tuohy, known as America's Guests for their willingness to drop in on friends. Her children were much loved and included in these meals, although the food might not have been on the table until after what should have been their bedtimes.

I was in love with Sarah. We were invited to the Tuohy family picnic, which many from O'Rourke's attended, thrown annually by a large Chicago Irish clan heavily invested in the police department, the law, and journalism. Jim Tuohy was a reporter for the *Sun-Times* and his wife, Michaela—Mike—was a freelance writer. They agreed one night at O'Rourke's that they were born to fill the roles of Drinking Companions to the World. I decided the Tuohy picnic would be a good occasion for my mother to meet Sarah and her children. "This is the woman I'm going to marry," I told her. Sarah looked lovely that day in a summer dress and big sun hat. Her cleavage was turned to the sun. My mother sparkled at the center of my friends. She was a live wire, remembered to this day as charming and funny.

I put her up at the Ambassador East and slept as usual at Sarah's house. At six a.m. the telephone rang. "I knew I'd find you there," she said. "How can you even think of marrying that woman, with her tits hanging out?" I'd never heard her use language like that. It came from the drinking that began with her second marriage, to George. I felt betrayed and treated unfairly. How could she put on such an act at the picnic, lead me to believe that it all might possibly work, and then start screaming at me about Sarah's tits? Why did the world think she was such a great character, when my stomach knotted every time the telephone rang? In those days I knew little about alcoholism and the personality changes that sometimes accompany it. I had been raised by one Annabel. Now I met a different one. This wasn't her fault. It was a disease, the same one that made it painful for me to deal with her.

Sarah and I continued to live together, but now the telephone calls came regularly. My aunt Martha, steady as a rock, took the train to Chicago to try to calm things. She and Annabel were friendly, but Martha saw her sister with clear eyes and was a realist free of any prejudice, a Catholic without malice, a liberal without even needing to think about it, and my best friend in the family. I looked more like her than any other Stumm. She clearly observed the situation, hit it off with Sarah while we ate cheeseburgers at Billy Goat's, and told me at the train station, "Your mother will never accept this. Do what you have to do."

The following Easter I invited my mother to attend Rita Marie's confirmation; I thought that might be a fire-free zone. The night before, we all went to dinner together, and then Sarah and I dropped her off at the hotel and continued drinking. I was certainly already by 1970 an alcoholic, and the next morning I overslept, fetched my mother late from the hotel, and arrived at Sarah's to find delay, disorganization, and Rita Marie sitting in the living room in her confirmation dress, in tears.

Martha had advised me to do what I had to do. For her that meant choosing Sarah. Martha herself had forthrightly lived for years with her friend Jean Sabo, another nurse. Their presence was necessary; Bob couldn't have taken care of their mother, Anna, and Jean and Martha in the house provided around-the-clock caregiving and nursing. Did I realize this involved a thankless sacrifice by Jean? After the deaths of my mother and Bob, Martha and Jean Sabo made households with my uncle Bill in Cape Girardeau, Missouri, and Wapella, Illinois. Together they bought the houses in both places. Martha had done what she had to do, and it had been best for everyone concerned.

What I should have done, she thought, was marry Sarah. That might have led to disaster. I had the decade of my worst drinking ahead of me. Sarah also drank too much, which is why, unlike Tal, she tolerated my own boozing. It's likely that the result for the kids would have been the misery of an alcoholic household. Once years later when Rita Marie and Britt were visiting Chicago for a family reunion, we had a long talk. I saw that while Rita had a clear view of the reality of those days, Britt felt abandoned by me. In his mind, I had left. He never knew his birth father, but I was the father who had walked out, and that still hurt.

After the turning point of the Tuohy family picnic, my relationship with Sarah was on a death watch. After Christmas I flew to London as I did every year, and when I returned, I had the taxi drop me at O'Rourke's and called Sarah. Her phone had been disconnected. It was after dark, bitterly cold. I drove to her house, used my key, and found it empty. I walked bewildered through the rooms, a few toys or socks scattered behind. I went to Mary Therese's house nearby. She told me Sarah and her children had moved in with her new friend Bob in Wicker Park. I guess I wasn't surprised.

Bob moved the family to Arizona, from whence came vague reports of the children being enlisted to manufacture sun-dried bricks for the construction of a house in the desert. I saw Sarah one last time, in Los Angeles in the 1980s. She was repping medical products to doctors. We had a long, nostalgic talk. All the chemistry was gone. We felt like comrades who had survived a battlefield where we might have been killed. That was what amounted to my first marriage.

Rita Marie, who later moved to Salt Lake City, raised two children on her own, put herself through school, and is an accounting and payroll manager. Our marathon cooking sessions may have had some influence on Greg and Britt. Greg taught himself guitar and piano, studied classical guitar, became a sous chef at the Space Needle in Seattle, and then, married with children, moved to Idaho, where he works in catering at a hospital. Britt put himself through school as a journeyman meat cutter, worked as a butcher and restaurant manager, and now works as a cook at one of the Utah resorts. He also has two children. Rita Marie tells me Bob, who died in 2011, kept her mother socially isolated; Sarah and Rita didn't speak for twenty years, staying in touch through Greg.

With Sarah as with Tal, alcohol had taken the place that should have been filled with a relationship. My alcoholism was masking deep problems, but it was a dependable friend, always there, never critical, making me feel good after it made me feel bad, so that I could sing and joke with a raucous crowd of newspaper friends and Old Town characters, forming those undying barroom friendships that never survived outside a bar. Never again did Annabel meet a woman I was dating, except Ingrid Magan Eng, my love of the 1980s, who was always carefully introduced as a "friend."

Ingrid had four children and had been divorced twice, and that made her ineligible according to my mother's Catholic beliefs, and more so because of her possessiveness and jealousy. I will write this book only once and might as well not make it fiction. Her beliefs were not mine after the early 1960s, but my life was chained and governed by hers.

In 1979 I took my last drink. Ingrid drank but never alcoholically; I never saw her drunk. In the 1970s she had been a friend who was always still there after various short-term romances; during some of the annual New Year's Eve parties I threw at O'Rourke's she had to ferry me home semiconscious at 10:30. While I was drinking she was to some degree my caregiver.

After sobriety and a hiatus when I plunged into AA, we resumed our relationship in a deeper and more meaningful way. For years before we started dating, we both traveled the same Chicago folk-song circuit: the Earl of Old Town, Holstein's, Somebody Else's Troubles, the Wise Fools, the Bulls. We were an item before we became a couple. Her first marriage had been to a Chinese-American man, the father of Monica, Magan, Scott, and Stuart. As I understand it his church beliefs led to conflict with Ingrid's folkie lifestyle.

I attended her second marriage, to a nice guy named Frenchie who ran a storefront restaurant on Armitage that later morphed into the Fifth Peg, another stop on the Chicago folk circuit. It was probably Ingrid who took me there the night I heard John Prine sing for the first time. He was still a mailman in the suburb of Maywood. I wrote an article for the *Sun-Times* and that was his first review. He is one of the great songwriters in American history. Ingrid followed folk music with a passion and introduced me to such artists as Queen Ida and Tom Waits.

She survived the upheaval of my transition from drunkenness to sobriety. That's a transfer of emotion that can require fundamental realignments of friendship, priorities, and your idea of yourself. I was completely immersed in Alcoholics Anonymous for the first two years, dating only women I met at meetings, who knew why I never drank. AA continued, but as I gained a footing in sobriety Ingrid was still there, and so were her children. I met the kids when they were all under ten, at her wedding, and when Monica was sixteen Ingrid took the two of us to a Mexican restaurant for our shared birthday on June 18.

I liked all four of them, but Monica was my Gemini twin (not that I subscribe to astrology). The boys and Magan had their own interests and priorities, but with Monica I can believe I had some influence. I was able to help both girls get jobs as copy clerks at the *Sun-Times*, and Monica stayed stuck in journalism; today she's still a writer for the *Chicago Tribune*, and considering how many fine newspapermen have been axed during bad times, that speaks for itself.

At the time Ingrid and I segued from friendship into romance I was well into *Siskel & Ebert* and had money to spend. Ingrid, the children, and I sailed on the *QE2* and visited London and Venice. Those were happy trips and happy years. Ingrid and I were close and loving companions, but I had no desire to face the wrath of my mother by declaring any serious plans. This is shameful and I cringe to write it, but I have to face the truth: I couldn't deal with tears, denunciations, and scenes from the Second Annabel.

This became more of a problem because as my drinking ended, my mother's began to increase. She was careful to conceal this from me, and it was during this time that I got a warning from her lifelong friend Ruby Harmon. Many people hardly knew that Annabel drank. It mostly took place in the evenings, and the caregivers I was paying for were essentially enablers. She grew thin and frail. I was never completely honest with Ingrid about my mother, but I believe she and many others guessed that I would never marry before my mother died.

I allowed my life choices to be limited by that fear. Now as I look back from the end, I clearly see that I should have broken free from Annabel as quickly as I could. It was not her fault that I didn't. Nobody ever makes you do anything. What they want to do is their decision. What you do is yours. If I am to be realistic, my life as an independent adult began after I met Chaz. I could write the story differently, but I wouldn't learn from it, and neither would you.

My mother was a good woman, and I loved her. I had a happy childhood and was loved and encouraged. Alcoholism changed her, and I should know as well as anyone how that happens. The Annabel people loved was lovable. She took baskets of food to poor people, not as a "volunteer" for some program, but because she personally knew people who needed it and she couldn't let them be hungry. She sat with the sick. She prayed with the dying. She was funny and very smart. She was a "businesswoman" in the 1940s when feminism was unheard of. She drove her own car. She helped her family and my father's. That was the mother I had. Alcoholism is a terrible disease and I am glad I had it because I can understand what happened to her, and how it damaged my own emotional growth. I buried myself in movies that allowed me to live vicariously.

There's nothing unique about my behavior. There is everything wrong with it. There must come a day when parents and children approach each other as adults or simply break off ties. This is in the nature of things. That day never came for me. From early in my childhood I developed a fear of my mother's storms, and perhaps observed my father's strategy of detachment. My aunt Martha told me, "Your father lived for you." This was true of both my parents and possibly explains the survival of their marriage and much of their undeniable happiness. If alcoholism brought me misery, it remained in abeyance long enough to allow me a happy childhood and adolescence, which took place after the end of my father's drinking and before the beginning of my mother's.

Why did the three most important loves of my life, Sarah, Ingrid, and Chaz, all happen to have children? I fell in love with them in the first place simply because of who they were. Then acting in the role of a stepfather came naturally. I took joy in the role and I loved the children. They represented children I believed I might never have. I never saw them as competing with me for their mother's attention, but as sharing their family with me. I have always had a great desire to be a father, and in my life this is how it worked out. I am a man who has never fathered yet has had a role in the raising of nine children and four grandchildren.

Twice in my life I had reason to believe a woman was pregnant with my child. There were no abortions, but there were apparently no children. One woman lived out of state and reported in urgent detail the progress of her pregnancy. She was overweight in a pleasing way and was plump enough to plausibly be pregnant. I sent her money for expenses. In the middle of one night I received a call that her water had broken and she was on the way to the hospital. My child was being born.

An hour later the phone rang again, and an unfamiliar voice said, "Roger, we've never met. I'm the woman who lives upstairs. I know what's been going on, and I want to tell you that woman has never been pregnant."

Was this fake mother simply a con-woman, shaking me down? I've never thought so. She was delightful and I liked her, but she was a fabulist. I met Robert Altman for the first time because she was running an event that she assured both of us Pauline Kael would attend. Pauline later told me she had never even been invited.

There were some months when I believed that child, my child, was on the way. The woman lived in another state. I never went to see a doctor with her, as I would have in Chicago. I flew out there. I saw her. She could have been pregnant. Or (I hesitate to say this because I found her quite attractive) she could have been fat.

If the child had been born, I would have claimed it as my own and wanted to raise it, while marrying the mother. That would have been absolute. I related this story of "my only child" to Chaz, and told her, "If the telephone were to ring today and the person on the other end were to say *You are my biological father*, I would weep with joy."

46 CHAZ

How can I begin to tell you about Chaz? She fills my horizon, she is the great fact of my life, she is the love of my life, she saved me from the fate of living out my life alone, which is where I seemed to be heading. If my cancer had come, and it would have, and Chaz had not been there with me, I can imagine a descent into lonely decrepitude. I was very sick. I might have vegetated in hopelessness. This woman never lost her love, and when it was necessary she forced me to want to live. She was always there believing I could do it, and her love was like a wind pushing me back from the grave.

Does that sound too dramatic? You were not there. She was there every day for two years, visiting me in the hospital whether I knew it or not, becoming expert on my problems and medications, researching possibilities, asking questions, making calls, even giving little Christmas and Valentine's Day baskets to my nurses, whom she knew by name.

Chaz is a strong woman, sure of herself. I'd never met anyone like her. At some point in her childhood a determination must have been formed that she would make a success of herself. She was born into a large family on the West Side of Chicago and already in high school was a tireless achiever. Her school yearbook shows her on every other page, a member of everything from the National Honor Society to Spanish Club, vice president of the senior class to best dancer. She won a scholarship to the University of Chicago but didn't accept it: "What did I know? Nobody told me it was a great university. I just wanted to get out of Chicago, to go somewhere on my own." She went to the University of Dubuque, and in keeping with the times she was a civil rights activist. There she met her first husband, Merle Smith, and soon they were married and raising their children, Josibiah and Sonia. She might easily have called off her professional dreams and returned to Chicago, where Merle was an electrical engineer. She went to the University of Wisconsin–Madison for a BA in sociology, and then graduated from the DePaul College of Law, the alma mater of generations of Chicago politicians and lawyers. And all this time raising her family, as she and Merle moved to the suburbs and bought a home. She was a litigator at Bell, Boyd and Lloyd, an important firm.

After seventeen years she and Merle were divorced, but remained friends. By the time I met her, about six years after that, she was a government trial attorney specializing in civil rights cases. We like to tell people we were "introduced by Ann Landers," which is technically true, although Eppie Lederer didn't know her at the time. The night I took Eppie to an open AA meeting, we decided to go out to dinner together afterward; this was the first and only time we ever had dinner for two. In the restaurant, Chaz was at a nearby table that included a couple of people I knew. I didn't know her, but I'd seen her before and was attracted. I liked her looks, her voluptuous figure, and the way she presented herself. She took a lot of care with her appearance and her clothes never looked quickly thrown together. She seemed to be holding the attention of her table. You never get anywhere with a woman you can't talk intelligently with.

Something possessed me to pull off one of the oldest tricks in the book. "I have a couple of friends over there I'd love for you to meet," I told Eppie, and got up to take her across. As the introductions went around, Chaz was included. When we went back to our own table, I had her card. She was an attorney with the Equal Employment Opportunity Commission. I studied the card and showed it to Eppie, who said, "You sly fox."

I came back from the Toronto International Film Festival with the card on my mind. I called Chaz and invited her to attend the Lyric Opera, which I'd subscribed to a year earlier because Danny Newman, the Lyric's press agent, had stood in my office door and said, "A man like you not going to the Lyric, you should be ashamed." Chaz, who later told me she never expected to hear from me again, said, "Actually, I'm on the women's board of the Chicago Symphony." I said I loved the symphony, but I had, cough, subscription seats at the Lyric for Monday night. The opera was *Tosca*. She said it was her favorite. "Does that scare you?" "No," I said, "why should it?" At the time I knew nothing about *Tosca*.

We went to dinner afterward at a restaurant in Greektown. Something happened. She had a particular quality. She didn't seem to be a "date" but an equal. She knew where she stood, and I found that attractive. I was going out to Los Angeles a few days later, and I asked her to come along. She said she would, but only with her mother's permission. We drove over to the near West Side to the senior center where Johnnie Mae Hammel lived.

To her family Chaz's mother was known as Big Mama, a common title in African-American families. Johnnie Mae, tall and courtly, took my hand in both of hers and steered me to a chair across from a coffee table on which rested a well-worn Bible. Chaz made us tea. Big Mama told me about her children, Chaz's four brothers and four sisters. "Charlie was the second youngest," Big Mama said, "but she was the boss." The next day Chaz said her mother's blessing had been conferred, and we flew to Los Angeles, not having yet slept together. I got us adjoining rooms at the Sunset Marquis, as I had promised Big Mama. On the sofa we emerged from exploratory passion and I told her she was incredibly sexy. She replied with words that held an erotic charge: "You haven't seen anything yet."

We formed a serious bond rather quickly. It was an understood thing. I was in love, I was serious, I was ready for my life to change. I had been on hold too long. She lived on the eighty-second floor of the Hancock Center and started sending me daily e-mails, even after we'd seen each other earlier the same evening. Her love letters were poetic, idealistic, and sometimes passionate. I responded as a man and a lover. As a newspaperman, I observed that she never, ever, made a copy-reading error. I saved every one of her letters along with my own and have them encrypted on my computer, locked inside a file where I can't reach them because the program and the operating system are now twenty years out of date. But they're in there. I'm not about to entrust them to anyone at the Apple Genius Bar.

On Thanksgiving two months after our first date, Chaz held a dinner at her apartment in the Hancock. I'd already met her children, but now I met Ina New-Jones and Myrin New, her closest niece and nephew, Myrin announcing he was an expert in turkey carving before assaulting the bird so savagely that it was fit for turkey salad. At a later family gathering I met Chaz's first husband, Merle Smith, an electrical engineer. I liked him then and like him today. I sensed no awkwardness. They'd been apart long enough that I hadn't been poaching.

Josibiah, always called Jay, was tall and taciturn, starting to grow his dreadlocks, easy to talk to. I was pleased that he confided in me. Sonia, a poised beauty with an outgoing personality, was attending Texas Southern in Houston and brought home Marquette Evans, the son of a Chicago minister. They were married not long after, and one day in Evanston Hospital I held in my arms one-day-old Raven, our first grandchild. Mark and Sonia filled my unrealized need to be a grandfather. In due course Sonia and Mark also presented us with Emil and Mark Taylor, and Jay became the father of Joseph. He and Joseph's mother never married, but I met Sheena soon after he did, and her Joseph is one of ours.

Our lives grew together. One day in May at the Cannes Film Festival we rented a car and drove over to San Remo in Italy to visit the grave of Edward Lear, and on the way back we stopped in Monte Carlo and in a café over coffee I proposed marriage. Why did I choose Monte Carlo, a place I have no desire ever to see again? I should have chosen London or Venice or for that matter Chicago. I wasn't thinking in those terms. We were sitting there talking in a little café at the end of a happy day and I became overwhelmed with the desire to propose marriage. Chaz filled my mind. She excited me physically. She was funny. She made a reading of my life rather quickly, understood what I did and how I had to do it, and after I proposed marriage I asked if she would resign as a lawyer because I wanted her to travel more than she would otherwise be able to.

Chaz became the vice president of the Ebert Company. It wasn't merely a title. She organized my contracts, protected my interests, negotiated, wheeled and dealed. I've never understood business and have no patience with business meetings or legal details. I had a weakness for signing things just to make them go away. She observed this and defended me. It was a partnership.

I'd been told that if I thought I knew about extended families, I didn't know anything until I married into an African-American family. This was true. My downstate relatives extended only to my uncles, aunts, and first and second cousins, the only cousins still living. Grandma Stumm's six grown children between them produced only three children. Chaz's family was large and stayed in constant communication. At a birthday party for Big Mama soon after I met Chaz, every one of her children and most of their children attended, some from Minneapolis, Atlanta, and Washington, and I met cousins to the third degree. There was a ceremony at which each child presented Big Mama with a rose and made a speech about her importance in their lives. At the center of the ceremony was a photograph of Big Daddy, who had been dead for some years.

Chaz's childhood wasn't deprived. She didn't feel poor. She remembers Big Daddy taking them for Sunday drives in the family car, a Chevy Corvette: "When I see one today I realize how small it is. All I remember from those days was that everyone seemed to fit inside." Her family was a great stable center, and

I have become especially close with her oldest brother, Johnnie, who is kind right down to his toes. She talks about growing up when everybody knew everybody and kids joked about the Nasty Man, who was always good for a lollipop but then you had to get outta there before he got you on his knee and started squeezing you. Big Mama was a precinct captain in the Daley machine. She was also a Spiritualist and healer and had the gift of the laying on of hands. I don't believe in any such gift, but Chaz told me she knew what she knew.

Chaz's family is in constant communication. She has a memory that retains the names of all children, grandchildren, great-grandchildren, present and former spouses, any of their previous or subsequent spouses, the offspring from those marriages, former boyfriends and girlfriends, and neighbors who have been appointed honorary uncles and aunts. All of these people are in touch with one another. They seem to know who everybody is dating, how marriages are going, who got hired or fired, who might have a drinking or health problem, how grades are in school, and who is being invited to weddings. Her family can effortlessly fill a church for a funeral. Keeping track of everyone, which I have never been able to do, makes remembering all the characters in *War and Peace* seem like a breeze.

We had times together I will always remember. Right after our first Christmas, we flew to Venice, where I promised Chaz it would be rainy, cold, deserted, and we would have it all to ourselves. That was how I'd first seen Venice in 1966, and it was the same. It was romantic, sleeping late in the Royal Danieli and then waking up and making love and looking out across the Grand Canal. The hotel was half empty, the rooms a fraction of the summer cost. The city was shrouded in mist and always haunting. Romance in the winter in Venice is intimate and private, almost hushed. One night we went to the Municipal Casino, carefully taking only as much money we were ready to lose, and lost it. In a little restaurant we had enough left for spaghetti with two plates and afterward lacked even the fare for the canal bus. We walked the long way back through the night and cold, our arms around each other, figures appearing out of the fog, lights traced on the wet stones, pausing now and again to kiss and be solemn. It was one of those experiences that seals a marriage.

At Cannes we bought a chicken sandwich for Quentin Tarantino in a beach restaurant, after *Reservoir Dogs* had been a success but he was broke. The next time we saw him at Cannes was after *Pulp Fiction*, when Miramax had rented a ballroom in the Carlton for him. It was the first time we remembered.

Another night, after seeing *Boyz n the Hood* and being awed by it, we drove out of town for dinner with John Singleton, so young and filled with plans. Chaz seemed to know everybody and to remember all the names.

We had fun together. In Salvador, the capital of Bahia in Brazil, we decided to go to a Macarena nightclub and practiced the dance in our hotel room. Wandering around the town, we saw a dress shop with local fashions and Chaz bought a low-cut white summer gown with lots of ruffles. She looked sexy as hell when we left the hotel. When we walked into the club, an odd silence fell. Something was wrong. People seemed to be smiling for the wrong reasons. An English-speaking waitress took mercy on us and explained the dress was a national costume intended for pageants and such. Wearing it to a nightclub was like me dressing as Uncle Sam.

In London, we stayed at 22 Jermyn Street, the former Eyrie Mansion. Chaz drew me into the contemporary art scene. I'd started collecting my Edward Lear watercolors in the 1980s, but after we moved into our town house with expanses of bare wall, we could think in terms of larger paintings. In the Purdy Hicks Gallery on the South Bank, where we'd gone to look at work by our friend David Hiscock, we saw a spacious canvas in a storeroom and found ourselves side by side just gazing at it. This was by Gillian Ayres, a formidable abstract expressionist who covered huge areas with bright impasto. It was a work inspired by a kite festival in India, and its energy flooded the room. Over a few years we obtained five works by Ayres and even had dinner with her one night at the Groucho Club, where the raffish atmosphere matched her roots in London's 1950s.

The greatest pleasure came from annual trips we made with our grandchildren Raven, Emil, and Taylor, and their parents Sonia and Mark. Josibiah and his son Joseph came on one of those trips, where we made our way from Budapest to Prague, Vienna, and Venice. We went with the Evans family to Hawaii, Los Angeles, London, Paris, Venice twice, and Stockholm. We walked the ancient pathway from Cambridge to Grantchester. Emil announced that for him there was no such thing as getting up too early, and every morning the two of us would meet in the hotel lobby and go out for long walks together. I took my camera. One morning in Budapest he asked me to take a photo of two people walking ahead of us and holding hands.

"Why?"

"Because they look happy."

At last I could show off my city secrets. I had been happy enough to drift for years lonely and solitary through strange cities, but it was more fun with the family. One quality the children had was the ability to feel at home anywhere, in restaurants, theaters, museums. They were attentive and absorbed. They had been well raised.

Those times seem more precious now that they're in the past. I don't walk easily anymore. When we were married I told Chaz that in 1987 I'd had a salivary tumor removed. Good Dr. Schlichter observed the surgery and told me, "They got it all. Every last speck." But I was warned my cancer was slow growing and sneaky and might return years later. That's what happened, and it set into motion all of my current troubles.

I mentioned how expert and exacting Chaz became in my care. Now I must tell you of her love. In the hospital, day after day, she was my staff of strength. In the rehabilitations she cheered me through every faltering step, and when I looked at a flight of three steps I was intended to climb, it was her will that helped me lift my feet. To visit a hospital is not pleasant. To do it hundreds of times is heroic.

The TV show was using "guest co-hosts," and Richard Roeper held down the fort. But after the first surgery failed and I nearly died, Chaz had faith, she encouraged me, her presence gave me strength so I would return to TV. That's why I had the two later surgeries—not to remove cancer, but to restore my speech and appearance. She brought my friends to see me. Studs came several times. Father Andrew Greeley was cheerful and optimistic. She brought McHugh and Mary Jo, Gregory Nava, Jon and Pamela Anderson, the mayor's wife Maggie, the actress Bonnie Hunt (who had once been an oncology nurse at Northwestern). She had become friends with the healer Caroline Myss and brought her to my bedside to evoke positive thoughts. I did not and do not believe in that kind of healing, but I see only good in the feelings it can engender. I am no longer religious, but every single day Chaz took my hand before she left and recited the Twenty-third Psalm and the Lord's Prayer, and from this I took great comfort.

After I was allowed to return home for the first time, Chaz decided I was ready for the Pritikin Longevity Center near Miami. We'd been going to Pritikin, first in Santa Monica and then Florida, since before we were married, and their theories about diet and exercise became gospel to me (sometimes more in the breach than the observance). I had for years been an enthusiastic walker, but now, after rehabilitation, I was using a walker and it was slow going.

I couldn't eat the largely vegetarian diet at Pritikin, but Chaz knew the cooks would blend a liquid diet to supplement my cans of nutrition. She also informed me that I *was* going to walk, exercise, and get a lot of sunshine. Because it was painful to sit in most chairs, Pritikin found me a reclining chair that faced a big TV. I had brought along a pile of books. I cracked open the sliding doors and a fragrant breeze came in, and I would have been completely content to stay there just like that. It was not to be. Chaz ordered me on my feet for morning and afternoon walks, with my caregivers Sandi Lee or Millie Salmon trailing along. I'd go as far as I thought I could, and Chaz would unfailingly pick out another farther goal to aim for. She was relentless.

In the gym every day I cranked through twenty minutes on the treadmill and then worked out with weights and exercise bands. After the gym she took me outside to sit in the sun for half an hour. She explained how natural vitamin D would help strengthen my bones, which were weakened during the degeneration of weeks of postsurgical bed rest. I resented her unceasing encouragement. I was lazy. It was ever so much preferable to sit and read. But she was making me do the right thing.

She did it all over again after my next three tours through the Rehabilitation Institute. Four times I learned to walk again, and each time she took me to Pritikin or Rancho La Puerta in Tecate, Mexico, which I had grown to love. I parked the wheelchair for good, I was no longer using a walker. I was walking, not quickly or for miles, but walking. And getting vitamin D. At home, we took walks around the neighborhood and down to the Lily Pond in Lincoln Park. We began to go to all the screenings again. She found Dr. Mark Baker, an exercise therapist, to work regularly with me.

It must not have been the most pleasant thing in the world to trail along as I walked slowly. She must have wished we could still be taking our trips overseas. When she thought I was ready for it, she took me back to London and Cannes, and every autumn to the Toronto festival. I know that left on my own I would have stayed at home in my favorite Relax the Back chair. That I am still active, going places, moving, in good health, is directly because of her.

We planned all along to produce a show that would continue the Siskel & Ebert & Roeper tradition. Chaz did all the heavy lifting, the negotiations, the contracts. We were going to be the coproducers, but I told her she was born for the job. She repeatedly told me I needed to appear more on the show, even with my computer voice. My instinct was to guard myself; I can never again be on television as I once was. She said, "Yes, but people are interested in what you have to say, not in how you say it." The point is not which of us is correct. The point is that she's encouraging me. She has more faith in me than I do.

I sensed from the first that Chaz was the woman I would marry, and I know after twenty years that my feelings were true. She has been with me in sickness and in health, certainly far more sickness than we could have anticipated. I will be with her, strengthened by her example. She continues to make my life possible, and her presence fills me with love and a deep security. That's what a marriage is for. Now I know.

47   GOOD NEWS AND BAD NEWS

AFTER A MOVIE at the Lake Street Screening Room, there was a note for me to call Bob Havey. "I have good news and bad news," my doctor said.

"What's the bad news?"

"The tests came back. You have thyroid cancer."

"What's the good news?"

"You have the kind you want to have. It's one of the rare cancers with a ninety-nine percent cure rate."

He explained that I would have thyroid surgery, a common operation. After I recovered, I would check into a hospital room for two days and drink a shot glass of radioactive iodine. The Achilles' heel of my particular cancer was that it finds iodine delicious. It soaks it in and the radiation kills it, no matter where those cells may have spread to.

Bob Havey has stayed in general practice in an age when many physicians specialize. He is a great and brilliant man whose knowledge is wide and whose mind is open. Many sick people search the Internet and bring their findings (usually loony) to their doctors. Havey searched the specialist sites and found the latest developments for me. He discusses my condition with me thoroughly and honestly. Some patients probably prefer to be lied to. I find the truth a great comfort. If I'm going to die, I'd rather know.

I've had a conviction of invulnerability through all of my illnesses, never mind how misplaced it may have turned out to be. I don't have a lot of fear. Like many people, I fear pain more than death. I've had doctors I trust, and if I should die during surgery it will be no more an event than falling asleep. Now I know something I didn't know before, which is that after my surgeries failed, I could live a perfectly happy life.

The thyroid surgery was successful. The radiation treatment was bizarre. I was shown into a hospital room where surfaces were covered with white paper. I drank the tasteless cocktail. For two days no one was permitted to enter my room, and my meal trays were pushed through the door. I wore clothes I could throw away and resurrected an old laptop that would have to be mothballed for radioactivity. At the end of the time a nurse came in wearing protective gear and checked me with a Geiger counter, and I was sent home with instructions to not sleep in the same bed with Chaz for two weeks, or sit next to a pregnant woman on an airplane. The radioactivity in the iodine, I was told, was about 5 percent as powerful as the monthly radiation treatments I, and thousands of children, had been given in the 1950s for ear infections and acne. Those treatments paid off half a century later in a boom for the formerly rare thyroid cancer. Now all I had to do was figure out the correct dosage of Synthroid to take every day for the rest of my life. I discovered Synthroid is the most commonly prescribed prescription medication in the world.

A few years later, I went in for a routine scan to check for any new problems. This time the news was not good. Bob Havey sent me to Harold Pelzer, a specialist, who explained cancer had been seen in my right lower jawbone. It wasn't the same cancer as affected my thyroid, and I guessed exactly what it was. In 1988, a cancer had been found in my right salivary gland. There was a lump there clearly visible in a photograph of Siskel and me. When Christopher Hitchens fell ill, people wondered why he hadn't noticed a lump on his clavicle that even they could see in his photos. Maybe it was because you don't want to notice such things. I had been shaving over the lump for some months in the 1980s before Doc Schlichter palpated it and sent me to George Sisson, who was impressed; this cancer was so rare he'd never seen one in thirty-five years of practice. He was like a hunter bagging a unicorn and told me with some pride that a color slide from my tumor had made the cover of the Walter Reed military hospital's research magazine. It was the kind of publicity difficult to turn into Nielsen ratings. My tumor grew less rare in the years to come. The childhood radiation had probably caused it. Because I was born four or five years earlier than most of the boomers, I was the canary in their coal mine.

"He is a good surgeon," Doc Schlichter told me. "I was in the OR every minute. He took his time and got everything, and a little bit more around it. You have no more tumor." Yes, but Dr. Sisson warned me, "It is very, very slow growing, but the odds are it may return after some years." It did. It had probably hidden in my mandible. Pelzer took one of those plastic models you always see in medical offices and measured a length of mandible a few inches long. This, he explained, would be removed and replaced with a bone graft taken from the fibula in my calf—one of the bones we don't need. Dr. Neil Fine, an expert plastic surgeon, would do this and patch me up so that after healing there was every reason to expect I'd be back on the television show.

That's not how it worked out. All by myself, with nobody to blame, I found out about the work in neutron radiation being done at a handful of hospitals. It was much more powerful and narrowly targeted than gamma radiation. The leading specialist was said to be Dr. George Laramore at the University of Washington Medical Center in Seattle. "My equipment is made for your tumor," he told me. "Of course you should have surgery first." Pelzer also recommended surgery first. So did Havey. But no. I became convinced there was a shortcut that would avoid plastic surgery and a healing period and have me back on the air much more quickly. I insisted. It was a great temptation. My doctors and Chaz advised the path of caution, but I cited reams of Web printouts indicating what a miracle this neutron radiation was. Eventually it was decided to give it a go.

The Internet is said to be responsible for helping patients take control of their own diseases. Few movies are ever made about sick people courageously taking doctors' advice. No, they get bright ideas online. I believe my infatuation with neutron radiation led directly to the failure of all three of my facial surgeries, the loss of my jaw, loss of the ability to eat, drink, and speak, and the surgical damage to my right shoulder and back as my poor body was plundered for still more reconstructive transplants. Today I look like an exhibit in the Texas Chainsaw Museum.

I have vague memories after my first surgery of Chaz holding a pad on which I could write notes. She says they didn't always make much sense. I was on a good deal of pain medication and my memories of that period are often hallucinations. I imagined myself in a hospital that doesn't exist in Chicago, with a broad flight of stairs leading down to the Chicago River. I saw myself in one of a row of barber chairs, while medical personnel rotated us for obscure reasons. Gradually my mind began to clear, and my assistant Carol Iwata brought three-ring notebooks and a box of pens.

On these I wrote out everything I wanted to say. I also began various random writing projects, including my memoirs. None of those words are included in this book; they were more like exercises in total recall from long ago events that were more clear to me than whatever had happened that day. Chaz dated and preserved every one of these dozens of notebooks. "You'll want to look at these someday," Chaz told me. I never have. I think I would find them depressing and would discover I was sicker and more confused than I care to remember.

I'm sure there are long painful pages written very late at night on the subject of pain medication. I was on a form of OxyContin, an addictive drug that supplies euphoria for thirty minutes or so, relative calm for another hour, and then increasing uneasiness and anxiety until it is finally time for the next dose. The final hour became almost unbearable, and I wrote out pleas that I asked the nurses to take to the overnight residents, who would have to approve additional medication. They never did. My meds were being injected using the "push" method, by which a liquid is supplied intravenously, and this produced an instant rush that seemed to expand my consciousness to fill the entire room, and then subsided into intense energy and a feeling of well-being. I think I learned something of what heroin and morphine addicts feel. I certainly learned something of the agonies of withdrawal.

I was put on the drugs while unconscious after surgery and regained consciousness already addicted. I told Chaz I felt I needed more pain medication, and she told me I was hooked and needed to detox. Finally I couldn't take the withdrawals anymore. By then I was in the Rehabilitation Institute of Chicago and wrote out a note to the doctor in charge, Dr. James Sliwa, saying I was "turning myself in." He took charge of the withdrawal process, joined by Dr. Susan Pearlson.

From those days I remember hallucinations that are startlingly vivid. I imagined a house in Michigan I thought was ours, which wasn't, but I had returned there with Chaz all the same. I found myself driving down country roads outside Urbana at dusk, the earth and sky unnaturally beautiful, a mournful song filling the air. I remember repurchasing my childhood home on Washington Street, moving back to Urbana, and buying the *Daily Illini* so I could edit it. During the presidential primaries, Chaz tells me, I thought Hillary Clinton had rescued me in a helicopter. I would often be interrupted from these hallucinations by one of my physicians making his rounds with half a dozen interns. It was like being captured by aliens.

So no, I don't want to look at those notebooks. Much of what happened is confused and lost. Let it stay that way. I have, however, identified the mournful plaintive beautiful song I heard on my drive through the Illinois cornfields. It was "Calling You" from *Bagdad Cafe*, waiting in my memory all those years.

48

WHEN I MENTIONED in my blog that I can no longer eat, drink, or speak, a reader wrote, "That sounds so sad. Do you miss it?" Not so much really. Not anymore. The new reality took shape slowly. Understand that I was never told that after surgery I might lose the ability to eat, drink, and speak. Eating and drinking were not mentioned, and it was said that after the first surgery I might be able to go back to work on television. Success in such surgery is not unheard of. It didn't happen that way. The second surgery was also intended to restore my speaking ability. It seemed to hold together for a while, but then, in surgeon-speak, also "fell apart." In both cases the idea was to rebuild my face with bone and flesh transplants from my legs to restore an acceptable appearance. Both surgeries failed because microsurgery to reattach blood vessels broke down. Dr. Neil Fine had done an exemplary job both times, but the neutron radiation was there ahead of him and the tissue could not hold. In the second, a vein was used to carry blood from a healthier area into a more threatened one. Dr. Fine instructed nurses and interns how to listen to this vein, and I listened in myself: a soft pulsing flow. One day it could not be heard. The transplanted flesh would die and had to be removed. Both of these surgeries eventually resulted in catastrophic bleeding of a carotid artery.

I was flat on my back for long periods after the surgeries, to avoid stress on the sutured areas. Muscular degeneration took place, and I graduated from intensive care to the Rehabilitation Institute of Chicago to learn to walk again. At the start they winched me out of bed in a sling. I eventually walked well enough, but never again with the happy stride of the ten-thousand-steps-a-day period.

Neil Fine was a human being, a caring man. He had a national reputation and was known as a perfectionist. I could tell he was disappointed that his best efforts had failed. He and Dr. Pelzer came to me with a third idea, which they felt might be safely attempted. By now there was no pretense of "restoration," and the goal became simply to repair the opening in my chin.

Both of my fibulas and both of my thighs had already been plundered. It would be necessary to transplant tissue from elsewhere. Fine proposed what he considered a very conservative approach. Chaz and I flew to Houston to get an opinion from Pierong Yu, a surgical specialist at the MD Anderson Cancer Center. He proposed moving a flap of tissue from my right shoulder and rotating it to fasten under my chin. This had the advantage of preserving its existing blood supply. We returned to Chicago and had a long, serious talk with Fine and Pelzer. Fine did me the honor of being absolutely honest. Yu's approach would be the one he himself might attempt, he said, but after two surgeries had failed, he preferred to be very conservative on the third attempt.

Surgery at MD Anderson worked better than we'd dare to hope. Dr. Yu was a master. In a mirror I saw myself looking familiar again. But after a little more than a week, that surgery failed, too. Radiation damage again. A fourth surgery has been proposed, but I flatly rejected the idea. To paraphrase a line from the orchid collector in *Adaptation*, I'm done with surgery. I should actually have stopped after the first, but then I had no idea of the troubles ahead. If I'd had no surgery, the cancer would have continued to spread, and today I might probably be dead. Since removing the cancer was the primary objective of the first surgery, it's unfair to call it a failure. I'm very aware of what Dr. Sisson told me long ago: My cancer is very slow growing and insidious. The bastard is quite likely lurking somewhere as I write. I'm sixty-nine, but in excellent health. I'm happy and working well. I would be obscurely pleased if something else carries me off before that insidious cancer wins its waiting game.

During the entire period of my surgeries, I was Nil by Mouth. Nobody said as much in so many words, but it gradually became clear that it wouldn't ever be right again. There wasn't some soul-dropping moment for that realization. It just...developed. I never felt hungry, I never felt thirsty, I couldn't be angry because the doctors had done their best. But I went through a period of obsession about food and drink. I came up with the crazy idea of getting some Coke through my G-tube. My doctors said sure, a little, why not? For once the sugar and a little sodium wouldn't hurt. I even got some tea, and a little coffee. I couldn't taste it, of course.

I dreamed of tastes. I was reading Cormac McCarthy's *Suttree*, and there's a passage where the hero, lazing on his riverboat on a hot summer day, pulls up a string from the water with a bottle of orange soda tied to it. I tasted that pop so clearly I can taste it today. Later he's served a beer in a frosted mug. The frosted mug evoked for me a long-buried memory of my father and me driving in his old Plymouth to the A&W Root Beer stand (gravel driveways, carhop service, window trays) and his voice saying "and a five-cent beer for the boy." The smoke from his Lucky Strike in the car. The heavy summer heat. Night after night I would wake up already focused on that small, heavy glass mug with the ice sliding from it, and the first sip of root beer. I took that sip over and over. The ice slid down across my fingers again and again.

One day in the hospital my brother-in-law Johnnie Hammel and his wife, Eunice, came to visit. They're two of my favorite people. I described my fantasies about root beer. I could smell it, taste it, feel it. I desired it. I said I'd remembered that day with my father for the first time in sixty years. They're Jehovah's Witnesses and interpreted my story in terms of their faith.

"You never thought about it before?" Johnnie asked.

"Not once."

"Could be, when the Lord took away your drinking, he gave you back that memory."

Whether my higher power was the Lord or Cormac McCarthy, those were the words I needed to hear. And from that time I began to replace what I had lost with what I remembered. If I think I want an orange soda right now, it is after all only a desire. People have those all the time. For that matter, when I had the chance, when was the last time I held one of those tall Nehi glass bottles? I hardly drank it when I could.

All sorts of memories now come welling up almost alarmingly. It's all still in there, every bit. I saw *Leap Year*, with its scenes in Dublin, and recognized the street where I stayed in the Shelbourne Hotel, even though the hotel wasn't shown. That started me thinking of Trinity College nearby, where I remembered that McHugh and I saw the Book of Kells in its glass case. And then I remembered us walking out the back gate of Trinity and finding a pub where we were to join two of his brothers. And meeting Kitty Kelly sitting inside the pub, who became legendary in our stories as the only whore in Dublin with her own coach.

"Are you two students?" McHugh's younger brother Eugene asked them innocently.

"I'm a working girl meself," the first said.

"Her name is Kitty Kelly," her friend volunteered. "I'm her coach."

I walked into *Leap Year* with the Book of Kells and Kit Kelly's coach and Eugene McHugh far from my mind. The story itself had long since fallen from our repertoire. But it's all in there in my memory.

When it comes to food, I don't have a gourmet's memory. I remember the kinds of foods I was raised to love. Chaz and I stayed once at Les Prés d'Eugénie, the inn of the famous Michel Guérard in Eugénie-les-Bains. We had certainly the best meal I have ever been served. I remember that fact, the room, and specific people at other tables, but I can no longer remember what I ate. It isn't hardwired into my memory. Yet I could if I wanted to right now close my eyes and reexperience an entire meal at Steak 'n Shake, bite by bite in proper sequence, because I always ordered the same items and ate them according to the same ritual. It's stored in there for me.

Another surprising area for sharp memory is the taste and texture of cheap candy. Not fancy imported chocolates, but Red Hots, Good & Plenty, Milk Duds, PayDays, Chuckles. I dreamed I got a box of Chuckles with five licorice squares, and in my dream I thought, "Finally!" With Necco wafers, there again, the licorice were the best. The peculiar off-purple wafers were space wasters. As a general rule in candy, if anything is black, red, or green, in that order, I like it. In my mind I went to Cracker Barrel and bought paper bags filled with licorice, root beer, horehound, and cinnamon drops. But the last thing I want to start is a discussion of such age-old practices as pouring Kool-Aid into a bottle of RC Cola to turn it into a weapon. Returning to the original question: Isn't it sad to be unable to eat or drink? Not as sad as you might imagine. I save an enormous amount of time. I have control of my weight. My blood pressure and cholesterol would make Nathan Pritikin cheer with joy. Everything agrees with me. And so on.

What I miss is the society. Meals are when we most easily meet with friends and family. They're the first way we experience places far from home. Where we sit to regard the passing parade. How we learn indirectly of other cultures. When we feel good together. Meals are when we get a lot of our talking done—certainly most of our recreational talking. That's what I miss. Because I can't speak that's another turn of the blade. I can sit at a table and vicariously enjoy the conversation, which is why I enjoy pals like my friend McHugh so much, because he rarely notices if anyone else isn't speaking. But to attend a "business dinner" is a species of torture. I'm no good at business anyway, and being forced to listen to a lawyer for much more than half an hour must be a violation of the Geneva Conventions.

When we drive around town I never look at a trendy new restaurant and wish I could eat there. I peer into little storefront places, diners, ethnic places, Asian noodle joints, and that's when I feel envy. After a movie we'll drive past a Formica restaurant with only two tables occupied, and I'll wish I could be at one of them, having ordered something familiar and reading a book. I never felt alone in a situation like that. I was a soloist. When I moved north to Lincoln Park and the Dudaks' house, Glenna Syse, the *Sun-Times* drama critic, told me about Frances' Deli on Clark Street. "They make you eat your vegetables," she told me. There were maybe a dozen tables inside, and you selected from a steam table the day's dishes like roast chicken, lamb stew, lake perch, and the veggies, although one of them was rice pudding. You want roast chicken, here's your roast chicken. It was so simple it almost made you grin. You didn't even have to ask for the bed of dressing on which it slumbered. Frances' has moved into a larger space across the street but nothing much else has changed. Nobody will look at you funny if you bring in the Sunday paper and spread it out. And breakfast? Talk about the breakfast. If a place doesn't advertise "Breakfast, Lunch and Dinner" and serve tuna melts, right away you figure they're covering up for something.

Until 2010 there was a place called the Old Timers Restaurant across the street from the Lake Street Screening Room in Chicago. I loved that place. No fuss, no muss, friendly, the owner stands behind the cash register and chats with everybody going in and out. I've ordered breakfast at lunchtime there. "You're still serving breakfast now?" I asked. "Hey, an egg's an egg." This sentence, in a Web review, perfectly describes the kind of place I like: "A Greek-style chow joint replete with '70s wood paneling, periwinkle padded booths, a chatty waitstaff and the warble of regulars at the bar. Basically, if you've ever had it at any place that starts with Grandma's, Uncle's or any sort of Greek place-name, you can find it here." Yes. The Old Timers was busy, popular, and *needed*. In the summer of 2010, it closed without notice and was replaced by a high-rent Einstein Bros. Bagels. Formica eateries are the lifeblood of a city. On Lake, between Michigan and Wabash, Chicago has opened a dead zone.

What's sad about not eating is the experience, whether at a family reunion or at midnight by yourself in a greasy spoon under the L tracks. The loss of dining, not the loss of food. Unless I'm alone, it doesn't involve dinner if it doesn't involve talking. The food and drink I can do without easily. The jokes, gossip, laughs, arguments, and memories I miss. I ran in crowds where anyone was likely to start reciting poetry on a moment's notice. Me too. But not me anymore. So yes, it's sad. Maybe that's why writing has become so important to me. You don't realize it, but we're at dinner right now.

49 MUSING MY MIND

I WOULD FANTASIZE about being blind or deaf. As a child of four or five I went through a weird stage where while lying in bed at night I would pretend I was paralyzed and imagine people coming to admire the brave little saint. I smiled and told them to pray the rosary. It never occurred to me that I might lose my voice. People on the street would try to sell those little cards showing a few symbols of sign language, and I assumed they were con artists.

On campus, some group had a day every year where their members walked around blindfolded to raise money for charity. They depended on the kindness of strangers. They said they were "finding out what it's like to be blind." They weren't doing any such thing. They were finding out what it's like to be blindfolded for a day. Someone who doesn't speak for a day has no idea what it's like to not speak at all. If you're in a country where no one understands you, that's not the same, because you can speak.

After losing my speech, there was never a single day when I realized that was what had happened. It became real to me gradually over a period of months, as one reconstruction surgery and then another failed. I edged into it, eased by a muddle of pain medication that for the first year made things foggy in general. My throat didn't hurt; my shoulders and legs were giving me the trouble, after they had been plundered for spare parts.

Blind people develop a more acute sense of hearing. Deaf people can better notice events on the periphery and comprehend the quick movements of lips and sign language. What about people who lose the ability to speak? We expand other ways of communicating. I can use my own pidgin sign language, combining waving, pointing, shrugging, slapping my forehead, tracing letters on my palm, mime, charades, and more uses of "thumbs-up" and "thumbs-down" than I ever dreamed of. Yet I know all about people responding "I don't know what you're saying." I especially know about having the answer and not being able to express it, and how the flow of a meeting gets away from you while you're desperately trying to write, or type, or signal what you want to say. People respond as if they're being sensitive and polite, but unconsciously they've started to think of me as a little slow.

I'm stuck with this and there's no fix. I'm fortunate that I'm a writer and can express myself that way, but in a meeting or a group conversation I'm always behind. I want to contribute and people want me to, but it just doesn't work. In the back of my head there's the hope that maybe somebody with a bright idea will pop out of the woodwork and give me a solution. Not in my lifetime. I began to find some measure of serenity when I finally accepted that I would never speak again, and that was that. I went through three surgeries intended to restore some measure of speech, however imperfect. All three failed. All three removed just a little more flesh in an unsuccessful attempt to attach spare parts.

So how can I communicate—not on the Internet, which I do easily, but in person at a meeting, a dinner party, or a social situation? I can (1) write by hand or on an iPad, (2) type spoken words for text to speech, or (3) select words and phrases from the selection on Proloquo or similar, more elaborate programs and devices. Signing doesn't work at meetings unless you want to say things like yes, no, so-so, or shrug your shoulders—things everybody understands. True sign language is an elegant and complete medium and I have learned something about it, but one thing I've learned is that most people don't understand it and never will. I may be inept, but in my experience of the Proloquo class of programs, the visual menus are slow and frustrating and hard to even see on a device like, for example, the iPhone. You find yourself with phrases like you find in those traveler's books: *Where is the toilet? What is the price? I am sick and need a doctor. Fill it up.* My mind goes back to Monty Python's Hungarian Phrase Book sketch.

Text to speech has the advantage of being more precise and responsive. You type it, a program says it. There are purpose-built voice devices that are said to be quite helpful, but I find that my laptop computer is handiest. I've tried several voices and find that Alex, which comes built into the Macintosh, is the easiest for most people to understand. Chaz prefers Lawrence and his British accent.

Writing on little notepads is quick and easy, but your messages have to be short, and people have to be able to read them. It amazes me how many people forget they use reading glasses. They take your notepad and move it closer or farther away from their eyes, trying to get it into focus, and finally say, "I think I need my reading glasses," and then start patting their pockets or searching through their purses. Meanwhile, everyone else in the group is smiling politely. If even one of them tries to get in a few quick words, the conversation moves on and the moment is lost.

A related problem is that some people don't seem to keep conversations loaded in current memory. If something I've written is a reference or a punch line to what was said two comments ago, they have no idea what I'm talking about. If I try to explain, the flow is even more seriously interrupted. Do people assume I make random statements out of context? Fifty years as a newspaperman have trained me to listen and follow through. The conversations of some people seem to drift in an eternal present. I didn't realize this so clearly before my current troubles.

Here's the point I'm at now. I find that I can weather about an hour of a business meeting before the bottled-up thoughts make my head explode. It's so hard for me to express myself that I've become aware of the words ordinary people waste. It used to drive Gene Siskel crazy when people would call him on the phone and tell him where they were calling from and that they'd tried earlier or meant to call yesterday and ask him how the weather was. "Lip flap," he called it. "What is the message?" he would interrupt.

At dinner parties or social gatherings, I deliberately dial down and just enjoy the company and conversation. I've given up trying to participate very much. People mean well, but it just doesn't work for me. I keep myself company. I don't feel especially lonely by myself. I feel lonelier at a party, when I'm sitting to one side. I like our family and close friends because they're used to me. But I'm never going to speak, and I may as well make the best of it.

At first after losing my speech, I could not read easily, because sedation had undermined my attention span. I was depressed. I could turn on the TV, but why? My wife brought a wonderful DVD player to my hospital room, but I could not make myself watch movies. My life was stale and profitless. I would spend hours in a murky stupor. Knowing I had always been reading a book, my concerned wife began reading the mainstays to me: Jane Austen and Charles Dickens. I couldn't follow.

Curiously, my love of reading finally returned after I picked up Cormac McCarthy's *Suttree*, a book I had already read not long before my first surgery. Now I read it two more times, reentering the same experience, the same occult and visionary prose, the life of Suttree so urgently evoked. As rarely before, a book became tactile to me. When Suttree stopped at the bus station for a grilled cheese, I ate it, and the pickle, and drank the black coffee. I began to live again through this desperate man's sad life. In my chilly hospital room late at night, a blanket pulled around me in a wheelchair, a pool of light on the page, I found myself drawn into the story of Suttree with an intensity I hadn't felt from fiction in years. I hungered for that book. I yearned toward it. Suttree was alive. He lived for me. How strange that a novel about such a desperate man could pull me back into living. I had no use for happy characters. What did they know?

50   PUTTING A NEW FACE ON THINGS

Would I want to start over with a new face? Would I like to eat, drink, talk, and look like a normal person? Even if that person was a stranger? In theory, this is now possible. In Spain and America experimental face transplants have been carried out. The damage to my face is considerable, involving the loss of my lower jaw, but in *New Scientist* magazine I read an article about a ravaged face: "The team then replaced this with practically the entire face of a dead donor, including all the skin, muscles and nerves, the entire nose, the lips, palate, all the teeth, the cheekbones and the entire lower jaw. These were grafted by microsurgery to what remained of the patient's own face, and the blood supply reconnected. In the final part of the operation, the surgeons transplanted bones and connecting nerves to the patient's own face."

The lower jaw! After all, I have much more real estate still intact than the Spanish patient. My first surgery was planned to restore my appearance to something close to normal, and the next two were to bring me "closer" to normal. At first it was hoped my drinking, speaking, and talking would return. All three surgeries failed, leaving me as I am today, damaged but happy and productive. I appear to be cancer free. Why should I complain?

I'd need to undergo rehabilitation to learn to speak again, but a Cleveland doctor says one of her face transplant patients, after two years, "can say all her vowels and has such normal sensation in her face that she can feel a kiss." This is encouraging. After the day in first grade when Sister Ambrosetta taught us to chant "A, E, I, O, U...and sometimes Y," I never thought the day would come when I couldn't say my vowels. But I can't, and don't bother asking about my consonants.

What if I could go to Spain and return with a complete face? If you passed me on the street, you might mistake me for a normal man. Smaller children would no longer stare and ask their mommies about me. Actually, that part, I might miss. These days children look at me frankly, with natural curiosity. I smile and wave, and they often smile and wave back. I'm not your everyday face. I provide entertainment value. I also believe our society has grown more tolerant of disabilities; never once has a mother snatched the child away from such a sight as me.

All the same, I don't have any desire for a face transplant. I knew that even while I was still reading about the transplants. I knew it for so many different reasons that it was hard to sort them out. Let's set aside medical reasons and assume for the sake of argument that the operation would be a success. I still don't want one.

I feel it would be an act of disloyalty to my own face. I have lived with it so long. In adolescence I studied it with fierce concentration in the mirror, convinced my nose was too long, my lips too fat, and my zits would colonize all available facial skin. Later, I saw it idealized in one of those unreal high school graduation pictures. Later still, recorded in states of hilarity during long nights of celebration and days with the friends of a lifetime. I saw my hair grow long and then longer. I saw sideburns appear and retreat. Twice I saw the beginnings of a beard and shaved it off. I saw it fatter and thinner. I saw my face grow smaller with diet and exercise. I saw it for the last time on the night before surgery, when I looked in a mirror and took a photograph that appears in this book.

For better or worse, it was my face, and today most of it remains. After a face transplant it would be somebody else's face. Something within me might recoil at the sight. I have no squeamishness about wearing another man's face after he has no need of it; I support transplants of all sorts, and when I die I hope my poor organs can be of use to someone. I wish happiness to the farmer in Spain and the woman in Ohio. I was tremendously moved to learn Robert Altman had lived for more than ten years with a transplanted heart. Think of the films he was able to make, the joy he was able to bring. All of that is good. If I should someday need a heart or liver, I will seek one. But this face, however imperfect, is still mine. I own it. I look out of it. I'm rather fond of it.

For some time after taking that "final photo" of myself, I avoided looking in mirrors. I knew the first operation had gotten the cancer but the reconstruction had failed. I vaguely knew what I must look like, but I didn't want to see. I was still inside, right here, in my head looking out, and in my mind I still had the same face. I could even feel sensations in places I no longer possessed—the "ghost limb" phenomenon. How did I know I'm in my head? How do any of us know? That's where my brain lives and where my eyes sit. I am not in my chest, my hand, or my foot. I live in *here* and operate all the rest like Iron Man.

And in *here*, I still imagine the same face, no matter what you see.

Of course eventually I looked in mirrors and grew to accept my new appearance. After the first surgery it looked...well, better than it does now. After the second surgery, Chaz said I looked pretty good. For the third surgery, I went to the famous man at the hospital in Houston. He labored for hours. My memory is cloudy because of pain medication, but a few days later I clearly remember Chaz holding up a mirror so I could see what looked like an acceptable version of myself. A specialist at the hospital had studied my tongue, professed herself satisfied with its motion, and told me I might talk again. Things were looking up.

That surgery failed, too. I sensed that my surgeons on all three procedures were personally saddened by the outcomes. I was not just a case for them. Microsurgery is painstaking, long, and unimaginably difficult. The surgeon invests so much of his skill in the process that when a procedure fails, he mourns. I never thought it was their fault.

It was probably the fault of earlier presurgical radiation I insisted on, hoping for an easy way around surgery. In Seattle every day for a month, I was strapped to a table suspended over a huge open space so the neutron beam equipment could rotate around me in 360 degrees. A tightly molded mask prevented my head from moving. A clamp held my jaws immobile. Precise readings were used to target the beam.

The radiation created nausea. Ordinary food became impossible. I was given antiradiation shots in my stomach wall—so powerful the first was to cushion against the impact of the second. I was forced to drink Ensure, which actually tastes pretty good, but during those days I could hardly keep it down. In the mornings Chaz would order me two eggs and I'd do my best. It wasn't until four months later that I ate another real meal.

But the radiation seemed to have worked. I could still talk. I went back on TV and did more shows with Richard Roeper. I went to Cannes. And then the cancer reappeared.

I've written before about how I've come to terms with my current appearance. The best thing that happened to me was a full-page photo in *Esquire*, showing exactly how I look today. No point in denying it. No way to hide it. Better for it to be out there. You don't like it, that's your problem. I'm happy I don't look worse. I made a simple decision to just get on with life. I was a writer, and so I was lucky. I wrote, therefore I lived. Another surgical attempt was proposed, but I said no. Enough is enough. I will look the way I look, and express myself in print, and I will be content.

51 HIGH SCHOOL REUNION

At our fiftieth Urbana High School class reunion in the summer of 2010, I watched as every class member walked to the microphone and said a few words. I saw a double image: the same person in 1960 and 2010. The same smile, the same gait, the same body language, the same eyes. I was witnessing a truth. Within our bodies of sixty-seven or sixty-eight years lived all the people we had ever been or seemed to be.

That spring of 1960, when we graduated, John F. Kennedy was running for president, and there was change in the air. It was the beginning of something—a new decade, a new kind of freedom vaguely predicted by rock and roll. Many of our hopes were delusions. One of our class members would die as a helicopter pilot in Vietnam. Another would die mysteriously fighting with the rebels in Nicaragua. At least one was lost to Alzheimer's. Others to accidents and disease. Most got married, had children and grandchildren, and now those still alive were gathered at a new hotel located more or less where we used to pick strawberries for ten cents a quart on the university's South Farms, passing around family photos on their cell phones.

This would probably be my last reunion. At our tenth reunion, held at the now-disappeared Moose Lodge in Champaign, there was still a little unfinished romantic business in the air. Twinges of old jealousies and heartbreaks. We noticed those who had once gone steady, the boy's class ring worn on a chain around the girl's neck, resting between her breasts in a gloat of possession. Now they had married others, but that night they took the dance floor together.

There had been little drinking in high school—none, in fact, that I ever saw. Or much smoking. At the Moose Lodge in 1970 a lot of us were smoking or drinking, and one classmate wanted to ride back to Urbana on top of my car. Here he was in 2010, one of the most respected men in Champaign County. But still—this is the point—still absolutely the same man, sober now but with the same sardonic grin, the same sideways amusement at life. Here were girls I dated and parked with in the moonlight to quote Thomas Wolfe on his trembling romantic destiny—his, and of course, ours. Then we kissed not so much in a sexual way as with the tender solemnity we thought of at the time as love. In 2010 that is all so long ago, but the same persons live inside, and while we live we have memories. Most of our memories are still in there somewhere, needing only a nudge to awaken. Here was Pegeen Linn, a girl who appeared with me in a class play. I hadn't thought about that play once in all these years, but now into my mind came the memorized monologue. From where? From where everything still is.

I went to school with these people for four years. With those who attended St. Mary's, for twelve. They evoke associations more fully than most of those I experienced later. One of the most noble undertakings in the history of the cinema is Michael Apted's *Up Series* of documentaries, which begins with a group of British seven-year-olds, and revisits them every seven years, most recently in 2005 when they were forty-nine. The films are the proof of Wordsworth's belief that "the child is father of the man." Looking at my classmates, I wondered if perhaps the person we are in school is the person we will always be, despite everything else that comes our way. All that changes is that slowly we become more aware of what matters in life.

On the Saturday morning we took a bus tour around the twin cities. Down the leafy old streets we remembered as children, past our old houses, past Lorado Taft's statue *Lincoln the Lawyer*, which faces the high school. We saw ghost buildings on every street and called out what used to be but was no more: the Elbow Room, the Urbana Lincoln Hotel, Mel Root's all-night restaurant, the old Steak 'n Shake, Hood's Drugs with its chocolate and marshmallow sundaes. We drove out into vast new "developments" rising from the farmland southeast of town, $500,000 homes surrounding a golf course, looking exactly like similar "developments" all over the nation and not at all like our Urbana neighborhoods.

We drove around the enormous campus, half the buildings new since our time, most of the old buildings still there. Past Memorial Stadium with ungainly sky boxes now surmounting the grandstands where rich and poor once froze alike. Past the Morrow Plots, the nation's oldest agricultural research field; the Undergraduate Library next to it was buried five levels into the ground to avoid casting shade on it. Past the Assembly Hall, now threatened with obsolescence because it wasn't large enough to accommodate the new scoreboards. *The new scoreboards!*

We passed the Taylor Thomas subdivision, named in honor of our history teacher, possibly the first African American to teach at Urbana High. In his civics class he taught me much of what I believe about politics. When he attempted to buy a house in a neighborhood mostly populated by professors at the university, the house was snatched up by a neighbor to keep him from moving in. He bought a lot just outside the city limits and built the home he and his wife occupied until he died. He never mentioned that in class.

Our sightseeing trip took us down a road through the university farms, where we once parked to make out. There in a cornfield, the university is building the new Blue Waters supercomputer. Our hometown, the birthplace of HAL 9000, would now give birth to a computer more powerful than the next five hundred largest supercomputers combined, operating at a quadrillion instructions per second.

Incredibly, four of our teachers were at the reunion. Here was Dan Perrino, our bandmaster and music teacher. Paul Smith, who told me I was one of his best physics students, although that's not how I recall it. Carolyn Conrad, who inspired me in English and drama. The poetic Carolyn Leseur, who turned me on to Charles Dickens for a lifetime, and who told Chaz I was always reading a book during class. Here was John Rasmussen, whose house I stopped at many mornings before grade school, so we and his sister Jeanne and brother Jerry could ride there together on our bikes. Here was this year's emcee, Dick James, the best-selling psychologist, who has probably forgotten he once threw a hard-packed snowball that gave me a black eye, but I haven't.

There were many women in the room I'd dated in that naïve time. I noticed all evening classmates smiled at one another in a subtly different way if they had reason to remember private tenderness. Marty McCloy wasn't there because she was Class of 1961, but somehow high school romance for me is evoked by the two of us on a hot summer night on the dance floor of the Tigers' Den, holding each other closely, very serious and inward of mind, while the Everly Brothers played "Dream." Under our armpits, sweat formed dark circles, and our cheeks were moist as they touched. Many years later Marty posted a comment on my blog saying I was the best kisser in school. Why don't we ever learn these things when they could do us some good?

THE GREATEST MAN I knew well was Studs Terkel. I met him very soon after I moved to Chicago.
It was in the Old Town apartment of Herman and
Marilou Kogan; Herman was the *Chicago Daily News*
editor responsible for getting me hired at the *Sun-
Times*. The evening was all conversation, nonstop,
and all consequential: no small talk or idle chat for
these people. I felt as if I'd been put at the same table
with the grown-ups. Not long after, the Nobel Prize–
winning novelist Doris Lessing visited Chicago.
Studs knew I had read all her books while studying
at the University of Cape Town, and he also knew,
more importantly, that I had a car and knew how to
drive. Studs never learned how to drive; he enlisted

me as chauffeur and I spent two days observing Studs showing Lessing his own Chicago. We drove past the Jackson Park lagoon and Studs made us stop and sit on a park bench where, he said, his namesake Studs Lonigan had first kissed Lucy Scanlon.

I ran across Studs countless times over the years. He was an old man and couldn't drive and he was everywhere at everything. The opening nights of Second City. A bartender's birthday. A political rally. A picnic in somebody's backyard. Riccardo's every Friday night. Looking up from a page at Stuart Brent's bookshop. Handing in an article at the paper. The emcee standing on third base at Wrigley Field for Mike Royko's funeral. Three seats ahead on the No. 36 bus. Visiting friends in Michigan. I saw that man intentionally or by accident more than anyone else I wasn't related to, involved with, or employed by. So did many others. Two people meeting with Studs standing between them would hear from him how extraordinary they both were. He knew no one but invaluable people. He never forgot a thing. Even at the end, it was all there, present in his mind. It is melancholy fact that after my first illness Studs visited me in the hospital more times than I had visited him. When we visited Studs three days after he had open-heart surgery, I expected to find a sick man. I found Studs sitting up in bed, surrounded by books and papers, receiving friends. The author Garry Wills appeared at his door. Studs had just finished reading his new book. He was filled with questions.

The lesson Studs taught me is that your life is over when you stop living it. If you can truly "retire," you only had a job, but not an occupation. Among his books is one about this very subject: *Working: People Talk About What They Do All Day and How They Feel About What They Do.* It became a Broadway musical. One reason Terkel got people to talk so openly with him is that he came across as this guy sitting down with you to have a good, long talk. Pick up one of his books, and now you're sitting next to the guy. You can't stop reading. Studs had an interviewing technique I admired: He combined astonishment with curiosity. He couldn't believe his ears. He repeated with enthusiasm what his subject had just said, and the subject invariably continued and expanded and wanted to make his own story better.

It's curious how only two of Studs's books are technically about himself, but in a way they're all about himself. Reading a novel, we may identify with one of the characters. Reading Studs, we identify with him—with the questions. Through his example, we become inquiring minds. And his subjects range widely. Look at his book *Will the Circle Be Unbroken? Reflections on Death, Rebirth, and Hunger for a*

Faith. He provides not New Age malarkey, but real people having real thoughts about their real lives and the inevitability of their own real deaths. He started writing the book after the death of his wife, Ida, a beautiful woman who stood by him in the good times (he starred on one of the first sitcoms in network history) and the bad (he lost that job because of the blacklist). He was envious that her FBI file was thicker than his own.

When Ida grew older, she refused to use a cane, she told me, "because I fall so gracefully." He told his friends her last words to him, as she was wheeled into the OR for heart surgery, were: "Louis, what have you gotten me into now?" Some weeks after her death, Chaz and I talked Studs into sailing along with us on Dusty Cohl's Floating Film Festival. One afternoon, over coffee in the cafeteria, he interviewed Chaz on her thoughts about death for the book. Never a lost moment.

Studs died on October 31, 2008, at ninety-six, just missing the election of Barack Obama, which he had promised to witness. Was Studs the greatest Chicagoan? I cannot think of another. For me, he represented the generous, scrappy, liberal, wisecracking heart of the city. If you met him, he was your friend. That happened to the hundreds and hundreds of people he interviewed for his radio show and twenty best-selling books. He wrote down the oral histories of those of his time who did not have a voice. In conversation he could draw up every single one of their names.

Studs said many times in the final years, "I'm ready to check out." Around the time of his ninety-third birthday, Chaz and I had dinner with him, a few days before he was having a heart bypass. He was looking forward to it. "The docs say the odds are four to one in my favor," he told us, with the voice of a guy who studied the angles. "At age ninety-three, those are pretty good odds. I'm gonna have a whack at it. Otherwise, I'm Dead Man Walking. If I don't have the operation, how long do I have? Six months, maybe. That's no way to live, waiting to die. I've had ninety-three years—tumultuous years. That's a pretty good run."

It was a run during which his great mind never let him down. "This is ironic," he told me. "I'm not the one was has Alzheimer's. It's the country that has Alzheimer's. There was a survey the other day showing that most people think our best president was Reagan. Not Abraham Lincoln. FDR came in tenth. People don't pay attention anymore. They don't read the news." Studs read the news. He sang with Pete Seeger: *I sell the morning papers sir, my name is Jimmy Brown. / Everybody knows that I'm the newsboy of the*

*town. / You can hear me yellin' "Morning Star," run-
nin' along the street. / Got no hat upon my head no shoes
upon my feet.*

Studs knew jazz inside out, gospel by heart, the
blues as he learned them after being raised in the
transient hotel run by his mother on Wells Street.
He wasn't the only man who had a going-away party
when he left to fight in World War II. He might have
been the only one to have Billie Holiday sing at his
party. He was never a communist. He was a proud
man of the Left. J. Edgar Hoover thought he was a
subversive. "That guy Hoover," he said, "had a lifelong suspicion of those who thought the Constitution
actually meant something." Almost every single day
of his life he wore a red-checked shirt and bright red
socks. Of course he smoked cigars. He liked a drink
and loved to hang out in newspaper bars and in ethnic
neighborhoods with his pals. I never saw him drunk,
and believe me, I had plenty of opportunities to.

During his final illness, we received bulletins from
those who loved him and cared for him. This was
the stunner, in an e-mail from his dear friend Sydney Lewis, on September 11, 2008: "After hearing
his very clear wishes, his son Dan called hospice. The
admissions nurse, a lovely woman, said in her many
years of doing this work she'd never seen a person
more at peace over the decision. Really, all he wants

is for J.R. [his caregiver J. R. Millares] and Dan to be around and never again to have to leave his house."

He had been in touch through the summer, by e-mail. He wasn't receiving a lot of visitors. He never mentioned his health. He was online encouraging me. That was so typical of him. After I broke my hip, he e-mailed me but never mentioned the hip. He said: "You have added a NEW VOICE, a new sound, to your natural one. This—what you write now—is a richer one—a new dimension. It's more than about movies. Yes, it's about movies but there is something added: A REFLECTION on life itself." I thought twice about whether I should quote that. I did it because it is the voice of Studs Terkel's love. Studs reaching outside his failing body and giving encouragement, as he always did for me and countless others. He couldn't have written a shelf of books after listening to hundreds of people and writing down their words if his heart had not been unconditionally open to the world.

An e-mail on September 15, from Sydney: "When I got here today he was gloomy and hadn't eaten. He said he's half interested in leaving, half in staying. After I printed out the great *Booklist* review his new book *P.S.* got, he perked up, we talked about the election, and before I knew it he'd polished off some meat loaf and grapes and was demanding more grapes! So it goes. I suggested he hang around for at least a few things: book publication, World Series, election, and Garry Wills's Terkel retrospective for *NY Review of Books*. He's agreed to try." On October 23, his friend Andrew Patner e-mailed: "The man with the greatest spirit known to man is sitting up and taking nourishment. Swallow coaching, even some (cut-up) meat. Gained back a few pounds. Opining on the election (surprise!), the World Series (surprise!), how lousy his new book is being marketed (surprise!). He's looking now to New Year's Eve ('Why not?'), but pulling at least for Election Day ('I can't miss it!')."

He was the most widely and deeply loved man I ever hope to know. "When I go," he told us, "my ashes will be mixed with Ida's and scattered in Bughouse Square." There would be no stone, although being Studs he had written his epitaph: "Curiosity didn't kill this cat."

53   MY LAST WORDS

IT WAS AN inexplicable instinct that led me to agree when Chris Jones contacted me requesting an interview. The idea of *Esquire* appealed to me. I wrote a bunch of interviews for them in the 1970s, when it was the crucible of the New Journalism. What goes around, comes around. I'd read some of Chris's stuff. He's a good writer. You sense the person there. He's not holding his subjects at arm's length. I knew I'd have to play fair. I've done interviews for years. This was no time to get sensitive and ask for photo approval, or an advance look at the piece. I'd been the goose, and now it was my turn to be the gander. I've never known what that means, geese-wise.

Chaz is always my protector. She had her doubts.

She worries that I'm too impulsive and trusting. She is correct. Left entirely to my own devices, God knows what I might be capable of. She would follow me into the mouth of a cannon, but first she'd say, "Do you really think it's a good idea to crawl into that cannon?" Then I would explain that it was my duty as a journalist, a film critic, a liberal, or a human being, etc., to crawl into the cannon. And she'd suggest I sleep on it and crawl into the cannon fresh and early in the morning.

Chaz wondered if I really thought it was a good idea to invite Chris Jones or anyone else to do an interview that would involve being followed around and observed informally. I said I believed he wasn't looking for a kill but just wanted to write a good article. He was a real writer. We talked about it. I knew he was coming when Chaz started in with the housecleaning.

Chris Jones was a very nice man. He told us he lives in Ottawa, was teaching journalism at the University of Montana, and is married with two kids. So that tells you something. If the same man is also a senior writer for *Esquire*, he's my man. He arrived at the appointed hour, and he did an excellent job of describing everything that happened subsequently.

Actually, he left some things out. As our library was being cleaned, I noticed for the first time in some years the bound albums of our wedding photos sitting out. That lodged in my mind. When Chris was about to arrive and I was a little nervous, I told Chaz, "For God's sake, don't start showing him our wedding photos! That will make us look bourgeois." She looked at me in disbelief. "What makes you think I would ever show him our wedding photos?" I explained that because I had seen the albums sitting out, I thought it was for a purpose. Chris Jones arrived. He hadn't been in the house half an hour before the conversation turned to Gene Siskel. I said what a close friend he had been, apart from our fights and feuds and the rest of it, which were real, but didn't dislodge our friendship. "His daughters were even the flower girls at our wedding," I said. "Chaz, show Chris our wedding photos." She looked at me like the eighth wonder of the world.

A little later I was telling Chris that Siskel was secretive and I was the opposite, always blurting out what I should shut up about. "He said my middle names should be Full Disclosure." This started Chaz to laughing and in the spirit of full disclosure she told him about my dire warning to her about the wedding photos.

Well, that was okay with me, actually. My theory was that if Chris had an article to write it was not my place to write it for him as a favorable press release about myself. Let him write what he observed. Oliver Cromwell is said to have commissioned an official painting of himself, "warts and all." He apparently never said any such thing, was misquoted a century after his death, and his official portrait showed no warts, but never mind. He should have said it.

The best interview I ever wrote was for *Esquire*. It was told almost entirely in dialogue, and involved an afternoon I spent with Lee Marvin at his beach house in Malibu. He spent much effort ordering in fresh supplies of Heineken's. I took faithful notes, sent the piece in, and waited for the shit to hit the fan. *Esquire* ran it with the headline, "Saturday with Lee F——ing Marvin." They used dashes in those days. I never heard a word from Marvin.

A few years later, I interviewed Marvin in his house outside Tucson. I observed he was not drinking. "I'm alive, aren't I?" he said. I said I didn't know if he would want to talk with me after the *Esquire* piece and the earlier piece in the *New York Times*. He had married again a few years earlier, a girl he'd been in love with before he went off to the Marines. She started laughing. "That was Lee," she said. Marvin lit a cigarette.

That's all you can really ask: for Chaz to be able to read the article and say it was about me. It was. By and large, it was a faithful account of what happened over the course of two days and evenings. The errors were few, small, and understandable.

I knew going in that a lot of the article would be about my surgeries and their aftermath. Let's face it. *Esquire* wouldn't have assigned an article if I were still in good health. Their cover line was the hook "The Last Words of Roger Ebert." A good head. Whoever wrote that knew what they were doing. When I turned inside the magazine, I got a jolt from the full-page photograph of my jaw drooping. Nobody had seen me quite that way before. Not a lovely sight. But then I'm not a lovely sight, and in a moment I thought, what the hell, it's just as well it's out there. That's how I look, after all. I was a little surprised at the detail the article went into about the nature and extent of my wounds and the realities of my appearance, but what the hell. It was true. I didn't need polite fictions.

One strange result of the cover line was that many people got the idea that these were my dying words. The line Chaz liked least used the words "the time he has left." We're all dying in increments. I don't mind people knowing what I look like, but I don't want them thinking I'm dying. To be fair, Chris Jones never said I was. If he took a certain elegiac tone, you know what? I might have, too. And if he structured his elements into a story arc, that's just good writing.

He wasn't still in the room the second evening when he wrote that after Chaz had gone off to bed and I was streaming Radio Caroline and writing late into the night. But that's what I did. It may be, the more interviews you've done, the more you appreciate a good one. I knew exactly what he started with, and I could see where he ended, and he can be proud of the piece. It was sort of a relief to have that full-page photo of my face. Running it that big was good journalism. It made you want to read the article. What I hated most was that my hair was too neatly combed.

54   HOW I BELIEVE IN GOD

WHEN I WAS in first or second grade and had just been introduced by the nuns to the concept of a limitless God, I lay awake at night driving myself nuts by repeating over and over, *But how could God have no beginning? And how could he have no end?* And then I thought of all the stars in the sky: *But how could there be a last one? Wouldn't there always have to be one more?* Many years later I know the answer to the second question, but I still don't know the answer to the first one.

I took it up with a favorite nun, Sister Marie Donald, who led our rhythm band and was our basketball coach. "Roger," she said, "that is just something you have to believe. Pray for faith." Then I lay awake wondering how I could pray for faith to a God I could not believe in without faith. That seemed to leave me suspended between two questions. These logical puzzles were generated spontaneously within my mind. They didn't come from my school or my family. Most of my neighborhood friends were Protestants who were not interested in theories about God, apart from the fact that of course he existed.

I bought the teachings of the Roman Catholic Church lock, stock, and barrel, apart from the God problem. We started every school day at St. Mary's with an hour of religion, and it was my favorite subject. We were drilled in memorizing entries from the Baltimore Catechism, which was a bore, but I was fascinated by the theoretical discussions: What qualifies as a sin? What do you have to do to get to heaven? Can you go to hell by accident? and "Sister, what would happen if..." Those words always introduced a hypothetical situation in which an unsuspecting Catholic had blundered perilously close to the fires below.

Religion class began every day with theoretical thinking and applied reasoning and was excellent training. No matter what one ends up believing, it is good to learn to think in such terms. To think that you might sin by accident and be damned before you could get to confession in time! What if you had an impure thought at the top of Mt. Everest and couldn't get back down? We were exposed to the concepts of sins of omission, sins of commission, intentional sins, and, the trickiest of all, unintentional sins. Think of it: a sin you didn't intend to commit. But Sister, is it a sin if you didn't know it was? Then isn't it safer not to know?

Some of my classmates and I would lie on our backs in the front yard, ponder the stars, and ask ourselves, "If some kid started to play with himself but he didn't know what would happen, would that be his fault?" We concluded: only if he did it again. "Yeah, like four times every night," giggled a pal whose anonymity I will preserve after all these years. I remember one night a kid brother asked innocently, "But what *would* happen if you played with yourself?" We told him, "Just don't ever try it!" "Then how do you know anything would happen?" We decided you were allowed just one time, to find out.

I have the impression that all of my Dominican teachers were New Deal Democrats, and that for them Franklin D. Roosevelt had achieved a species of secular sainthood. Of course they were fervently anti-communist. People in the USSR could be thrown in jail just for going to church, and there was brave Cardinal Mindszenty, who was tortured by the Hungarian atheists. For many years I visualized the Soviet

Union as a land where the sun never came out and enslaved Catholic peasants labored under lowering skies for their godless rulers.

But our theology was often very practical: All men are created equal. Do onto others as you would have them do onto you. Follow the Ten Commandments, which we studied at length, except for adultery, "which you children don't have to worry about." A fair day's work for a fair day's wage. A good government should help make sure everyone has a roof over his head, a job, and three meals a day. The cardinal acts of mercy. Ethical behavior. The sisters didn't especially seem to think that a woman's place was in the home, as theirs certainly was not. You should "pray for your vocation." My mother prayed for mine; she wanted me to become a priest. "Every Catholic mother hopes she can give a son to the priesthood," she said, and spoke of one mother at St. Patrick's, who had given two, as if she were a lottery winner.

As I grew I no longer lost any sleep over the questions of God and infinity. I understood they could have no answers. At some point the reality of God was no longer present in my mind. I believed in the basic Church teachings because I thought they were correct, not because God wanted me to. In my mind, in the way I interpret them, I still live by them today. Not by the rules and regulations, but by the principles. For example, in the matter of abortion, I am pro-choice, but by personal choice would have nothing to do with an abortion of a child of my own. I believe in free will, and believe I have no right to tell anyone else what to do. Popes come and go, and John XXIII has been the only one I felt affection for. Their dictums strike me as lacking in the ability to surprise. They have been leading a holding action for a millennium.

Catholicism made me a humanist before I knew the word. When people rail against "secular humanism," I want to ask them if humanism itself would be okay with them if it wasn't so secular. Then I want to ask, "Why do you think it *is* secular?" This would lead to my opinion that their beliefs were not humanist. Over the high school years, my belief in the likelihood of a God disappeared. I kept this to myself. I never discussed it with my parents. My father in any event was a nonpracticing Lutheran, until a deathbed conversion that rather disappointed me. I'm sure he agreed to it for my mother's sake. Did I start calling myself an agnostic or an atheist? No, and I still don't. I avoid that because I don't want to provide a category that people can apply to me. Those who say that "believer" and "atheist" are concrete categories do violence to the mystery we must be humble enough to confess. I would not want my convictions reduced to a word. Chaz, who has a firm faith, leaves me to my beliefs. "But you know you're one or the other," she says. "I have never told you that," I say. "Maybe not in so many words, but you are," she says. "You're an atheist." I say that nothing is that simple. Absolutists frighten me. During all the endless discussions on my blog about evolution, intelligent design, God, and the afterworld, numbering altogether thousands of comments, I have never named my beliefs, although readers have freely informed me that I am an atheist, an agnostic, or at the very least a secular humanist— which I am.

Let me rule out at once any God who has personally spoken to anyone or issued instructions to men. That some men believe they have been spoken to by God, I am certain. That's for them to believe. I don't believe Moses came down from the mountain with any tablets he did not go up with. I believe mankind in general has a need to believe in higher powers and an existence not limited to the physical duration of the body. But these needs are hopes, and believing them doesn't make them true. I believe mankind feels a need to gather in churches, whether physical or social. I've spent hours and hours in churches all over the world. I sit in them not to pray, but to gently nudge my thoughts toward wonder and awe. I am aware of the generations there before me and the reassurance of tradition. At a midnight Mass on Christmas Eve at the village church in Tring in the Chilterns, I felt unalloyed elevation. My favorite service is the Anglican evensong. I agree with Annie Dillard, who says that in an unfamiliar area, she seeks out the church of the oldest established religion she can find, because it has the most experience in not being struck by lightning.

I have no interest in megachurches with jocular millionaire pastors. I think what happens in them is sociopolitical, not spiritual. I believe the prosperity gospel tries to pass through the eye of the needle. I believe it is easier for a Republican to pass through the eye of a needle than for a camel to get into heaven. I have no patience for churches that evangelize aggressively. I have no interest in being instructed in what I must do to be saved. I prefer vertical prayer, directed up toward heaven, rather than horizontal prayer, directed sideways toward me. I believe a worthy church must grow through attraction, not promotion. I am wary of zealotry; even as a child I was suspicious of those who, as I often heard, were "more Catholic than the pope." If we are to love our neighbors as ourselves, we must regard their beliefs with the same respect our own deserve.

I'm still struggling with the question of how anything could have no beginning and no end. These days I'm fascinated by it from the point of view of science. I cannot know everything, but I approach matters in terms of what I do and can know. Science is not "secular." It is a process of honest investigation. Take infinity. We know there must be an infinite number of numbers, because how could there be a last number? The more interesting puzzle is, how did there come to be a first number, and why do many mammals other than man know how to count, at least a little? I don't believe the universe can count. Counting is a mental exercise, and mathematics is useful to the degree it helps us describe and understand the universe and work within it in useful ways. A last number is not important; only the impossibility of one.

I know there cannot be a last star, because we know the universe to be curved. At least, that's what mathematicians tell us. I can't form the concept of a curved universe in my mind, but I think I know what they're trying to say. Nor can I comprehend five, six, or many additional dimensions. Nor do I understand the theory of relativity. Growing up I used to hear that Einstein was the only man smart enough to understand his own theory. Now countless people do, but I suspect few have a literal vision of what it means. What they understand, I think, is their mathematical proofs of it. If I'm wrong about this, I'm encouraged.

That the universe may expand indefinitely and die is a concept I can imagine. That all of its matter would cease to exist I cannot imagine. That the universe, as was once thought, expands and contracts indefinitely, one Big Bang collapsing into another one, seemed reasonable enough. But in both models of the universe, what caused the first Big Bang? Or was there a first Big Bang, any more than a last number? If there was a first cause, was there a first causer? Did Big Bangs just happen to happen? Can we name the first causer "God"? We can name it anything we want. I can name it after myself. It is utterly insignificant what it is called, because we would be giving a name to something that falls outside all categories of thought and must be unknowable and irrelevant to knowledge. So naming it is a futile enterprise. The word "God" is unhelpful because it implies it has a knowable definition.

Quantum theory is now discussing instantaneous connections between two entangled quantum objects such as electrons. This phenomenon has been observed in laboratory experiments and scientists believe they have proven it takes place. They're not talking about faster than the speed of light. Speed has nothing to do with it. The entangled objects somehow communicate instantaneously at a distance. If that is true, distance has no meaning. Light-years have no meaning. Space has no meaning. In a sense, the entangled objects are not even communicating. They are the same thing. At the "quantum level" (and I don't know what that means), everything may be actually or theoretically linked. All is one. Sun, moon, stars, rain, you, me, everything. All one. If this is so, then Buddhism must have been a quantum theory all along. No, I am not a Buddhist. I am not a believer, not an atheist, not an agnostic. I am more content with questions than answers.

GO GENTLY

I KNOW IT is coming, and I do not fear it, because I believe there is nothing on the other side of death to fear. I hope to be spared as much pain as possible on the approach path. I was perfectly content before I was born, and I think of death as the same state. I am grateful for the gifts of intelligence, love, wonder, and laughter. You can't say it wasn't interesting. My lifetime's memories are what I have brought home from the trip. I will require them for eternity no more than that little souvenir of the Eiffel Tower I brought home from Paris.

I don't expect to die anytime soon. But it could happen this moment, while I am writing. I was talking the other day with Jim Toback, a friend of thirty-five years, and the conversation turned to our deaths, as it always does. "Ask someone how they feel about death," he said, "and they'll tell you everyone's gonna die. Ask them, In the next thirty seconds? *No, no, no, that's not gonna happen.* How about this afternoon? *No.* What you're really asking them to admit is, *Oh my God, I don't really exist. I might be gone at any given second.*"

Me too, but I hope not. I have plans. Still, illness led me resolutely toward the contemplation of death. That led me to the subject of evolution, that most consoling of all the sciences, and I became engulfed on my blog in unforeseen discussions about God, the afterlife, religion, theory of evolution, intelligent design, reincarnation, the nature of reality, what came before the Big Bang, what waits after the end, the nature of intelligence, the reality of the self, death, death, death.

Many readers have informed me that it is a tragic and dreary business to go into death without faith. I don't feel that way. "Faith" is neutral. All depends on what is believed in. I have no desire to live forever. The concept frightens me. I am sixty-nine, have had cancer, will die sooner than most of those reading this. That is in the nature of things. In my plans for life after death, I say, again with Whitman:

*I bequeath myself to the dirt to grow from the grass I
  love,*
*If you want me again look for me under your boot-
  soles.*

And with Will, the brother in Saul Bellow's *Herzog*, I say, "Look for me in the weather reports."

Raised as a Roman Catholic, I internalized the
social values of that faith and still hold most of them,
even though its theology no longer persuades me. I
have no quarrel with what anyone else subscribes to;
everyone deals with these things in his own way, and
I have no truths to impart. All I require of a religion
is that it be tolerant of those who do not agree with
it. I know a priest whose eyes twinkle when he says,
"You go about God's work in your way, and I'll go
about it in His."

What I expect to happen is that my body will
fail, my mind will cease to function, and that will be
that. My genes will not live on, because I have had
no children. I am comforted by Richard Dawkins's
theory of memes. Those are mental units: thoughts,
ideas, gestures, notions, songs, beliefs, rhymes, ideals,
teachings, sayings, phrases, clichés that move from
mind to mind as genes move from body to body.
After a lifetime of writing, teaching, broadcasting,

and telling too many jokes, I will leave behind more memes than many. They will all also eventually die, but so it goes.

O'Rourke's had a photograph of Brendan Behan on the wall, and under it this quotation, which I memorized:

> I respect kindness in human beings first of all, and kindness to animals. I don't respect the law; I have a total irreverence for anything connected with society except that which makes the roads safer, the beer stronger, the food cheaper and the old men and old women warmer in the winter and happier in the summer.

That does a pretty good job of summing it up. "Kindness" covers all of my political beliefs. No need to spell them out. I believe that if, at the end, according to our abilities, we have done something to make others a little happier, and something to make ourselves a little happier, that is about the best we can do. To make others less happy is a crime. To make ourselves unhappy is where all crime starts. We must try to contribute joy to the world. That is true no matter what our problems, our health, our circumstances. We must try. I didn't always know this and am happy I lived long enough to find it out.

One of these days I will encounter what Henry James called on his deathbed "the distinguished thing." I will not be conscious of the moment of passing. In this life I have already been declared dead. It wasn't so bad. After the first ruptured artery, the doctors thought I was finished. Chaz said she sensed that I was still alive and was communicating to her that I wasn't finished yet. She said our hearts were beating in unison, although my heartbeat couldn't be discovered. She told the doctors I was alive, they did what doctors do, and here I am, alive.

Do I believe her? Absolutely. I believe her literally—not symbolically, figuratively, or spiritually. I believe she was actually aware of my call and that she sensed my heartbeat. I believe she did it in the real, physical world I have described, the one that I share with my wristwatch. I see no reason why such communication could not take place. I'm not talking about telepathy, psychic phenomenon, or a miracle. The only miracle is that she was there when it happened, as she was for many long days and nights. I'm talking about her standing there and knowing something. Haven't many of us experienced that? Come on, haven't you? What goes on happens at a level not accessible to scientists, theologians, mystics, physicists, philosophers, or psychiatrists. It's a human kind of a thing.

Someday I will no longer call out, and there will

be no heartbeat. I will be dead. What happens then? From my point of view, nothing. Absolutely nothing. All the same, as I wrote to Monica Eng, whom I have known since she was six, "You'd better cry at my memorial service." I correspond with a dear friend, the wise and gentle Australian director Paul Cox. Our subject sometimes turns to death. In 2010 he came very close to dying before receiving a liver transplant. In 1988 he made a documentary named *Vincent: The Life and Death of Vincent van Gogh*. Paul wrote me that in his Arles days, van Gogh called himself "a simple worshiper of the external Buddha." Paul told me that in those days, Vincent wrote:

> Looking at the stars always makes me dream, as simply as I dream over the black dots representing towns and villages on a map.
>
> Why, I ask myself, shouldn't the shining dots of the sky be as accessible as the black dots on the map of France?
>
> Just as we take a train to get to Tarascon or Rouen, we take death to reach a star. We cannot get to a star while we are alive any more than we can take the train when we are dead. So to me it seems possible that cholera, tuberculosis and cancer are the celestial means of locomo-

tion. Just as steamboats, buses and railways are
the terrestrial means.

To die quietly of old age would be to go there
on foot.

That is a lovely thing to read, and a relief to find
I will probably take the celestial locomotive. Or, as
his little dog, Milou, says whenever Tintin proposes a
journey, "Not by foot, I hope!"

ACKNOWLEDGMENTS

THIS BOOK BEGAN to take shape in my head after I began writing a blog and found myself drawn to the autobiographical. In that process, at a low time in my life, I was greatly encouraged by Chaz. She was my angel.

Mitch Hoffman, my editor at Grand Central, was unfailingly encouraging and helpful at every stage of the editorial process. His suggestions showed a deep sympathy with the enterprise. Lindsey Rose of Grand Central, his associate, was tireless throughout the proofreading process and in assembling the photographs.

Carol Iwata, my invaluable assistant for more than twenty years, was heroic in tracking down sources and permissions for the photos. She performed wonders. My caregiver, Millie Salmon, was a daily encouragement.

My agents, Joel Gotler and Brian Lipson, were instrumental right from the start. I also received much help from my lawyers Eliot Ephraim and Anita First.

Some of these words passed under the scrutiny of Laura Emerick, my editor at the *Sun-Times*, Sue Roush and Dorothy O'Brien at Universal Press/ Andrews & McMeel, and Jim Emerson, editor of rogerebert.com. They repaired countless errors.

ABOUT THE AUTHOR

ROGER EBERT HAS been reviewing films for the *Chicago Sun-Times* since 1967 and won the Pulitzer Prize for criticism in 1975. He has appeared on television for four decades, including twenty-three years as co-host of *Siskel & Ebert at the Movies*, and is now managing editor and reviewer for *Ebert Presents At the Movies*.

His previous books include *Scorsese by Ebert*; *Awake in the Dark*; *The Great Movies*, volumes I, II, and III; twenty annual volumes of *Roger Ebert's Movie Yearbook*; *Your Movie Sucks*; *Two Weeks in the Midday Sun: A Cannes Notebook*; *I Hated, Hated, Hated This Movie*; and the Norton anthology *Roger Ebert's Book of Film*.

The only film critic with a star on the Hollywood Walk of Fame, Roger Ebert is also an honorary member of the Directors Guild of America. He received the Carl Sandburg Literary Award of the Chicago Public Library, and won the Webby Awards Person of the Year in 2010. His website, RogerEbert.com, receives 110 million visits a year.

He lives with his wife, Chaz Hammelsmith Ebert, in Chicago.